Archaeology in South Carolina

Archaeology

in South Carolina

Exploring the Hidden Heritage of the Palmetto State

EDITED BY

Adam King

THE UNIVERSITY OF SOUTH CAROLINA PRESS

© 2016 Archaeological Research Trust of the South Carolina
Institute of Archaeology and Anthropology

Published by the University of South Carolina Press
Columbia, South Carolina 29208

www.sc.edu/uscpress

Manufactured in the United States of America

26 24 23 22 21 20 19 18 17 16   10 9 8 7 6 5 4 3 2 1

Library of Congress Cataloging-in-Publication Data can be
found at http://catalog.loc.gov/.

ISBN: 978-1-61117-608-7 (hardcover)
ISBN: 978-1-61117-609-4 (ebook)

CONTENTS

following page 132

COMPLETING A BOOK SUCH AS THIS ONE requires the efforts of a great many people, and here I would like to thank them. The idea for the volume has been around for a very long time and has taken the continued efforts of many members of the South Carolina Institute of Archaeology and Anthropology's Archaeological Research Trust (ART) Board to bring it to fruition. Key among these is Russ Burns, who like others donated materially to this project and created the means by which ART has been able to offset the cost of the color images that appear in the volume.

Of course, the book would not have been possible without authors willing to contribute, some of whom received relatively short notice. I appreciate very much their hard work and patience and the confidence they placed in me to take their research and bring it to an audience. I also want to express my gratitude to James Legg, Sharon Pekrul, Tommy Charles, George Wingard, and Tammy Herron for playing a large part in creating and assembling the collection of images that appears in this volume. I especially appreciate that they each put other pressing matters aside to contribute.

I also wish to thank my employers, Steven D. Smith of the South Carolina Institute of Archaeology and Anthropology and Mark Brooks of the Savannah River Archaeological Research Program, for supporting my efforts. Without their continued support and prodding, this volume might never have seen the light of day. A special thanks must also go to Nena Rice Powell for keeping the idea of this book alive for so many years. Finally, credit must go to Thorne Compton for obtaining the original author commitments, because without his leadership and strong arm this volume still might be just an idea.

IT HAS BEEN A LONG TIME since an entire book devoted to current research in South Carolina archaeology has been published. Honestly, this book has been a long time in the making, and the vision for what it was to look like has changed over the years. In this book the authors and I have tried to balance two important considerations. On the one hand, we wanted the book to stand up to scholarly scrutiny and be a resource for our colleagues to use. At the same time, we all realize that we need to communicate directly to the interested public what we do and what we have learned. After all, in one way or another, that public pays for most archaeology and certainly keeps the political will in the state positively predisposed to our shared past. This book is written to be accessible to nonarchaeologists while presenting information that is interesting and informative to both our research colleagues and those in our state who support us. That can be a tricky pair of objectives to meet. Some papers in this book are more technical than others, some are longer than others, and some are more easily accessible to nonspecialists than others. If we have done our jobs, all the essays should have something that everyone can gain from them.

This book is a collection of essays written by archaeologists currently doing research in the state of South Carolina. As such it is not written in one voice but, like the archaeology in South Carolina, has many voices and perspectives. This is an important aspect of archaeology for everyone to understand. Archaeology is not a unitary science: it has multiple ways of gathering data, and there are often multiple ways of interpreting the past. That makes perfect sense when you remember that we are ultimately studying people and their behavior in the past. The reasons why people do what they do are varied, complex, and often contradictory. Given the complexity and variability of what we study, it remains important to be as broad and flexible as we can as a profession.

In this book we have contributors from universities, state agencies, and private consulting companies. This is not uncommon and reflects the variety of entities that collect information about our past and interpret it. The essays discuss everything from the earliest people in the state to Native Americans at the dawn of European colonization to colonial Charleston and even some Civil War history. Archaeology is a way to collect information about the past, and lots of people use it as part of their study of the past—from anthropologists to historians to ecologists. In general, our intent is to capture the breadth of interests archaeologists pursue in the state. This is by no means an exhaustive showing, but it is fairly representative.

What Is Archaeology?

At its most fundamental level, archaeology is a set of methods designed to gather information about past behavior. Those methods range in scale from detailed excavations to the use of satellite imagery, and in technology from digging in the dirt with shovels to using nuclear physics to derive chemical compositions or estimate age. It is the great borrowing discipline, as it has and will always borrow methods of collecting and analyzing data as well as theory from other academic fields to understand the past.

In most of North America, archaeology is considered to be one of the four subfields of anthropology. One way (of many) to explain anthropology is to consider it the study of humankind as biological organisms and users of elaborate culture. In Europe archaeology is often set off as its own intellectual discipline. Wherever you want to put it, archaeology, as a set of methods, is used in many different scholarly fields—anthropology, history, art history, paleoecology, and even landscape architecture and history.

For anthropological archaeologists, the goal of exploring the past is not to find treasure or rare artifacts but to understand how people in the past lived. Ultimately, all American archaeologists are interested in contributing to anthropology's attempt to understand humanity's past, present, and future.

Who and Why

Because many different disciplines use the methods of archaeology to learn about the past, most of the people who do archaeology in South Carolina have done graduate training in anthropology or at least work under someone with a graduate degree. As a general rule, you need to have a graduate degree (at least a master's degree) to be considered a professional archaeologist with the credentials to conduct archaeological research, as well as to apply for grants and contracts to do archaeology. That does not mean you need a graduate degree to do archaeology. Anyone who knows the methods of archaeology and has practiced them in the field can work as a volunteer or be hired to do the actual field work of archaeology.

The typical view of archaeology is that it is largely done by college professors working with money from grants. In reality there is not very much grant money available, and many college professors apply for what there is. Thus only a small number of proposals get funded in any one year. Most of the archaeology done in our state and across the country is funded not by grants but by federal agencies that are mandated to comply with federal laws requiring some kind of archaeology. The main law driving federally sponsored archaeology is the National Historic Preservation Act (NHPA). You may know the NHPA as the law that creates the National Register of Historic Places and helps private individuals preserve old buildings and turn them into enterprises such as inns. Another part of that law requires federal agencies to consider impacts by projects to archaeological sites, buildings, structures such as bridges and dams, landscapes, and other places that might be eligible for the National Register of Historic Places.

Anything that is funded, required, or permitted by a federal agency and has the potential to negatively affect some place eligible for the National Register must follow a process set out in the NHPA. That process involves some level of looking for archaeological sites. If some are discovered that are considered important enough to be on the National Register, and are threatened by a federal project, then the federal agency must consider any damages as part of their planning. Contrary to popular belief, federal agencies do not have to save archaeological sites or dig them up; their only requirement is to consider how archaeological sites might be affected. In most cases reason prevails, and sites are avoided or money is made available to document and learn from them before they are destroyed.

This requirement of the NHPA effectively mandates some level of archaeological review for any new federal construction projects. It does the same for highway projects, U.S. Forest Service timbering operations, private developments that require wetlands or storm water permits from the Army Corps of Engineers, cell phone towers that require Federal Communications Commission permits, and many other kinds of activities. With a reach so potentially broad, it should not be surprising that most archaeology is funded by federal requirements, nor should it be surprising that most archaeologists in the state are employed by private companies that compete for federal money and projects.

What, Where, and When

To use information from the past to reconstruct the ways of life in the past, archaeologists need to know *what, where,* and *when*. The *what* refers to evidence of past human behavior, and it can come in the form of artifacts (portable objects made or used by people), features such as fire pits or postholes (nonportable things made or used by people), and assemblages of artifacts and features that may make up campsites, quarries, villages, cemeteries, plantations, battlefields, factories, and so on. Finding the what is the thing that brings many people into archaeology, myself included. No one can deny that it is exciting and inspires the imagination to find a thing or a place that no one has seen or understood for thousands or even tens of thousands of years. And no one can deny the satisfaction of revealing a way of life that was lost to history.

But remember, archaeology is about figuring out the past, not just appreciating or possessing pieces of it. That means we must look beyond the artifacts to the patterns they reveal. One key to all this is the idea of context. This is the *where* of archaeology. An object by itself can reveal things about its function, its method of manufacture, its place of origin, and even its age. However, if we know exactly where that object was found and what was around it (its archaeological and cultural context), we can learn a great deal more. For example, an arrowhead (or projectile point, as most archaeologists call them) by itself can tell us a lot. We can tell its age by its shape and size and also how it was used (not all stone projectiles were arrowheads; some were spear points or knives). Based on the kind of stone used to make it, we can tell where that stone came from.

However, if we find that arrowhead as it was left by the people who last used it, we can learn a great deal more. For example, if that arrowhead was found at a site in Beaufort County and was made of rhyolite found only in North Carolina, we can infer that the stone or the finished projectile was traded or carried to the site from far away. This tells us important things about trade and territory size. If that projectile was found at a small campsite that was part of a set of sites in a river valley that included permanent communities and nut-gathering camps, we can learn something about how people living in that valley made a living. They lived in permanent villages but went out into the valley to hunt and gather foods.

Context is critical to archaeologists because it gives us the rest of the story. And remember, that is what archaeology is really all about. We want to understand how people in the past lived and how that changed over time. Context is also one of the reasons why archaeologists have a problem with nonarchaeologists digging up sites or even collecting artifacts from plowed fields. If the digging is done without keeping track of exactly where the objects in a site were found (down to the centimeter) and what was found with them and where, then we all lose information about the past. The same goes for collecting artifacts without keeping track of the places they came from. Many people think that archaeologists do not like nonarchaeologists digging or collecting because we want the artifacts for ourselves. Actually, we want the information that context provides and not the artifacts. Doing archaeology without paying attention to context is not much different from simply running a bulldozer through a site or crushing up an arrowhead or pottery sherd.

That does not mean archaeologists want to keep all the fun of discovery to themselves, nor does it mean that only trained archaeologists can do archaeology. There are organizations throughout South Carolina that offer nonarchaeologists the chance to take part in doing archaeology. No matter where you are in the state, you can find one of those organizations. Below is a list of projects, organizations, and museums and university departments that either offer or provide information about hands-on experiences.

PROJECTS

Allendale Paleoindian Expedition
Dorchester State Park
Historic Columbia Foundation
Johannes Kolb Site

NONPROFIT ORGANIZATIONS

Archaeology Society of South Carolina
Chicora Foundation
Diachronic Research Foundation
Piedmont Archaeology Studies Trust
ScienceSouth
South Carolina Archaeology Public Outreach Division

UNIVERSITIES AND MUSEUMS

Aiken County Historical Museum
The Charleston Museum
Clemson University Department of Anthropology
College of Charleston Department of Anthropology
Savannah River Archaeological Research Program
South Carolina Institute of Archaeology and Anthropology
South Carolina State Museum
University of South Carolina Department of Anthropology

This leaves us with one critical piece of archaeology: the *when*. If we are interested in changes in the way people lived over the course of human history, we need to be able to tell and measure the passage of time. Since the very early stages of archaeology as a discipline the principle of stratigraphy has allowed people to tell which deposits were older than others—at least at individual sites or sometimes within larger sets of closely located sites. Stratigraphy is fundamental not just to archaeology but also to geology. It is the idea that soil layers and human activities deposited over time layer themselves one over the other in such a way that the oldest things are on the bottom and the newest are on the top. This is called a relative dating technique, because it really only tells you how old things are in relation to others found in the same setting. Of course, events such as flooding, erosion, and plate tectonics can all rearrange stratigraphic sequences and obscure relative temporal relationships.

Stratigraphy is fundamental to archaeology, but it is not very useful in helping us assign a particular year, decade, or century to an artifact, feature, or site; this is especially true when dealing with really old things. To obtain those absolute dates, archaeologists in South Carolina most often turn to a couple of different absolute-dating techniques: radiocarbon dating and luminescence dating.

Both of these techniques have their roots in the efforts to understand atomic structure and the search for the ultimate weapon during World War II. Out of nuclear science came radiocarbon dating as well as a host of other absolute-dating methods that work on a radioactive decay principle. The principle is not hard to understand. Atoms energized by some external source, such as the sun or extreme heating, take on electrons and therefore a particular form of the element. Over time, the energy dissipates, and the element loses electrons and transitions to another element or elemental form. As atoms lose energy, they change, and that loss of energy happens at a known rate and can be measured.

Rather than going too far into how these techniques work, I want to explain some more practical issues that affect how and when we use them. One of those issues concerns what one needs to collect from an archaeological site to obtain these dates. The radiocarbon method uses changes in elemental carbon, so to get a radiocarbon date one must find something that has carbon in it—something that was once alive. Finding once-living things in the archaeological record can be difficult because most organic matter decays relatively rapidly except in very dry, very wet, and very cold settings. Most often, material suitable for radiocarbon dating is found in the form of charred plant remains (such as wood charcoal and burned seeds or fibers), bone, and shell.

Luminescence dating works by counting electrons trapped in the crystal matrix of certain minerals—often feldspar or quartz. To obtain one of these dates, you must collect grains of sand or something with grains of sand in it. That sounds pretty easy because sand is often found in the soil matrix of archaeological sites. It is not quite that simple. Elements in the structure of sand grains must have been excited by high energy, either through exposure to sunlight or high heat, and then not reenergized again until they are collected for dating purposes. That means you need something that was heated or exposed to sunlight once, because you ultimately date the last time the elements in those crystals were energized.

The most important consideration for either of these techniques is the context of the samples collected for dating. Context is critical because what you actually date is the death of a living thing or the energizing of a crystalline structure. Therefore, you need to be sure that the samples you choose actually are directly linked to the artifacts, features, or archaeological context you want to date. The surest way to do that is to find carbon adhering to artifacts or sand grains within actual artifacts. Unfortunately, that is not always possible, so charcoal or sand grains are collected from the fills of features or the strata of interest. The less direct the connection between your samples and the things you want to date, the greater the chance you will obtain dates that have nothing to do with the contexts or artifacts of interest.

Another thing to keep in mind is that neither of these methods produces a date expressed as a single year or even decade. These methods produce probabilistic estimates of the true time elapsed since the death of the organism or the energizing of a sand grain. That means what you get is a mean and a standard deviation, not a single year. For radiocarbon dates, those standard deviations usually range from 40 to 100 years and for luminescence dating they can be as wide as 200 years or more. Thus, what you learn is this: the true age of your sample has a very good chance of falling somewhere in a range that may be as small as 80 years and as large as 400 years. That is a lot better than not having any information on absolute age, but it can be frustratingly imprecise. Human behavior happens on a much shorter time scale, measured in months or years. Think about what has happened to your town or American society over the past 200 years—a lot. Our most commonly used methods for absolute dating do not get us very close to the time scale we need to really understand human behavior over time.

One final thing to consider about these dating techniques is that they have their limits in terms of time. The radiocarbon method does not produce very accurate results for things that have been dead less than a few hundred years or things that have been dead for more than 50,000 years. Luminescence dating has a wider range, reaching back at least 100,000 years. Fortunately, these both work fine for North American archaeology because human occupation does not go back much further than 20,000 years, and within the last few hundred years we have written records that help provide more precise dates for recent materials, activities, and deposits.

When dealing with archaeological materials and deposits created at a time when written records also were made, it is possible to date things more precisely. In some cases, the contexts under study may be described in written records so the dating is known already. In other instances historical records make it possible to place specific locations, kinds of features, events, or even kinds of artifacts in time. Records such as deeds and tax assessments can date the construction of houses, factories, churches, and later improvements to them. Military records can place specific battles, encampments, and military features in time. Economic documents such as ship manifests, records of trade, and industrial production also make it possible to date particular kinds of artifacts.

Archaeologists in South Carolina have been asking the when question for as long as they have been doing archaeology. Over time, we have developed a pretty good idea of how artifacts and lifestyles changed before the coming of Europeans—in a general sense. That general understanding is presented in Table 1 as a list of time periods and dates used by most South Carolina archaeologists.

History and Prehistory

This concern about *when* leads to a distinction often made in American archaeology and certainly here in South Carolina. That distinction is one made between historical and prehistoric archaeology. In this context, the term *prehistoric* is used

TABLE 1. General Timeline

PERIOD	DATE	DATE	SUB-PERIOD	DATE	DATE
			Late Mississippian	1400 A.D.	1600 A.D.
Mississippian	1000 A.D.	1600 A.D.	Middle Mississippian	1200 A.D.	1400 A.D.
			Early Mississippian	1000 A.D.	1200 A.D.
			Late Woodland	500 A.D.	1000 A.D.
Woodland	1000 B.C.	1000 A.D.	Middle Woodland	100 B.C.	500 A.D.
			Early Woodland	1000 B.C.	100 B.C.
			Late Archaic	3800 B.C.	1000 B.C.
Archaic	9500 B.C.	1000 B.C.	Middle Archaic	6800 B.C.	3800 B.C.
			Early Archaic	9500 B.C.	6800 B.C.
Paleoindian	13000 B.C.	9500 B.C.			

specifically to refer to time periods before things were written down—the time before written history. Native Americans of the past in what is now the United States did not have a writing system, so they had no written history. Does that mean Native Americans had no tradition of keeping track of their history before Europeans came to the continent? The answer, of course, is an emphatic no. Their tradition, like many around the world even today, is oral history—that is, history was and is passed down through the telling of that history. Some have argued that oral history is less likely to be a true history because it can be changed with each telling. They also argue that it is biased because the individuals who remembered it and retold it injected their own biases into it. In reality, those same criticisms of oral history apply to written history. Written histories are always told from a perspective and so include biases of authors. Additionally, written histories, especially very old ones, are recorded (or retold) more than once and in the process changed. So, in the end history is history with changes and biases regardless of whether it is oral or written.

The continued use of the terms *historical* and *prehistoric* reveals the Western bias embedded in American archaeology. What happened deep in the past did not happen before history (prehistory); it only happened before westerners learned about it and incorporated it into their written system of history keeping. Not surprisingly, many Native Americans take offense at the use of the term prehistoric to describe their past. In part this is because the popular conception of prehistoric perpetuated in our popular culture is that of dumb, brutish cavemen wielding clubs and running from dinosaurs. No one would be pleased to have their past thought of in that way. More Native Americans dislike the term prehistoric because it seems to make only Western (European) history a legitimate history.

Some have attempted to address this concern by switching to the term pre-Columbian, as in before Columbus. That may be a more precise term and also gets away from the "whose kind of history is legitimate" concerns. However, it still suffers from a glaring problem. No one can deny that Columbus's accidental "discovery" of the Caribbean was an enormous moment in the course of human history. For the West and for many modern countries in North and South America, it is a moment to be celebrated as a key time in our becoming what we are today. But again, that is a Western perspective. I think it would be very easy to find many Native Americans who do not look so positively on the arrival of Columbus. That arrival and its aftermath helped bring about things that we today are horrified to see happen elsewhere in the world: the destruction of cultures, genocide, ethnic cleansing, and slavery.

All of this reveals what lies behind the fundamental tension between archaeologists and Native Americans. Taking archaeology as part of a Western intellectual tradition, it seeks to study the past of people and cultures that were radically changed or destroyed by that very intellectual tradition. And who is doing the studying? It is mostly people of European descent who practice the discipline of archaeology as a profession. Moreover, the way we did it in the past was not even remotely sensitive to the concerns of the living descendants of the people we study. Mainstream nineteenth-century anthropological thought saw Native Americans as inferior. It often questioned whether they had anything to do with the incredible cliff dwellings, giant earthen mounds, and elaborate art objects clearly produced by people who occupied our country in the past. This kind of thinking led to a history of objectification of Native Americans (treating them as specimens to be studied) and a taking of their history and culture for the edification and entertainment of Western society.

I get it, as do most archaeologists of my generation and younger, and there are plenty of Native Americans who can see how archaeology (as a method of exploring the past) can help them understand themselves. Still, when terms like *prehistoric* persist and old debates are revived about them, bringing archaeologists and Native Americans together becomes very difficult. Unfortunately, use of terms that reveal old biases and an ugly past persist, and they are likely to remain a part of the intellectual discipline of archaeology here in the United States. This is not because we archaeologists really do not care whether other people, especially the people whose history we study, like the way we do things. It is more because of intellectual inertia—the idea that a body at rest tends to remain at rest until acted upon by an external force. In this case we are talking about terminology. It is embedded into our intellectual system of dialogue. Is that a good excuse to keep using it? No, but it does mean that it is going to take well-meaning and thoughtful archaeologists a long time to get rid of its use.

Who Owns the Past?

This problem of terminology irritating a nerve kept raw by history is part of a broader issue in all archaeology. Whose past is it? What rights do different interest groups have to exploring, interpreting, and possessing pieces of the past? The answers to these questions are not always clear and sometimes very messy. That is because those answers require the balancing of sometimes conflicting interests of different groups, each with distinct and legitimate claims to the remains of the past.

One group with a claim to the past is the intellectual or scholarly community, of which professional archaeologists are members. This group is interested in learning from the past, but with the explicit purpose of sharing that knowledge and enriching humanity's understanding of its collective past. This group focuses on the systematic study of the past and insists that archaeological data must be collected in a specific and detailed way. They further insist that those materials must be kept available for study by scholars—and, at some level, the general public—in perpetuity. Finally, that intellectual community believes that the knowledge gained from the study of archaeological materials, and the materials themselves, must be shared with other scholars and the general public.

These lofty goals are often at odds with the interests and desires of people descended from the people whose history archaeologists study. This group is referred to as descendant communities and they may include direct, lineal descendants—such as Thomas Jefferson's kin. They may also include people who are clearly cultural descendants, but they may not have (or feel the need to produce) the historical records to show lineal descent. While many in descendant communities are anxious to learn what archaeology can tell them about their past, they also have other concerns.

Those may have to do with privacy, summarized by the classic question posed to archaeologists, "Would you be OK with me digging up your grandmother to study?" They may also have to do with the secrecy required for proper religious observance or concerns about vandalism, unwanted visitors, and nontraditional uses of sacred landscapes or medicinal plants. Their concerns may stem from the long-term consequences of inequality, discrimination, and exploitation. For most of American archaeology's history, archaeologists have been allowed to visit and excavate archaeological sites, take the materials they found (including human remains), and do what they wanted with them—all without involving the living people whose ancestors lived and died on those archaeological sites. I think any reasonable person can see that if you and your ancestors have been mistreated at the hands of any particular group, you are less likely to be positively disposed to that group and their interests. This impact of history may be the greatest impediment to archaeologists and descendant communities finding common ground.

There is a third group of people whose interests and claims often conflict with those of the previous two. They are members of the interested public who want to find, possess, and control access to pieces of the past but who have no interest in playing by the rules insisted upon by professional archaeologists. This group, like the others, tends to be very diverse. They range from people who hunt arrowheads in plowed fields to those who unsystematically dig for their own collections or to sell to others and even to those who simply buy artifacts found by others. They view the remains of history to be as much theirs to find, possess, and interpret as any anyone else's. They often view their claims to the past to be in direct opposition to those of the intellectual community and descendant communities, whom they view as trying to keep them from exploring the past. Professional archaeologists and descendants often see these people as destroyers of the past—mainly through unsystematic digging and creating a private market that keeps pieces of the past from their cultural heirs, the general public, and scholarly study.

This group is empowered or protected (depending on how you want to view it) by private property laws in our country. Those laws give legal rights of ownership of archaeological materials to the owner of the land. The exceptions to these are human remains and, in some states, associated grave goods, which are protected by state grave laws. Private property rights are a fundamental part of our culture. They are fiercely guarded by individual property owners and unlikely to be compromised or changed despite the fears of this group.

There is one final group with a stake in the past and its material remains, and that is the interested general public that wants to learn about the past. This group can argue that ours is a shared past that cannot and should not be owned or controlled by any single group. It is a past of which we are all a part and from which we all should be able to learn. At a more practical level, this group has a claim to the remains of the past because they are the primary funders of archaeological research through private donations and taxes. They have a right to benefit, see, and understand what their money produces.

As you can see, this is a messy business that forces into conflict humanitarian concerns (a shared past we can all learn from), moral claims (lineal and cultural descent), private property rights, and economic interests. Whose claims are the strongest? Frankly that is a question that can and must be worked out in multiple arenas. It is something individual property owners should consider. There is no question about who owns antiquities on private property, but there is plenty of room to think about how best to treat archaeological sites and the things they contain. It also is something that must be dealt with by individual professional archaeologists. It is our responsibility to think about the interests of the descendant communities, the scholarly community, and various public groups and try to balance their claims with our own interests. Finally, it is up to the people of South Carolina, through their elected representatives and private giving, to insure that a good-faith effort is made to find a reasonable balance among these different and sometimes competing claims.

In sum, archaeology is a varied and diverse field whose results are of interest to several different groups of people. Conducting archaeological research often requires investigators to navigate very complex modern social issues created by recent and ancient histories. Fortunately, in our state it also is a vibrant discipline that enjoys a great deal of public support in an atmosphere where the various stakeholders work well together. The research represented in this book is a product of that positive intellectual climate. In the pages that follow, not all areas of the state are equally represented, and not all time periods are discussed. Still, the essays here represent reasonably well the current state of South Carolina archaeology.

Archaeology in South Carolina

The Search for the Earliest Humans in the Land Recently Called South Carolina

TRADITIONALLY THE STUDY of archaeology evokes the imagery of finding old things, artifacts that are not of our culture. Old, of course, is relative, depending on where you are in the world. Part and parcel to this is not only old but also the earliest. Whether it is South Africa with its 100,000-year-old Archaic Homo sapiens or South Carolina with its Ice Age prehistoric humans, the question always remains a local one: Who were the first people who lived here?

Until just a few years ago, that question as applied to the Western Hemisphere seemed to have been settled. Basically the first people were thought to be those of what archaeologists call the Clovis culture and other contemporary groups that dated to the very end of the last Ice Age, or about 13,000 years ago. The Clovis story or what has been called Clovis First, dominated the thinking of North American archaeologists until about the 1970s, when earlier sites in South America and the United States began to be discovered. Sites such as Taima-Taima in Venezuela and Monte Verde in Chile showed that people were present well south of Mexico some 1,000–2,000 years before the Clovis culture (Dillehay 2000). In North America, the Meadowcroft Rockshelter in southwestern Pennsylvania created quite a controversy with its radiocarbon dates of 14,000–15,000 years, indicating people present from 2,000 to 3,000 years before Clovis (Adovasio and Page 2002). Continuing into the 1990s, other sites in North America, such as Cactus Hill in Virginia and Topper in South Carolina (Figure 1), have been added to an ever-increasing group of sites showing that humans inhabited this hemisphere several thousand years before the Clovis culture (Goodyear 2005a). Today the idea of people being in the Americas starting at the end of the Last Glacial Maximum (LGM) some 18,000 years ago is increasingly accepted, with some sites likely older than that (Collins et al. 2008). Archaeological research in what is now known as South Carolina has paralleled many of the national trends in what can be referred to as Paleoamerican research.

In 1927 the notable Folsom discovery occurred in New Mexico. A distinctive, well-made fluted spear point known as the Folsom point was found with the bones of a now-extinct form of bison. Based on the indisputable association of stone tools with Ice Age animals, the scientific community became convinced of the great antiquity of the American Indians in North America (Meltzer 2009). This was followed in 1932 by the discovery near Dent, Colorado, of another type of fluted point known as Clovis, this time with other Ice Age or Pleistocene animals, including mammoths (Wormington 1957). Although radiocarbon dating had not been developed, it was abundantly clear that humans were in North America at least by the end of the Pleistocene.

These discoveries spawned numerous reports in the East of "Folsomoid" or other fluted lanceolate points (Caldwell 1952). In 1939 Robert Wauchope published an article in *American Antiquity* describing obvious fluted points found near the city of Columbia, South Carolina, that he attributed to "Paleoindians" (Wauchope 1939). Years later in the same journal, Antonio Waring, a medical doctor and avocational archaeologist, reported Clovis points from the coast near Beaufort (Waring 1961). At about the same time, Eugene Waddell (1965) published photos and proveniences of several South Carolina fluted points in what was the first attempt to list the then-known examples of Paleoindian points in the state.

In 1967 the South Carolina Institute of Archaeology and Anthropology (SCIAA) was officially established at the University of South Carolina, marking the beginning of full-time professional archaeological research in the state (Stephenson 1975; Anderson 2002). The first director was Robert L. Stephenson

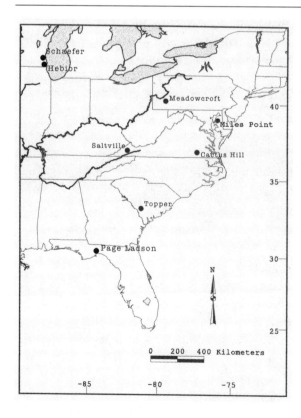

Figure 1. Location of sites in the eastern United States with evidence of human occupation more than 14,000 years ago. Courtesy of the South Carolina Institute of Archaeology and Anthropology.

Figure 2. Archaeologists historically involved in the search for early sites in South Carolina: Robert L. Stephenson (upper left), James L. Michie (upper right), Tommy Charles (lower left), and Albert C. Goodyear (lower right). Courtesy of the South Carolina Institute of Archaeology and Anthropology.

(Figure 2), who previously had a distinguished career with the River Basin Survey of the Smithsonian Institution. Dr. "Bob," as he was known by many, had worked in the West with prominent prehistorians such as Luther Cressman and Frank H. H. Roberts and had himself a strong interest in the earliest humans of the Americas (Goodyear 1994). Intellectually he was open to the possibility of people being in America well back into the Pleistocene, and he even attended the international meeting at the famous and controversial Calico Early Man site in California (Stephenson 1971). In 1969 Stephenson hired E. Thomas Hemmings, a newly minted Ph.D. from the University of Arizona, who did his dissertation work on the Murray Springs Clovis site with C. Vance Haynes. At about this time, a standardized form was instituted for the recording of lanceolate Paleoindian points for the state, a form that is still in use today.

The first systematic study of South Carolina Paleoindian artifacts was done by James L. Michie (1977). Michie was a self-taught avocational archaeologist and native South Carolinian (Figure 2). He pioneered Paleoindian-point studies in South Carolina and published typologies of fluted points (Michie 1965). Using mostly private artifact collections, Michie compiled a comprehensive inventory of 95 points during the 1960s and 1970s, resulting in a B.A. honors thesis with the Department of Anthropology at the University of South Carolina (1977). He later went on to graduate school and became an archaeologist at SCIAA and lastly at Coastal Carolina University (Goodyear 2005b).

At the urging of Michie, and realizing the wealth of information contained in private artifact collections, Stephenson received a series of yearly grants from the South Carolina Department of Archives and History to begin to inventory sites and privately held collections around the state. Tommy Charles, also a native South Carolinian and former collector, was hired to conduct these statewide surveys (Figure 2). Using the Archives and History Planning Grants, Charles did five seasons of collector surveys, starting in 1979 and continuing through 1986. One of the objectives of the surveys was to systematically record Paleoindian lanceolate points. During his tenure, Charles recorded over 300 examples from nearly all parts of the state. The standard typology in use at that time included Clovis, Suwannee, and Simpson points (Figure 3). Late Paleoindian Dalton points were recorded by collection but until recently have never been included in the statewide Paleoindian point survey. In an effort to synthesize the findings of Paleoindian studies to date, Goodyear, Michie, and Charles (1989) published a summary of various Paleoindian artifacts and sites. Up to that point, few sites with good contexts suitable for excavation had been found, and the study was essentially typological and distributional in nature. The types employed were derived from stratigraphic and radiocarbon studies from other states (see, for example, Hemmings 1972).

The South Carolina Paleoindian Point Survey, as developed largely by the work of Charles and Michie, continues to this day, with over 600 points recorded. Since the retirement of Tommy Charles, the survey has been continued as a function of the Southeastern Paleoamerican Survey (SEPAS) (Goodyear 2006). The South Carolina data have been incorporated into David Anderson's national database known as Paleoindian Data Base of the Americas (Anderson et al. 2010) where it can be viewed online (http://pidba.utk.edu/). As of 2012 the South Carolina survey is over 40 years old and has great potential for identifying significant geographic patterns in artifact types and raw materials as well as for formulating hypotheses about Paleoamerican groups in South Carolina and adjacent states (Goodyear 2010).

Figure 3. Examples of South Carolina Paleoindian point types historically used in recording point data: (a) Clovis, (b) Redstone, (c) Suwannee, (d) Simpson, and (e) Dalton. Drawing by Darby Erd, courtesy of the South Carolina Institute of Archaeology and Anthropology.

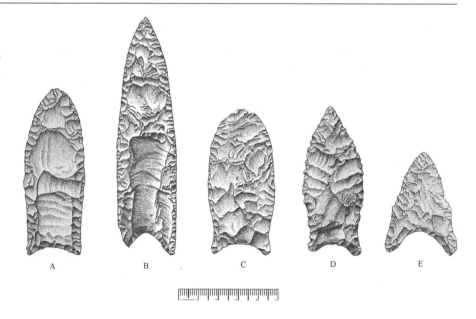

A   B   C   D   E

Beginning in the 1980s, systematic survey and testing were initiated in order to locate buried sites with interpretable geoarchaeological contexts. The Coastal Plain chert outcrops and quarries of Allendale County, South Carolina, were targeted since high-quality, fine-grained cryptocrystalline lithic raw material sources were known to be a good predictor of Paleoindian sites in the eastern United States (Gardner 1983). Though mostly restricted to Allendale County, extensive quarries and stratified sites are also known in neighboring Burke and Screven counties of Georgia (Goodyear and Charles 1984; Brockington 1970). These surveys resulted in a comprehensive inventory of prehistoric chert quarries of what has been called Allendale chert in South Carolina and Brier Creek chert in the adjacent counties of Georgia, named for the extraordinarily rich chert sources within the Brier Creek drainage. Nine new terrestrial and underwater quarries were found in the Allendale County survey, located on the property of what was then known as Sandoz Chemical Corporation (Goodyear and Charles 1984), later owned by Clariant Corporation. These nine quarries were nominated to the National Register of Historic Places as a district in 1985. Because of their rich artifact inventory and evident stratified nature, some of these sites, such as Charles (38AL135), Big Pine Tree (38AL143), and Topper (38AL23), have received significant excavations (Goodyear 1999). Topper in particular has provided extensive evidence of Clovis and pre-Clovis occupations (Goodyear 2005a).

The results of initial testing led to the realization that substantial funding and labor would be required to excavate these sites effectively. Being quarry-related sites, the bulk of artifacts represent waste debris from chert quarrying and unsuccessful tool manufacture. To meet these needs, in 1996 the Allendale Paleoindian Expedition was founded, which is an excavation program for members of the public (http://www.allendale-expedition.net/). The expedition utilizes volunteers from the public who sign up for a week or more and make a financial donation to the University of South Carolina. This approach has provided the resources necessary to conduct excavations every year since 1996, with plans being made for 2013. As of 2010, over 1,000 people from all across the United States have participated in this program, with many returning year after year.

Because of the extraordinary implications of the Topper site discovery, it was decided to expand the scope of the Allendale Expedition and rename the program the Southeastern Paleoamerican Survey. With the founding of the survey in 2005 (Goodyear 2006), the aim is to expand the scope of inquiry to gather data on a geographic scale commensurate with low-density Pleistocene-age human populations, who in the ancient past were likely to be distributed over what is now a multistate area. Since most archaeological sites are on private land, the approach has been to reach out to private landowners and artifact collectors, concentrating especially on the lower Southeastern Coastal Plain from the Carolinas to Florida. This area of North America was never glaciated and should provide a prime area to prospect for traditional Paleoindian as well as pre-Clovis sites. Given the temporal remoteness and ephemeral preservation of such ancient remains, the involvement of private landowners and collectors is critical to the discovery and documentation of what no doubt is a small universe of sites to begin with, virtually necessitating help from the interested public. This philosophy has been articulated before regarding the matter of involving the public in the search for what must be inherently rare sites (Goodyear 1993).

The previous history of research on the early human occupation of South Carolina as briefly outlined here has led to several interesting discoveries and results. The most prominent of these both scientifically and in the media concern the pre-Clovis and Clovis occupations at Topper and related sites in Allendale County.

Pre-Clovis at Topper

In 1998, because of severe flooding of the Savannah River, the expedition had to be moved to higher ground. Though on the river, the Topper site was unaffected by the flooding, and the project was relocated there. Clovis was already known to be present at Topper, located about a meter below surface. Because of discoveries such as Meadowcroft Rockshelter, Monte Verde, and Cactus Hill, it was decided to dig deeper to see if anything artifactual might be found. Topper is a chert quarry overlooking a major river in the Southeast, enhancing, it was thought, the possibility of an earlier occupation. Some 50–60 cm below the Clovis zone, chert cores and choppers, waste flakes, and small tools were discovered, initiating a flurry of media coverage (Petit 1998; Begley and Murr 1999).

To prove the existence of a pre-Clovis site, three main criteria must be met. There must be genuine artifacts found in valid stratigraphic context with dates in excess of 13,500 years (Haynes 1969; Meltzer 2009). This requires an interdisciplinary geoarchaeological approach. The matter of stratigraphy and dating in ancient Pleistocene deposits is the purview of geologists. A geoscience team worked on these issues at Topper from 1999 to 2004, resulting in the sound establishment of stratigraphic layers with approximate dates (Waters et al. 2009). Because of a general lack of datable carbon, a newly developed sediment-dating technique known as optically stimulated luminescence (OSL) was employed. OSL dating of Topper revealed that the Clovis layer that lies above the pre-Clovis archaeology dated to approximately 13,000 calendar years ago, the expected time range. Because these sediments had moved slowly down from the adjacent hillside by slopewash or colluvium, they are amenable to OSL dating. The base of this deposit dated from 14,000 to 15,000 years ago, which is pre-Clovis in age. Thus, any sediments below this zone and any artifacts they might contain would be at least that old or older.

The upper pre-Clovis assemblage at Topper lies in a Pleistocene alluvial sand deposit (Figure 4) that was deposited before some 15,000 years ago when the Ice Age Savannah River flowed at elevations higher than it does today. Direct dating of these alluvial sediments was not achieved as they were not amenable to OSL dating. Thus, while they are at least 15,000 years old, they are likely several thousand years older. The alluvial sands lie unconformably on an eroded terrace (Figure 4) formed by overbank flooding, resulting in back swamp deposits containing fine clay and silt sediments. This terrace is at least 20,000 years old based on radiocarbon dates obtained from adjacent lower alluvial deposits toward the river. Charcoal was found about 2 m down in the terrace and dated in excess of 50,000 years uncalibrated B.P. (before present), which also represent minimal ages since they are likely beyond the range of radiocarbon dating (Waters et al. 2009). Artifacts similar to the upper alluvial sands have also been found in the terrace (Goodyear 2009). Thus, the geochronology studies at Topper resulted in an anomalously long date range from 15,000 to at least 50,000 or more years (Waters et al. 2009).

Clovis

White Pleistocene Alluvial Sands

Pleistocene Terrace

Big Core

50,300 RC yr. BP
51,700 RC yr. BP

Figure 4. Photo of the 4-m artifact-bearing stratigraphy at Topper from modern ground surface to the 50,000-years-before-present-plus terrace deposit. Courtesy of the South Carolina Institute of Archaeology and Anthropology.

The pre-Clovis artifact assemblage in both the upper Pleistocene alluvial sand layer and down in the terrace is essentially the same. Cores and resultant flakes were produced by some type of smash-core method such as bipolar and anvil flaking (cf. Jones 2002). No large hammerstones and few large flakes with bulbs of force have been found, which would indicate hammerstone reduction. Some of the cores have retouched margins, creating chopping and cutting implements. Cores were retouched unifacially and bifacially, although they are not bifaces in the usual sense of that word. No bifaces have yet been found in the Topper pre-Clovis assemblage. Flakes were modified in many cases by unifacial retouch, creating standard side and end scrapers as well as spokeshaves. Occasional prismatic blades also were made. The most common artifacts are burin-like pieces known as a bend-break flakes, which number in the hundreds

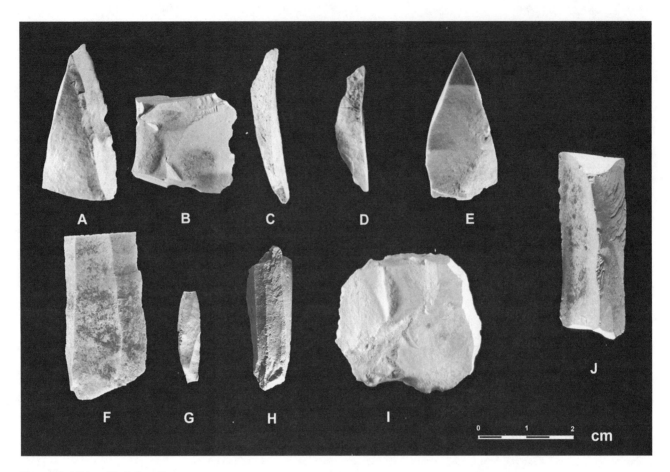

Figure 5. Lithic artifacts from the pre-Clovis occupation at the Topper site: (a, b, e) bend-break tools, (c, d) bend-break spalls, (f, g) blades, (h) possible microblade core, (i) scraper, and (j) blade-like tool. Photograph by Daryl P. Miller, courtesy of the South Carolina Institute of Archaeology and Anthropology.

(Figure 5). Altogether, apart from the larger core/chopper–like implements, the assemblage can be described as microlithic (Goodyear 2005a).

The Topper pre-Clovis artifacts are somewhat unique in New World prehistory in that they are not bifacial and tend to be rather small—that is, microlithic in nature. This is the case even though the site is situated on a chert outcrop. While larger artifacts such as cores and choppers are present, the small-sized flake-tool assemblage might be best suited for working organic artifacts made of wood, bone, ivory, and antler. The Topper site is also unusual owing to its apparent antiquity. Pre-Clovis sites dating from 18,000 to 14,000 years ago are being found increasingly in the New World (Goebel et al. 2008). While Topper may date as late as this interval, radiocarbon dating would indicate several thousand years earlier. Additional OSL dating is planned to resolve this dating issue.

Clovis at Topper

The original objective of the Allendale Paleoindian Expedition was to locate and excavate classic fluted-point sites, especially Clovis. Both Topper and the Big Pine Tree site were tested, with Clovis being recognized at both sites, particularly the latter (Goodyear 1999). Topper was thought to have some evidence of Clovis, but like Big Pine Tree and the Charles site (38AL135), this was based on suspected Clovis-point preforms and not finished points. At Topper, Clovis bifaces were encountered on the terrace as part of the pre-Clovis excavations (Goodyear

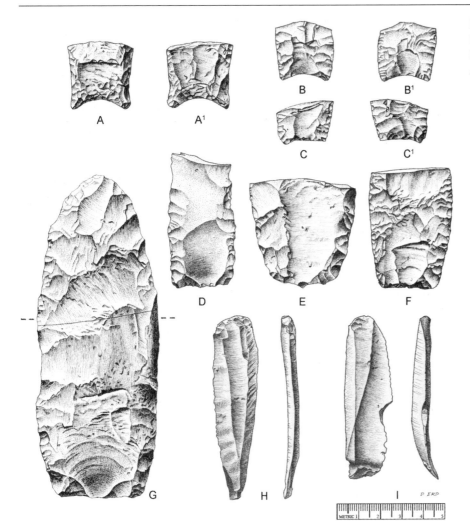

Figure 6. Representative Clovis bifaces and blades from the Topper site. Drawing by Darby Erd, courtesy of the South Carolina Institute of Archaeology and Anthropology.

and Steffy 2003), which eventually included macro-prismatic blades (Steffy and Goodyear 2006). Even in the absence of fluted points, Clovis-point preforms and macroblades have come to be as diagnostic as the points themselves (Figure 6). Starting in 2004, testing on the hillside overlooking the terrace produced large numbers of Clovis artifacts in easily recognized floors (for example, Miller 2011). The size of the Clovis occupation of what is called the Hillside at Topper is immense, with the northern and eastern limits still undefined. Excavation of the Hillside Clovis occupation has continued every year since 2004, yielding a number of important discoveries.

As of 2012 over 800 m² of the Clovis occupation have been excavated, including the terrace and the hillside. The typical Clovis biface is a broken- or unfinished-point preform with over 190 excavated. Only four Clovis points have been recovered (Figure 6), indicating that hunting was probably not a major activity when the quarries were occupied. Enough whole and broken-point preforms have been recovered to reconstruct the manufacturing processes of Clovis points made of Allendale chert, as revealed in the dissertation research of Smallwood (2010, 2012). It is clear that fluting or end thinning was carried out throughout biface manufacture and not necessarily done at the end (Figure 6). Prismatic blades and their cores also have been found in abundance in all parts of the site. The blades have received special study in a master's thesis (Sain 2010, 2012). One significant finding was the low incidence of blades modified as tools on site. Only 3 percent of the 257 blades showed evidence of use based on retouching, suggesting that blades and perhaps cores were prepared at Topper to be transported out into the settlement system (Sain and Goodyear 2012).

Other types of artifacts, including unifaces, are commonly found in the Clovis floors, indicating that activities besides quarrying and stone tool manufacture took place (Smallwood et al. 2013). These include end and side scrapers, retouched flakes, and denticulates. The latter type of artifact was created by unifacial retouch, which produced teeth-like projections, probably for shredding plant materials, perhaps for fiber. The majority of tools appear to be expediently made, probably for on-site use and discarded there. Taken altogether, the evidence for Clovis use of Topper would be for processing lithic artifacts, especially bifaces and blades for transport off site with some habitation implied by the extensive inventory of expedient tools. More excavation and analysis of the site is needed to fully define the technological inventory, as well as potential spatial variation in activity areas of Clovis at Topper. As it stands now, it is one of the largest Clovis sites found in North America, ranging over an estimated 35,000 m^2 and possibly larger.

Conclusion

The search for archaeological evidence for the first peoples in what we now know as South Carolina has been going on for several decades. As I have shown here, the work being conducted today in reality had its beginnings with observations and investigations of earlier generations of researchers. The diverse, multidisciplinary research and multi-institutional involvement now taking place at Topper and related sites in the central Savannah River Valley can ultimately be traced back to these archaeologists, both professional and avocational. Because of the continuing presence of the South Carolina Institute of Archaeology and Anthropology, it has been possible to maintain a sustained research focus on these many fascinating questions. The traditional understanding and the search for classic Paleoindian cultures such as Clovis continues—but now with the added possibility of even earlier peoples who only a few years ago were thought probably not to exist. The continued maintenance of the South Carolina Paleoindian Point Survey, whose data have mostly come from collectors and other members of the public, as well as the intense public involvement with the Allendale Paleoindian Expedition, serve to illustrate the value of archaeology for and with the interested public and the kinds of research contributions that can be made.

Acknowledgments

Research on the earliest South Carolinians has spanned several decades and has benefited from a host of individuals and institutions. At SCIAA, the administration of Robert L. Stephenson, Bruce Rippeteau, Jonathan Leader, Thorne Compton, and Charles Cobb have supported this work in countless ways. At the USC Salkehatchie campus, Dean Ann Carmichael provided storage space and sponsored the Topper artifact exhibit. Colleagues at the institute include

Tommy Charles, Nena Powell Rice, Keith Derting, Mark Brooks, Christopher Moore, Daryl P. Miller, Kenn Steffy, and John Kirby. Funding has been provided by the Archaeological Research Trust Board of SCIAA, the Robert L. Stephenson Archaeology Fund, the National Geographic Society, the Harper Family Foundation through Tony Harper, Elizabeth Stringfellow, and the numerous participants of the Allendale Paleoamerican Expedition. The sites referred to here are on the land owned by Clariant Corporation, and before that Sandoz Chemical Corporation. The crucial support of Mike Anderson and Bill Hartford of those companies cannot be overestimated. Fellow Paleoamerican scholars—including David G. Anderson, Rob Bonnichsen, Mike Waters, Tom Stafford, Steve Forman, Dennis Stanford, Pegi Jodry, Randy Daniel, John Foss, Scott Harris, Barbara Purdy, Allen West, David Leigh, Joel Gunn, Shane Miller, Ashley M. Smallwood, Doug Sain, Derek T. Anderson, Kara Bridgman Sweeney, Sean Taylor, and Megan Hoak King—all contributed to our work. Field laboratory work was provided by Erika H. Shofner and Elizabeth Bell. Scott Jones provided lithic replication studies that aided analysis and public education. The artistic skills of Darby Erd and video production of SCETV's Steve Folks are acknowledged. The formation of the Allendale Paleoamerican Expedition led to the expansion of the fieldwork to include numerous individuals from the avocational field. There is not enough space to acknowledge fully the work of Tom Pertierra in fashioning the expedition into a logistically efficient field operation and making numerous programmatic improvements with internet technology, laboratory development, and conference production. Expedition members who functioned as staff include Tom Pertierra of SEPAS, DSO, director of operations and logistics; Joan and Ernie Plummer; Bill Lyles; Bill and Ann Covington; Judith Scruggs; Terry Hynes; Jean Guilleux; Leon Perry; Carol Reed; Paula Zitzelberger; John and Alison Simpson; John White; and Steve Williams. In the avocational community, John Arena, Dr. Robert Costello, Danny Greenway, Sam and Anne Rice, Stan Smith, Frank and Andee Steen, and Dr. Larry Strong provided useful data over the years. To all these people and organizations go my heartfelt thanks.

References Cited

Adovasio, James, and Jake Page

2002   *The First Americans: In Pursuit of Archaeology's Greatest Mystery.* Random House, New York.

Anderson, David G.

2002   A History of Archaeological Research in South Carolina. In *Histories of Southeastern Archaeology,* edited by Shannon Tushingham, Jane Hill, and Charles H. McNutt, pp. 145–159. University of Alabama Press, Tuscaloosa.

Anderson, David G., D. Shane Miller, Stephen J. Yerka, J. Christopher Gillam, Erik N. Johanson, Derek T. Anderson, Albert C. Goodyear, and Ashley M. Smallwood

2010   PIDBA (Paleoindian Database of the Americas) 2010: Current Status and Findings. *Archaeology of Eastern North America* 38:1–28.

Begley, Sharon, and Andrew Murr

1999   The First Americans. *Newsweek.* April 26:50–57.

Brockington, Paul B.

1970   A Preliminary Investigation of an Early Knapping Site in Southeastern Georgia. *The Notebook* 3:34–46. South Carolina Institute of Archaeology and Anthropology, University of South Carolina, Columbia.

Caldwell, Joseph R.

1952   The Archeology of Eastern Georgia and South Carolina. In *Archeology of Eastern United States,* edited by James B. Griffin, pp. 312–321. University of Chicago Press, Chicago.

Collins, Michael B., Michael R. Waters, Albert C. Goodyear, Dennis J. Stanford, Tom Pertierra, and Ted Goebel

2008   2008 Paleoamerican Origins Workshop: A Brief Report. *Current Research in the Pleistocene* 25:195–197.

Dillehay, Thomas D.

2000   *The Settlement of the Americas: A New Prehistory.* Basic Books, New York.

Gardner, William

1983   Stop Me If You've Heard This One Before: The Flint Run Paleoindian Complex Revisited. *Archaeology of Eastern North America* 11:49–59.

Goebel, Ted, Michael R. Waters, and Dennis H. O'Rourke

2008   The Late Pleistocene Dispersal of Modern Humans in the Americas. *Science* 319:1497–1502.

Goodyear, Albert C.

1993   Origins: Some Thoughts and Reminiscences Concerning Florida Archaeology, 1963–1993. *Florida Anthropologist* 46:212–214.

1994   Robert Lloyd Stephenson. *American Antiquity* 59:264–269.

1999   The Early Holocene Occupation of the Southeastern United States: A Geoarchaeology Summary. In *Ice-Age People of North America: Environments, Origins and Adaptations,* edited by R. Bonnichsen and K. Turnmire, pp. 432–481. Center for the Study of the First Americans, Corvallis, Oregon.

2005a   Evidence of Pre-Clovis Sites in the Eastern United States. In *Paleoamerican Origins: Beyond Clovis,* edited by Robson Bonnichsen, Bradley T. Lepper, Dennis Stanford, and Michael R. Waters, pp. 103–112. Texas A&M University Press, College Station.

2005b   A Special Tribute to James L. Michie. *Legacy* 9(1–2):50. Newsletter of the South Carolina Institute of Archaeology and Anthropology, University of South Carolina, Columbia.

2006   The Southeastern Paleoamerican Survey. *Legacy* 10(2):16–19. Newsletter of the South Carolina Institute of Archaeology and Anthropology, University of South Carolina, Columbia.

2009   Update on Research at the Topper Site. *Legacy* 13(1):8–13. Newsletter of the South Carolina Institute of Archaeology and Anthropology, University of South Carolina, Columbia.

2010   Lithic Raw Material Studies in South Carolina and Their Implications for Paleoindian Mobility Patterns and Exchange. *South Carolina Antiquities* 42:40–41.

Goodyear, Albert C., and Tommy Charles

1984   *An Archaeological Survey of Chert Quarries in Western Allendale County, South Carolina.* Research Manuscript Series 195. South Carolina Institute of Archaeology and Anthropology, University of South Carolina, Columbia.

Goodyear, Albert C., and Kenn Steffy

2003   Evidence of a Clovis Occupation at the Topper Site, 38AL23, Allendale County, South Carolina. *Current Research in the Pleistocene* 20:23–25.

Goodyear, Albert C., James L. Michie, and Tommy Charles

1989   The Earliest South Carolinians. In *Studies in South Carolina Archaeology: Essays in Honor of Robert L. Stephenson,* edited by

A. C. Goodyear and G. T. Hanson, pp. 19–52. Anthropological Studies 9, Occasional Papers of the South Carolina Institute of Archaeology and Anthropology. University of South Carolina, Columbia.

Haynes, C. Vance, Jr.

1969   The Earliest Americans. *Science* 166:709–715.

Hemmings, E. Thomas

1972   Early Man in the South Atlantic States. *South Carolina Antiquities* 4:1–9.

Jones, Scott

2002   Smashing Success: Pleistocene Lithic Replication in South Carolina. *Bulletin of Primitive Technology* 23:44–51.

Meltzer, David J.

2009   *First Peoples in a New World: Colonizing Ice Age America.* University of California Press, Berkeley.

Michie, James L.

1965   Fluted Point Types of South Carolina. *The Chesopiean* 3(5):107–113.

1977   The Late Pleistocene Human Occupation of South Carolina. Manuscript on file with the South Carolina Institute of Archaeology and Anthropology, University of South Carolina, Columbia.

Miller, D. Shane

2011   *Clovis Excavations at Topper 2005–2007: Examining Site Formation Processes at an Upland Paleoindian Site along the Middle Savannah River.* Occasional Papers—Southeastern Paleoamerican Survey 1. South Carolina Institute of Archaeology and Anthropology, University of South Carolina, Columbia.

Petit, Charles W.

1998   Rediscovering America. *U.S. News and World Report,* October 12:56–64.

Sain, Douglas A.

2010   Clovis Blade Technology at the Topper Site (38AL23). Unpublished master's thesis, Department of Anthropology, Eastern New Mexico University, Portales.

2012   *Clovis Blade Technology at the Topper Site: Assessing Lithic Attribute Variation and Regional Patterns of Technological Organization.* Occasional Papers—Southeastern Paleoamerican Survey 2. South Carolina Institute of Archaeology and Anthropology, University of South Carolina, Columbia.

Sain, Douglas A., and Albert C. Goodyear

2012   A comparison of Clovis Blade Technologies at the Topper and Big Pine Tree Sites, Allendale County, South Carolina. In

Contemporary Lithic Analysis in the Southeast: Problems, Solutions, and Interpretations, edited by Philip J. Carr, Andrew P. Bradbury, and Sarah E. Price, pp. 42–54. University of Alabama Press, Tuscaloosa.

Smallwood, Ashley M.

2010   Clovis Biface Technology at the Topper Site, South Carolina: Evidence for Variation and Technological Flexibility. *Journal of Archaeological Science* 37:2413–2425.

2012   Clovis Technology and Settlement in the American Southeast: Using Biface Analysis to Evaluate Dispersal Models. *American Antiquity* 77:689–713.

Smallwood, Ashley M., D. Shane Miller, and Douglas Sain

2013   Topper Site, South Carolina: An Overview of the Clovis Lithic Assemblage from the Topper Hillside. In *In the Eastern Fluted Point Tradition,* edited by Joseph A. M. Gingerich, pp. 280–98. University of Utah Press, Salt Lake City.

Steffy, Kenn, and Albert C. Goodyear

2006   Clovis Macro Blades from the Topper Site, 38AL23, Allendale County, South Carolina. *Current Research in the Pleistocene* 23:147–149.

Stephenson, Robert L.

1971   Thoughts on the Calico Mountains Site. *The Notebook* 3(1):3–9. South Carolina Institute of Archaeology and Anthropology, University of South Carolina, Columbia.

1975   An Archaeological Preservation Plan for South Carolina. *The Notebook* 12:41–109. South Carolina Institute of Archaeology and Anthropology, University of South Carolina, Columbia.

Waddell, Eugene C.

1965   South Carolina Fluted Points. *Southeastern Archaeological Conference Bulletin* 2:52–54. Proceedings of the Twentieth Southeastern Archaeological Conference, edited by Stephen Williams. Cambridge, Massachusetts.

Waring, Antonio

1961   Fluted Points on the South Carolina Coast. *American Antiquity* 26:550–552.

Waters, Michael R., Steven L. Forman, Thomas W. Stafford, and John Foss

2009   Geoarchaeological Investigations at the Topper and Big Pine Tree Sites, Allendale County, South Carolina. *Journal of Archaeological Science* 36:1300–1311.

Wauchope, Robert

1939   Fluted Points from South Carolina. *American Antiquity* 4:344–346.

Wormington, H. M.

1957   *Ancient Man in North America.* Popular Series No. 4. Denver Museum of Natural History, Denver, Colorado.

KENNETH E. SASSAMAN

The Multicultural Genesis of Stallings Culture

SOME 4,000 YEARS AGO in the river valley shared today by South Carolina and Georgia, people of at least two distinct ancestries joined together to create a cultural tradition known to archaeologists as "Stallings." They persisted as a people for some 15 generations before embarking on other historical paths. Their time

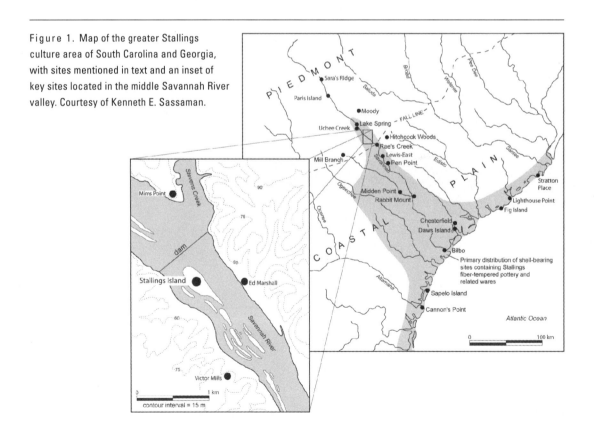

Figure 1. Map of the greater Stallings culture area of South Carolina and Georgia, with sites mentioned in text and an inset of key sites located in the middle Savannah River valley. Courtesy of Kenneth E. Sassaman.

in the region was actually quite short lived compared to others who came before and since, but they left an indelible footprint on the landscape, particularly in the middle Savannah River valley near Augusta, Georgia, and along the coast (Figure 1). In these locations they collected shellfish—primarily oysters on the coast and freshwater clams along the river—and placed the inedible remains in piles that sometimes gained monumental proportions. This conspicuous record of their life aquatic is evident in the large assemblages of sherds of pottery sporting distinctive stylistic and technical qualities (Figure 2). Tempered with plant fiber and decorated elaborately, this pottery is among the oldest in North America, giving Stallings culture enough relevance to be featured in major textbooks on North American archaeology (Fagan 2005; Neusius and Gross 2007:464–465).

Although the shell deposits and pottery of Stallings culture are well known to archaeologists, its genesis is not fully understood. We can trace the local history of cultural development from the time pottery appears, but ultimately, we do not have much knowledge of the ancestry of the first pottery-using communities. Sea-level rise since 5,000 years ago has obliterated remnants of the early centuries of coastal settlement, the presumed venue for the oldest pottery (Sassaman

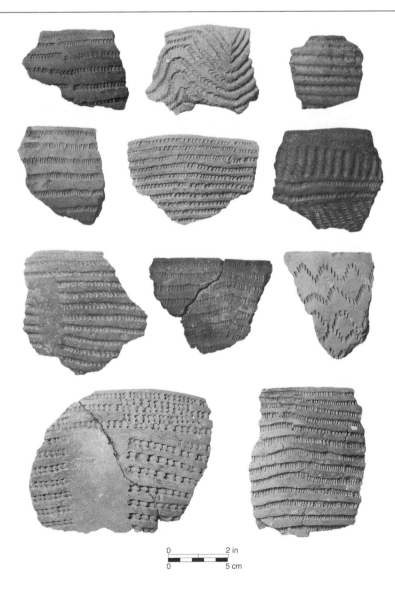

Figure 2. Sherds of Stallings drag-and-jab fiber-tempered pottery. Courtesy of Kenneth E. Sassaman.

0   2 in
0   5 cm

2004). Pottery and a shell-fishing economy were likely to have been homegrown innovations, but they also may have been stimulated by developments farther south, in the Caribbean, and even in South America, as the famous archaeologist James Ford (1969) once opined.

We may never know the ultimate source of innovation, but we do know that when pottery first appeared on the coast and in the coastal plain, about 5,000 years ago, the Piedmont province of the upper Savannah River valley was inhabited by people of a different cultural tradition. The history of these upcountry communities traces back many centuries, even millennia. Over the many centuries of interacting with their neighbors in the lowcountry, they underwent several cultural changes, including their own displays of ostentatiousness, but they never adopted pottery or fully assimilated into Stallings culture, at least not at first. Eventually, at about 4,100 years ago, certain Piedmont descendants and immigrant bands of coastal dwellers converged in the middle Savannah River valley to form the namesake community of Classic Stallings times. Other episodes of multicultural community formation likely transpired in other places on the landscape, but none is as well known as that of the middle Savannah valley, centered on the premier site of cultural identity, Stallings Island (Figure 1).

This recounting of ancient culture history begins with a sketch of life during the heyday of Stallings culture, a three-century-long era I refer to as "Classic Stallings." After considering the coastal roots of this tradition and its connection to ancestral people of the Piedmont, I revisit Classic Stallings culture to examine the circumstances of its ultimate transformation. If there is a thread of continuity in this history of genesis, flamboyance, and demise, it is that people of distinct cultural identity interacted routinely across vast geographies and through these interactions culture change ensued (see Sassaman 2006 for a detailed exposition of this culture history and the archaeology that enabled its writing).

This story is informed by a suite of observations and hard data, but it is also structured by anthropological theory about the sociality of small-scale societies. Stallings people were hunter-gatherers, people who lived off of natural resources alone, many of which, in this case, they harvested from river, swamp, and sea. Since the early twentieth century, hunter-gatherer studies have been dominated by an ecological approach that emphasizes the relationship people have to the environment. In the middle of the last century, the concept of "culture core," promoted by Julian Steward, became nearly synonymous with hunter-gatherers. Steward (1955) suggested that hunter-gatherers were so closely tied to the land and its resources that their entire cultural being, their culture core, was understood best as an adaptation to nature. Only after the advent of farming, the old story goes, were humans able to free themselves of the vagaries of nature and embark on the pathways of cultural development that would lead to city-states, religious and political institutions, and the arts, among other accoutrements of civil society.

But Steward's perception of hunter-gatherer life was heavily biased toward observations of people in relatively inhospitable locales, such as the Great Basin of the American West, where his Shoshone subjects resided. Living in an environment where access to food and water is tenuous at times, cultural dispositions and routine practices had better obey the rhythms and limits of nature. Conversely, hunter-gatherers who occupied more benevolent and forgiving environments attained levels of settlement permanence and economic surplus that would rival or surpass many agricultural communities. Examples in North America include the Chumash of coastal California (Gamble 2008), the Calusa of southwest Florida (Marquardt 2004), and numerous populations of the Northwest Pacific Coast (Ames and Maschner 1999). These remarkable exceptions to Steward's model of hunter-gatherer society have never been regarded as good analogs for ancient hunter-gatherers because both the rich environments that enabled them and the technological means to exploit rich resources were considered relatively recent phenomena. Now that we have a good sense that so-called complex hunter-gatherers can be traced back millennia in many locations across the globe, archaeologist engage in debate on the extent to which their genesis can be attributed to the resource abundance of certain locales (Arnold 1996; Hayden 1994).

Expanding on this sort of environmental perspective, archaeologists are increasingly investigating the effect of intergroup interactions in shaping hunter-gatherer diversity. Over the past few decades, anthropologists have reexamined the histories of ethnographic hunter-gatherers for clues of widespread and influential interactions with agricultural and state-level societies (Headland and Reid 1989). We now know that even the simplest hunter-gatherers of the modern era, such as those of the Kalahari desert of southern Africa, have been in contact with farmers, herders and states for centuries. Arguably, the cultural dispositions of these small-scale, simple societies—as well as their circumscription in less-than-ideal locations on the globe—resulted directly from interactions with others, many of which were and continue to be hostile and exploitative. This appears to have been the fate of some Mountain Shoshone groups (Scheiber and Finley 2011) and may very well prove to be the case for the Great Basin groups studied by Steward.

Anthropologists now generally agree that the cultural dispositions of hunter-gatherers in the modern era cannot be understood apart from their interaction with the food-producing communities and nation-sates in which they are encapsulated. Two deductions follow from this conclusion. First, given the webs of social interaction that shaped hunter-gatherer culture of the modern era, it is imprudent to reduce explanations of hunter-gatherer diversity to (natural) environment alone. Second, only archaeology can provide information on what hunter-gatherer society and culture was like in a world of exclusively hunter-gatherers (that is, before agriculture). Unfortunately, this latter deduction can be misconstrued as a warrant for archaeologists to ignore the lessons of recent history. It would be a mistake to assume that the time before history, the time of "prehistory," was free of the sorts of intercultural encounters that had the capacity to shape culture (Sassaman 2011). This ill-founded assumption perpetuates a continuing dominance of ecological paradigms in the interpretation of ancient hunter-gatherers, as if prehistoric cultures were self-contained adaptations to particular environmental conditions.

Stallings culture defies any such simple ecological explanation. Sure, the people of this culture lived in a world structured by seasonal change, fluctuations in the availability of food and raw materials, and energetic limits to growth and expansion. However, the cultural dispositions that determined what was and was not edible, where to pitch camp, or the best way to process plant foods were not simply the long-term outcome of communing with nature. Rather, they were constructed from a mélange of diverse experiences in far-flung places and shifting relationships to other people. The diversity of their dispositions was both precedent and product of technological choice, labor relations, and coresidency—the very factors that would determine their ability to successfully exploit their environment and sustain themselves in a given locale. Classic Stallings culture owes its genesis to interactions among people of diverse cultural traditions. In this sense it was an historical phenomenon, a history that was enacted over a vast geographical expanse.

Classic Stallings

For three centuries, ca. 4,100–3,800 years ago, the middle Savannah River valley was dominated by a people determined to leave their mark on the landscape. Classic Stallings culture was an era of apparent florescence. I use the term "classic" to signify a heightened and unified sense of cultural identity, a distinctive cultural tradition. In Classic Stallings times, distinctiveness is seen in a variety of ways, but none is more conspicuous than pottery making (Sassaman 1993a).

The repertoire of Classic Stallings pottery includes a diversity of stylistic expression. Indentations in the wet-clay surfaces of pottery vessels were executed with styluses made from a variety of materials, notably wood, bone, and shell. The size and tip shape of styluses varied widely, and even more varied were the uses of repetition in linear, geometric, and random fashion. Throughout the middle Savannah River valley, no two punctated Stallings vessels were identical. It seems reasonable to suggest that the extreme variation in Stallings pottery reflects a sense of individuality, but when we look past the specific execution of punctations to consider the broader motifs expressed in lines, zonation, and spacing, we can appreciate that Stallings potters were strongly allied as a community.

The technology of Stallings pottery is nearly as distinctive, if less diverse, than variations on punctations. Classic Stallings pottery from the middle Savannah area, like its antecedents and some regional cognates, was made from clay that was tempered with plant fiber, mostly Spanish moss. Vessels were generally shaped from slabs and occasionally coiled into simple, open bowls. Averaging about 30 cm in diameter and 20 cm in height, Classic Stallings bowls were usually thin walled but occasionally thickened, often owing to larger vessel size.

It is difficult to state with authority the absolute geographic limits of Classic Stallings pottery. The core of its distribution is the middle to lower Savannah River valley, but it is attenuated to the south, and its ultimate origins likely fall to the Georgia coast (Sassaman 2004). On the apparent edges of its regional distribution, Classic Stallings pottery gives way to related wares that were presumably used by related, yet separate people. The St. Simons wares of coastal Georgia, Thoms Creek of coastal and coastal plain South Carolina, and the Ogeechee pottery of Georgia are among the larger cognates. In some of these related wares, fiber gives way to sand for temper, and surface treatments include variations on punctations and incisions not found in the middle Savannah area.

No site in the Savannah River is known to have more fiber-tempered pottery than Stallings Island. The Peabody Museum at Harvard has collections of many thousands of sherds from the work of Claflin and the Cosgroves (Claflin 1931). Among the numerous examples of linear punctate and other Classic Stallings wares are rim sherds with carinated profiles (Figure 3). This form occurs occasionally at other sites in the area, but only at Stallings Island does it occur with appreciable frequency (about 15 percent of all vessels). The form appears again much later in the Mississippian period and is interpreted by David Hally (1986) as a vessel designed for serving. Because many of the ones from Stallings Island have large volumes and highly ornate decoration on the rim (like the fine china used today for special occasions), I suspect they were not simply everyday serving vessels but rather used on occasions of social gatherings. Given the evidence of feasting at coastal sites of Classic Stallings culture (see below), the carinated bowls at Stallings Island are likely the remnants of large social gatherings.

The remainder of the Stallings material repertoire is a plethora of stone, bone, and antler tools and ornaments. The typical chipped-stone tool is a stemmed hafted biface, a form with precedence in older Late Archaic phases in the region. Classic Stallings bifaces, however, exhibit great diversity in the size and shape, and they were made from a variety of raw materials. Other chipped-stone tools were generally expedient in design and use, with a few formal tools for boring, scraping, and cutting functions. Groundstone tools include hand-sized hammers and grinding stones and larger basins and mortars. They apparently had few polished stone items, such as the bannerstones of the preceding Late Archaic phase (see below). They did, however, continue to use the grooved axe of their predecessors in the Piedmont, and the age-old custom of shaping soapstone into perforated slabs for indirect-heat cooking persisted into at least the first century or two of Classic Stallings times. Soapstone vessels were never part of the Classic Stallings repertoire.

From bone Stallings craftspeople made pins, awls, fish hooks, fleshers, blunt-edged tools, and spearthrower handles and hooks (Figure 4). Pins made from split deer bone were often adorned with flanges at the top and incised in a variety of geometric motifs. Occasional deer jaws and other bone parts were likewise decorated with incising and sometimes with red paint, most likely made from hematite. Deer antler was used to make handles for knives, billets for chipping stone, and socketed projectiles. Other organic media used by Stallings people, such as wood and fiber, have not been preserved in archaeological contexts but are presumed to have been used for nets, baskets, mats, and elements of domestic architecture.

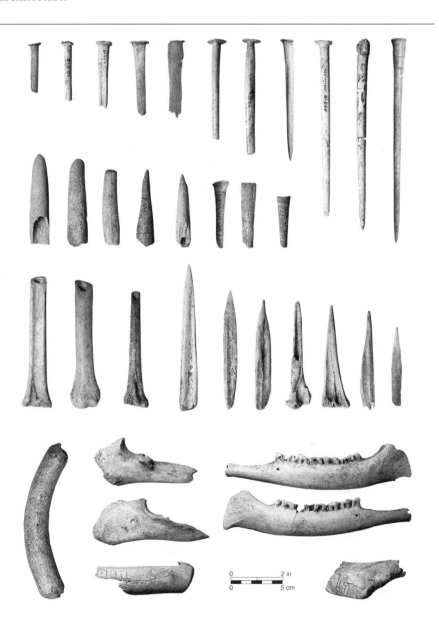

Figure 4. Bone and antler tools from the Classic Stallings assemblage at Stallings Island. Courtesy of Kenneth E. Sassaman.

Direct evidence for the sorts of houses built and occupied by Classic Stallings people eludes us. However, an important line of circumstantial evidence comes from the spatial array of pit features and hearths they dug into the earth (Sassaman et al. 2006). At some sites that have been excavated in middle Savannah, feature assemblages cluster in circular or semicircular arrays between 30 and 40 m in diameter. These patterns are what remains, I have argued, of circular compounds of seven or eight houses in communities estimated to consist of 25–40 individuals. Evidence to support this inference is so far restricted to few sites, the best example of which is known as Mims Point (Figure 1).

Mims Point is a small Classic Stallings settlement at the confluence of Stevens Creek and the Savannah River, a mere kilometer upriver from Stallings Island (Sassaman 1993b). Through funding and support of the U.S. Forest Service, excavations at Mims Point in the 1990s exposed a large portion of a compound of several households encircling a central, open area (much like a plaza). Each household in the compound was surrounded by a series of pits. The largest ones were storage pits that at first held hickory and maybe acorn but were converted to trash receptacles after stored food was removed. Among the items of refuse in abandoned pits were Classic Stallings sherds, stemmed bifaces, soapstone cooking stones, bone tools, grooved axe fragments, fish hooks, and abundant animal food remains.

Although the Mims Point circular compound was not fully exposed, the portion observed expressed an advanced level of clarity because uses of the site before and after did not obscure spatial patterning of the Classic Stallings settlement. Certainly the artifacts of earlier and some later people are common at the site, but aside from a few intrusive burials and a Late Woodland structure at the north end of the compound, much of the Stallings compound was free of unrelated features.

Such was not the case at Stallings Island, where earlier Late Archaic occupations involved human interments and innumerable pit features and hearths. The amalgam of early and late features in the excavation made by the Cosgroves provides little evidence of patterning, aside, that is, from being concentrated at the center and high point of the site. However, coupled with the collections housed at the Peabody Museum at Harvard, the field notes made by the Cosgroves enable us to infer a circular compound similar to the Mims Point compound (Sassaman et al. 2006). The Cosgroves recorded information of the depth, diameter, and content of the 110 pit features they excavated, and of these 38 contained Classic Stallings pottery. The spatial distribution of these 38 pits is decidedly arcuate, and clusters of several pits within the arc, spaced about 8 m apart, each contain a combination of storage "silos," shallow pits, basins, and hearths. Like the deep pits at Mims Point, the silos at Stallings Island were chock full of debris and food remains, including ample hickory nutshell. As far as we know, silos were not used by the Late Archaic people who lived at Stallings Island and vicinity in the centuries before Stallings culture appeared. Nor has evidence for circular compounds been observed at any of the excavated sites in the area of pre-Stallings age.

One peculiar feature of the Stallings Island residential compound suggests that it was a special locus on the landscape of Classic Stallings times. In the projected center of the circular compound at Stallings Island were the interments of at least 32 humans. An additional 12 were located in the area of the houses, and another 40 were scattered across areas excavated by the Cosgroves and Claflin. C. C. Jones (1861), the nineteenth-century antiquarian, exhumed many other graves and was so impressed with the mortuary function that he considered the site to be a "huge necropolis." I believe he had good reason to do so, for only one other Stallings site in the middle Savannah area, Lake Spring, upriver from Stallings Island, contained more than an occasional burial (Miller 1949).

Because humans were interred at Stallings Island before, during, and after the Classic Stallings period, it is not often possible to date any particular burial to any particular period based on artifacts alone. None of the cultural traditions involving human interments on the island included diagnostic artifacts with every grave. Still, the concentration of burials in the center of the residential compound is not likely to be random and most likely reflects a tendency for Classic Stallings residents to place their dead in the center of the village. Moreover, subtle differences in the placement of individuals in the center suggest that mortuary practice was structured by very specific cultural values. That is, the specific locations of individuals by gender and perhaps age, like the arrangement of houses in a circle, followed a proscription that sets Classic Stallings apart from its immediate forebears and its contemporary neighbors. At the same time, it embodies the multiple strands of cultural heritage that converged and then morphed into this particular suite of cultural practices. No strand of heritage is more obvious than that of the coast.

Stallings Coastal Roots

The coast of Georgia or northeast Florida is the likely source area for two of the defining features of Classic Stallings culture: pottery and circular settlement. The exact timing and sequence of these features on the coast are complicated by preservation factors and the vagaries of radiometric age estimates taken from marine shell. The oldest radiometric dates for pottery come from both riverine (Stoltman 1974) and coastal sites (Saunders 2004a), but we have good reason to suspect that even older occupations existed on the coast and were long ago destroyed or buried under a mantle of marsh mud. Archaeologists generally acknowledge that the record of coastal dwelling is truncated at ca. 4700 cal B.P., after which the rate of sea-level rise slowed considerably. Coastal sites predating 4,700 years ago are indeed rare. Archaeologists suspect that there was sustained coastal settlement along the coast well before pottery appeared about 5,000 years ago, and evidence from northeast Florida is beginning to bear this out (Russo 1996:189–190).

Circular settlement has great antiquity on the coast, in forms known to archaeologists as "shell rings" (Russo and Heide 2001). Shell rings of the South Atlantic coast are circular or semicircular accumulations of shell ranging from tens to hundreds of meters in diameter and 1–5 m in height. The oldest is from northeast Florida and dates to roughly 5,300 years ago, at least 500 years before pottery appeared locally. The youngest date to several centuries after the Classic Stallings era and are concentrated on the South Carolina coast. Those coeval with Classic Stallings times and the centuries immediately prior extend from the southern South Carolina coast to northeast Florida.

Our knowledge of the function, internal configuration, and sociality of shell rings has been greatly enhanced lately by a series of independent projects (such as Russo et al. 2002; Saunders 2004b; Saunders and Russo 2002; Thomas 2008;

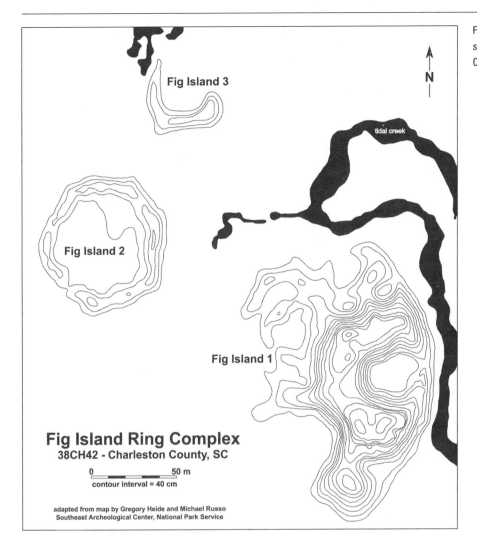

Figure 5. Topographic map of the Fig Island shell ring complex, Charleston County, South Carolina. Courtesy of Kenneth E. Sassaman.

Fig Island 3

tidal creek

Fig Island 2

Fig Island 1

Fig Island Ring Complex
38CH42 - Charleston County, SC

0   50 m

contour interval = 40 cm

adapted from map by Gregory Heide and Michael Russo
Southeast Archeological Center, National Park Service

Thompson 2006). Given the brevity of this essay and our present interest in examining the roots of Classic Stallings culture, I must refer the reader to this body of new literature for more detail (see Russo 2008 and Russo and Heide 2001 for cogent summaries). I do, however, find it useful to summarize the findings of one project in particular that has fundamentally reshaped the way we think about shell rings.

Fig Island is South Carolina's largest and most complex shell ring complex (Figure 5) (Saunders and Russo 2002). Located in an estuary near Edisto Island, the shell rings at Fig Island include a more or less circular deposit about 77 m in diameter, an arcuate midden 50 m in diameter, and an arcuate deposit some 157 m long, 111 m wide, and 5.5 m tall. This latter deposit features smaller, ring-like appendages on the west side. All told, the shellworks cover an area of about 5 acres and were laid down from ca. 4600 to 4200 cal B.P.

Like other coastal shell rings, the Fig Island rings consist mostly of oyster. Fish bones dominate the vertebrate food remains, and a variety of other aquatic and terrestrial species occur in much lesser abundance. Nothing in the food inventory of Fig Island deviates all that much from any other coastal settlement of this age, but the structure of the deposits strongly suggests that food remains accumulated in large batches. Massive lenses of whole, clean oyster were deposited at the base and in successive layers throughout the rings. Atop these large dumps of shell are lenses of soil or crushed shell indicative of interruptions in the accumulation of shell and temporary periods of surface stability. Similar deposits of whole clean shell and overlying "floors" have been observed at other shell rings along the coast (Russo 2006).

Saunders and Russo (2002), among others, regard these large dumps of shell as the byproduct of communal feasts. The sheer scale of these activities is alone enough to support this hypothesis (that is, the level of shellfish consumption exceeds that expected of a single episode of consumption by a small residential unit), but strong, ancillary support is seen in the composition of the pottery assemblage. Vessel lots from Fig Island are dominated by simple, open bowls that were ornately decorated. Paralleling the circumstances discussed earlier about Stallings carinated bowls, the bowls of Fig Island were arguably the wares of social consumption, of feasts. Elsewhere Saunders (2004a) has documented that shell rings in general have a much higher frequency of decorated wares compared to other types of shell-bearing sites along the coast. Michie (1979) made a similar observation long ago when he argued that shell rings were ceremonial locations of gathering for an otherwise dispersed population.

How dispersed people were integrated into ring ceremonialism is a matter of speculation at this point, but we can begin to assemble the rudiments of a sociopolitical model of shell-ring populations from clues to the spatial configuration of the rings themselves. This has been the approach of Michael Russo (2004), who sees in the asymmetries of shell-ring form the economic basis of social differentiation within the Fig Island community.

Variations in the height and breadth of shell-ting segments at Fig Island led Russo to deduce that activities involving rapid accumulations of shell (either feasting or purposeful construction) varied with social status. Competitive feasts, such as those practiced by Northwest Coastal groups in ceremonial potlatches, implicate some level of social differentiation whereby one's ability to compete varies with one's ability to muster obligatory labor, which is often tied to one's ability to collect and dispense of wealth as a means of accumulating social debt. The rich keep getting richer, so to speak. The consequence for asymmetry in the shell rings is that locations occupied by households of wealth (social, if not material) grew higher and broader through time, compared, that is, to households of lesser wealth. Russo has been able to show that asymmetries in height and breadth occur in regular locations at shell rings across the region. For instance, the highest and broadest parts of rings are typically opposite any sort of opening or some other distinctive features. Fig Island Ring 2, despite its seeming asymmetry, clearly has nodes of higher and broader shell accumulation opposite an apparent opening to the southwest and adjacent to an apparent causeway linking it with Fig Island 3 to the northeast. If these sorts of asymmetries resulted from the fixed spatial arrangements of certain types of personnel over many generations, then social roles may have been inherited. But even if the spatial patterning evident at rings had little to do with particular individuals or households, the redundancy in use signals a proscription for how rings were to be constructed or at least occupied. At the minimum, the recurrent geometry of rings precludes any argument that rings were the de facto or even deliberate product of a community consisting of interchangeable personnel. Social or cultural differentiation of some manner is encoded in the geometry and internal structure of rings.

Fig Island dates to the centuries just prior to the emergence of Classic Stallings culture in the middle Savannah, but there is no evidence to suggest that Fig Island denizens figured directly in the genesis of Stallings. Fig Island pottery is classified as Thoms Creek, meaning that it is sand tempered, not fiber tempered. Also, Fig Island potters often used a periwinkle shell to punctate the exterior surfaces of their bowls, something that is very rare in the middle Savannah area, despite access to freshwater snail shells that mimicked the shape of periwinkle shells. Moreover, periwinkle designs were executed in lines of separate punctation, not in the continuous drag-and-jab manner of middle Savannah pottery.

Pottery assemblages from other shell rings on the southern coast of South Carolina bear greater affinity to Classic Stallings wares than does Fig Island. No assemblage exemplifies this better than the one from Chesterfield Shell Ring on Port Royal Island. A sizeable fraction of sherds from this 55-m diameter ring are fiber-tempered, drag-and-jab punctate that would fit comfortably in any collection from Stallings Island and vicinity. In fact, the type description for Stallings pottery was written by the late James B. Griffin (1943) from analysis of sherds from this ring. A single radiocarbon age estimate from a sooted sherd at Chesterfield (3660 ± 50 cal B.P.) falls squarely in the middle of the Classic Stallings period in the middle Savannah; its historical affinity to Stallings Island appears certain. However, this is not to suggest that Chesterfield and Stallings Island are simply two sites of the same people. Some of the pottery from Chesterfield suggests otherwise. A sizable portion of the Chesterfield assemblage consists of periwinkle punctate designs, like those from Fig Island. Although the technology of these wares is the same as the drag-and-jab wares, the decorative motifs are very distinctive.

Better understanding about the coexistence of two distinct decorative motifs at Chesterfield must await better chronology, but noteworthy nonetheless are implications for dual social organization at the site. In many nonwestern societies, village communities consist of two or more major units of descent, what are called lineages or clans. Such divisions are implicated in all manner of social interactions, from organized labor to rules of marriage, and from conflict resolution to ritual practices. They sometimes also signal the historical union or coalescence of formerly distinct communities, as in certain tribal societies of the Amazon and the American Plains. Circular settlement in these cases unify and integrate disparate people into "one," which may well be the case with shell rings. And yet, even in the symmetrical circular villages of Amazonia or the Great Plains, social identities and cultural heritage are not blended or lost through union; indeed, the divisions are manifest in spatial regularities that underpin distinctions of rank and privilege. In each of these cases, there is always a social faction that asserts its dominance over the other(s) by asserting its ancestral primacy. In these cases, there are always "first people."

Evidence for duality in social organization can be inferred from a variety of sites in the region, but we have to be careful not to confuse this sort of patterning with the duality to living that Williams Sears (1973) dichotomized as "sacred" and "secular." That is, the differences between ritual life and everyday living may be manifested in the distinction between decorated and plain pottery, communal feasting and domestic consumption, and even between shell rings and all other site types. In exploring causes for these possible dualities, archaeologists may find it useful to expand their spatial and time scale to consider the extent to which emergent ritual structures, like shell rings, provided contexts for integrating people of distinctive culture.

Upcountry Traditions

Small communities of coastal people using plain fiber-tempered pottery started to occupy lower Coastal Plain sites in the Savannah River valley as early as 5,100 years ago. Rabbit Mount (Stoltman 1974) in Allendale County and Bilbo near Savannah (Waring 1968) are good examples of this upriver encroachment by communities with ties to the coast. The occupants of these early Coastal Plain sites had connections to upcountry neighbors as well. Throughout the period I call Early Stallings, Coastal Plain residents acquired perforated soapstone slabs from their counterparts in the Piedmont and used these items with shallow, flat-bottomed pottery vessels in the age-old method of indirect cooking, otherwise known as "stone boiling." These long-distance connections to the upcountry may have facilitated or even encouraged the relocation of some Coastal Plain groups to the middle Savannah area, at least temporarily. By about 4,700 years ago, groups from the Coastal Plain traveled into the lower Piedmont to collect and store hickory nuts and acorns for the winter. A century or two later, the apparent descendants of these interlopers established more or less permanent residence in the middle Savannah.

The establishment of trade relations between upcountry and lowcountry groups and the eventual relocation of some of the latter to the area around Augusta was accompanied by abrupt shifts in the way people expressed themselves through material culture. There can be no doubt that Piedmont populations in the fledgling years of this history traced their ancestry to people and places far different from those of Coastal Plain and coastal peoples. Interactions between the two clearly resulted in transfers of items, ideas, and even personnel though intermarriage, but it did not fully erase the heritage of these distinctive people. In fact, interactions heightened the expression of difference, at least among those factions who elaborated tradition to assert autonomy or to resist change. Both compliance and defiance are evident in the social histories of upcountry groups as their world was drawn into closer contact with coastal groups.

Two instances of cultural change among upcountry communities exemplify the heightened sense of cultural identity emanating from interactions with "foreigners." The Paris Island phase of ca. 5350–4700 cal B.P., centered on the Piedmont province of the Savannah River valley, is well known to archaeologists thanks to the excellent work of Dean Wood and his colleagues (1986). The onset of this phase coincides with the oldest pottery on the coast, and its close coincides with the movement of Coastal Plain communities into the lower Piedmont. Throughout this phase and the succeeding Mill Branch phase (ca. 4700–4200 cal B.P.), pottery was never adopted by indigenous, upcountry communities, despite lasting and varied contacts with pottery-using people downriver. They all shared in the use of perforated soapstone slabs, but upcountry groups never strayed from the traditional practice of using cooking stones in earth ovens and perhaps hide-lined pits.

The calling card of Paris Island culture is the Paris Island Stemmed point, a smallish triangular blade fitted with a square to slightly expanding stem, rounded shoulders, and slightly rounded bases. Stemmed points were sometimes reworked into drills, which were likely the tool of choice for perforating soapstone slabs. Excavations in the Richard B. Russell Reservoir area suggest that Paris Island communities were seasonally mobile and relied heavily on mast resources, seed-bearing plants, white-tailed deer, small terrestrial game, and aquatic resources (Anderson and Joseph 1988; Wood et al. 1986). None of the sites excavated to date are larger than an encampment for a few households, and none appear to have been occupied year-round.

Although there is little evidence for formal community structure at any of the Piedmont sites, some evidence from Stallings Island and Lake Spring suggest that Paris Island residents convened at these shell-bearing sites to dispose of their dead. Until recently, the first use of shellfish was long believed to coincide with the appearance of Stallings culture in the middle Savannah; we now have good evidence that shellfish were collected by Paris Island people and their Mill Branch successors at Stallings Island. Shellfishing, however, is not a pervasive pattern and may well have been exclusive to locations of human interment. Indeed, the very oldest use of shell anywhere in the middle Savannah is for covering the graves of the ancestors of Paris Island people (Sassaman 1993b).

A particularly distinctive feature of the Paris Island phase is the winged bannerstone (Figure 6). These are oval to subrectangular objects sculpted from soapstone or harder materials and drilled through a central, perpendicular spine with

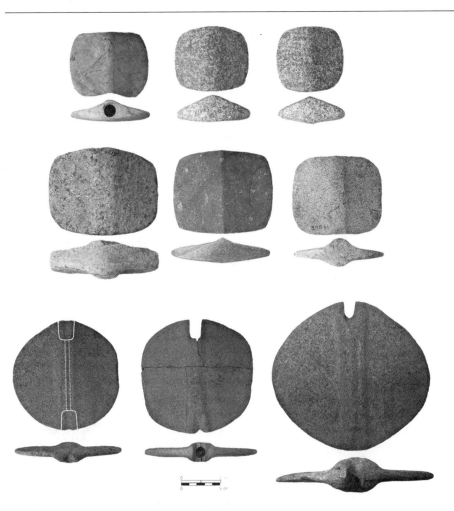

Figure 6. Bannerstone preforms of the Paris Island and Mill Branch phases: southern ovates (top two rows) and notched southern ovates (bottom row). Courtesy of Kenneth E. Sassaman.

a hole roughly 1 cm in diameter. Although I refer to these objects as bannerstones, others prefer the term "atlatl weight" because of the demonstrable use of these stones on spearthrowers of the middle South and lower Midwest (Webb 1957). In the Paris Island phase, however, and even more so in the following Mill Branch phase, bannerstones took on proportions and refinements that suggest they were far more than hunting technology. Moreover, they began to be traded far and wide, and several manufacturing locations in the Piedmont attest to large-scale production (Sassaman and Randall 2007).

The Mill Branch phase of ca. 4700–4200 cal B.P. follows directly from the Paris Island phase and is, in many ways, an elaboration of its ancestral existence. Two pervasive classes of material culture are essentially enlarged versions of Paris Island forms. Hafted bifaces during Mill Branch times were nearly twice the size, on average, as Paris Island points (Figure 7). As part of the pan-regional horizon of large stemmed forms in the Savannah River Stemmed tradition (Coe 1964), Mill Branch "points," were actually large hafted knives whose multifunctional use and edge maintenance are registered in diverse blade forms (incurvate,

Figure 7. Stemmed hafted bifaces of the Mill Branch phase. Courtesy of Kenneth E. Sassaman.

excurvate, straight). Stemmed bifaces with drill tips are especially common and signal the continuation, if not intensification, of soapstone slab production.

Bannerstones also take on much larger proportions in the Mill Branch phase (Figure 6). Early in the phase, the ovate forms of Paris Island times nearly doubled in size and gained notches at either end of the central spine. The notched southern ovate, as dubbed by Knoblock (1939), was often manufactured to exacting standards. Tapered to a fine tolerance, the enlarged "wings" of this form were joined at the center by an intricately sculpted raised spine. Greenstone and related igneous rocks were the raw materials of choice for the largest specimens. A high frequency of unfinished preforms at Stallings Island and nearby sites is suggestive evidence for craft specialization (Elliott and Doyon 1981; Sassaman and Randall 2007).

Stallings Island is without question an important place during Mill Branch times, at least early on. But by about 4,500 years ago the site appears to have been abandoned. We cannot be sure if other riverine sites in the vicinity were also abandoned then, but it is not likely coincidental that in the last half of the Mill Branch phase, from about 4,500 to 4,200 years ago, most known sites of Mill Branch affiliation are located deep in the tributary drainages of the river, tens of miles from the main channel. It is during this period that sites of Early Stallings affiliation appear in the middle Savannah region. One of the earliest of these is Victor Mills, one kilometer south of Stallings Island on the Georgia bluff overlooking the river (Sassaman 2006:108–111). An assemblage of large storage pits but limited habitation debris suggest that roughly 4,500 years ago, Early Stallings people ventured into the Fall Zone to collect and store mast. The first evidence we have of actual settlement in the area comes at about 4450 cal B.P., at the Ed Marshall site, where Early Stallings residents used clay to construct house floors over shell (Sassaman 2006:75, 113). After this time, further interactions between Coastal Plain and Piedmont denizens took one of two directions: (1) the formation of a new community combining elements of both cultures (presumably through intermarriage), which is what Classic Stallings culture is surmised to be; and (2) resistance to change among certain factions of the Mill Branch population, resulting in first a retreat into upland sites and then, when Classic Stallings culture first appears at ca. 4200 cal B.P., complete abandonment of the middle Savannah River valley.

The first of these responses by Mill Branch descendants is exemplified by upland settlements involving dispersed pit houses (Ledbetter 1995). These may very well signal merely the cold-season dispersal of riverine groups into the uplands, but again, key sites of riverine habitation during the period of upland settlement, notably Stallings Island, are completely abandoned. It is noteworthy that the production of notched southern ovates persisted through this two- to three-century period of dispersed settlement, but without the extremely large forms. The bannerstone tradition disappeared altogether at the onset of Classic Stallings culture.

Regional abandonment of the greater middle Savannah region by descendants of Mill Branch culture is not so well known to us, although we can be certain that after 4200 they were nowhere locally to be found. However, appearing at this same time to the west, in north Georgia, is a phase known as Black Shoals (Stanyard 2001). The material inventory of Black Shoals sites matches Mill Branch closely, but with one major addition. Appearing for the first time in the area are soapstone vessels, an innovation that quickly became not only an alternative to cooking with pottery (which neither Mill Branch nor Black Shoals people embraced) but also an important trade item. It is tempting to assert that soapstone vessels were the symbolic union of traditional technology (cooking with soapstone) and innovative forms (vessels), but irrespective of the historical links to the middle Savannah, the Black Shoals people seeded an industry that was to become the medium for interaction with people downriver, this time down the Chattahoochee River. The commerce in soapstone vessels that was part of a massive exchange network centered on Poverty Point in northeast Louisiana (Gibson 2001) may owe its beginnings to the Black Shoals phase.

Stallings Demise

The florescence that was Classic Stallings culture lasted about 250–300 years. About 3,800 years ago the namesake site, Stallings Island, was abandoned thoroughly by Classic Stallings people, as were many of the surrounding locations of riverine settlement. This time local abandonment seems to have anticipated or accompanied larger-scale regional processes that would affect much of the Southeast. The dissolution of societies such as those of Classic Stallings times occurred repeatedly, albeit for varied reasons, across other parts of the region. Often local changes came abruptly, as in the abandonment of Stallings Island, but we have too few data to say much about the synchronicity of local events. Natural phenomena certainly have to be considered, as in the massive flooding T. R. Kidder (2006) has documented at this time in the lower Mississippi Valley, or the sorts of long-term droughts that reduced the capacity of the land to sustain human life. Considering the history of interconnections, relocations, and immigrations recounted above, one can appreciate that even highly localized events can have reverberations over much space and across many generations.

Environmental causes for the demise of Classic Stallings culture in the middle Savannah have yet to be found. Seeking direct evidence for the ecological circumstances of abandonment, researchers at the University of Florida examined a series of paleoecological and subsistence records from Stallings Island. Although the analysis was hardly exhaustive, nothing in the vertebrate, invertebrate, or plant records registered evidence for any gradual reduction in the capacity of the locale to support human settlement. Also missing is any direct evidence for catastrophic flooding. Stratigraphic evidence for late-period floods is pervasive, but no scoured surfaces or unconformities have been observed in strata dating to Classic Stallings times. The top of the island is itself a high spot on the landscape, and even higher are the bluffs on either side of channel. As they did in the historic era, these locales would have provided refuge even during the most severe floods.

Abandonment of Stallings Island signaled the end of the Classic Stallings phase in the middle Savannah, but aspects of the culture persisted in modified form both near and far. Lineal descendants of Stallings culture established small sites throughout the upland tributaries of the middle Savannah and down into the Coastal Plain, and even occasionally along upriver stretches of the Savannah (Anderson and Joseph 1988). Continuing settlement into the ensuing Early Woodland phase was likewise dispersed throughout the region, with few large sites along the first terrace of the main channel but innumerable small assemblages far into tributary headwaters. Accompanying this change in settlement was a diminished level of stylistic elaboration on pottery surfaces. Combined with a dispersed settlement pattern and seemingly small-scale coresidency, the growing "anonymity" of stamped and plain pottery was a likely outcome of more open, flexible rules of inclusion and interaction, including marriage, and less fixed social relationships at the local level than the integrative structures that enabled Classic Stallings society to exist. The circular settlement of Classic Stallings times likewise disappeared from the region, although shell rings on the coast persisted for several more centuries. By about 3,400 years ago, these too were largely abandoned.

Conclusion

Causes for change in the way Stallings people created communities, distributed themselves on the landscape, and established alliances among them are not likely to be understood at the local scale and with reference to environment alone. As we have seen in this outline of culture history, the cultural traditions that made up Classic Stallings culture were spread across three or more physiographic provinces and several centuries. With such diverse cultural influences, Classic Stallings culture, like others, harbored the seed of its own transformation.

Despite its distinctive flair and flamboyance, Classic Stallings culture was not a unitary phenomenon and cannot be understood apart from its contemporaries and predecessors of distinct cultural disposition. It was not the evolutionary fate of local people in the Middle Savannah, as if they existed in a vacuum, and it was not a wholesale replacement of indigenes by foreigners. Rather, it was a complex process of ethnogenesis, a coming together of diverse elements and the assertion of a new cultural identity that would, on the surface, mask diverse streams of heritage. Classic Stallings culture was the unity of opposites, the integration of diversity.

The formalized and flamboyant nature of Classic Stallings culture is what we can expect of a multicultural community trying to establish itself as a "people." Formalized living, such as the circular settlements, elaborate pottery, and dedicated cemeteries, is self-imposed structure. It reflects the efforts of a people to bring discipline to social life, to establish rules of order. Imposed structure such as this is not needed when everyone is like-minded, when everyone in the community is familiar.

Insofar as it lasted 15 generations, the Classic Stallings multicultural experience in the middle Savannah River valley was a success. That it eventually dissolved is testament to the fragile nature of alliances and communities built from diverse, perhaps even contentious elements. Still, the dynamic nature of Stallings culture in general shows how quickly people adjust to new circumstances. It also goes to show how even the smallest, presumably simplest form of human societies determine their own fate through the actions they take to create and transform the communities and alliances that determine their relationship to the environment. Classic Stallings culture was one of South Carolina's first multicultural revolutions.

References Cited

Ames, Kenneth M., and Herbert D. G. Maschner

1999 *Peoples of the Northwest Coast: Their Archaeology and Prehistory.* Thames and Hudson, London.

Anderson, David G., and Joe Joseph

1988 *Prehistory and History Along the Upper Savannah River: Technical Synthesis of Cultural Resource Investigations, Richard B. Russell Multiple Resource Area.* Russell Papers, Interagency Archeological Services Division, National Park Service, Atlanta.

Arnold, Jeanne E.

1996 The Archaeology of Complex Hunter-Gatherers. *Journal of Archaeological Method and Theory* 3:77–126.

Claflin, William H., Jr.

1931 *The Stalling's Island Mound, Columbia County, Georgia.* Peabody Museum of American Archaeology and Ethnology Papers 14(1).

Coe, Joffre Lanning

1964 *The Formative Cultures of the Carolina Piedmont.* Transactions of the American Philosophical Society, New Series, Vol. 54, Pt. 5. American Philosophical Society, Philadelphia.

Elliott, Daniel T., and Roy Doyon

1981 *Archaeological and Historical Geography of the Savannah River Floodplain Near Augusta, Georgia.* Laboratory of Anthropology Series Report 22. University of Georgia, Athens.

Fagan, Brian M.

2005 *Ancient North America.* 4th ed. Thames and Hudson, London.

Ford, James A.

1969 *A Comparison of Formative Cultures in the Americas: Diffusion or the Psychic Unity of Man.* Smithsonian Contributions to Anthropology 11. Smithsonian Institution Press, Washington, D.C.

Gamble, Lynn H.

2008 *The Chumash World at European Contact: Power, Trade, and Feasting among Complex Hunter-Gatherers.* University of California Press, Berkeley.

Gibson, Jon L.

2001 *The Ancient Mounds of Poverty Point: Place of Rings.* University Press of Florida, Gainesville.

Griffin, James B.

1943 An Analysis and Interpretation of Ceramic Remains from Two Sites near Beaufort, South Carolina. *Bureau of American Ethnology Bulletin* 133:159–168. Washington, D.C.

Hally, David J.

1986 The Identification of Vessel Function: A Case Study from Northwest Georgia. *American Antiquity* 51:267–295

Hayden, Brian

1994 Competition, Labor, and Complex Hunter-Gatherers. In *Key Issues in Hunter-Gatherer Research,* edited by E. S. Burch, Jr., and L. J. Ellana, pp. 223–239. Berg, Oxford, United Kingdom.

Headland, Thomas N., and Lawrence A. Reid

1989 Hunter-Gatherers and Their Neighbors from Prehistory to the Present. *Current Anthropology* 30:43–66.

Jones, Charles C., Jr.

1861 *Monumental Remains of Georgia.* John M. Cooper and Company, Savannah, Georgia.

Kidder, Tristram R.

2006 Climate Change and the Archaic to Woodland Transition (3000–2600 cal BP) in the Mississippi River Basin. *American Antiquity* 71:195–231.

Knoblock, Byron

1939 *Banner-stones of the North American Indian.* Published by the author, LaGrange, Illinois.

Ledbetter, R. Jerald

1995 *Archaeological Investigations at Mill Branch Sites 9WR4 and 9WR11, Warren County, Georgia.* Technical Report No. 3. Interagency Archeological Services Division, National Park Service, Atlanta.

Marquardt, William H.

2004 Calusa. In *Handbook of North American Indians,* Vol. 14, *Southeast,* edited by R. D. Fogelson, pp. 204–212. Smithsonian Institution Press, Washington, D.C.

Michie, James L.

1979 *The Bass Pond Site: Intensive Archaeological Testing at a Formative Period Base Camp on Kiawah Island, South Carolina.* Research Manuscript Series 154. South Carolina Institute of Archaeology and Anthropology, University of South Carolina, Columbia.

Miller, Carl F.

1949 The Lake Spring Site, Columbia County, Georgia. *American Antiquity* 15:254–258.

Neusius, Sarah W., and G. Timothy Gross

2007 *Seeking Our Past: An Introduction to North American Archaeology.* Oxford University Press, Oxford, United Kingdom.

Russo, Michael

1996 Southeastern Mid-Holocene Coastal Settlements. In *Archaeology of the Mid-Holocene Southeast,* edited by Kenneth E. Sassaman and David G. Anderson, pp. 177–199. University Press of Florida, Gainesville.

2004 Measuring Shell Rings for Social Inequality. In *Signs of Power: The Rise of Complexity in the Southeast,* edited by J. L. Gibson and P. J. Carr, pp. 26–70. University of Alabama Press, Tuscaloosa.

2008 Late Archaic Shell Rings and Society in the Southeast U.S. *Archaeological Record* 8(5):18–22.

Russo, Michael, and Greg Heide

2001 Shell Rings of the Southeast USA. *Antiquity* 75:491–492.

Russo, Michael, Gregory Heide, and Vicki Rolland

2002 *The Guana Shell Ring.* Report submitted to the Florida Department of State, Division of Historical Resources, Tallahassee, by the Northeast Florida Anthropological Society, Jacksonville.

Sassaman, Kenneth E.

1993a *Early Pottery in the Southeast: Tradition and Innovation in Cooking Technology.* University of Alabama Press, Tuscaloosa.

1993b *Mims Point 1992: Archaeological Investigations at a Prehistoric Habitation Site in the Sumter National Forest, South Carolina.* Savannah River Archaeological Research Papers 4. Occasional Papers of the Savannah River Archaeological Research Program. South Carolina Institute of Archaeology and Anthropology, University of South Carolina, Columbia

2004 Common Origins and Divergent Histories in the Early Pottery Traditions of the American Southeast. In *Early Pottery: Technology, Function, Style and Interaction in the Lower Southeast,* edited by R. Saunders and C. T. Hays, pp. 23–39. University of Alabama Press, Tuscaloosa.

2006 *People of the Shoals: Stallings Culture of the Savannah River Valley.* University Press of Florida, Gainesville.

2011 History and Alterity in the Eastern Archaic. In *Hunter-Gatherer Archaeology as Historical Process,* edited by K. E. Sassaman and D. H. Holly, Jr., pp. 187–208. University of Arizona Press, Tucson.

Sassaman, Kenneth E., Meggan E. Blessing, and Asa R. Randall

2006 Stallings Island Revisited: New Observations on Occupational History, Community Patterning, and Subsistence Technology. *American Antiquity* 71:539–566.

Sassaman, Kenneth E., and Asa R. Randall

2007 The Cultural History of Bannerstones in the Savannah River Valley. *Southeastern Archaeology* 26:196–211.

Saunders, Rebecca

2004a Spatial Variation in Orange Culture Pottery: Implications and Function. In *Early Pottery: Technology, Function, Style, and Interaction in the Lower Southeast,* edited by Rebecca Saunders and Christopher T. Hays, pp. 40–62. University of Alabama Press, Tuscaloosa.

2004b The Stratigraphic Sequence at Rollins Shell Ring: Implications for Ring Function. *Florida Anthropologist* 57(4):249–270.

Saunders, Rebecca, and Michael Russo (editors)

2002 *The Fig Island Ring Complex (38Ch42): Coastal Adaptations and the Question of Ring Function in the Late Archaic.* South Carolina Department of Archives and History (45–01–16441), Columbia.

Scheiber, Laura, and Judson Finley

2011 Mobility as Resistance: Colonialism among Nomadic Hunter-Gatherers in the American West. In *Hunter-Gatherer Archaeology as Historical Process,* edited by Kenneth E. Sassaman and Donald H. Holly Jr., pp. 167–186. University of Arizona Press, Tucson.

Sears, William H.

1973 The Sacred and the Secular in Prehistoric Ceramics. In *Variation in Anthropology: Essays in Honor of John MacGregor,* edited by Donald Ward Lathrop and Jody Douglas, pp. 31–42. Illinois Archaeological Survey, Urbana.

Stanyard, William F.

2001 *Archaic Period Archaeology of Northern Georgia.* Georgia Archaeological Research Design Paper No. 13, Laboratory of Archaeology Series 37. University of Georgia, Athens.

Steward, Julian H.

1955 *The Theory of Cultural Change: The Methodology of Multilinear Evolution.* University of Illinois Press, Urbana.

Stoltman, James B.

1974 *Groton Plantation: An Archaeological Study of a South Carolina Locality.* Monograph of the Peabody Museum No.1. Harvard University, Cambridge.

Thomas, David Hurst

2008 *Native American Landscapes of St. Catherine's Island, Georgia.* Anthropological Papers 88. American Museum of Natural History, New York.

Thompson, Victor D.

2006 Questioning Complexity: The Prehistoric Hunter-Gatherers of Sapelo Island, Georgia. Unpublished Ph.D. dissertation, University of Kentucky, Lexington.

Waring, Antonio J., Jr.

1968 The Bilbo Site, Chatham County, Georgia. In *The Waring Papers: The Collected Works of Antonio J. Waring, Jr.,* edited by Stephen Williams, pp. 152–197. Papers of the Peabody Museum of Archaeology and Ethnology, Vol. 58. Harvard University, Cambridge. Originally written in 1940.

Webb, William S.

1957 *The Development of the Spearthrower.* Occasional Paper in Anthropology 2. Department of Anthropology, University of Kentucky, Lexington.

Wood, W. Dean, Dan T. Elliott, Teresa P. Rudolph, and Dennis B. Blanton

1986 *Prehistory of the Richard B. Russell Reservoir: The Archaic and Woodland Periods of the Upper Savannah River.* Russell Papers. Interagency Archeological Services Division, National Park Service, Atlanta.

ADAM KING AND KEITH STEPHENSON

Foragers, Farmers, and Chiefs

The Woodland and
Mississippian Periods in the
Middle Savannah River Valley

THROUGHOUT MUCH OF SOUTH CAROLINA'S HISTORY, archaeological research has been funded and conducted by scholars at universities and other educational institutions. Increasingly archaeological research is being funded by federal agencies in their effort to comply with the National Historic Preservation Act, and those efforts continue to produce important information about our state's past. At the Department of Energy's Savannah River site, located near Aiken, South Carolina, federally funded archaeological investigations have been conducted since the early 1970s, and the result is a vast body of data on the prehistory of the Aiken Plateau and middle Savannah River valley. Our concern is with the history of people living in the middle Savannah River Valley during the Woodland (1000 B.C.–A.D. 1000) and Mississippian (A.D. 1000–1600) periods.

Across the southeastern United States some interesting things happened during the Woodland and Mississippian periods, from the adoption of agriculture to mound building and long-distance exchange to the creation of large and complex societies. People living in the middle Savannah River valley were part of these broader social trends, but they participated in their own unique way. What emerges is a unique history characterized by population fluctuations, ethnic diversity, and sometimes dramatic social change, all played out against the backdrop of a fairly consistent use of the natural landscape.

The Middle Savannah Valley

For almost 40 years archaeological research has been conducted on the Department of Energy's Savannah River Site (SRS). The SRS is a 310-square-mile facility that stretches from the floodplain of the Savannah River to the Sand Hills uplands of the Aiken Plateau in east-central South Carolina (Figure 1). In 1990 Kenneth Sassaman and his colleagues synthesized the prehistory of the SRS region using data collected from some 17 years of compliance archaeology (Sassaman

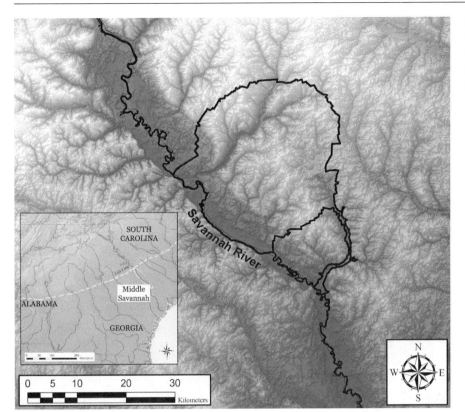

Figure 1. Savannah River Site in the middle Savannah River valley. Drawing by Christopher L. Thornock, courtesy of the South Carolina Institute of Archaeology and Anthropology.

et al. 1990) and that work has continued for the past 22 years. In 1994 David Anderson (1994; see also 1990a, 1990b, 1991, 1996) published an entire volume devoted to the Mississippian period in the Savannah River Valley, based in part on his work at the SRS. Building upon these bodies of research, we summarize the current understanding of how this landscape was used from the Early Woodland through Late Mississippian periods (see Table 1).

TABLE 1. Pottery Sequence of the Middle Savannah River Valley

PERIOD	PHASE	DATES
Early Woodland	Refuge	1000–500 B.C.
Middle Woodland	Deptford	500 B.C.–500 A.D.
Late Woodland	Savannah I	900–1200
Early Mississippian	Sleepy Hollow	900–1100
Early Mississippian	Lawton	1100–1250
Middle Mississippian	Hollywood	1250–1350
Late Mississippian	Silver Bluff	1350–1450

Woodland

According to Sassaman (1993), the Early Woodland period in the middle Savannah valley represented a time of both settlement and sociopolitical dispersal. During the previous Late Archaic period, as described by Sassaman in this volume, dispersed social groups collected into larger communities on the Savannah River floodplain. That aggregation created more complex societies whose members maintained far-flung connections through trade. By the Early Woodland period, people spread out on the landscape forming more loosely integrated, dispersed communities situated in the uplands of the Aiken Plateau. While people were experimenting with growing plant foods in other parts of the Southeast, in the middle Savannah valley people of the Early Woodland period continued to be generalized foragers exploiting a broad spectrum of wild foods. In many respects this pattern established in the Early Woodland persists throughout the Woodland and even Mississippian periods.

Throughout the rest of the Southeast, the Middle Woodland period is associated with complex mortuary ceremonialism, the creation of elaborate symbolic objects, more complex forms of society, and increasing reliance on gardening. There is little direct evidence that many of these broader trends impacted contemporary settlement in the middle Savannah valley. Extant data indicate a continuation of permanent, loosely integrated settlements in the uplands, whose inhabitants practiced a generalized foraging subsistence strategy. In contrast to the Early Woodland, larger sites where people congregated and lived at least seasonally appear again along the Savannah River. One of these aggregation sites, the G. S. Lewis site, did contain evidence for long-distance contacts in the form of a copper bead, fragments of marine shell, and nonlocal pottery (Sassaman et al. 1990). The appearance of these aggregation sites along the natural communication corridor of the Savannah River does suggest that broader regional social changes inspired local changes as households began to integrate into larger social groups.

With the advent of the Late Woodland Savannah I phase, settlement data suggest a continuation of permanent upland residence but a loss of the riverine aggregation sites—signaling a decrease in the efforts to integrate households at some higher level (King and Stephenson 2003; Cabak et al. 1996). Site location data suggest that the same kind of generalized foraging strategy in use during earlier periods continued to be used at this time. The overall trend is a continuation of a fairly generalized use of the landscape by small-scale groups with no evidence of social differences brought about by wealth or rank.

The Late Woodland–Mississippian Transition

What makes this time interesting is that we see a diversity of material culture, particularly in pottery assemblages. Between A.D. 900 and 1200 , the landscape of the middle Savannah valley appears to be occupied by people making three different pottery traditions: Cordmarking of the Savannah I phase (DePratter 1991), Etowah Complicated Stamped of the Lawton phase (Anderson 1994), and Pisgah Complicated Stamped of the Sleepy Hollow phase (Brummitt 2007). What makes this situation even more difficult to sort out is that the Pisgah-like material of the Sleepy Hollow phase seems foreign in this area. Pisgah motifs do appear in Early Mississippian contexts to the north in the piedmont portion of the Savannah valley, and we suspect that it represents a Late Woodland–Early Mississippian phase equivalent to the Woodstock phase in northern Georgia (see Cobb and Garrow 1995). During the Late Woodland period, cordmarking seems to be a coastal and coastal plain pottery tradition, while throughout Georgia and South Carolina complicated stamping appears first in the Ridge and Valley, Piedmont, and Blue Ridge provinces.

What seems plausible to us is that these three pottery traditions overlapped in the middle Savannah valley at this time, potentially creating a situation where as many as three distinct ethnic groups used the same landscape. Site numbers tell us that the people associated with the Lawton and Sleepy Hollow phases were in the distinct minority (Stephenson 2011). However, as far as we can tell, they all used the landscape in much the same way.

This period becomes even more interesting because it represents the time across the Southeast when ranked Mississippian societies emerged. These kinds of societies were different from the Woodland groups that came before them because, instead of all people being essentially equal, they had social differences built into their structure. Some people were more important than others, often through birth, and those differences were visible in the kinds of houses used, better cuts of meat and special foods, special dress and regalia, and close association with platform mounds. Also, these Mississippian societies were made up of several distinct communities spread over an area at least a day's walk across, but united under one leadership—either a council or an individual chief. The Mississippian economy focused much of its energy on the production of food by growing tropical crops such as corn and beans.

Cordmarked pottery is usually associated with Woodland society and economy. Those societies were dominated by small communities made up of households scattered through the uplands, whose members were all roughly equal in social rank. Their economies were fueled by broad-spectrum hunting and gathering with varying amounts of effort devoted to the growing of local starchy seed food crops. In contrast, complicated stamped pottery is associated with Mississippian lifeways, consisting of social ranking, multiple communities united under one leadership, and a greater emphasis on food production. While it is tempting to think of the Savannah I phase adaptation (with its cordmarked pottery) as essentially Late Woodland and the Sleepy Hollow and Lawton phase adaptations (with their complicated stamped pottery) as Mississippian, there really does not seem to be a great deal of difference in how people of the different traditions used the landscape (King and Stephenson 2003).

Our best evidence indicates that people of both pottery traditions used the landscape largely for foraging, possibly mixed with small-scale food production. The clearest indirect evidence for food production appears during the Lawton phase (A.D. 1150–1250), when corncob-impressed pottery is added to local ceramic assemblages. We strongly suspect that gardening was added to the subsistence mix before that point, but evidence supporting this idea has not yet been found. We can say that at no time during this period did horticulture seem to affect the choice of site locations (King and Stephenson 2003). This is likely because of environmental limitations on intensive production of cultivated plants in the Aiken Plateau and coastal plain in general. Neither the Savannah River floodplain nor those of smaller drainages are particularly well suited for large-scale horticulture. Most of the Savannah River floodplain is seasonally inundated and the secondary drainages are small and given to high-energy flash flooding. Small-scale gardening could have been practiced on a shifting basis on river terraces and in the uplands. However, the soils in the Aiken Plateau are typical of the coastal plain in being well drained and low in organics. This would have limited the productive potential and necessitated a shifting system.

It might be reasonable to think of the Lawton phase as Mississippian in the broad cultural sense. There is evidence for the production of corn, and the phase shares ceramic attributes with societies up the Savannah River where platform mounds were being built; there is also some evidence for social ranking (Anderson 1994). It is possible that the people in the middle Savannah River valley were part of very young or incipient chiefdoms where the evidence of the ranked social structure might be hard to find in the archaeological record. It also remains possible that they lived in more decentralized social formations on the margins of the Mississippian world.

Social Centralization and Labor Mobilization

By A.D. 1250, the social landscape underwent significant changes. The culture history was marked by a transition to the complicated stamped and check-stamped ceramic assemblage of the regional middle Mississippian Hollywood phase (Anderson 1994; Anderson et al. 1986; Hally and Rudolph 1986). More significantly, at least five nucleated towns with one or more mounds were established in the area (Figure 2). Based on the available information, all five towns were occupied during the Hollywood phase (Stephenson 2011; Wood 2009). Settlement data on the Savannah River site, which is positioned between two sets of mound towns (Mason's Plantation and Hollywood upriver; Lawton, Red Lake, and Spring Lake downriver), indicates that permanent use of areas between mound towns declined significantly (King and Stephenson 2003). We suspect this reflects a shift in settlement focus toward the areas around the mound towns.

The mounds and associated towns represent surplus in the form of voluntary, collective labor that was put to such specific tasks as the construction of

Figure 2. Hollywood-phase mound sites in the Middle Savannah River Valley. Drawing by Christopher L. Thornock, courtesy of the South Carolina Institute of Archaeology and Anthropology.

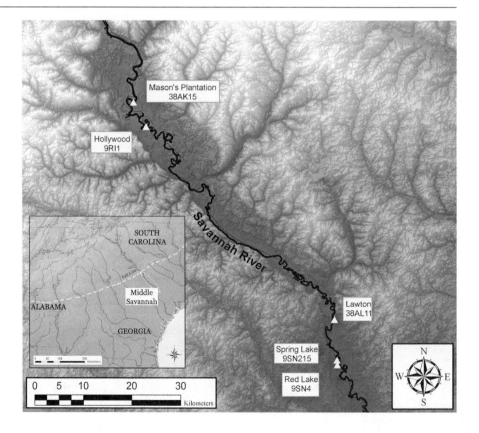

fortification ditches, palisades, and mounds. A political economic analysis informs us that "class relations derive from the making and taking of surplus labor" (McGuire 1992:183). Dean Saitta (1987:4) defines surplus labor as "that amount of socially determined labor time expended beyond the amount . . . required to meet the subsistence needs of the direct producers." With this notion, surplus labor exists in all societies and thus the potential for some persons or corporate group to obtain more control over this labor than others (McGuire 1992:183). We further hypothesize that the ideological means to collective labor mobilization came in the form of a set of beliefs revolving around mounds as monuments and their manipulation.

As Jared Wood's (2009) dissertation research recently disclosed, both the North Mound at Lawton and Mound A at Red Lake are preceded by a dense midden of mainly freshwater mussel shell. The dense and localized nature of these middens suggests to us that they were produced through redistributive feasting. Around the world, communal feasts have been and continue to be used as a means of attracting and employing labor (Dietler and Hayden 2001). The close association between these middens and mounds further suggests to us that feasting was related to the construction and use of at least the initial stages of the associated mounds. Knight (1981, 1986, 1989) has long argued that mounds stood as metaphorical earth symbols and their manipulation was part of efforts to purify or renew the world and in turn human society. By so doing, the fertility and productivity of the earth also was guaranteed. Thus, the control of surplus production and mobilization of labor, coupled with the ideological disguise of social values, forms the basis of power for emerging elites where status is achieved (Benn 1995:114–121; Muller 1997:270–287).

Those individuals or corporate groups that facilitated these earth-renewal activities certainly laid claim to some material and social benefit for their efforts on behalf of all. We suspect that this opportunity to leverage social position through symbolic capital and opportunistically reformulate the social relations of production to favor a few elite was a key factor in the rather sudden appearance of mound towns in the middle Savannah valley. Mounds had been present in the Deep South for millennia, and there is little reason to doubt that people in the middle Savannah valley knew of them and their association with the earth. Furthermore, the manipulation of mounds and world-renewal beliefs was a strategy that had been used by emerging elites throughout northern Georgia since A.D. 1000. King (2003) has argued that the earliest chiefdom centered at Etowah was created as competing corporate groups came together in a strategic alliance facilitated by a common need to renew the earth and society. In this instance, corporate group competition most likely led to intensified food production, thereby generating surpluses that could be used to support prestige-building activities (Benn 1995; Bender 1985; Brumfiel and Earl 1987; Scarry 1993:88–89). Logically, there is no reason to think that people in the Savannah valley were unaware of social developments in northern Georgia or even central Georgia, where Macon Plateau was located. In fact, the presence of pottery styles similar to those found in northern Georgia confirms the connection between these regions.

Thus, we see the emergence of ranked societies or chiefdoms in the middle Savannah valley as part of a calculated effort by individuals or specific family groups to use a prevailing belief system to mobilize, appropriate, and expend labor for their own material and social benefit.

The polities that emerged in the middle Savannah valley do not necessarily look or function as traditional models of Mississippian chiefdoms predict. These suggest Mississippian chiefdoms should have permanent towns with mounds and mound-top architecture and should be associated with maize gardening at some level. However, unlike our notions of chiefdoms, there is little material evidence for differential social ranking in the middle Savannah valley, especially in the case of mortuary practices. Here we are working largely with indirect evidence and secondhand accounts of looting. In our work at both Lawton and Red Lake, we have discovered no burials, and what we have heard from local collectors suggests that there are no burials to be found at these sites. Enough looting has occurred at Lawton and Red Lake so that if burials were present at these sites, they would have been ravaged thoroughly.

The only place that large numbers of burials have been found are on a series of natural sand ridges located at various points along the Savannah River floodplain. Except for a regional survey done by Leland Ferguson (1971) 40 years ago, no systematic work has been done at these sites. However, Chester DePratter (1993) conducted salvage work at a looted sand-ridge cemetery site along the floodplain of Groton Plantation, which gives us a good idea of Middle Mississippian burial practices. These isolated sand-ridge sites appear to have been community cemeteries where people were most often buried as cremations in burial urns. There is little evidence of social differentiation, either indicating that these were undifferentiated societies or that ranking was not expressed in mortuary treatment.

The settlement systems associated with these towns do not necessarily meet expectations of ranked social structures either. Our best evidence, which is not great, indicates that Red Lake and Lawton are surrounded by dispersed households and possibly small multiple-household hamlets. Some would argue that this is the kind of settlement organization associated with simple chiefdoms (Anderson 1994; Hally 1996; Wright 1984). However, as David Hally (1993) and John Blitz (1999) have discussed, short distances, such as that separating Lawton and Red Lake, go against conventional ideas about the structure of Mississippian chiefdoms. Using the spacing of mound towns in the Deep South, Hally (1993) has argued that closely spaced mound sites, like Lawton, Red Lake, and Spring Lake should be primary and secondary centers in a single complex chiefdom. However, as Hally (1993) and Blitz (1999) have pointed out, it is difficult to see which site (Lawton or Red Lake) should be considered more important in a complex administrative structure. In this instance, Wood (2009) maintains that Lawton would be paramount because of the amount of social labor invested in constructing this palisaded mound precinct.

There are obviously many questions to be answered about these towns that will inform us about their political place on the regional landscape. However, the layout and distribution of the mound towns in this part of the middle Savannah valley may provide some insights into those issues. The regional settlement system, as far as we understand it, is reminiscent of the *talwa* or town organization of the Creek Indians, particularly of the seventeenth and eighteenth centuries. Creek communities had a sacred core that included a winter council house, a square ground where summer councils and important ceremonies took place, a ball pole and field, and sometimes one or more small mounds (Howard 1968; Knight 1994). This civic-ceremonial space was surrounded by households that often were strung up and down the major drainages on which the towns were located (Etheridge 2004; Knight 1994; Worth 2000). This is a classic dispersed-settlement system. Following Bruce Smith's (1978) arguments for Mississippian settlement in the Mississippi River valley, the middle Savannah valley system makes ecological and social sense in the ridge-and-swale floodplain setting of the Coastal Plain.

In many instances, Creek towns were scattered up and down major drainages, sometimes close enough to one another that the scatter of households from one town butted up on the households associated with a nearby town. Town affiliation was important among the Creeks, and although some towns were more important than others, each had a great deal of autonomy (Knight 1994; Saunt 1999).

It is possible that what we are looking at in the middle Savannah valley may be a social formation not unlike the Creeks of the eighteenth century. There was social ranking, but it was embedded within some kind of corporate kin group system and expressed in terms such as "older brother" or as part of the Red and White symbolism of war and peace (King 2002). If there was a social segment in the middle Savannah valley that achieved a measure of prominence through its control over mound manipulation, that prominence did not translate into great material differences. In fact, it appears that it never succeeded in breaking out of the bounds of the nested and complementary nature of kin organization.

Decentralization and Fragmentation

By the end of the fourteenth century, it looks as though all of these mound towns in the middle Savannah valley were abandoned. At that same time, dispersed Mississippian occupations reappeared in upland, interriverine settings on the Savannah River site (King and Stephenson 2003). We have interpreted these settlement changes to indicate the collapse of the Hollywood-phase polities centered on the mounds and a return to a more dispersed settlement organization.

We think the reason for the disintegration of these young chiefdoms can be found in their structure. As noted, extra labor and probably food were collected by social leaders and used to fund projects such as mound building and community fortification and probably also to feed and house those social leaders. This extraction of surplus can be sustained as long as the demands are not too great or overly burdensome to the producers. If those demands interfere with the ability of regular people to make a living, then producers will begin to resent them and ultimately resist them. If the perceived benefits of the social system to the producers do not outweigh the costs of maintaining that system, then those who produce surpluses can and will cease to participate. This could happen as social leaders increase their demands for surplus labor and food. It could also happen if it becomes more difficult for regular people to produce a surplus. Both might have been caused by decreased rainfall, evidence of which Anderson (1994; Anderson et al. 1995) reports in tree-ring data from the middle Savannah valley during the Hollywood phase.

Social Collapse and Abandonment

It appears that the Late Mississippian dispersal eventually led to outmigration from the Savannah valley. The prevailing idea is that as polities below the Fall Line collapsed along the Savannah River, people gravitated to emerging or powerful polities in other regions, particularly those up the Savannah River, to the east in central Georgia, and to the west in central South Carolina. David Anderson (1994) summarizes evidence for this dispersal and population movement to the Oconee Valley in central Georgia, and it is presumed the same evidence will be found for a movement to the Wateree Valley. By the time Hernando de Soto and his army tried to cross the Savannah River in A.D. 1540, few if any people seemed to be living in the valley below the Fall Line (Hudson 1997).

References Cited

Anderson, David G.

1990a The Mississippian Occupation and Abandonment of the Savannah River Valley. *Florida Anthropologist* 43(1):13–35.

1990b Stability and Change in Chiefdom Level Societies: An Examination of Mississippian Political Evolution on the South Atlantic Slope. In *Lamar Archaeology: Mississippian Chiefdoms in the Deep South,* edited by Mark Williams and Gary Shapiro, pp. 187–213. University of Alabama Press, Tuscaloosa.

1991 Mississippian Settlement in the Savannah River Basin. *Early Georgia* 19(2):47–60.

1994 *The Savannah River Chiefdoms: Political Change in the Late Prehistoric Southeast.* University of Alabama Press, Tuscaloosa.

1996 Chiefly Cycling and Large-Scale Abandonments as Viewed from the Savannah River Basin. In *Political Structure and Change in the Prehistoric Southeastern United States,* edited by John F. Scarry, pp. 150–191. University Press of Florida, Gainesville.

Anderson, David G., David J. Hally, and James L. Rudolph

1986 The Mississippian Occupation of the Savannah River Valley. *Southeastern Archaeology* 5:32–51.

Anderson, David G., D. W. Stahle, and M. K. Cleaveland

1995 Paleoclimate and the Potential Food Reserves of Mississippian Societies: A Case Study from the Savannah River Valley. *American Antiquity* 60:258–286.

Bender, Barbara

1985 Prehistoric Developments in the American Midcontinent and in Brittany, Northwest France. In *Prehistoric Hunter-Gatherers: The Emergence of Cultural Complexity,* edited by T. Douglas Price and James A. Brown, pp. 21–57. Academic Press, New York.

Benn, D. W.

1995 Social and Political Causes for the Emergence of Intensive Agriculture in Eastern North America. In *Beyond Subsistence: Plains Archaeology and the Postprocessual Critique,* edited by Philip Duke and Michael C. Wilson, pp. 113–128. University of Alabama Press, Tuscaloosa.

Blitz, John

1999 Mississippian Chiefdoms and the Fission-Fusion Process. *American Antiquity* 64:577–592.

2010 New Perspectives on Mississippian Archaeology. *Journal of Archaeological Research* 18(1):1–39.

Brumfiel, Elizabeth M., and Timothy K. Earle

1987 Specialization, Exchange, and Complex Societies: An Introduction. In *Specialization, Exchange, and Complex Societies,* edited by Elizabeth M. Brumfiel and Timothy K. Earle, pp. 1–9. New Directions in Archaeology. Cambridge University Press, Cambridge, United Kingdom.

Brummitt, Aaron G.

2007 The Sleepy Hollow Phase: Mississippian Emergence in the Middle Savannah Valley. Unpublished master's thesis, Department of Anthropology, University of South Carolina, Columbia.

Cabak, Melanie A., Kenneth E. Sassaman, and J. Christopher Gillam

1996 *Distributional Archaeology in the Aiken Plateau: Intensive Survey of E Area, Savannah River Site, Aiken County, South Carolina.* Savannah River Archaeological Research Papers 8. Occasional Papers of the Savannah River Archaeological Research Program. South Carolina Institute of Archaeology and Anthropology, University of South Carolina, Columbia.

Cobb, Charles, and Patrick Garrow

1995 Woodstock Culture and the Question of Mississippian Emergence. *American Antiquity* 61:21–38.

DePratter, Chester B.

1991 W.P.A. Archaeological Excavations in Chatham County, Georgia: 1937–1942. *Laboratory of Archaeology Series* 29. University of Georgia, Athens.

1993 Looting and Site Destruction at Ware Creek Ridge, Hampton County, South Carolina. In *Site Destruction in Georgia and the Carolinas,* edited by David G. Anderson and Virginia Horak, pp. 67–76. Interagency Archeological Services Division, National Park Service, Atlanta.

Dietler, Michael, and Brian Hayden (editors)

2001 *Feasts: Archaeological and Ethnographic Perspectives on Food, Politics, and Power.* Smithsonian Books, Washington, D.C.

Etheridge, Robbie

2004 *Creek Country: The Creek Indians and Their World.* University of North Carolina Press, Chapel Hill.

Ferguson, Leland G.

1971 Middle/Lower Savannah River Survey. Notes and records on file at the Savannah River Archaeological Research Program, South Carolina Institute of Archeology and Anthropology, University of South Carolina, Columbia.

Hally, David J.

1993 The Territorial Size of Mississippian Chiefdoms. In *Archaeology of Eastern North America, Papers in Honor of Stephen Williams,* edited by James B. Stoltman, pp. 143–168. Archaeological Report No. 25. Mississippi Department of Archives and History, Jackson.

1996 Platform Mound Construction and the Instability of Mississippian Chiefdoms. In *Political Structure and Change in the Prehistoric Southeastern United States,* edited by John F. Scarry, pp. 92–127. University of Florida Press, Gainesville.

Hally, David J., and James L. Rudolph

1986 *Mississippi Period Archaeology of the Georgia Piedmont.* Laboratory of Archaeology Series Report No. 24. Department of Anthropology, University of Georgia, Athens.

Howard, James H.

1968 *The Southeastern Ceremonial Complex and Its Interpretation.* Memoir 6. Missouri Archaeological Society, Columbia.

Hudson, Charles

1997 *Knights of Spain, Warriors of the Sun: Hernando de Soto and the South's Ancient Chiefdoms.* University of Georgia Press, Athens.

King, Adam

2002 Creek Chiefdoms at the Temporal Edge of the Mississippian World. *Southeastern Archaeology* 21:221–226.

2003 *Etowah: The Political History of a Chiefdom Capital.* University of Alabama Press, Tuscaloosa.

King, Adam, and Keith Stephenson

2003 From Potsherds to Political Cycling: The Mississippian Occupation of the Middle Savannah Valley. Paper presented at the 60th Annual Meeting of the Southeastern Archaeological Conference, Charlotte.

Knight, V. James, Jr.

1981 Mississippian Ritual. Unpublished Ph.D. dissertation, Department of Anthropology, University of Florida, Gainesville.

1986 The Institutional Organization of Mississippian Religion. *American Antiquity* 51:675–687.

1989 Symbolism of Mississippian Mounds. In *Powhatan's Mantle: Indians in the Colonial Southeast,* edited by P. H. Wood, G. A.

Waselkov, and M. T. Hatley, pp. 279–291. University of Nebraska Press, Lincoln.

1994   Aboriginal Population Movements in the Postcontact Southeast. In *The Forgotten Centuries: Indians and Europeans in the American South, 1521–1704,* edited by Charles Hudson and Carmen Chaves Tesser, pp. 257–275. University of Georgia Press, Athens.

McGuire, Randall H.

1992   *A Marxist Archaeology.* Academic Press, Orlando.

Muller, Jon

1997   *Mississippian Political Economy.* Plenum Press, New York.

Saitta, Dean

1987   Economic Integration and Social Development in Zuni Prehistory. Unpublished Ph.D. dissertation, Department of Anthropology, University of Massachusetts, Amherst.

Sassaman, Kenneth E.

1993   *Early Woodland Settlement in the Aiken Plateau: Archaeological Investigations at 38AK157, Savannah River Site, Aiken County, South Carolina.* Savannah River Archaeological Research Papers 3. Occasional Papers of the Savannah River Archaeological Research Program. South Carolina Institute

of Archaeology and Anthropology, University of South Carolina, Columbia.

Sassaman, Kenneth E., Mark J. Brooks, Glen T. Hanson, and David G. Anderson

1990   *Native American Prehistory of the Middle Savannah River Valley: A Synthesis of Archaeological Investigations on the Savannah River Site, Aiken and Barnwell Counties, South Carolina.* Savannah River Archaeological Research Papers 1. Occasional Papers of the Savannah River Archaeological Research Program, South Carolina Institute of Archaeology and Anthropology, University of South Carolina, Columbia.

Saunt, Claudio

1999   *A New Order of Things: Property, Power, and the Transformation of the Creek Indians, 1733–1816.* Cambridge University Press, Cambridge, United Kingdom.

Scarry, C. Margaret

1993   Variability in Mississippian Crop Production Strategies. In *Foraging and Farming in the Eastern Woodlands,* edited by C. Margaret Scarry, pp. 78–90. University of Florida Press, Gainesville.

Smith, Bruce D.

1978   Variation in Mississippian Settlement Patterns. In *Mississippian Settlement Patterns,* edited by Bruce D. Smith, pp. 479–503. Academic Press, New York.

Stephenson, Keith

2011   Mississippi Period Occupational and Political History of the Middle Savannah River Valley. Unpublished Ph.D. dissertation, Department of Anthropology, University of Kentucky, Lexington.

Wood, M. Jared

2009   Mississippian Chiefdom Organization: A Case Study from the Savannah River Valley. Unpublished Ph.D. dissertation, Department of Anthropology, University of Georgia, Athens.

Worth, John E.

2000   The Lower Creeks: Origins and Early History. In *Indians of the Greater Southeast: Historical Archaeology and Ethnohistory,* edited by Bonnie G. McEwan, pp. 265–298. University Press of Florida, Gainesville.

Wright, Henry T.

1984   Prestate Political Formations. In *On the Evolution of Complex Societies: Essays in Honor of Harry Hoijer, 1982,* edited by Timothy Earle, pp. 41–78. Undena Publications, Malibu, California.

CHARLES R. COBB AND
CHESTER B. DEPRATTER

Carolina's Southern Frontier

Edge of a
New World Order

THE IDEA OF THE FRONTIER looms large in the American imagination and concept of who we are as a people: entrepreneurs in search of more open space on the fringes of political systems, rugged individualists, a melting pot, risk-takers. Is it any accident that in what is probably the most successful American science-fiction franchise of all time, Captain Kirk (and subsequent generations of captains) and the *Enterprise* crew of *Star Trek* were charged with conquering space as the Final Frontier? The weekly introduction intoned that the *Enterprise* was going where no "man" (later amended to "one") had gone before, but as Trekkies know, there was still a heck of a lot of life out there, friendly and otherwise.

Despite the romance of the frontier, it does have a darker side. The historian Frederick Jackson Turner has often been vilified for entrenching the view of a triumphal and inevitable westward migration of the American frontier (Turner 1920). Forgotten in this expression of manifest destiny were the histories of the Native Americans on the other side of this imaginary dividing line. Of course, Turner was a product of his times, and he has to be credited with making the frontier a centerpiece of research for historians as well as anthropologists, who have since made many strides toward correcting the one-sided perspective over the past decades. Indeed, recent archaeological and ethnohistorical research in eastern North America has begun to show how frontiers were highly complex zones of convergence, where cultures were highly intermingled and interactions were much more subtle and multisided than the popular idea of the colonial juggernaut rolling over indigenous groups (Barr 2006; Cayton and Teute 1998; Lightfoot and Martinez 1995).

The territory that is now South Carolina was a highly contested ground in early colonial times, and what we would construe as a geographic frontier changed constantly with the fortunes of various European and Native American groups. Spain considered the region part of its northern margin of Florida,

England viewed it as a western toehold in the Americas, and both powers were continually concerned about possible French encroachment from bases along the Gulf Coast to the west. Needless to say, the many Native American groups already occupying the region had their own convictions about the expanse of their own territories, which typically conflicted with European boundaries.

Given the widely differing worldviews and aims of all the parties who had a vested interest in what is today South Carolina, we think it is useful to narrow down to a set of historical particulars to gain some insight into the complexity of the history of frontiers in the state. Specifically, we explore the founding of a southern borderland between indigenous groups and Carolina after the colony took root in the 1670s. Beginning with a philosophical and political-economic background to the development of that frontier, because it helps explain who lived there and why, we consider how archaeology plays a crucial role in understanding the lives of the many different groups who converged at multiethnic settlements along the southern frontier during a particularly dynamic period that lasted for about a century, from the late 1600s to the late 1700s.

Reshaping the New World in the Old World's Image

It is all too easy to attribute the colonization of the Atlantic Seaboard of eastern North America to a single-minded lust by individuals for resources that left thousands of victims in its wake. To be sure, we will never accurately know how many Native Americans died enslaved, from Old World epidemics, or as a result of conflict with Europeans, even if that number must have been tragically large. Nonetheless, the actual causes and mechanisms of colonialism were complex and ranged from economic to theological, and varied from person to person as well as from country to country. For example, many European powers adhered to variants of a mercantile philosophy that viewed wealth as a zero-sum game rather than as a function of productivity. In other words, there was only a finite amount of territory and bullion in the world, and the viability of emerging nation-states and the well-being of their citizens was crucially dependent upon out-competing other nation-states for those resources. The accumulation of colonies was an important component of that policy. These political and economic underpinnings of expansionism were complemented by a growing ethnocentric belief on the eve of the Enlightenment (that is, the late 1600s) that Europe served as a template for how the rest of the world should be modeled, ranging from agrarian practices to political institutions.

In England, this notion of reenvisioning the world was greatly spurred by two chains of events (Bauman and Briggs 2003). First, the tumult of the Protestant Reformation spawned by Martin Luther in the 1500s had led to a century of theological and physical conflict between the Catholic and Protestant Churches in England. This dispute was resolved decisively in favor of the English Protestants (primarily the Church of England) by the 1600s. Second, the costly English Civil War had drawn to a close with the restoration of the monarchy in 1660 under Charles II. As part of the process of attempted closure to these events, many English intellectuals became increasingly concerned with the nature of order in the world and how to offset the chaos they associated with the premodern era prior to their own times. A prominent figure in this intellectual quest was the philosopher John Locke. Of his many contributions, one that had far-reaching impact on England's rationale for imperial expansion was the idea of *res nullius*. In brief, this idea from Roman common law asserted that ownerless property belonged to the first taker, and in postfeudal Europe it was extended to the colonial enterprise to justify the taking of land that not only appeared ownerless but was "unimproved" (Gosden 2003:27–28).

Projecting the concept of *res nullius* to North America immediately threatened indigenous lands. Some regions might appear unused when in reality they were a critical seasonal food source to mobile groups who inhabited different localities on a temporary basis. In areas such as the Southeast that were occupied by agriculturists, European prejudices toward the perceived inefficiency or archaic nature of native agricultural practices (multicropping rather than monocropping, lack of irrigation, absence of enclosing features such as fences) were used to justify the appropriation of rich farming regions.

Of more direct historical relevance to South Carolina is the fact that John Locke for a time served as secretary to the First Earl of Shaftesbury, Anthony Ashley-Cooper, who in turn was one of a close inner circle of influential and powerful friends around Locke who debated matters philosophical, political, and economic. The Earl of Shaftesbury was one of the eight Lords Proprietors titled to a huge tract of land in North America that eventually became South Carolina. Although neither Locke nor Sir Anthony were to visit the New World, their mutual concern with order was expressed in the *Fundamental Constitutions of Carolina*, which some historians believe may have been a collaboration between the two (Edgar 1998:42). This document, adopted by the Lords Proprietors in 1669, envisioned a disciplined society overseen by a titled, landed gentry, who in turn fell under the purview of the Lords Proprietors. Although this model clearly reflected the English class-based political system, the *Constitutions* also outlined several democratic overtures that were very liberal for the era: notably, modest property requirements for (male) voting rights, elections by secret ballot, and a guarantee of religious freedom (Edgar 1998:43–46).

The *Constitutions* was not a popular document in Carolina, nor was it ever ratified by the colonial legislature, but many of its provisions became accepted practice in the colony. By the 1800s the English vision of how the world should look became a cornerstone of the westward movement of the young American republic through the ideal of manifest destiny. Yet, in the late 1600s the implementation of European ideas about resculpting the world in North America was still confronted by the harsh reality of small numbers of colonials clinging on in precarious ports along the Atlantic seaboard. In South Carolina, the Spanish Empire attempted several explorations and settlements in the 1500s. On Parris Island, archaeologists have discovered Santa Elena—which served for a time as the capital of Florida—as well as the short-lived French occupation of Charlesfort. Spanish commitment to its northerly ambitions eventually faltered because of a lack of resources, as the Crown was occupied by its more lucrative colonial enterprises elsewhere at the same time that it was experiencing misfortune in its imperial conflicts in Europe. With the establishment of Charleston and the Carolina colony in 1670, the English initiated an expansion that managed to push the Spanish increasingly southward. However, the large numbers of Native Americans in the region presented a number of problems to Charleston's leaders. The natives knew the land more intimately, were increasingly armed with guns, and were the procurers of the deer hides and (Indian) slaves that were a source of great wealth.

The fact that Indians were simultaneously potential threats as well as lucrative trading partners led the English to a policy of accommodation and assimilation of Native Americans along the coast. Colonial powers throughout the Southeast were also adept at fostering antagonisms between groups, relying on a divide-and-conquer approach when more peaceful means were unsuccessful (Ramsey 2008; Taylor 2002). It must be added that Indian groups were equally capable at playing off the European powers against one another. The unpredictable terrain of geopolitical alliances in and around Carolina led leaders in Charleston to encourage the development of a frontier inhabited by allied Indians in a larger arc around the coastal settlements, a borderland where the colony's hold on daily affairs was very tenuous. The key frontier region to the west and south was along the Savannah River and to the south of Port Royal. The Yamasee Indians living alongside Port Royal constitute a unique historical grouping discussed elsewhere in this book (Sweeney and Poplin), so we turn our attention northward to the Savannah River.

Why a Savannah Frontier?

The Savannah River region has been home to Native American settlements dating to the earliest occupation of the Americas. As Albert Goodyear describes in his essay, there were a number of Clovis encampments dating to about 13,000 years ago, and he argues that the Topper site near Allendale, South Carolina, may have a pre-Clovis occupation that reaches as far back as 25,000–50,000 years before present. Beginning with the Clovis tradition, there are 13,000 years of uninterrupted settlement along the Savannah River. This is not to say that groups consistently occupied the same spot, but through time the river and its adjoining lands provided ample resources for communities with greatly differing lifeways—whether they were mobile Archaic peoples hunting, fishing, and gathering along the rich flood plain, or Mississippian towns cultivating fields of maize in the fertile bottomlands.

The one exception to this history of occupation occurred around A.D. 1450 when most of the Savannah River Valley was abandoned by the Mississippian peoples who had been building sizable mound centers and villages there for at least 400 years (Anderson 1994; DePratter 1991; King and Stephenson, this volume). The inability of archaeologists to identify Mississippian sites dating after 1450 in the region does have an independent source of verification: chroniclers with the de Soto expedition that passed through less than a century later also observed that the region was devoid of settlements (DePratter 1991). Whether Mississippian peoples relocated for social, ecological, climatic, or other reasons is still debated. We do know that the flood of Native American groups returning to the region in the late 1600s coincided with the founding of Charleston.

There was an important prelude to the arrival of the English, however, and that was the appearance of the Westo Indians. Believed to be an Iroquoian group—likely the Erie—the Westo apparently vacated what is now western Pennsylvania because of losses from conflict with their neighbors, primarily the Seneca (Bowne 2005). Migrating slowly southward, they established their last known settlement somewhere on the western bank of the Savannah River in 1659. The arrival of the Westo in the Southeast was to have profound consequences on the Native American landscape. Their experiences in Iroquoia had taught them the importance of European weaponry, and they arrived in the Southeast as the first group widely equipped with firearms. The mobility and military prowess of the Westo, combined with their growing reliance on slaving, prompted a literal reign of terror and dispersal of native groups throughout the Southeast (see Sweeney and Poplin, this volume). As the English were building the early stages of the Carolina colony, they recognized the might of the Westo, who were provided with firearms in exchange for defending the southerly reaches of the colony. But the depredations and destabilization of the Westo continued, leading the English to defeat and disperse them in 1683 with the assistance of the Shawnee.

As the English presence began to grow in the late 1600s, native groups flocked to the Savannah drainage to take advantage of lucrative trade possibilities (Figure 1). The economic advantages to both sides were substantial. Native Americans were eager to obtain apparel items (trade cloths, glass beads), muskets, spirits, and a range of other goods. The English colony continued to encourage slaving on native groups by their Native American allies into the early 1700s, sending many of the captives to plantations in the Caribbean (Gallay 2002). Hides were the other commodity highly valued by colonials, and trade in deerskins steadily grew throughout the eighteenth century. With the Savannah River promoted as a southern frontier to the growing Carolina colony, friendly native groups were either enticed to the region or diverted there by the English as they raided areas under nominal Spanish control. Because of these political, economic, and military impetuses, by the second decade of the eighteenth century the Savannah drainage—effectively empty 50 years previous—had been transformed into a

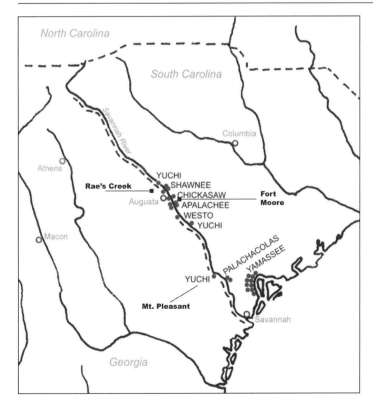

Figure 1. Known Savannah River colonial-era Native American settlements and sites discussed in text. Courtesy of the South Carolina Institute of Archaeology and Anthropology.

thriving and multiethnic frontier region. A census in 1715 by the colonials enumerated 233 Shawnee in 3 towns, 638 Apalachee in 4 towns, 214 Apalachicola in 2 towns, and 400 Yuchi in 2 towns, all along the Savannah River (Haan 1982). In addition, 1,273 Yamasee, who had particularly close ties with the colony, were tallied in 10 towns around Port Royal Sound, where they presented a bulwark to possible Spanish land excursions (Sweeney and Poplin, this volume).

The More Things Change . . .

One of the continuing topics on the South Carolina legislative agenda throughout the first decades of the twenty-first century has been the attempt to rein in so-called "payday" lending. This practice—outlawed in many states—allows lenders to provide short-term loans to persons at interest rates considered well above the going rate. Typically relied upon by low-income persons or families undergoing recurring bouts of economic crisis, these loans have been viewed in the state as either highly predatory or as a salvation, depending upon one's economic outlook. Similar arguments were aired in the late 1990s concerning video poker in South Carolina (banned in 1999), and they center on one of the seemingly intractable debates in American politics: does government regulation of such activities represent a form of necessary consumer protection from the avarice of others; or, should people be held accountable for their actions and not anticipate being bailed out from poor decision making on their part?

We will hardly lay claim to resolving this philosophical quandary here. But we do observe that this debate is the latest iteration of a centuries-long struggle over the role of government in free-market economies that has had particular salience in South Carolina, beginning with the early days of frontier building and trading with Native Americans along the Savannah River and elsewhere. Although the many different groups strung out along the Savannah River and below Port Royal appeared to live without major outbreaks of regional conflict for many years, by the early 1700s matters were quickly coming to a head. Since the late 1600s there had been a litany of accusations by Native Americans against independent European fur traders. These complaints included violent attacks on men, raping of women, cheating in trade negotiations, and leveraging huge debts against Native Americans unversed in the calculus of market exchange and credit (Oatis 2004).

Leaders in Charleston were understandably concerned about this state of affairs. Suspicious and intolerant as they often were of the strange cultures living around them, the colonial leaders were well aware of the importance of Native Americans to the economic well-being of Carolina. Just as important, the friendly communities arranged in a large swath around the English coastal settlements also provided a defensive barrier against Indians who might be allied with European rivals, as well as against those rival themselves. Spain's intentions were always a concern (the Scottish colony of Stuarts Town at Port Royal and adjacent Yamasee towns were razed by a Spanish expedition in 1686), and after 1700 the expanding presence of the French settlements along the Gulf Coast was likewise viewed with growing alarm. So, appeasing Native American allies became a major goal of the Lords Proprietors and colonial governors, who issued a variety of laws and regulatory bodies pertaining to trade relations. In 1677 colonial traders were required to obtain special licenses; in 1680 a commission was established to hear complaints between Native Americans and English; in 1691 traders were restricted to the coastal region between the Savannah River and Winyah Bay to the north; and in 1707 another commission was established to formally supervise Indian affairs (Smith 1903:213–214). Despite these moves to regulate the economy and the behavior of English traders, relations continued to sour and the Yamasee War erupted in 1715. The surprise attack by the Yamasee and many of their allies briefly posed a grave threat to the Carolina colony (Oatis 2004). The conflict was largely dampened by 1716 but continued to fester as small skirmishes for years.

As a response to the Yamasee War and in its anxiety to allay Native American complaints, the colonial government established in 1716 a monopoly and a public trading corporation with direct oversight over the Indian trade, thereby eliminating private traders from living and working among Indian groups. Although the monopoly was voided in 1718, the public trading company continued to tax and strongly regulate Indian commerce—to the great ire of former and aspiring traders—until 1721, when it too was voided. It should be pointed out that the government's strategy was not purely an altruistic move on behalf of beleaguered Indian allies. The colony's leaders well recognized that their control of the hide trade potentially diverted a huge source of income away from troublesome traders and into their own coffers. For their part the Native American groups were not altogether pleased at the loss of local independent traders (at least the benign ones) since the new system restricted their trading options and forced them to travel considerable distances with loads of hides.

Nevertheless, the trade in hides continued to grow in importance, in part because enslavement of Indians sharply declined after the Yamasee War. As Alan Gallay (2002:338) has observed: "The trade did not cease entirely, but the wars to obtain Indian slaves ended abruptly. No longer could South Carolina enlist Indian peoples to conduct slave raids. Indians were too discontented with the English to do their bidding and only slowly, and at arm's length, reconstituted trade relations: a generation of traders had been wiped out, leaving the colony shorn of men skilled at inducing groups to 'go-a-slaving.'"

Another outgrowth of the Yamasee War, and a natural segue to the archaeology of the region, was the fortification of the frontier. No longer secure in the allegiance of old allies, Carolina felt compelled to build several small forts in 1715–1718 at points in an arc around Charleston. Some of these forts were also intended as economic entrepôts ("factories"), occupying strategic locations that would facilitate the government's ability to clamp down on the deer hide trade. Fort Moore was the most important of these since it effectively was a gateway to the sizable Creek settlements to the southwest. It was constructed in 1715–1716 near a former trade settlement known as Savano Town (see Figure 1).

Before we leave the historical background of the Savannah frontier, it is important to emphasize that the Native American presence did not end with the Yamasee War. A few groups apparently remained in the area through the conflict. After peace was reestablished, the allure of trade drew Native Americans back to the region. Some new groups also appeared from somewhat surprising distances, such as the Chickasaw from the northern Mississippi region, who were old allies of the English by this time. Not until the Cherokee War of 1760–1761 did Native tribes opt to permanently vacate the middle to lower reaches of the Savannah River.

The Archaeology of the Southern Frontier

Despite the historical importance of Carolina's southern frontier, the region has received relatively little in the way of sustained or systematic archaeological investigation. Within the Savannah drainage proper, only five settlements have been the subject of relatively intensive work: Fort Moore, Palachacolas Town, Mount Pleasant, Rae's Creek, and the North Augusta site. The latter two sites are still a mystery with regard to their tribal or ethnic affiliations. The work at the North Augusta site is recent and yet to be published, so it will not receive further mention here, although it is undoubtedly a very important part of the frontier picture. Considerable work at varying levels of intensity has also been carried out among some of the ten Yamasee towns, and these likewise provide important information on the development of the southern Carolina frontier (Sweeney and Poplin, this volume). In sum, the artifacts and other remains from these varied occupations have provided important insights into the ways in which both Native Americans and Euro-Americans swapped and mixed the objects and lifeways from their respective worlds, thereby creating new and hybrid lifestyles that were a foreshadowing of the melting-pot metaphor that we associate with the United States today.

PALACHACOLAS TOWN

Located in the southerly reaches of the Savannah Valley (Figure 1), Palachacolas Town was established by a group of Apalachicola Indians who originated from what is today eastern Alabama along the Chattahoochee River. It is believed that they arrived around the late 1600s to late 1700s and departed with the onset of the Yamasee War. Palachacolas Town has been the subject of excavations by Cobb and DePratter (and Chris Gillam) from 2009 to 2012, with support from the National Science Foundation. Here we describe some of the initial findings from that work.

Like many Indian communities of the colonial era, Palachacolas Town appears to have been highly dispersed. The core of the town was at a strategically located point on a bluff on the Savannah River, providing a clear view up and down the drainage. Before our recent investigations, a number of avocational and professional archaeologists had carried out small-scale work at this location over the past century, finding evidence for burials (with numerous associated artifacts), houses, and other features associated with a thriving community. Our own work has indicated that considerable damage has occurred at this spot because of modern disturbance, but that intact colonial-period deposits and features still remain. We have located what appears to be a fortification line that runs parallel to the edge of the bluff (Figure 2). The artifact assemblage is characteristic of other Indian towns of this period (such as described by Sweeney and Poplin for the Yamasee in this volume). In other words, there are remnants of many European trade goods such as bottle glass, lead shot and firearms fragments, and European kaolin smoking pipes.

There are three categories of remains where we see a strong persistence in Native American traditions. First, the Apalachicola continued to rely heavily on their ceramic traditions. European pottery is relatively rare, whereas Native pottery is commonplace. Second, our initial botanical analyses suggest a continued

Figure 2. Fortification trench at Palachacolas Town: (a) top-down view of exposed trench, and (b) profile of trench. Courtesy of the South Carolina Institute of Archaeology and Anthropology.

reliance on a diverse diet, consisting of a number of wild plants in addition to the cultivation of maize. We do see the introduction of a few Old World imports, however, such as peach and cowpea (or black-eyed pea). Third, Indians continued to dig pits large and small into the ground for storage, food preparation, and other uses (Figure 3). Artifacts and botanical remains from these contexts have provided some of our best, undisturbed evidence for life at Palachacolas Town. We should add here that it is likely that the Apalachicola continued to live in some variation of traditional housing; however, we have yet to identify any of these structures.

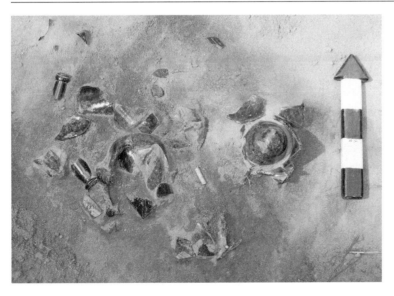

Figure 3. Broken glass bottle in pit feature at Palachacolas. Many of the glass shards from the site had been recycled into cutting and scraping tools. Courtesy of the South Carolina Institute of Archaeology and Anthropology.

Archaeological survey in the region indicates that Palachacolas Town had several satellites. We have discovered a contemporary community across the Savannah River in Georgia, in addition to what appear to be small, discrete residential areas to the south of the core community on the east side of the river. All the locations share strong similarities in their strong integration of European material culture but continued persistence on native pottery technologies. There is considerable stylistic and technological variation in the native pottery, and this may suggest that the Apalachicola adopted other Indian groups. The dispersed residential pattern may be due in part to the segregation of groups by their ethnic affiliation, but it is possible that the use of shifting forms of agriculture may also have led Indian towns to extend themselves in a broad pattern across the landscape.

MOUNT PLEASANT

The Mount Pleasant site is on the Georgia side of the Savannah River about 15 km north of Palachacolas Town (Figure 1). One likely reason for the occupation of this location, aside from its access to the river, is that it bordered a major trail that linked Charleston with Native American groups and trading opportunities to the south. Indian encampments occurred at this strategic spot at least as early as the early 1700s. A more sizable settlement appears to have been established by the Yuchi Indians in the early 1720s after the tumult of the Yamasee War had died down. The Yuchi likely migrated here from somewhere around eastern Tennessee.

Archaeological investigations at Mount Pleasant in 1989 by Daniel and Rita Elliott showed that the settlement covered an area of about 360 by 200 m on a bluff edge overlooking the Savannah River (Elliott and Elliott 1990). Although there were prehistoric occupations in the vicinity, there is no long sequence of overlapping time periods represented in one discrete area as found at Rae's Creek (described below). Similar to Rae's Creek, however, archaeologists did find two levels of occupation dating to the colonial period. The lower of the two zones contained large frequencies of indigenous pottery and the recovered animal bone was dominated by wild species such as white-tailed deer. Nevertheless, a wide variety of European objects was recovered, the likely result of trade with colonials. The upper level contained numerous remains of domestic animals, such as cows and pigs, as well as large numbers of European ceramics and a greater diversity of objects of European origin. Elliott and Elliott (1990) have attributed the upper occupation to a small military garrison established by the fledgling Georgia colony in 1741.

Colonial records observe that the Yuchi had moved upriver a few years before the garrison was established, but the locality continued to serve as a trade post and it was likely visited on a regular basis by the Yuchi and other groups. A recent shovel-test investigation of the site has revealed artifact concentrations that may coincide with Yuchi households (Figure 4).

The artifacts from the presumed Native American deposit are typical of the intermingling one associates with a frontier. While Native Americans continued to rely heavily on their own traditions for pottery manufacture, European objects and practices were being widely incorporated. Particularly noteworthy are the numbers of European kaolin clay smoking pipe fragments, the remains of firearms and ammunition (gunflints, lead shot, musket fragments), and clothing

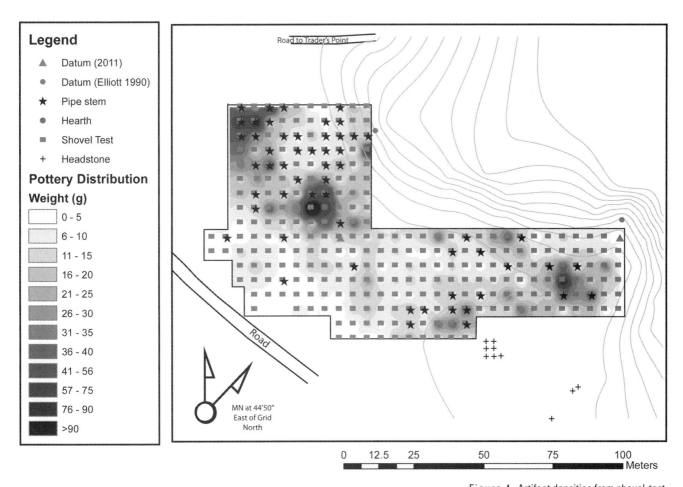

Legend

▲ Datum (2011)
● Datum (Elliott 1990)
★ Pipe stem
● Hearth
■ Shovel Test
+ Headstone

Pottery Distribution

Weight (g)

	0 - 5
	6 - 10
	11 - 15
	16 - 20
	21 - 25
	26 - 30
	31 - 35
	36 - 40
	41 - 56
	57 - 75
	76 - 90
	>90

Road to Trader's Point

Road

MN at 44'50"
East of Grid
North

0   12.5   25   50   75   100
Meters

Figure 4. Artifact densities from shovel-test investigations at Mount Pleasant. Courtesy of the South Carolina Institute of Archaeology and Anthropology.

items such as pewter buttons. The prevalence of indigenous pottery and wild food remains suggests that Native Americans were retaining certain traditional aspects of their lifeways, notably food preparation and serving, while adapting to foreign influences in the form of clothing, hunting, and self-defense. This evidence, combined with that from Rae's Creek (such as the continuity of native housing styles), indicates that Native Americans were selectively incorporating certain aspects of colonial influences, while rejecting others.

FORT MOORE

Unlike the other sites mentioned in this essay, Fort Moore was built by the colonials (Figure 1). However, it appears to have been built next to Savanno Town, an important trade village established by the Shawnee before the Yamasee War. The fort was one of a series of fortifications rapidly thrown up as a result of the Yamasee War. It also served as a factory in the fur trade. Its construction on a high bluff on the South Carolina side of the Savannah River, proximity to a major trail that ran to the heart of Creek country to the west and southwest, and placement next to a well-known Indian town all worked to make this location optimal for trade and defense.

Fort Moore was a relatively modest affair. There are no existing maps, but descriptions of the era put its size at roughly 150 by 150 ft (Ivers 1970). With the demise of the monopolistic factory system in the 1720s, and with French and Spanish threats never materializing on this border of the colony, the staffing and upkeep of Fort Moore by Carolina seems to have been half-hearted at best. Nevertheless, it remained an important trading post until 1766, when it was abandoned following the construction of Fort Charlotte farther up the river.

There have been several archaeological investigations at Fort Moore, but the most wide-scale and systematic one took place in 1971 under the supervision of Stanley South and Richard Polhemus (Polhemus 1971). Their large block excavation uncovered a significant portion of the fort, including the entrance area, a trade house in the interior, and segments of the wall fortifications (Figure 5). The distribution of artifacts and features is particularly interesting in light of Carolina's sensibilities regarding the appropriate segregation of Native Americans and colonials. For example, the fort's commandant, Captain Charlesworth Glover, was cautioned, "We repeat our former desire, by direction of the governor, council and assembly, that on no account whatsoever you will admit any Indian, of any nation or quality soever, into the fort" (JCIT 1717:224). Accordingly, the fort's plan called for the trade house or storeroom to be located within the stockade itself to separate Native Americans from the interior. Trade was to take place in an antechamber in front of the storeroom, which was uncovered in the 1971 excavations. Similar policies, intended to segregate Native Americans from Europeans in as many spheres of life as possible, were common among colonial powers (Stoler 1989).

As the archaeological record from Fort Moore demonstrates, the intimacy of daily life on the frontier often undermined imperial anxieties about rubbing

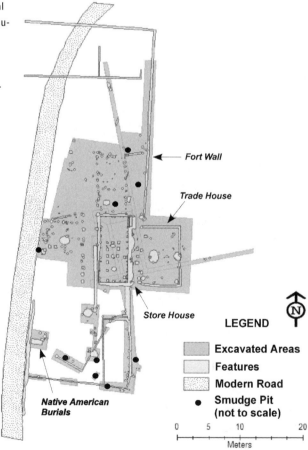

Figure 5. The archaeological remains of Fort Moore, as documented by Stanley South and Richard Polhemus (Polhemus 1971). Courtesy of the South Carolina Institute of Archaeology and Anthropology.

Fort Wall

Trade House

Store House

Native American Burials

LEGEND

Excavated Areas
Features
Modern Road
● Smudge Pit (not to scale)

0   5   10   20
Meters

shoulders with Native Americans. Although the storeroom cellar has the concentrations of kaolin pipe fragments and European ceramics that one would expect of a trade facility, there is also a scattering of stone tool debris and indigenous ceramic sherds as well. Although these artifacts do not necessarily reflect the physical presence of Native Americans, they do suggest that the somewhat impoverished colonial inhabitants of the fort may have been somewhat dependent on locally made Native objects. One particularly compelling example of this possibility was the discovery by archaeologists of part of a colonoware bowl on the storeroom floor (Figure 6). This is a ceramic type made with an indigenous clay paste but with some of the attributes of a European shape—in this case a raised circular foot on the bottom of the vessel, which is very typical of European pottery but absent in prehistoric ceramic types. Other intriguing results from Fort Moore excavations include the discovery of two Native American burials and a concentration of smudge pits inside the fortification wall (see Figure 4). Apparently Native Americans enjoyed a very close relationship on many levels with the colonials.

The lesson we take from Fort Moore is the very porous nature of social boundaries along the frontier and the reality that Native Americans provisioned colonials as well as vice versa. Despite the concerns in London and Charleston about the orderly way in which the colonial enterprise should proceed, life along the frontier reflected the gritty reality of peoples from many backgrounds pitched together and struggling to make a go of it together.

RAE'S CREEK

The Rae's Creek site is located north of present-day Augusta, Georgia, about 200 m west of the Savannah River (Figure 1). This is a multicomponent site with occupations extending as far back as Stalling Island culture, about 3,500 years before

Figure 6. Colonoware vessel from trade house basement at Fort Moore. Courtesy of the South Carolina Institute of Archaeology and Anthropology.

the present (see Sassaman, this volume). The likely allure of this spot to many generations of Native Americans was its location on the Fall Line, the transition between the hilly Piedmont and the Coastal Lowlands that is marked by a high degree of biodiversity in both plant and animal life. In addition, the stretches where drainages run through the Fall Line transition are often richly abundant in fish and mollusks. While this so-called ecotone was always critical to Native Americans in a swath running from Alabama to North Carolina, it apparently resumed a strong importance in the colonial era. Ethnohistorian Robbie Ethridge (2003:36–37) has suggested that the frequent population movement of Native Americans during this era, combined with concerns about European encroachment on agricultural lands, may have made the Fall Line particularly enticing as a way of ensuring a reliable food supply of wild resources. In addition, access to trail crossings, defensive concerns, and other factors likely affected where Native Americans built their towns.

It is still unclear whether the Rae's Creek site is a town that is represented in the colonial surveys. Although the artifacts recovered from Rae's Creek undoubtedly belong to the colonial era, the ethnic affiliations of its inhabitants remain a mystery. Morgan "Ray" Crook's excavation of portions of the site in 1988 (Crook 1990) represents the only synthesis of the materials. He was able to discern two discrete layers dating to the final occupations of the site and which were likely associated with both Native American and English activities. Crook attributed the lower of the two horizons to primarily Native American occupants since the artifact assemblage weighed heavily toward objects of apparent indigenous manufacture, such as ceramics. The upper level had significantly larger numbers of objects and materials of European origin, which Crook believed reflected the increasing presence of either colonials or intensified trade relations with them.

Artifacts and features at the Rae's Creek site typified the flux of peoples moving in and out of the frontier region. Possible domestic structures were represented by the many post molds identified at the site. These reflected the architectural style of the region, where walls were built from rows of single posts set in the ground. However, Crook also identified a wall-trench structure where vertical wall posts were aligned within a pre-excavated trench that was subsequently filled in with soil as a support. This style is much more typical of the eastern Tennessee region and is somewhat unusual for South Carolina. As archaeologists throughout the Southeast have discovered, domestic architecture was one of the categories of tradition that was most resistant to colonial influence. European-style cabins were not widely adopted until the late 1700s, after the Revolutionary War (Hally 2002).

The diagnostic indigenous ceramic sherds were typical of traditions from both the Chattahoochee drainage (sand-tempered wares) between Georgia and Alabama, and from the eastern Tennessee region or farther west (shell-tempered wares). Crook also believed some of the pottery types embodied stylistic and technological elements from multiple traditions simultaneously—perhaps the result of different cultures sharing their decorative and manufacturing techniques. In another instance of cultural borrowing, Native Americans were using shards from green European wine or rum bottles to create scrapers and other tool forms usually made from local stones such as chert. The scrapers may have been used for preparing the deer hides that were so important to the trade with the colonials. Further support for this idea comes from the number of smudge pits that were found at Rae's Creek. These small pits filled with carbonized corncobs are described in historical documents as being important for producing a black, oily smoke important for the preparation of deer hides by Native Americans.

Discussion

To date, archaeological research along the Savannah River frontier region has revealed the rapid changes that were taking place among all peoples in the colonial era. The frontier was populated by a number of diverse Indian groups. Many of them had little interaction with one another prior to their migration to the region, so the development of the frontier led to new neighbors and new relationships among Indians, as well as between indigenous peoples and colonials. Just as interestingly, we see a diverse mix of pottery types with the archaeological sites, suggesting that people of different backgrounds and ceramic traditions were migrating between towns. Thus, when the English referred to a town as "Shawnee" or "Yuchi," the reality is that those groups may have been in the majority at that location but that other peoples were likely represented as well.

Many of the traditional objects and technologies associated with the homelands of the various Indian groups rapidly disappeared as they moved closer to the Carolina orbit. We see several patterns that hold for all the Indian colonial sites along the Savannah River, despite their diverse origins. Stone tools are very rare on the sites we have discussed and were apparently replaced with glass shards and metal forms. Gauging from the widespread presence of gun parts and musket balls, firearms had become widely adopted. Objects of European clothing (buckles, jewelry, glass beads) and glass bottles (which likely held alcoholic beverages) are also common on all these sites.

A major thread of Native persistence can be seen in the ceramic assemblages, which are dominated by indigenous forms of pottery. The continuity of tradition can also be seen in the botanical remains, which demonstrate a continued reliance on North American domestic and wild plants, with the appearance of a few imported species such as peach (Wagner forthcoming). There may be a gendered element to these distinctions of borrowing and persistence, as ethnohistoric evidence suggests that women were traditionally engaged in food preparation whereas males are known to have been heavily involved in trading deer hides for guns and alcohol (Hudson 1976).

Although some of these trends have been documented for colonial-period Indian sites elsewhere in the Southeast, we cannot assume that all peoples underwent exactly the same transformations. For example, the Apalachee, who lived alongside the Spanish around modern-day Tallahassee in the seventeenth century, created a wide variety of "copy-wares" (Vernon 1988; Vernon and Cordell 1993). These are pottery types made with Native pastes (temper and clay) but which mimicked Spanish shapes, such as pouring vessels or plates. Such forms are extremely rare along the Savannah River towns. The Chickasaw, who lived in northern Mississippi but were strongly allied with the Carolina colony, show a much stronger reliance on traditional technologies and ornamentation later in time than do the frontier towns we have described—perhaps because of their greater distance from Charleston (Johnson et al. 2008). In short, various Indian communities reacted very differently to the appearance of colonial powers as a result of their own cultural traditions and their own complex mix of relationships with other Indian groups and the different European colonies in the Southeast.

Conclusion

The sites we have introduced are not the only ones along the Carolina southern frontier that have been investigated by archaeologists, only those with significant Native American presences that have received the most intensive scrutiny. Other important occupations have received more limited testing, and many others await discovery. These include forts, Indian communities, and locations such as trading posts. In the latter category, the Silver Bluff site, home and trading outpost of the highly influential entrepreneur George Galphin, has been investigated archaeologically (see Herron and Moon, this volume). Given the diverse history represented by these camps, towns, forts, and outposts, it is fair to say that understanding the changes along Carolina's southern frontier over a period spanning a century is a major challenge to archaeologists. The mixing of artifact and housing styles makes it difficult to attribute material culture to specific groups, such as the Shawnee or Yuchi, and to assess precisely who was interacting with whom at specific points on the landscape. At the same time, this is what one would anticipate in a highly dynamic and volatile frontier region.

In many respects the land that is now South Carolina was one of the key proving grounds for the English colonial expansion in the New World. The development of the colony conceived in the ideal by the Lords Proprietors on one side of the Atlantic was quickly altered in the face of harsh realities on the other side. Faced with relatively meager resources in its early going, the colonial government constantly struggled to balance an unstable triangle: its concern with defense against other European powers, its oversight of an economy strongly reliant on fiercely independent traders, and its own territorial ambitions in a region already occupied by an unpredictable mix of hostile and friendly Native Americans. By the end of the seventeenth century, as the colony began to thrive along the coast, the region along the Savannah River and below Port Royal emerged as a relatively stable southerly boundary. The wide variety of Native American groups and Europeans attracted to the area led to the formation of a frontier distinguished by remarkable ethnic diversity, held together in large part by the promise of trade. The archaeology that has been conducted on some of these important settlements has begun to reveal how a new and rich mixture of practices emerged from the convergence of multiple traditions and cultures.

Acknowledgments

We are grateful to the many people who have shared their ideas based on their own experiences in working in the Savannah Valley, notably Dan Elliot, Stan South, and Richard Polhemus. We also thank the undergraduate and graduate students who worked with us in the field and lab for several gratifying seasons. Portions of this research are based upon work supported by the National Science Foundation under Grant No. 0852686.

References Cited

Anderson, David G.

1994 *The Savannah River Chiefdoms: Political Change in the Late Prehistoric Southeast.* University of Alabama Press, Tuscaloosa.

Barr, Daniel P. (editor)

2006 *The Boundaries between Us: Natives and Newcomers along the Frontiers of the Old Northwest Territory, 1750–1850.* Kent State University Press, Kent, Ohio.

Bauman, Richard, and Charles L. Briggs

2003 *Voices of Modernity: Language Ideologies and the Politics of Inequality.* Cambridge University Press, Cambridge, United Kingdom.

Bowne, Eric E.

2005 *The Westo Indians: Slave Traders of the Early Colonial Southeast.* University of Alabama Press, Tuscaloosa.

Cayton, Andrew R. L., and Fredericka J. Teute

1998 Introduction: On the Connection of Frontiers. In *Contact Points: American Frontiers from the Mohawk Valley to the Mississippi, 1750–1830,* edited by Andrew R. L. Cayton and Fredericka J. Teute, pp. 1–15. University of North Carolina Press, Chapel Hill.

Crook, Morgan R., Jr.

1990 *Rae's Creek: A Multicomponent Archaeological Site at the Fall Line Along the Savannah River.* Report submitted to the Georgia Department of Transportation, Atlanta. Department of Anthropology, Georgia State University, Atlanta.

DePratter, Chester B.

1991 *Late Prehistoric and Early Historic Chiefdoms in the Southeastern United States.* Garland, New York.

Edgar, Walter

1998 *South Carolina: A History.* University of South Carolina Press, Columbia.

Elliott, Daniel L., and Rita Elliott

1990 *The Lost City Survey: Archaeological Reconnaissance of Nine Eighteenth Century Settlements in Chatham and Effingham Counties, Georgia.* Report submitted to the Georgia Department of Natural Resources, LAMAR Institute, Inc., Savannah.

Ethridge, Robbie

2003 *Creek Country: The Creek Indians and Their World.* University of North Carolina Press, Chapel Hill.

Gallay, Alan

2002 *The Indian Slave Trade: The Rise of the English Empire in the American South, 1670–1717.* Yale University Press, New Haven.

Gosden, Chris

2003 *Archaeology and Colonialism: Cultural Contact from 5000 BC to the Present.* Cambridge University Press, Cambridge, United Kingdom.

Haan, Richard L.

1982 The "Trade Do's Not Flourish as Formerly": The Ecological Origins of the Yamasee War of 1715. *Ethnohistory* 28(4):341–358.

Hally, David J.

2002 "As Caves Beneath the Ground": Making Sense of Aboriginal House Form in the Protohistoric and Historic Southeast. In *Between Contacts and Colonies: Archaeological Perspectives on the Protohistoric Southeast,* edited by Cameron B. Wesson and Mark A. Rees, pp. 90–109. University of Alabama Press, Tuscaloosa.

Hudson, Charles

1976 *The Southeastern Indians.* University of Tennessee Press, Knoxville.

Ivers, Larry E.

1970 *Colonial Forts of South Carolina, 1670–1775.* University of South Carolina Press, Columbia.

JCIT

1715–1717 *Journal of the Commissioners of the Indian Trade.* On file, South Carolina Department of Archives and History, Columbia.

Johnson, Jay K., John W. O'Hear, Robbie Ethridge, Brad R. Lieb, Susan L. Scott, and H. Edwin Jackson

2008 Measuring Chickasaw Adaptation on the Western Frontier of the Colonial South: A Correlation of Documentary and Archaeological Data. *Southeastern Archaeology* 27:1–30.

Lightfoot, Kent G., and Antoinette Martinez

1995 Frontiers and Boundaries in Archaeological Perspective. *Annual Review of Anthropology* 24:471–492.

Oatis, Steven J.

2004 *A Colonial Complex: South Carolina's Frontiers in the Era of the Yamasee War.* University of Nebraska Press, Lincoln.

Polhemus, Richard

1971 Excavation at Fort Moore—Savano Town (38AK4&5). *SCIAA Notebook* 3(6):132–133.

Ramsey, William L.

2008 *The Yamasee War: A Study of Culture, Economy, and Conflict in the Colonial South.* University of Nebraska Press, Lincoln.

Smith, W. Roy

1903 *South Carolina as a Royal Province, 1719–1776.* Macmillan, London.

Stoler, Ann Laura

1989 Rethinking Colonial Categories: European Communities and the Boundaries of Rule. *Comparative Studies in Society and History* 31:134–61.

Taylor, Alan

2002 *American Colonies: the Settling of North America.* Penguin, New York.

Turner, Frederick Jackson

1920 *The Frontier in American History.* H. Holt, New York.

Vernon, Richard

1988 17th Century Apalachee Colono-Ware as a Reflection of Demography, Economics, and Acculturation. *Historical Archaeology* 22:76–82.

Vernon, Richard, and Ann S. Cordell

1993 A Distributional and Technological Study of Apalachee Colono-Ware from San Luis de Talimali. In *The Spanish Missions of La Florida,* edited by B. G. McEwan, pp. 418–441. University Press of Florida, Gainesville.

Wagner, Gail E.

Forthcoming The Food of Colonial South Carolina Indians. In *Are We What We Eat? Continuity and Change in Food During the Colonial Era in North America,* edited by J. G. Douglass and S. N. Reddy. Archaeological Papers of the American Anthropological Association. Washington, D.C..

ALEX Y. SWEENEY AND ERIC C. POPLIN

The Yamasee Indians of Early Carolina

THE YAMASEE INDIANS were a multiethnic conglomeration of Native Americans who lived in the lower coastal plain of South Carolina during the late seventeenth and early eighteenth centuries. During their tenure in South Carolina, the Yamasee and the colonists from Carolina shared a dynamic relationship. The relationship between these two groups evolved over a 30-year period from close military allies and trading partners to enemies and warfare.

Much of what is known regarding the Yamasee has been discovered through ethnohistorical and archaeological research. The *Journals of the Commissioners of the Indian Trade* (McDowell 1955) provide some of the accounts and details regarding the relationship between the Yamasee and the colonists, as well as Yamasee political structure and settlement. The origins and history of the Yamasee have been documented through research projects that have examined Natives Americans throughout South Carolina, Georgia, and Florida (Gallay 2002; Green 1992; DePratter and Green 1990; Hann 1988, 1990, 1991, 1996; McKivergan 1991; Worth 1995, 1998a, 1998b). Numerous archaeologists have been able to identify Yamasee cultural materials and settlements within South Carolina (for example, Elliot and Cable 1994; Fletcher and Harvey 2000; Jordan et al. 1999; Green 1992; McKivergan 1991; Rust et al. 1995; Southerlin et al. 2001; Sweeney 2003) and Georgia and Florida (Bushnell 1994; Saunders 2000; White 2002). Combined, the archaeological and historic data provide a concrete view of the Yamasee, although much remains to be known about them.

We seek to describe the lifeways of the Yamasee Indians during their stay in South Carolina by comparing archaeological evidence from three South Carolina sites with the historical accounts of the Yamasee and their interactions with the early Carolina colonists. Interpretation of the historical accounts provides some insight into the beliefs and actions of the Yamasee, while information from the archaeological sites provides a more detailed view of how the Yamasee lived while in Carolina and how their interactions with both the English and Spanish colonists of the seventeenth and early eighteenth centuries changed their material culture and lifeways.

Ethnohistorical Overview of the Yamasee

The Yamasee had three massive migration episodes in Carolina (Figure 1). The earliest known Yamasee settlement in Carolina was on Hilton Head Island in 1683 (Worth 1995:37). Sometime in late 1686–1687, the Yamasee migrated inland and north, settling near the Ashepoo River (McKivergan 1991:49). Between 1695 and 1715, the Yamasee lived in ten towns in modern-day Beaufort and Jasper counties in South Carolina (Table 1). These towns were divided into two distinct clusters, the Upper and the Lower Yamasee (Figure 2). Ethnohistorical research has traced the cultural origins of four of the Upper Yamasee towns (Pocotaligo, Huspah, Sadketche, and Tulafina) to Guale settlements within Spanish Florida along the Georgia coast during the mid- to late seventeenth century. All four of the Lower Yamasee towns (Altamaha, Chechessee, Euhaw, and Okatee) can be traced back to earlier sixteenth- and seventeenth-century Indian provinces located in the interior of Georgia (Green 1992:24; Sweeney 2005).

TABLE 1. South Carolina Yamasee Town Names

YAMASEE TOWN NAME	POSSIBLE ORIGIN
Upper Towns	
Pocotaligo	Ocotonico (Guale/Mocama)
Pocosabo	Ospo (Guale/Mocama)
Sadketche	Unknown
Tulafina	Tulafina (Guale/Mocama)
Tomatley	Tomatley (Cherokee?)
Lower Towns	
Altamaha	Altamaha (Interior Georgia)
Chechessee	Ichisi (Interior Georgia)
Euhaw	Toa (Interior Georgia)
Okatee	Ocute (Interior Georgia)

SOURCE: All origins are adapted from Green (1992:24) and Green et al. (2002:18) except for Pocotaligo (Sweeney 2005)

The interior Georgia Indian provinces were located in the Oconee River Valley in central Georgia. In the spring of 1540, Hernando de Soto's quest to the chiefdom of Cofitachequi (located in the Wateree Valley of central South Carolina) encountered people from the provinces of Toa, Ichisi, Altamaha, and Ocute (Ranjel 1904 in Smith and Hally 1992:100). During this time, Ocute was described as the paramount chiefdom over Toa, Ichisi, and Altamaha, and was currently at war with the chiefdom of Cofitachequi (Green 1992:8 after Ranjel 1904). Gifts of supplies (such as food, guides, burden bearers, and canoes) were provided to de Soto and his men during their visits to these interior chiefdoms (Gentleman of Elvas 1968).

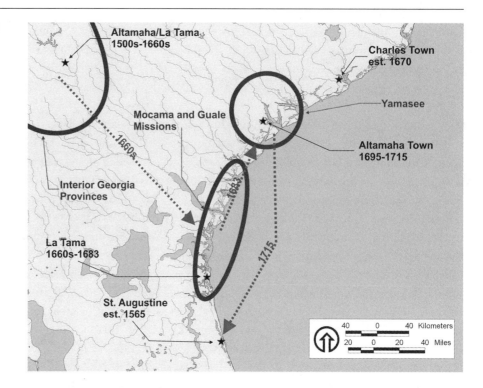

Figure 1. Location of Yamasee Migrations between the 1540s and 1715. Courtesy of Brockington and Associates.

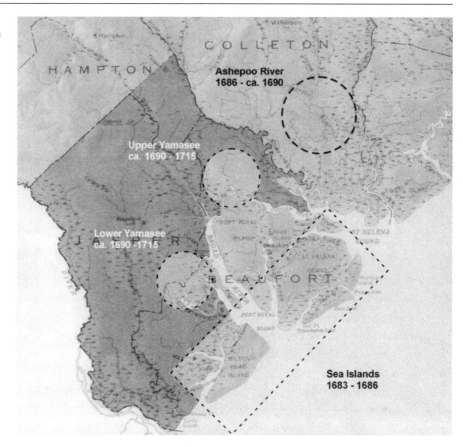

Figure 2. General location of Yamasee settlements within South Carolina. Courtesy of Brockington and Associates.

During the next 150 years, the political fortunes of Altamaha (referred to as La Tama in Spanish documents) and Ocute shifted. Ocute's power waned and Altamaha/La Tama rose to emerge as the paramount chiefdom (Green 1992:13). Altamaha/La Tama's power over Toa, Ichisi, and Ocute remained intact as their constituent populations migrated into the coastal areas of Georgia and South Carolina. This shift in power between Ocute and Altamaha may have come about when initial contact with the Spanish led to widespread epidemics and population loss, which in turn caused a disruption in indigenous sociopolitical systems (Smith 1987:58–60).

Following attacks from the Westo Indians to the north in 1662, Native Americans from the Georgia interior provinces migrated toward the missionized areas of Spanish Florida to the east (among the Guale along the Georgia coast) and to the south (among the Timucuans near St. Augustine and the Apalachee in western Florida). In 1663 a group of Indians called the Yamasis occupied five towns in the Escamaçu province, a peripheral area to Spanish Florida north of the Guale (Anguiano 1663 in Worth 1995). This is perhaps the first mention of the Yamasee by name, and perhaps they were also refugees from the Georgia interior fleeing the Westo raids. Further assaults by the Westo forced these Yamasee living in Escamaçu south into the Guale mission province sometime between 1663 and 1665 (Worth 1995:20–21).

The Yamasee became incorporated into the Spanish mission system for several decades. Archival documentation makes a clear distinction between the Guale and the Yamasee; the latter are often described as pagans and heathens, and many Spanish writers questioned the effectiveness of converting the Yamasee to Christianity (Deagan 1978; Worth 1995). The Yamasee were less likely lured to the Spanish mission area by the spiritual benefits of Christianity than by the protection offered by living in close proximity to other nonhostile native groups and the Spanish. During their tenure in the Guale province, the Yamasee participated in the annual *repartimiento* labor draft, which provided Indian laborers to work for the Spanish government in St. Augustine. Although all Indian groups living under the Spanish mission systems contributed laborers, the Yamasee provided a higher percentage of laborers than other groups (Worth 1995:35; 1998a:128–129).

Within the Guale province, the Yamasee occupied the areas in the southern portion of the province that were formerly occupied by the Mocama. A 1675 Spanish census among the indigenous population in the Guale territory identifies six towns on two islands inhabited by the Yamasee (Worth 1995:28). The Yamasee towns of San Simon and Ocotonico were located on St. Simons Island. Ocotonico had the most non-Christianized Indians (n=160) in the region and was the second most populated town in the Guale province (Worth 1995:28–29). To the south on Amelia Island, the Yamasee lived in four towns: a former Mocama village, Ocotoque (Ocute), La Tama (Altamaha), and Santa Maria. Amelia Island was the second highest populated island of Guale in 1675 with 190 occupants, all of whom were Yamasee (DePratter and Green 1990; Green 1992:17; Hann 1990:497; Worth 1995:28). Yamasee Indians also were reported living in the towns of San Felipe, Talapo, Ospogue, Fascule, and Alests, mixed among the Guale population on Cumberland Island (Deagan 1978:101–102; Hann 1996:251; Worth 1995:106).

In 1683 French and English vessels under the command of the French pirate Grammont attacked St. Augustine and raided the Yamasee towns of Santa Maria and San Pedro, as well as the mixed Yamasee/Guale town of San Felipe (Bushnell 1994:162; Worth 1995:36). Shortly after these attacks, the Yamasee and much of the Guale population migrated together to the north, away from Spanish control to Hilton Head Island in South Carolina. Spanish Ensign Alonso Solana identified a "town of pagans" on Hilton Head later in 1683. Inadequate Spanish protection from hostile raids, abuses during the *repartimiento* drafts, and perhaps better opportunities presented by living closer to the English colonists in newly established Charles Towne all likely contributed to this desertion of the Georgia coast (Crane 1929:20–21; Worth 1995:37–38).

Over the next couple of years, more Yamasee continued to migrate into the Port Royal area. Former mission Indians from Sapelo, Asao, and Tupiqui arrived in the region (Crane 1929:25). A month later, English trader Caleb Westbrook reported that over a thousand Yamasee had moved into the area as well (Green 1992:23). Westbrook was informed by the cacique of Altamaha that his people were in the region and expanding farther into the Port Royal area. By 1686 nearly 2,000 Yamasee were living in the lower Coastal Plain of South Carolina (Rowland et al. 1996:72–73).

In 1684 Scottish settlers under the leadership of Henry Lord Cardross established Stuart's Town in the Port Royal area (Crane 1929:25, 28). Stuart's Town, which retained political autonomy from English authority in Charles Towne, became an exclusive trading partner and ally to the neighboring Yamasee. In February 1685, 50–60 Yamasee under the leadership of Cacique Altamaha raided the Timucuan mission Santa Catalina de Ajoica. The Yamasee captured 21 Timucuans and sold them as slaves to the Scots at Stuart's Town (Worth 1998:140). On the return trip home, the Yamasee boasted to English explorer Henry Woodward that they had killed as many as 50 Timucuans and claimed that they were motivated and armed by the Scots (Crane 1929:31).

In August 1686 the Spanish retaliated for the raid on Santa Catalina by assaulting Stuart's Town. After three days of ransacking the homes and butchering livestock, Stuart's Town and its fortifications were burned and destroyed (Rowland et al. 1996:74). In December 1686 the Spanish conducted a second raid and "utterly destroyed what they left before at Port Royal" (Gallay 2002:84).

Following the destruction of Stuart's Town, the Yamasee relocated inland and to the north along the Ashepoo River within five towns: Altamaha, Chechessee, Pocotaligo, Tuskegee, and Chehawes (McKivergan 1991:49). During this time, the Yamasee allied themselves with the English colonists from Charles Towne. Sometime after 1690, but likely no later than 1695, the Yamasee relocated back to the Port Royal area (Green 1992:28).

Separated by the Broad River, the Yamasee divided into two distinct clusters, the Upper and Lower Yamasee (Crane 1929:164). Each cluster consisted of a primary town and multiple secondary towns. Each primary town served as a capital and contained a council house and may have held diplomatic responsibilities regarding the relationships between the secondary towns and the English settlers and traders. Accounts of the Commissioners of the Indian Trade indicate that Indian trade agents frequently met within the primary towns to conduct trade with all Indians within either the Upper or Lower Yamasee clusters (McDowell 1955).

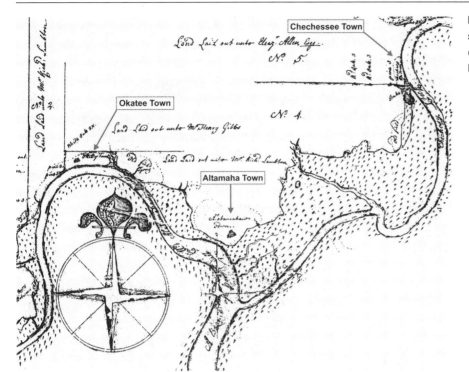

Figure 3. Vogue and Hunter map of 1732 showing the location of Altamaha Town, Chechessee Town, and Okatee Town. Courtesy of Brockington and Associates.

Associated farmsteads and agricultural fields were situated around the secondary towns and the primary towns (Green et al. 2002:19). A portion of a 1732 map shows the location of Altamaha Town, flanked by the Yamasee towns of Chechesy Town to the east and Okatie Town to the west (Figure 3). Within each town, a larger structure is shown that may represent a council house for each town. Areas marked as "old fields" are seen near Chechesy and Okatie; however, none are depicted on this map near Altamaha. Since Altamaha was the capital of the Lower Yamasee, perhaps some crops grown in these old fields of the adjacent secondary towns were given as tribute to Altamaha.

In 1703 the Euhaw band joined the Yamasee and became the fourth town within the Lower Yamasee (Crane 1929:26, 76). As previously stated, all four Lower Yamasee towns originated as sixteenth-century interior Georgia chiefdoms, and four of the six Upper Yamasee towns were descended from Guale mission settlements. It appears that despite being grouped within the same cultural designation of Yamasee, the individual towns chose to affiliate politically and culturally based on their distinct origins. Boundaries and group membership of these towns during this period was likely fluid, and members of individual villages also likely included refugees and survivors of other groups that are not presently known.

Colonial documents name King Lewis the leader of Pocotaligo and "King Altimaha" the chief of Altamaha Town (McDowell 1955:37–38, 41, 50). Lewis's European name suggests that perhaps he was to some degree Christian, or at least baptized; Altamaha was likely not. The influence of Christianity introduced within the Guale mission villages in coastal Georgia likely remained among many members of the Upper Yamasee after the Guale were absorbed into the Yamasee (Sweeney 2003:151). Education in language and religion for children was requested by some Yamasee (Klingberg 1960:5).

The Yamasee towns were located on the buffer region between the Spanish in Florida and the English in Carolina. For the English colonists, it was beneficial to have allied native groups situated between themselves and their enemy in Florida. The Lords Proprietor recognized this advantage, and designated the "Indian Lands" in 1707 to maintain Yamasee allegiance to the English. These "Indian Lands" were the mainland bounded by the Combahee River, the marsh and islands of the Coosa and Port Royal rivers, the Savannah River, and an arbitrary line connecting the head of the Combahee River to the head of the Savannah River (Cooper and McCord 1836:317–319). Yamasee settlements were limited within this specified reservation, and settlers were to be penalized for encroachment into these lands. All non-Indian settlers living within the lands had one year to vacate or pay a fine of 100 pounds; settlers with titles within those lands were to be reimbursed by the colonial government upon compliance and removal from their lands (Gallay 2002:218).

The Yamasee served as slave raiders and a military force for the English colonists. They were expected to defend their lands from the Spanish to the south. To ensure this, the English government provided them with firearms, gunpowder, and knives (Green 1992). The Yamasee raided neighboring Native groups and sold captives as slaves to work on English plantations. The English benefited from the raids in numerous ways. Aside from the increase in slave labor, the Yamasee removed other native groups from desired land for future colonial settlement (Green 1992:74). These raids also severely depleted the Spanish-allied Native Americans, which weakened Spanish defenses and increased their vulnerability to English assault (Gallay 2002:128). Figure 4 shows a portion of Thomas Nairne's 1711 map that indicates the Yamasee slaving activities in Spanish Florida. On this map near the headwaters of the St. Johns River, it states, "Here the Carolina Indians leave their Canoes when they go to war against the Floridians."

These slave raids were often joint ventures with Indian and colonial forces. In 1702 Governor James Moore and a thousand troops consisting of colonial soldiers, Yamasee, and Creeks captured and enslaved over 500 Timucuans between

Figure 4. A portion of Nairne's 1711 map showing Spanish Florida and depicting the location of a Yamasee canoe landing for slaving ventures. Courtesy of Brockington and Associates.

Amelia Island and St. Augustine (Lanning 1935:186, 227–228). The Yamasee were also responsible for enslavement of the Calusa Indians near Tampa Bay. Fear of the Yamasee in Florida forced surviving Indians southward into the Florida Keys, seeking refuge and protection from the Spanish in Cuba (Gallay 2002:148–295).

As a military force, the Yamasee assisted the colonists during the Tuscarora War in 1712. Not only did the Yamasee provide soldiers during this war, but they also led battles and provided tactical guidance to Colonel John Barnwell's troops (Gallay 2002:269). The Yamasee participated in the siege at Fort Neoheroka, a pivotal battle in the Tuscarora War (Southerlin et al. 2001:49).

The Yamasee traded deerskins to the English colonists, which became highly profitable in trade to Great Britain. In 1693 Indians allied to the English were required to provide deerskins to the government annually (Green 1992:71). As the Yamasee increased their hunting of wild deer to gain more European goods, the deer population became severely depleted. This depletion, along with reported unethical trading practices, increased the Yamasee debt to the traders. These unethical trading practices included providing rum to Indians prior to trading for skins and slaves, resulting in the traders acquiring more goods at less expense (Johnson 1980:59). This led to several prohibitions by the government restricting rum or alcohol provisions to the Yamasee. Despite these prohibitions, English traders still provided alcohol to the Indians (Johnson 1980:63–64). Upon hearing that the Yamasee had received rum in 1713, the Commissioners of Indian Trade ordered traders to search all Yamasee towns and destroy all bottles of rum and alcohol (McDowell 1955:50).

Tensions between the colonists and Yamasee escalated, and Captain Thomas Nairne was assigned the Commissioner of Indian Trade to the Yamasee. Nairne was ordered to conduct routine visits to the Yamasee and help assure their allegiance to the colonial government by regulating trade as well as recording and settling disputes between Indians and traders. Nairne documented numerous complaints by the Yamasee against traders and settlers for murder, beatings, abduction, illegal enslavement (particularly against women), thefts, demands for labor, and encroachment upon their lands (McDowell 1955). Disputes also often occurred following joint slave raids and warfare episodes, with the division of plundered goods and captured slaves giving rise to disagreement (Crane 1929; Gallay 2002; Green 1992).

The alliance between the Yamasee and the English continued to be strained, and a census conducted in early 1715 by Colonel Barnwell of all natives living in South Carolina increased Indian fears that perhaps they had become the next target of the colonists' enslaving efforts (Merrell 1989:66). The 1715 census revealed that the Yamasee were the only Native group in Carolina to have fewer women (n=345) than men (n=413). This imbalance supported Yamasee allegations of illegal enslavement of their women (Gallay 2002:207).

On April 12, 1715, a warning was issued to William Bray's wife from a member of the Yamasee town of Euhaw. This warning claimed that the nearby Creek Indians had devised a plan to first eradicate the Carolina traders and then destroy the entire colony. In response to this, the governor ordered Indian trade agents to visit the Yamasee, the Apalachee, and the Creek to address grievances (McDowell 1955:65).

Two days later, Nairne, Bray, Samuel Warner, John Wright, John Cochran and his wife, and several other traders arrived at the Upper Yamasee capital of Pocotaligo. After a meeting with the Yamasee chief, presumably King Lewis of Pocotaligo, the alliance between the groups appeared to be intact. The traders stayed the night "in the round-house, with the King and chief War captains, in seemingly perfect friendship" (Carroll 1836:548). The next morning, however, the traders were abruptly awakened by an attack by their Yamasee hosts, who were now painted in red and black. Most of the traders were slaughtered that day, several by torture (Milling 1940:141). Nairne suffered a slow and painful death over several days as his body was pierced with burning splinters of wood (Gallay 2002:328).

Immediately following the incident at Pocotaligo, the Yamasee attacked Port Royal. Over 300 of Port Royal's colonists quickly boarded a ship and escaped prior to the attack. The Yamasee "destroyed homes and cattle, sacked the deserted plantations, and murdered those few unfortunates who fell into their hands" (Crane 1929:169). Simultaneously, the Yamasee assaulted several plantations in St. Bartholomew's Parish to the north, located between the Edisto and Combahee rivers. Fleeing settlers escaped to the protection of Charles Towne; however, nearly 100 settlers were taken prisoner as their homes were burned and their goods plundered. These events sparked the Yamasee War, and several other native groups, including the Creeks, Choctaws, Yuchi, Apalachee, Catawba, and Cherokee, joined the Yamasee resistance against the English colonists (Carroll 1836:549; Crane 1929:169).

Carolina quickly responded to the Yamasee resistance with militia forces led by Governor Craven and Colonel Barnwell. Craven's forces defeated Yamasee forces near the Salkahatchie Swamp along the Combahee River. Barnwell's forces captured Pocotaligo and reclaimed plundered goods and seized Yamasee supplies. Captain Mackay established a colonial encampment at Pocotaligo and dispatched soldiers from there to confront other Yamasee (Crane 1929:170–171).

Near the end of May, less than two months after the start of the Yamasee War, the surviving Yamasee were expelled from South Carolina and temporarily lived along the Georgia coast to the south. On May 28 and 29 four Yamasee caciques met with the Spanish governor in St. Augustine and requested pardons from the Spanish government for their hostilities over the previous two decades. The Spanish Governor forgave the Yamasee and allowed them to resettle to the south around St. Augustine (Lanning 1935:230). The Yamasee eventually merged into the Creek Confederacy (Sattler 1996:42).

Spanish accounts of this meeting in St. Augustine indicate that prior to the Yamasee War, the English told the Yamasee that "if they failed to pay them in slaves" for their traded English goods, the English would "take payment by making slaves of the debtors themselves, and their children and wives, and carry them off for sale to the other places" (Corcoles y Martinez 1716). This statement supports the Yamasee fears of being enslaved by the English colonists. The account also supports the Yamasee perception of the Pocotaligo meeting that started the Yamasee War. According to the Yamasee, the objective of the English traders was to "get the Indians drunk with strong drinks, and afterwards kill those who were men at arm, and carry off the women and children in order to embark them and carry them for sale" (Corcoles y Martinez 1716).

Archaeological Evidence of Yamasee Lifeways

The historical accounts we have summarized above provide some information about the unique cultural origins of the Yamasee, how they organized themselves in Carolina, and a little about their material culture. We know that they had a fierce reputation as warriors in support of the colonial government of early Carolina and surmise that there may have been a round central house or building in each town that represented a council house or the town leader's residence. However, we must look to archaeological evidence to interpret in more detail how the Yamasee lived.

Archaeological evidence has provided much insight into the Yamasee occupations in South Carolina. Green (1992) identified an archaeological signature for Yamasee sites based upon his work at Altamaha Town. This signature consists of the presence of Altamaha series ceramics in association with European (both English and Spanish) trade goods. The use of Altamaha ceramics extends beyond the Yamasee, as several other native groups (including the Guale, Timucuans, and Apalachee) produced this pottery between the late sixteenth and early eighteenth centuries in coastal Georgia and Florida. However, Altamaha ceramics are associated exclusively with the Yamasee settlements in South Carolina.

The exteriors of Altamaha-series ceramic vessels often are decorated with a variety of paddle-stamped designs (rectilinear, line blocked, cross-simple stamped, and curvilinear). These designs are often over-stamped, partially obliterating or obscuring the original stamped motif (Figure 5). Several researchers have noted that the primary motif found on Altamaha pottery vessels—a line-blocked stamp—is derived from the filfot cross commonly found on earlier Irene-period vessels (A.D. 1500–1700). Several researchers have proposed that the

Figure 5. Altamaha line-blocked stamped vessel. Courtesy of Brockington and Associates.

curvilinear and central dot elements of the filfot cross were dropped, leaving only the central line-block element of the original motif on Altamaha pottery (Braley et al. 1986:14; DePratter 1984:48; Saunders 1999:422–424). Following Saunders (2000), this simplification of the filfot cross may reflect changes in worldview and belief. Overall, curvilinear elements are substantially rarer than rectilinear designs in the Altamaha series. Also, incising on Altamaha vessels is infrequent, and vessels that are scraped/brushed or fabric-impressed are exceptionally rare.

The changes in the decorative motifs between the preceding Irene series ceramics and Altamaha ceramics appear to be a direct result of the interactions of the Yamasee (and other Native American groups) with the Spanish explorers and colonists of Florida. While the Yamasee retain central elements of their former decorative motifs, they abandon other parts. As discussed below, they also changed the nature of the ceramic vessels they made and decorated. All these changes occurred after they moved to the coast in the 1660s and began regular contacts with the Spanish missions and settlements of Florida. Thus, they adopt a ceramic assemblage in use by other Indians associated with the Spanish but retain very specific aspects of their former ceramic traditions. Further research is needed to explore the meaning of these retained traits.

Trends in the use of different exterior decorations may vary among the Yamasee clusters and towns. Sweeney's (2003) research at Pocotaligo recovered a diamond-shaped motif, a design which has yet to be identified on other Yamasee sites. The diamond stamp may have been a local manifestation and its preference was not shared among all the Yamasee. Furthermore, the recovery of these diamond-stamped ceramics is almost exclusively limited to one area of the site, indicating that the stamp may have been the preference of only one or a few particular potters at Pocotaligo.

A common trait on Altamaha ceramics is the presence of a wide folded rim (Southerlin et al. 2001:170–171). These rims are substantially wider than the preceding Irene period rims, where a thin rim strip is applied near the lip of the vessel. Wide folded rims appear to be present only on larger vessels used for storage and cooking. Other decorative elements common on these wide folded rims include reed punctations and finger pinching and, to a significantly lesser degree, shell punctations. These decorative elements are usually found on the bottom of the rim fold where it meets with the top of the vessel body.

Detailed analyses of the pottery from Yamasee sites have identified five different vessel forms: jars, bottles, simple bowls, carinated bowls, and brimmed bowls. Jars tend to be the largest vessel type and were used for storage and cooking. Bottles, which are exceptionally rare, were used for storage and transportation of water and other liquids. Simple bowls and carinated bowls were likely used for cooking and serving needs. Brimmed bowls (deep bowls with wide marelys), which exhibit influence from European potters, were likely serving vessels. Further evidence of European influences on Yamasee potters can be seen in the incorporation of strap handles and foot rings on some Altamaha series vessels.

Another marker of Altamaha ceramics is the presence of red-filmed interiors, which are likely made from a ferrous material to create a red ochre–like paste (Figure 6). This paste is applied to the interior portion of the vessel near the rim. Although red filming is a minority component of Altamaha ceramics, its recovery on archaeological sites in South Carolina is generally used to infer a Yamasee

Figure 6. Altamaha vessel with red-filmed interior. Courtesy of Brockington and Associates.

presence. The exterior surfaces of red-filmed Altamaha ceramics exhibit a variety of decorative surface treatments, including stamping (rectilinear, curvilinear, simple, and line blocked), plain, and burnished.

Yamasee sites also yield a number of European trade goods. These trade goods were coveted items that propelled the Yamasee to become slavers against other Indian groups. Evidence for the Yamasee use of firearms is seen in the recovery of musket balls and gun flints. Recent excavations at Altamaha Town by Sweeney and Poplin (2007) recovered a substantially higher amount of artifacts related to firearms than related to traditional bow-and-arrow technology. This presence of firearms and related artifacts in high frequencies reflects the arming of the Yamasee by the Carolinians and their prowess as warriors and slavers.

Jewelry is the most common trade item recovered from Yamasee sites. Glass beads of various colors are abundant on Yamasee sites, with the majority being blue. These beads range in size and shape from small seed beads to larger tubular-shaped and gooseberry beads. Jesuit rings and silver earrings were also recovered from the recent excavations at Altamaha Town. Other trade items include kaolin pipes, metal tools, glass rum bottles, iron kettle fragments, and European manufactured pottery (Green 1992; McKivergan 1989; Southerlin et al. 2001) (Figure 7).

Many trade items received by the Yamasee were modified for additional uses. For example, brass from kettles was cut and rolled to create tinkler cones, which were attached to clothing. Glass from rum bottles was knapped in traditional fashion to create tools such as arrow points and hide scrapers. In addition, coin-like tokens and the butt plates from muskets were sometimes pierced to create pendants or adornments (Figure 8).

The Yamasee undoubtedly used many of these artifacts to distinguish themselves among their neighbors and the Europeans with whom they traded. Yamasee adornments helped create an identity for them as they adapted to the roles they played in the frontier society and the pressures they faced during the rapidly changing social, political, and economic worlds of early Carolina (Lightfoot 1995;

Figure 7. Sample of trade items recovered from Yamasee sites. Courtesy of Brockington and Associates.

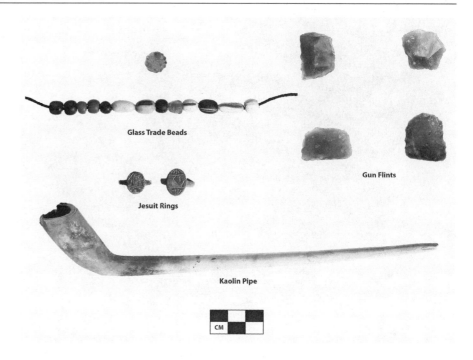

Figure 8. Modified trade goods recovered from Altamaha Town. Courtesy of Brockington and Associates.

Lohse 1988; Plane 2004). Numerous firearms gave the Yamasee an advantage over the Spanish-allied Indians to the south, upon whom they routinely preyed for captives to trade for additional European goods. Their conversion of gun parts into adornments provided visual evidence of their wealth and military prowess. The weaker and poorer groups raided by the Yamasee would not miss the import of these talismans. Perhaps, like the Catawba who became the native military arm of Carolina in the late eighteenth century, the Yamasee decorated themselves as fiercely as possible to enhance their martial appearance and thereby intimidate their foes and prey (Heath 2004). Other artifacts, like the Jesuit rings and St. Johns pottery (discussed in more detail below), may reflect the people the Yamasee captured and sold into slavery in Carolina. Jesuit missionaries presented rings like those recovered from Altamaha Town to Indians as they converted to Christianity during the seventeenth century. Were the rings at Altamaha Town loot taken from captives before they were sold as slaves? Or do they reflect the interactions of the Yamasee with the Spanish in coastal Georgia in the decades before they moved to Carolina? Or had these rings lost their religious connotations by this time (see Hauser 1983) and become merely other evidences of the wealth and interconnections of the Yamasee with their European neighbors?

Excavations by Southerlin et al. (2001) at a farmstead associated with the Lower Yamasee town of Chechessee contribute to our understanding of Yamasee diet. The Yamasee still relied heavily upon the hunting of wild game species such as bear, deer, raccoon, squirrel, turtle, and various fish and shellfish. This traditional diet was supplemented by the incorporation of a few Old World domesticates such as chickens, pigs, and cows. Plant species also followed this trend as New World species of maize, beans, a variety of berries, walnuts, and acorns were more common than European-introduced plants such as peaches (Southerlin et al. 2001).

Recent excavations by Sweeney and Poplin (2007) provide data regarding Yamasee settlement within town settings. Their excavations at the Lower Yamasee capital of Altamaha Town are the most extensive ever conducted at a Yamasee site in South Carolina. The eastern third of Altamaha Town lies in a tract that was slated for residential development. Excavations sponsored by the developer and required by the South Carolina Office of Ocean and Coastal Resource Management, Beaufort County, and the South Carolina State Historic Preservation Office recovered information that would have been lost. Six nearly identical circular structures were identified (Figure 9), representing some of the only examples of well-defined Yamasee houses in South Carolina. All of these houses are approximately 7 m in diameter and contained interior posts that were remnants of either sleeping platforms or wall partitions. No hearths were found inside any of the houses, suggesting that perhaps these were summertime houses. One of the houses contained storage pits that were filled with Altamaha pottery vessels and trade items. These buildings are similar in size and shape to the round Mississippian-period buildings recorded in the Oconee River Valley, the general location of Yamasee cultural origins. This suggests that despite migrations and long interactions with Europeans and several other Indian groups, Yamasee houses reflected their descendent tradition over several hundred years (Sweeney 2009).

Previous investigators of Yamasee sites described their communities as non-nucleated, consisting of buildings spaced from 50 to 120 m apart (DePratter 1994; Green et al. 2002; Southerlin 2000). The houses at Altamaha conform to this pattern, where the houses are spaced from 60 to 100 m apart. The exception to this was one locale where two houses were only a few meters apart. We suspect that the occupation of these two particular houses was episodic, with a new house built adjacent to the older one when the latter deteriorated and became unlivable.

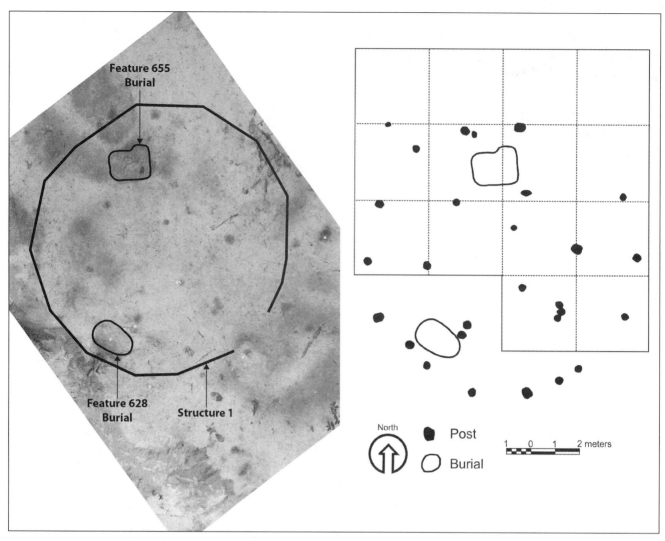

Figure 9. View of Structure A from Altamaha
Town. Courtesy of Brockington and Associates.

Within five of the six Yamasee houses from Altamaha, six human burials were identified. These are the first Yamasee burials that any archaeologist has discovered in South Carolina. All of the burials are just inside the exterior walls of the houses and were situated approximately 50–80 cm below the house floors. Five of the six graves were situated in the western side of the house. An exception to this was one particular house that contained two Yamasee graves, one of which was located in the western portion of the house and the other situated on the northern side.

Yamasee burials were filled with a variety of grave goods. One particular grave (Figure 10) contained a person buried in a flexed position wrapped in cane matting and wearing blue glass seed beads. These seed beads were identified near the neck and hands of the individual, while the fragile remains of a woven mat were identified near the skull. The woven mat was likely wrapped around the individual, and iron nails were used to pin the mat in place. Other items identified in Yamasee graves include Altamaha pottery vessels, kaolin pipes, rum bottles, and an iron sickle/scythe (Sweeney and Poplin 2007; Sweeney 2009).

The nature of this burial and the locations of the other graves within houses appears to reflect the traditional burial customs of the Yamasee. This is very

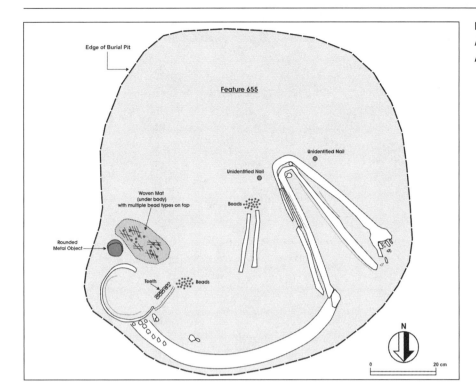

Figure 10. Sketch of burial identified at Altamaha Town. Courtesy of Brockington and Associates.

similar to the burial practices of Indians during the Late Mississippian period through the Southeast. These burials do not appear to reflect any Christian influences, confirming that the Yamasee did not accept the proselytizing of their former Spanish neighbors. Burials of Christianized Indians in Spanish missions in Florida and Georgia are found within defined cemeteries or beneath the floor of the mission church, with the individuals laid in a face-up extended position with their heads to the west.

Note that the graves at Altamaha Town were excavated to the extent necessary to confirm that they were human burials. All human remains and grave goods (artifacts found within the graves) were left in place in the grave. The first grave excavated at Altamaha Town, the one described in detail above, was the most fully exposed since no archaeologist had seen a Yamasee burial before that time. Using the knowledge gained from this initial excavation, excavation of subsequent graves stopped when researchers were sure that the pit was a human burial. This procedure was developed in consultation with the Catawba Indian Nation and the South Carolina State Historic Preservation Office (SHPO). Once a grave was identified, a plan to preserve each one was developed through consultations with the Catawba and the SHPO, with the preferred option being preservation in place through protective coverings (buried concrete slabs) and protective deed covenants.

In the yard areas outside of the Yamasee houses, several features, including trash pits, linear trenches, various shell piles, and smudge pits were identified. Substantial amounts of animal bone, several pottery vessels, and a bone point used for fishing were among the items collected from the trash pits. The shell piles resulted from the cooking and eating of shellfish, particularly oysters, collected from the nearby streams. Smudge pits are small pits filled with burned

material that are generally assumed to have been used to make dense smoke for
repelling inspects and pests. Additional patterns of post holes were found in yard
areas of houses that likely represent screens or racks. These were possibly used
for drying and smoking animal hides and fish (Sweeney and Poplin 2007; Sweeney 2009).

Evidence for defensive fortifications at Altamaha Town were identified by
the exposure of 71 round posts spaced 25–30 cm apart (Figure 11) around the
southeastern portion of the site. The wall is approximately 25 m long and opens
up facing a point overlooking Chechesee Creek. This point offers the easiest access to the town from the water. The position and alignment of the wall suggests
that it was part of a palisade surrounding some portion of the site, perhaps even
serving as a fortification against intruders traveling on the creek (Sweeney and
Poplin 2007; Sweeney 2009).

Possible archaeological evidence related to Yamasee slaving forays into
Spanish Florida also was recovered during the excavations at Altamaha Town.
A heavily sooted St. Johns–series ceramic bowl was recovered from a trash pit
outside one of the Yamasee houses (Figure 12). This vessel is diagnostic because
of its chalky paste made from freshwater sponge spicules found only found along
the coastal areas of Florida and not in South Carolina. It is likely that the only
native group who continued to make St. Johns pottery into the early eighteenth
century was the Ais, who lived in the central portion of eastern Florida. Archival
evidence suggests that this group was raided and enslaved by the Yamasee sometime between 1704 and 1711. This vessel may have been brought back to Altamaha
Town from a raid into that area, possibly even carrying small plundered items.

Conclusion

Since Green's (1992) identification of an archaeological signature for Yamasee material culture and McKivergan's (1989) investigations into the migration

Figure 12. Heavily sooted St. Johns bowl recovered from a Yamasee trash pit at Altamaha Town. Courtesy of Brockington and Associates.

patterns of the Yamasee, archaeologists and ethnohistorians have been able to produce a more concrete perception of the Yamasee. To date, more than 30 archaeological sites have been identified with Yamasee components. This adds to our comprehension of a group of Native Americans who had a complex history and interaction with Spanish and English colonists. Despite their interactions and relationships with these foreign groups, the Yamasee were able to retain many aspects of their traditional cultural identity as expressed through their material culture, architecture, and diet. All that we know today of Yamasee material culture, settlement patterns, and subsistence practices are derived from archaeological investigations. While English and Spanish colonial documents provide much information about the number and location of the Yamasee and their relationships with the colonial powers, these documents provide little information about their daily lives and their efforts to maintain their identity as Yamasee in a very dynamic setting. As evidenced by the archaeological record, the Yamasee were successful in establishing and maintaining themselves as a cultural entity with great military and political power within the swirling currents of the colonial competition in Carolina and the greater Southeast.

References Cited

Anguiano, Carlos de

1995 [1663] Certification Regarding the State of Guale, translated by John E. Worth. In *The Struggle for the Georgia Coast: An Eighteenth Century Retrospective on Guale and Mocama,* by John E. Worth, pp. 92–94. Anthropological Papers of the American Museum of Natural History No. 75, University of Georgia Press, Athens.

Braley, Chad O., Lisa D. O'Steen, and Irvy R. Quitmyer

1986 *Archaeological Investigations at 9McI41, Harris Neck National Wildlife Refuge, McIntosh County, Georgia.* Southeastern Archaeological Services. Submitted to U.S. Department of the Interior, Fish and Wildlife Service, Contract No. 14–16–004–84–019.

Bushnell, Amy

1994 *Situado and Sanbana: Spain's Support System for the Mission Provinces of Florida.* Anthropological Papers of the American Museum of Natural History no. 74.

Carroll, B. R. (editor)

1836 *Historical Collections of South Carolina.* 2 vols. Harper and Brothers, New York.

Cooper, Thomas, and D. J. McCord (editors)

1836 *The Statutes at Large of South Carolina.* 10 vols. A. S. Johnston, Columbia, South Carolina.

Corcoles y Martinez, Governor Francisco de

1716 Letter dated January 25, 1716 Regarding the Arrival of Four Caciques in St. Augustine. Selected documents from Archivo General de Indias, Santo Domingo 843, relative to the Yamasee War, preliminary translations by John E. Worth, March 2007.

Crane, Verner W.

1929 *The Southern Frontier, 1670–1732.* Duke University Press, Durham.

Deagan, Kathleen A.

1978 Cultures in Transition: Fusion and Assimilation among the Eastern Timucua. In *Tacachale, Essays on the Indians of Florida and Southeastern Georgia during the Historic Period,* edited by Jerald Milanich and Samuel Proctor, pp. 89–119. University Press of Florida, Gainesville.

DePratter, Chester B.

1984 Irene Manifestations on the Northern Georgia Coast. *Early Georgia* 12(1):44–58.

1994 *National Register of Historic Places Registration Form.* U.S. Department of the Interior, National Park Service.

DePratter, Chester B., and William Green

1990 Origins of the Yamasee. Paper presented at the Forty-Seventh Annual Meeting of the Southeastern Archaeological Conference, Mobile, Alabama.

Eliot, Daniel, and John Cable

1994 *Cultural Resources Survey of the Bull Point Tract, Beaufort County, South Carolina.* Prepared for Metropolitan Properties, Inc., West Columbia, South Carolina, Report No. 256. New South Associates, Inc., Irmo, South Carolina.

Fletcher, Joshua N., and Bruce Harvey

2000 *Cultural Resources Survey of the Hassell Point Tract, Beaufort County, South Carolina.* Prepared for D'Amico Management Associates, Hilton Head Island, South Carolina. Brockington and Associates, Inc., Charleston.

Gallay, Alan

2002 *The Indian Slave Trade: The Rise of the English Empire in the American South, 1670–1717.* Yale University Press, New Haven.

Gentleman of Elvas

1968 Relation of a Gentleman of Elvas. In *Narratives of De Soto,* edited by Buckingham Smith, pp. 5–203. Palmetto Books, Gainesville, Florida.

Green, William

1992 *The Search for Altamaha: The Archaeology and Ethnohistory of an Early 18th Century Yamasee Indian Town.* Volumes in Historical Archaeology XXI, edited by Stanley South. South Carolina Institute of Archaeology and Anthropology, University of South Carolina, Columbia.

Green, William, Chester B. DePratter, and Bobby Southerlin

2002 The Yamasee in South Carolina: Native American Adaptation and Interaction Along the Carolina Frontier. In *Another's Country: Archaeological and Historical Perspectives on Cultural Interactions in the Southern Colonies,* edited by J. W. Joseph and Martha Zierden, pp. 13–29. University of Alabama Press, Tuscaloosa.

Hann, John H.

1988 *Apalachee: The Land Between the Rivers.* University Press of Florida, Gainesville.

1990 Summary Guide to Spanish Florida Missions and Vistas. *The Americas* 56:417–513.

1991 *Missions to the Calusa.* University Press of Florida, Gainesville.

1996 *A History of the Timucua Indians and Missions.* University Press of Florida, Gainesville.

Hauser, Judith A.

1983 *Jesuit Rings from Fort Michilimackinac and Other European Contact Sites.* Mackinac State Historic Park Archaeological Completion Report Series 5. Mackinac Island, Michigan.

Heath, Charles

2004 Catawba Militarism: An Ethnohistorical and Archaeological Overview. *North Carolina Archaeology* 53:80–120.

Johnson, David Lee

1980 The Yamasee War. Unpublished master's thesis, Department of History, University of South Carolina, Columbia.

Jordan, William R., Whitney Smith, Joe Sanders, and Bobby Southerlin

1999 *Archaeological Survey of the Cedar Point Tract, Beaufort County, South Carolina.* Prepared for the Chechessee Land and Timber Company, Okatie, South Carolina. Brockington and Associates, Atlanta.

Klingberg, Frank J.

1960 Early Attempts at Indian Education in South Carolina, a Documentary. *South Carolina Historical Magazine* 61(1):1–10.

Lanning, John T.

1935 *The Spanish Missions of Georgia.* University of North Carolina Press, Chapel Hill.

Lightfoot, Kent G.

1995 Prehistoric and Ahistorical Archaeology in Culture Contact Studies. *American Antiquity* 60:199–217.

Lohse, E. S.

1988 Trade Goods. In *History of Indian-White Relations,* edited by W. E. Washburn, pp. 396–401. Handbook of American Indians 4. Smithsonian Institution Press, Washington, D.C.

McDowell, William L., Jr. (editor)

1955 *Journals of the Commissioners of the Indians Trade, September 20, 1710–August 29, 1718.* South Carolina Department of Archives and History, Columbia.

McKivergan, David A., Jr.

1991 *Migration and Settlement Among the Yamasee in South Carolina.* Unpublished Master's thesis, Department of Anthropology, University of South Carolina, Columbia.

Merrell, James H.

1989 *The Indians' New World: Catawbas and Their Neighbors from European Contact through the Era of Removal.* University of North Carolina Press, Chapel Hill.

Milling, Chapman J

 1940   *Red Carolinians.* University of South Carolina Press, Columbia.

Nairne, Thomas

 1711   Map of South Carolina Shewing the Settlements of the English, French, and Indian Nations from Charles Town to the River Missisipi.

Plane, Mark R.

 2004   Catawba Ethnicity: Identity and Adaptation on the English Colonial Landscape. *North Carolina Archaeology* 53:60–79.

Ranjel, Rodrigo

 1904   Relation. In *Narratives of the Career of Hernando de Soto,* Vol. II, translated by Buckingham Smith and edited by E. G. Bourne. A. S. Barnes and Co., New York.

Rowland, Lawrence S., Alexander Moore, and George C. Rogers, Jr.

 1996   *The History of Beaufort County, South Carolina,* Vol. 1, *1514–1861.* University of South Carolina Press, Columbia.

Rust, Tina M., Elsie I. Eubanks, and Eric C. Poplin

 1995   *Archaeological Testing of Five Sites on the Bull Point Development Tract, Beaufort County, South Carolina.* Prepared for Metropolitan Properties, West Columbia, South Carolina. Brockington and Associates, Charleston.

Sattler, Richard A.

 1996   Remnants, Renegades, and Runaways: Seminole Ethnogenesis Reconsidered. In *History, Power, and Identity: Ethnogenesis in the Americas, 1492–1992,* edited by J. D. Hill, pp. 36–69. University of Iowa Press, Iowa City.

Saunders, Rebecca

 1999   Forced Relocation, Power Relations, and Culture Contact in the Missions of La Florida. In *Studies in Culture Contact: Interaction, Culture Change, and Archaeology,* edited by James G. Cusick, pp. 402–429. Occasional Paper No. 25, Center for Archaeological Investigations, Southern Illinois University, Carbondale.

 2000   *Stability and Change in Guale Indian Pottery, AD 1300–1702.* University of Alabama Press, Tuscaloosa.

Smith, Marvin T.

 1987   *Archaeology of Aboriginal Culture Change in the Interior Southeast: Depopulation During the Early Historic Period.* University Press of Florida, Gainesville.

Smith, Marvin T., and David J. Hally

 1992   Chiefly Behavior: Evidence from Sixteenth Century Spanish Accounts. In *Lords of the Southeast: Social Inequality and the Native Elites of Southern North America,* edited by Alex W. Barker and Timothy R. Pauketat, pp. 99–109. Archaeological Papers of the Anthropological Association, Number 3.

Southerlin, Bobby G.

 2000   *Archaeological Testing at the Cedar Point Development Tract, Beaufort County, South Carolina.* Prepared for Chechesee Land and Timber, Okatie, South Carolina. Brockington and Associates, Atlanta.

Southerlin, Bobby G., Dawn Reid, Connie Huddleston, Alana Lynch, and Dea Mozzingo

 2001   *Return of the Yamasee: Archaeological Data Recovery at Cedar Point (38BU1605).* Report Submitted to Chechesee Land and Timber, Okatie, South Carolina. Brockington and Associates, Atlanta.

Sweeney, Alex

 2003   Investigating Yamasee Identity: Archaeological Research at Pocotaligo. Unpublished master's thesis, Department of Anthropology, University of South Carolina, Columbia.

 2005   Identifying Pocotaligo, an Upper Yamasee Town in Jasper County, South Carolina. Paper presented at Sixty-Second Annual Meeting of the Southeastern Archaeological Conference, Columbia, South Carolina.

 2009   *The Archaeology of Indian Slavers and Colonial Allies: Excavations at the Yamasee Capital of Altamaha Town.* Paper presented at the Society for Historical Archaeology Annual Conference, Toronto, Ontario, Canada.

Sweeney, Alex Y. and Eric C. Poplin

 2007   *Altamaha Town, Site 38BU20/1206, Heyward Point Tract, Beaufort County, South Carolina- Management Summary, Road Right-of-Way.* Prepared by Brockington and Associates, Inc., for Hazel Pointe LP, Okatie, South Carolina.

White, Andrea P.

 2002   Living on the Periphery: A Study of an Eighteenth-Century Yamasee Mission Community in Colonial St. Augustine. Unpublished master's thesis, Department of Anthropology, College of William and Mary, Williamsburg, Virginia.

Worth, John E.

 1995   *The Struggle for the Georgia Coast: An Eighteenth-Century Retrospective on Guale and Mocama.* Anthropological Papers of the American Museum of Natural History No. 75, University of Georgia Press, Athens.

 1998   *The Timucuan Chiefdoms of Spanish Florida,* Vol. 2, *Resistance and Destruction.* University Press of Florida, Gainesville.

TAMMY FOREHAND HERRON
AND ROBERT MOON

George Galphin, Esquire

Forging Alliances,
Framing a Future, and
Fostering Freedom

FOR A NUMBER OF YEARS, the colonial settlement of New Windsor Township has been the subject of research by archaeologists from the Savannah River Archaeological Research Program, a division of the South Carolina Institute of Archaeology and Anthropology at the University of South Carolina. Established as part of a protective buffer for the English interests in the lowcountry, New Windsor essentially encompassed the area between present-day North Augusta and Silver Bluff in western Aiken County, South Carolina (Figure 1). Archaeologists have conducted surveys at a handful of eighteenth-century sites in this region; however, our focus is on research regarding the Galphin site (38AK7), an eighteenth-century trading post and plantation situated on the east bank of the Savannah River at Silver Bluff.

Since 1996 the primary focus of our research at the Galphin site has been to reveal the built environment during the ownership of the property by George Galphin, a native of County Armagh, Ulster, in Northern Ireland. Although a considerable amount of original written records survives concerning Galphin's business activities at Silver Bluff, specifics concerning the establishment of the trading post and eventual evolution of the site into a working plantation are scant. Because there is no known map of the site detailing building locations and/or functions, researchers employed the use of remote sensing and archaeology to aid in better understanding the historical landscape at Silver Bluff. In April 1996 a ground-penetrating-radar (GPR) survey was conducted at the site; this survey was executed by a class in training to use the equipment. Although numerous anomalies were detected, the archaeologists unfortunately never received a final report of the findings based on this survey.

As such, we were more than elated in 2001 when researchers with the Strategic Environmental Research and Development Program (SERDP) contacted us regarding the possibility of conducting a remote sensing survey at Silver Bluff.

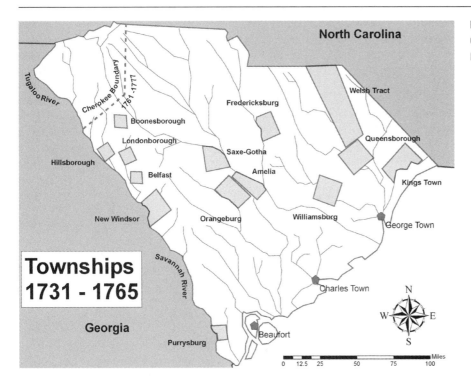

Figure 1. Colonial townships of South Carolina. Courtesy of the South Carolina Institute of Archaeology and Anthropology.

We were even more ecstatic when the Galphin site was finally chosen as one of four sites in the United States for participation in a project entitled "New Approaches to the Use and Integration of Multi-Sensor Remote Sensing for Historic Resource Identification and Evaluation." As part of a three-year study funded by the SERDP, researchers from the Center for Advanced Spatial Technologies and the Department of Anthropology, the University of Arkansas, the Engineer Research and Development Center, the Construction Engineering Research Laboratory (ERDC CERL), and the NASA-Marshall Space Flight Center employed various remote sensing technologies on four sites around the country to explore the benefits of integrating multiple remote-sensing techniques to detect subsurface archaeological features. While the comprehensive results of the remote-sensing project are presented in other reports, the specific focus here is on the Galphin site and how archaeology and remote sensing are leading to a new and better understanding of this frontier outpost (Maki n.d.; Herron and Moon 2006; Kvamme et al. 2006).

Natural Environment

Silver Bluff is situated at the extreme southwestern corner of what was known as New Windsor Township during the colonial period (Figure 2). A detailed chronology of Silver Bluff and surrounding lands can be found in the 1980 publication entitled *Initial Archeological Investigations at Silver Bluff Plantation Aiken County, South Carolina* by James D. Scurry, J. Walter Joseph, and Fritz Hamer. Preserved as part of the 3,154-acre Silver Bluff Audubon Center and Sanctuary (SBACS), the Galphin site is situated on a high bluff overlooking the Savannah River in the Upper Coastal Plain of South Carolina. The Savannah River marks the southern boundary of the Audubon wildlife sanctuary in this area.

The wildlife sanctuary located at Silver Bluff contains a mixture of planted

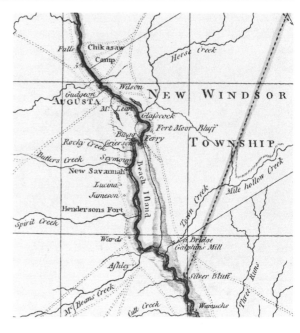

Figure 2. A portion of Faden's 1780 map of South Carolina and part of Georgia. Note Galphin's Mill and Silver Bluff at lower center. American Memory, Library of Congress, 2012.

pines, grassy fields, and hardwoods along ridge noses. The northern portion of the sanctuary contains three large stork ponds that are fed by Hollow Creek, a Rank 5 stream that cuts across the northern quarter of the property before forming a part of the western property line. Hollow Creek empties into the Savannah River approximately 1 km upriver from the Galphin site.

The sanctuary has a maximum elevation of approximately 173 ft above mean sea level (AMSL); however, most of the property is between 125 and 135 ft AMSL. In addition to Hollow Creek, there are numerous small depressional wetlands across the property. The majority of the property falls within the Troup-Lakeland-Fuquay series of soils, which are listed as sandy soils with loamy subsoils that are well to excessively drained (Rogers 1985). The Galphin site, in particular, has a gentle slope from northeast to southwest toward the Savannah River, with a steep drop from the bluff to the river at about 100 ft AMSL (Figure 3).

Figure 3. View of the bluff from the Savannah River. Courtesy of the South Carolina Institute of Archaeology and Anthropology.

Although the soils at Silver Bluff are not well suited for agricultural production, agriculture has been the primary land use since the latter part of the eighteenth century. Historically, Galphin turned his trade business over to his sons and nephew in the early 1770s so that he might concentrate on improving his plantation. Corn, tobacco, and indigo were planted at Silver Bluff during Galphin's tenure. After Galphin's death, the property passed through a number of owners, including James Henry Hammond, who served as a United States representative 1835–1836, the governor of South Carolina 1842–1844, and a United States senator 1857–1860 (Bleser 1981:4–5; Scurry et al. 1980:25–27).

Following extensive farming in the latter part of the nineteenth century, the area was used as a hunting preserve in the 1930s by then-owner Floyd Starr of Philadelphia, Pennsylvania. In more recent times, crops grown at the site included corn, cowpeas, peanuts, and soybeans. It was from Starr's estate that the land was bequeathed to the National Audubon Society in 1975. The Galphin site and 128 surrounding acres were placed on the National Register of Historic Places in 1977. There has been no cultivation on the site since the early 1980s (Dan Connelly 2005, personal communication). Currently, the area of the Galphin site under study is situated in an open field bordered to the west, north, and east by planted pine forests and to the south by a narrow strip of mixed hardwoods along the bank of the Savannah River (Figure 4).

Historic Occupation at the Galphin Site

Steeped in history, the story behind Silver Bluff has intrigued archaeologists and historians for years. As early as 11,000 years ago, Native Americans inhabited the region. Based on archaeological evidence, the land at Silver Bluff was occupied periodically by Native Americans well into the eighteenth century. Primary documents indicate that Kenedy [*sic*] O'Brian received the first land grant at Silver Bluff "on a place called Cundys" as certified on August 21, 1736 (South Carolina Department of Archives and History [SCDAH], Colonial Plat Books 1736–1737:3:309). The earliest documented purchase of land by George Galphin

Figure 4. View of the George Galphin site (38AK7). Courtesy of the South Carolina Institute of Archaeology and Anthropology.

at Silver Bluff is a deed of sale from Robert McMurdy to George Galphin dated August 12, 1757, and recorded August 22, 1757. Other early landowners at Silver Bluff included William Gascoigne, William McMullon, Archibald Neale, and Joshua Snowden (Scurry et al. 1980:13–15).

An Irish immigrant, George Galphin sailed to the American colonies in the 1730s and began his life in the New World working in the deerskin trade. He eventually joined forces with other traders in the area working with the Augusta Company—a company that controlled most of the Indian trade with groups west of the Savannah River. The Augusta Company was also known as Brown, Rae, and Company, so named for two of the primary partners. Galphin served as an interpreter in the Creek nation for the colonial government in Charleston conveying numerous "talks" between Native American groups and colonial officials. Through alliances forged, Galphin would ultimately become one of the most trusted traders in the Backcountry among both the colonists and natives (Sheftall 1980:44–76).

Initially, Galphin spent a great deal of his time in the backcountry trading with various tribes, while at the same time striving to establish operations at Silver Bluff. The savvy businessman likely chose this location because Silver Bluff was strategically located along the Savannah River near the intersection of Creek trading paths leading to the backcountry from Charleston (Figure 5). The selection of this location was no doubt crucial to framing a secure economic future for Galphin and his heirs. Galphin's trade industry ultimately extended from the central Savannah River valley to the Gulf Coast and as far away as the Mississippi River valley. Over the years, he spent less time in the backwoods and more time supervising operations at the Augusta Company, as well as developing his own trading post and plantation at Silver Bluff. At least two brick houses were constructed during Galphin's ownership of the site as documented in his will; however, no documentation to date has revealed the exact layout or location of the buildings during Galphin's ownership (Abbeville County Office of Probate Judge, 1776:Box 40, Package 898).

As the frontier continued to migrate farther to the west, Galphin expanded his operations by acquiring a 1,400-acre land grant along the Ogeechee River in Georgia in 1765 (Candler 1907:420–422). This area is still known as Ogeechee Old Town, or more simply Old Town, as it was one of the "old towns or old fields" previously inhabited by Native Americans (Sheftall 1980:7). Galphin established a second trading post at this location, along with cowpens, a mill, and a farm (Sheftall 1980:23; Moore 2003:32). Since the 1990s, Sue M. Moore of Georgia Southern University has led several futile attempts to locate Galphin's trading post at Old Town (Moore 2003:33–36).

John M. Sheftall has summarized Galphin's rise to prominence and wealth:

As a result of the overwhelming success of Galphin's many business ventures, his financial empire reached its zenith in the early 1770s. Silver Bluff, with its houses, saw and grist mills, stores, warehouses, and fort, remained a home-base for Galphin, but his operations at Old Town and Queensborough certainly vied with the older establishment for primacy in business matters. . . . How interesting it would be to understand fully the mastermind which built and managed this frontier kingdom, stretching from the micca-flicked bluff along the Savannah

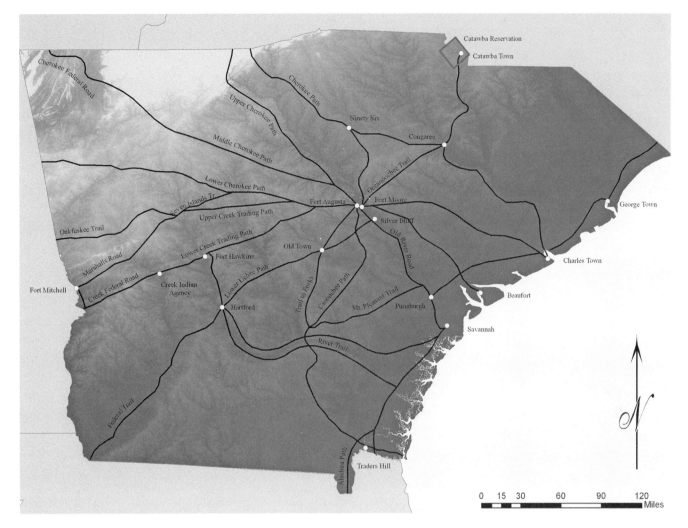

Figure 5. Map of Silver Bluff in relation to Native American trading paths. Georgia map adapted from Hodler and Schretter (editors) 1986; courtesy of the South Carolina Institute of Archaeology and Anthropology.

down the Yuchi trail to Old Town and on across the Ogeechee into the swamps and forests beyond! (Sheftall 1980:34).

Galphin exerted his influence over the Creek Indians to keep them neutral during the Cherokee War and in the impending war between the colonists and the Crown. In *History of the American Indians* (1974 [1775]:393), James Adair wrote the following about George Galphin and Lachlan McGillvery:

> Every Indian trader knows from long experience, that both these gentlemen have a greater influence over the dangerous Muskohge, than any others besides. . . . It was, chiefly, the skilful management of these worthy patriots, which prevented the Muskohge from joining the Cheerake, according to treaty, against us in the year 1760 and 1761,— to their great expence and hazard of life, as they allowed those savages to eat, drink, and sleep at Silver-Bluff, below New Windsor garrison, and at Augusta fifteen miles apart, and about 150 miles from Savanah. I write from my own knowledge, for I was then on the spot, with a captain's commission from South Carolina.

Members of the Provincial Congress met during the month of June 1775. During this session, "George Galphin, LeRoy Hammond, and David Zubly, Esqrs. for the Creek department; . . . [were elected to serve on] Committees of

Inquiry, to attend closely to Indian affairs, to correspond with and transmit every necessary intelligence to the Council of Safety" (SCDAH, *Extracts from the Journals of the Provincial Congress 1775–1776*:59). On October 2, 1775, Galphin's position was elevated to Federal Commissioner for Indian Affairs in the Southern District—a position he would hold until his death. As such, Galphin managed to keep the Indians from attacking the colonists on the side of the Crown for quite some time with only limited resources and his good name.

During America's pursuit of freedom, Silver Bluff continued to operate as a trading post and plantation but took on an even more important role as a diplomatic center for Indian affairs. With his time divided between Silver Bluff and his trading post at Old Town on the Ogeechee River, Galphin spent the waning years of his life trying to keep the Indians peaceful during the American Revolution, as well as attempting to keep squatters from invading Indian lands (Scurry et al. 1980:23; Sheftall 1980:45–47; Chesnutt 1985:10:190; Cashin 2000:158).

Unfortunately, as fighting during the Revolution shifted to the southern theater, traveling from Silver Bluff to Old Town became very hazardous. By 1779 Galphin's supply of trade goods was depleted because of the lack of access to British imports and pillaging of both his trading posts. Without the leverage of the trade goods as a bargaining tool, Galphin was at a loss. As such, the Creeks who had been his faithful allies for so long turned to the side of the Crown. While en route to reoccupy Augusta, Georgia, in the spring of 1780, Lieutenant Colonel Thomas Brown of the King's Rangers arrested Galphin at Silver Bluff and charged him with treason (Sheftall 1983:44–55).

With Silver Bluff now in the hands of the British, the stockade was renamed Fort Dreadnought. In turn, the British chose to use the post as a distribution center for transferring goods to the Native Americans. After witnessing his world crumble around him, Galphin died on December 1, 1780. The fort remained in British control until May 1781, when it was captured by troops under the command of Lieutenant Colonel Henry "Light Horse Harry" Lee and members of the South Carolina militia. In addition to capturing 126 prisoners, the militia also confiscated a large quantity of much-needed supplies from the storehouses at the fort that were originally to be delivered as annual gifts to the Native Americans (Lee 1812:2:89–91; Johnson 1822:2:130–134; Johnson 1851:354–357; Scurry et al. 1980:24; Sheftall 1983:55–58; Chapman 1988:155).

Previous Archaeological Excavation

The initial archaeological survey at the Galphin site was conducted in 1979–1980 by staff of the South Carolina Institute of Archaeology and Anthropology (SCIAA) and an all-volunteer labor force. An intensive surface collection was planned across a 200-acre area known to contain archaeological material. One hundred percent collections were made in random 10-m grid blocks within 50-m blocks identified as Priority Area 1. The systematic surface collection yielded over 9,000 artifacts, 57 percent of which were historic.

A detailed discussion of the artifacts recovered appears in the report by Scurry et al. from 1980. A number of the artifacts recovered are temporally diagnostic indicators that yield clues as to when the site was occupied. Through detailed research, archaeologists have discovered ways to calculate the median occupation of a historic site based on the types of ceramics recovered and through tobacco pipe stem analysis. Historic documents, when available, can also lend evidence as to the timeframe that someone owned or inhabited a particular tract of land.

Mean ceramic dating is "a statistical technique devised by Stanley South for pooling the median age of manufacture for temporally significant pottery types" (Thomas 1990:659). Armed with the knowledge that pipe bowl shape, stem thickness, stem length, and stem-bore diameter changed through time, J. C. "Pinky" Harrington, and later Lewis Binford (1962), developed systems to estimate the age of pipe stem collections based on stem-bore diameters. In essence, bore diameters decreased in size through time—that is, the oldest pipe stems tend to have larger holes through the length of the stem (Thomas 1990:336–338; Noël Hume 1991:297–299). Based on the artifacts recovered, two median occupation dates for the Galphin site were calculated using the mean ceramic date formula and via the Binford formula for pipe stem dating. The dates were 1765 for the ceramics and 1761 for the pipes, which clearly fall well within the time period documented in the historic records (Figure 6).

In addition to dating, researchers examined spatial distributions of artifacts across the site to identify various activity areas. Artifact density plots were created using SYMAP for various artifact categories. These projections revealed that historic artifacts were concentrated in an area along the bluff line just east of Bluff Landing Road (Figure 7). In contrast, areas containing a higher density of Native American artifacts were located farther to the west of the area of concentrated historic artifacts (Scurry et al. 1980:68). Perhaps the Native Americans conducting business at Galphin's trading post were not allowed into the interior of the fortifications but, rather, allowed to camp just outside of the trading complex. An example of such dealings is recorded in the Saturday, August 11, 1716, entry of the *Journals of the Commissioners of the Indian Trade.* This entry includes an instructional letter dated August 9, 1716, addressed to Capt. Charlesworth Glover, Assistant Factor at Savano Town/Fort Moore:

> Inclosed you have Invoice for sundry Goods and Merchandize amounting to one thousand nine hundred and thirty-four Pounds and five Pence, laden on board the Periago, for the Use of the Trade, which in the absence of Maj. Blakewey, you

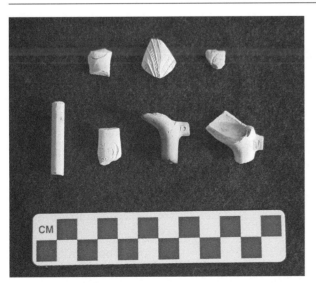

Figure 6. Tobacco pipe fragments excavated from the George Galphin site (38AK7). Courtesy of the South Carolina Institute of Archaeology and Anthropology.

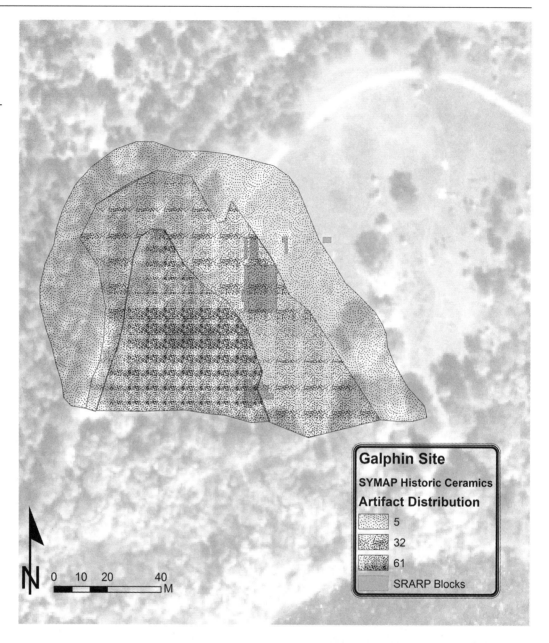

are to receive and put into a Store House, for that Purpose to be built within the Body of the Fort, (and a small trading Room or House in some of the Outworks of the same, for conveniency of Trading, intirely under the Command of the Fort) and in your Dealings with the Indians, you are not to suffer one of them (even the Charikees themselves) to come into our main Store; keeping the Doors thereof shut at such Times of Trading, otherwise, the greatest Precautions will be insufficient to secure you from their Treachery (McDowell 1992:100–105).

Following the 1979–1980 survey, no work was conducted at the site until 1996, when a team from the Savannah River Archaeological Research Program (SRARP) conducted subsurface testing in an area of high artifact concentration. A 100-by-100–m grid was established across the site and subsequently divided into 5-m intervals. With the aid of volunteers, an intensive surface collection was

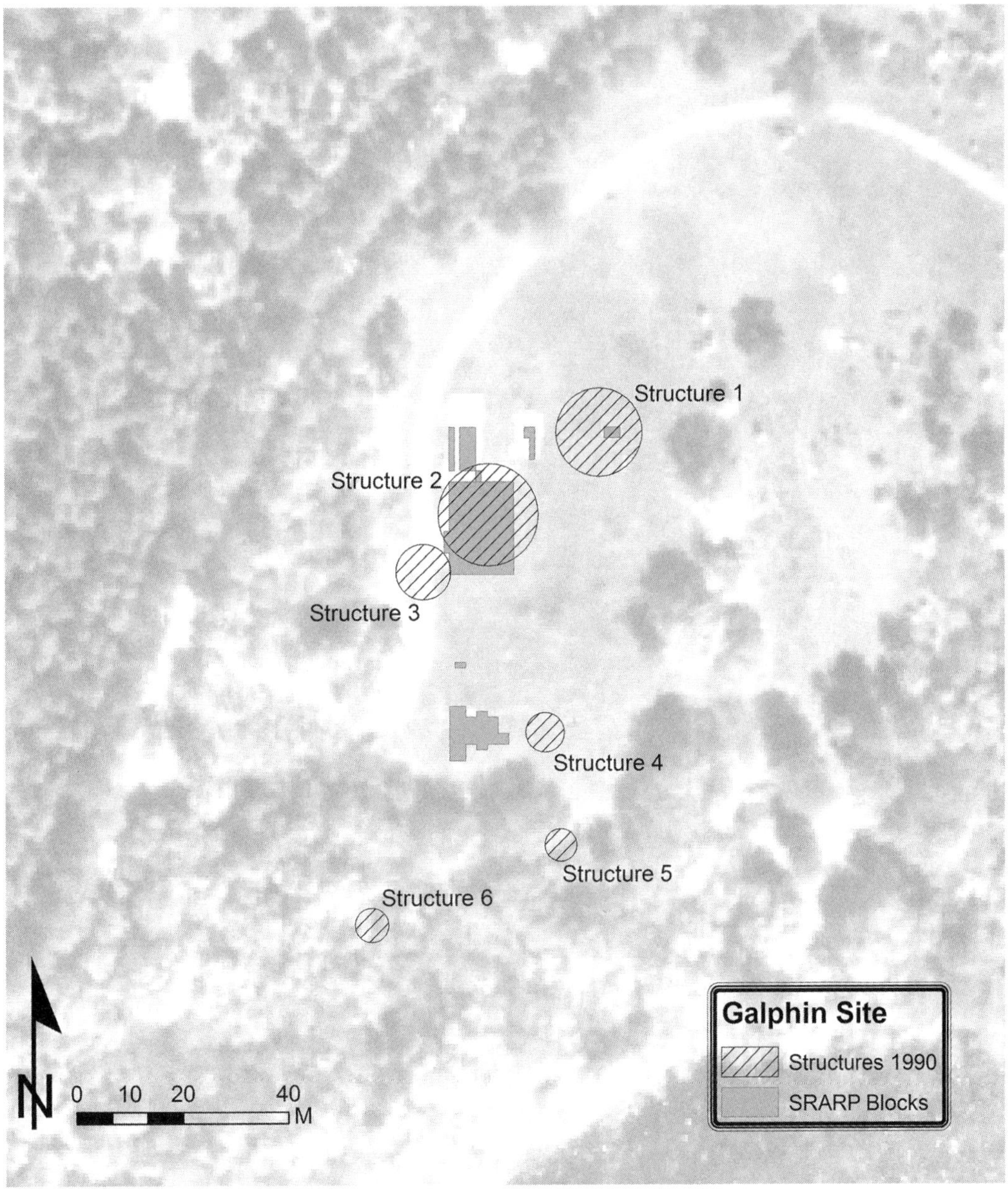

Figure 8. Potential structure locations based on 1990s survey at 38AK7. Courtesy of the South Carolina Institute of Archaeology and Anthropology.

carried out for each 5-by-5-m block of the grid. Throughout 1996 and 1997, volunteers also participated in close-interval shovel testing, limited test unit excavations, as well as observing a ground-penetrating radar survey at the site. These efforts located a large number of subsurface features and anomalies at the site, further demonstrating the potential for archaeological inquiry at Silver Bluff. Based on the results of the shovel-test survey and excavation of an additional eight 1-by-2-m units, a hypothetical model of the site layout was created, which included the locations of six potential structures (Figure 8).

Seeking to expand our involvement with the public and to provide fieldwork opportunities for interested students at a local university, we decided to conduct a historical archaeology field school in the spring of 1999. The field school was sponsored by Augusta State University, the SRARP, and the Silver Bluff Plantation Sanctuary (currently known as the SBACS). Based on previous knowledge

Figure 9. Field school students from Augusta State University at 38AK7, with concentration of brick fragments in foreground. Courtesy of the South Carolina Institute of Archaeology and Anthropology.

that Galphin owned at least two brick dwellings at Silver Bluff, efforts during the field school focused upon block excavations in the area encompassing Structure 2—a concentration of brick fragments identified through spatial analysis (Figure 9).

Although the remains of a brick chimney base were discovered during the excavation of Structure 2, there was no evidence of a builder's trench for a brick walled structure. Rather, several large structural postholes were located immediately adjacent to the chimney base, suggesting, along with the high occurrence of brick fragments identified from the spatial analysis, that the structure was perhaps a half-timbered earthfast dwelling with brick-filled walls that contained a brick chimney. Additional efforts will be required to clarify fully the architectural details associated with the dwelling.

In addition to the chimney base and postholes associated with Structure 2, a section of a defensive palisade trench was encountered a few meters west of the dwelling. Similar to a very substantial picket fence, the palisade appears to have consisted of post-and-paling construction with large buttress posts seated in substantial postholes. The spaces between the buttress posts were in turn filled with split rails that were seated in the trench. Recovered information suggests that Structure 2 and the palisade were built simultaneously. During this early site event, sometime between the late 1730s and early 1740s, brick debris from construction of the house was placed in the large postholes associated with the palisade.

A block of units was opened to locate the southern segment of the palisade immediately below Structure 2. The palisade extends to the south, where it seems to skirt around a large round feature, possibly a well, measuring 4 m in diameter, which appears to have been enclosed with a structure of timber frame construction. As revealed by the units located north of the original block, the palisade also extends north from the dwelling. A palisade corner appears to align with

Figure 10. Larry and Lois Potter excavating a shovel-test pit at 38AK7. Courtesy of the South Carolina Institute of Archaeology and Anthropology.

Structure 1. If the palisade indeed extends across the field to Structure 1, then this segment of the palisade probably served as the north wall of the trading post. Structure 5 may have been located near the southeast corner of the complex, while Structure 6 may have formed the southwest corner of the trading post.

As the field school came to a close in June 1999, excavations at the site continued with the help of local avocational archaeologists and volunteers. We were able to complete the shovel-test survey of the 100-by-100-m grid that was initially established across the site in 1996, as well as survey as far south toward the river bluff as possible with the help of a group of high school students who volunteered throughout the 1999–2000 school year. In all, 543 shovel-test pits were excavated across the site. Only 13 percent of the shovel-test pits failed to produce any historic material. Block excavations totaling 284 m² have also been excavated at the site, primarily with the help of volunteers, including members of the Augusta Archaeological Society, the Archaeological Society of South Carolina, and interested members of the local community and surrounding region (Figure 10).

Remote Sensing

In November 2002 Archaeo-Physics, LLC–Shallow Subsurface Geophysical Survey of Minneapolis, Minnesota, conducted a remote sensing survey at the Galphin site. The site was surveyed using three different methods: (1) electrical resistance, (2) magnetic field gradient, and (3) ground-penetrating radar (Figure 11). For the survey, a portion of the site was divided into 24½ survey grids measuring 20 by 20 m each. The total survey area equaled .98 ha (2.42 acres). Instrument readings were recorded at regular intervals throughout the grids. The electrical resistance and magnetic field gradient surveys were conducted over the entire .98 ha; however, the GPR survey was conducted only on the southern half of the grid (Maki n.d.:1).

Based on the work of Archaeo-Physics, LLC, several areas were identified by the SERDP team as representing potential subsurface archaeological deposits or some other type of subsurface anomaly. To quantify the reliability of archaeological interpretations based on the remote sensing results, these anomalies were tested using traditional archaeological methods, including both hand and mechanized excavation. A total area of 215 m^2 was originally targeted for excavation, primarily through the use of a backhoe (Figure 12).

Field Methods

Ground-truthing excavations were conducted at the George Galphin site during March 21–25, 2005. Locations of targeted anomalies were selected by the SERDP team prior to excavation and flagged by them just prior to beginning the excavations. Archaeological fieldwork included the excavation of 2 test units (1 by .5 m), 20 shovel-test pits, and 51 backhoe trenches. Results of these ground-truthing excavations appear in the *Ground Truthing of a Multi-Sensor Remote Sensing Survey at the George Galphin Site* (Herron and Moon 2006), excerpts of which form the basis for this essay.

Archaeological ground truthing of the subsurface anomalies was conducted using the following excavation techniques: mechanical excavation employing a backhoe, hand excavation of shovel tests, hand excavation of test units, and Oakfield soil probes. Backhoe trenches measuring approximately 1 by 4 m were placed across geophysical anomalies. These trenches were not excavated to a standard depth; however, most stopped in the transition zone between plowzone and sterile subsoil at approximately 30 cm below surface. Following excavation, all trenches were cleaned and photographed. Each trench was also drawn in profile, and most trenches were drawn in plan—the only exception being units with no discernible features in the plan view. In rare cases both profiles were drawn to illustrate major differences between the two.

Ground truthing also included the excavation of 20 shovel-test pits to identify magnetic anomalies. These excavations were halted once the source of the

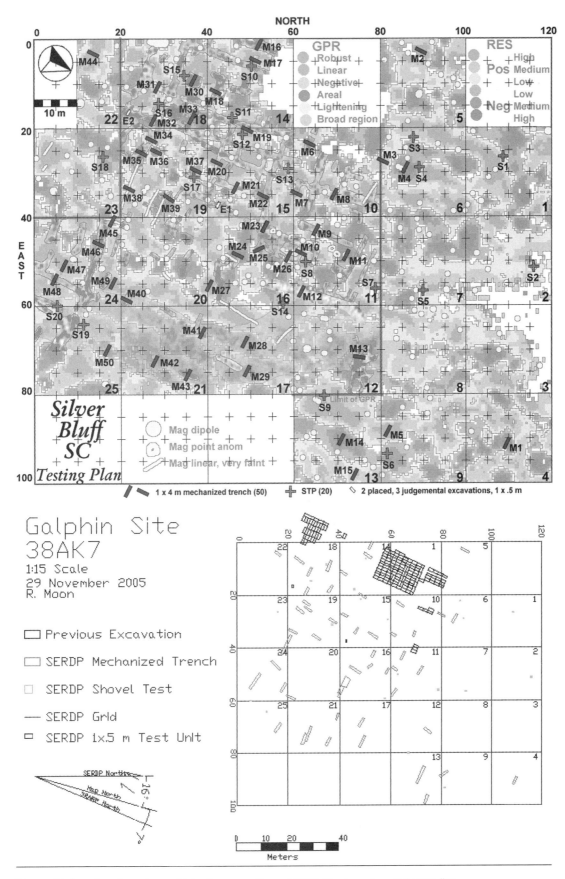

Figure 12. Location of trenches and 1-by-.5-m excavation unit (EU) laid out over targeted anomalies.
Courtesy of the South Carolina Institute of Archaeology and Anthropology.

anomaly was identified. As a result, most tests were concluded well above the transition between the plowzone and subsurface sterile soil. In addition to the shovel tests, two 1-by-.5-m test units were excavated in 10-cm levels. Significant deposits extending well below the usual depth of the transition from plowzone to sterile subsoil were encountered in both test units. Lastly, numerous Oakfield soil probes were conducted at nonregular intervals to test feature or deposit depths.

While all artifacts from the shovel-test pits and test units were collected, the Statement of Work called for the collection of diagnostic artifacts only from the backhoe trenches and backdirt piles. As a general rule, this practice was adhered to; however, in some cases a number of nondiagnostic artifacts were recovered depending upon the individual collector. As such, the collection of artifacts resulting from mechanized trench excavations may be more aptly described as a grab sample of artifacts.

Results

Mechanized excavations of a sample of the remote sensing anomalies produced some interesting results that are providing new direction for the course of study at the Galphin site. Prior to ground truthing, the full extent of the palisaded trading post was unclear. Secondary sources and historical documentation point toward at least two building episodes at Silver Bluff. A palisade was reportedly present during the Cherokee War in the 1760s. Later, when British troops occupied the site during the Revolutionary War, the palisaded enclosure at Silver Bluff was renamed Fort Dreadnaught or Dreadnought (Johnson 1822:2:130, 133; Johnson 1851:355; Jones 1883:479–481; Ivers 1971:47). Additionally, these excavations indicated potential new areas for structures within the enclosure, as well as a historic roadbed along the eastern edge of the site. As always seems to be the case, however, additional excavation will be necessary to confirm the initial observation (see Figures 12 and 13).

The west wall of the palisade was clearly defined through previous excavations; however, the other edges have remained somewhat elusive until now. Initial interpretations placed the north wall roughly in line with Structure 1. The southeast and southwest corners were thought to be in the vicinity of Structures 5 and 6, respectively. While some of the previous interpretations appear accurate, the mechanized excavations are offering new evidence in the overall size of the palisade. The northern extent does appear to be in line or in close proximity to Structure 1. Trenches M3 and M11 both yielded features that are consistent with remnants of buttress posts identified in previous excavations. Additionally, both of these areas have a fairly thin buildup of midden materials—potentially indicating that little activity occurred at the northern end of the palisade.

Along the southern end of the palisade, Trench M51 was excavated in an attempt to capture palisade features. Previous excavations suggested that the north-south wall trench stopped approximately 45 m south from where it was first identified. We have had difficulty identifying the southwest corner and hence the south wall; however, M51 potentially captured the southern boundary of the palisade. There is a clear break between mottled midden deposits in the northern part of the unit, and undisturbed sterile soil to the south, though the area is lacking in the heavy trench feature identified on the western wall. One possible

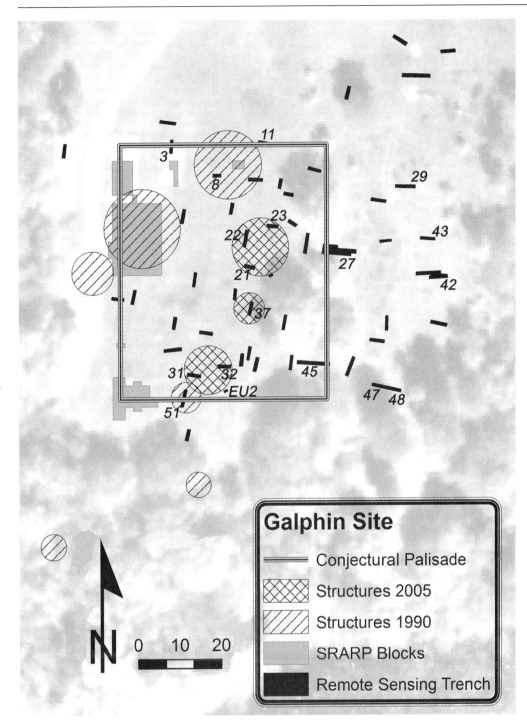

Figure 13. Aerial photo of 38AK7 with overlay of proposed structure locations and current project map. Courtesy of the South Carolina Institute of Archaeology and Anthropology.

theory, which will require additional excavation, is that the south wall trench runs into a structure that would have faced the river. This may represent the actual trading post, while the storehouses and living quarters were most likely located within the palisade. Additional excavations are necessary between Trench M51 and the previously excavated southern block to search for other structural remains.

There is potential evidence for the east palisade wall in two areas. Approximately 25 m east of the west wall, the GPR survey detected a long, linear anomaly

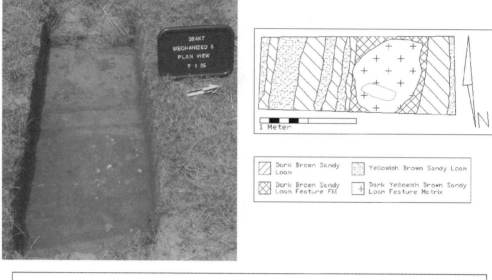

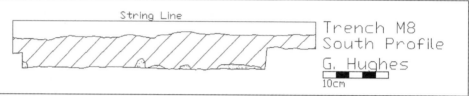

on a north-south axis running through a major portion of the site. Trenches M8 and M32, along with test unit EU2, straddle this linear anomaly. Excavation of M8 revealed a posthole similar to the buttress posts previously excavated in the west wall of the palisade (Figure 14). Trench M32 and EU2 both contain midden fill, which could be the result of refuse that was discarded periodically along the palisade wall, as seen along the west wall. Farther to the east, very ephemeral evidence exists in Trench M27, which was heavily expanded. This trench produced a large post consistent with others found along the known palisade wall. To the south of M27 lies M45, denoted as a subtle linear magnetic anomaly. Compacted soil runs the length of the trench and may be indicative of an interior floor space/living area.

If these theoretical wall locations are indeed accurate, the palisaded enclosure would measure approximately either 23 m (75 feet) or 50 m (164 feet) east to west by 60 m (197 feet) north to south. The area encompassed would measure roughly 1,407 m² or 3,000 m² respectively. These differing measurements could be because of multiple rebuilding and/or expansion of the palisade walls during the colonial occupation of the site. Significant additional excavations are necessary to determine the validity of the east wall trench or trenches.

Within the enclosures, ground-truthing excavations appear to have identified three additional structures. While the exact dimensions remain unclear, Trenches M21, M22, and M23 all produced possible post features. Given the proximity of the trenches (within 10 m of one another), this could indicate a sizable structure of roughly 83 m² (900 sq ft). An additional post was found in Trench M31. Trench M31 is also very close to the previously identified Structure 4 and along the southern edge of the palisade. Trench M37 produced a potential post as well. Unfortunately, the grab-sample collection method yielding only a few artifacts from the trenches precludes any interpretation of function for these structures at this time; however, additional controlled excavations at those locations should aid in defining their role within the palisade.

Lastly, mechanized excavations produced evidence of a lane located along the eastern edge of the Galphin site. Starting at Trench M48 along the southern edge, similar areas of densely compacted soil were found in Trenches M42 and M29 extending to the north. A small post feature, possibly a fence post, was discovered in Trench M43 just to the east of the proposed roadbed. The use of modern satellite imagery has recently confirmed the presence of a road at this location. Whether this road dates to the colonial occupation of the site or to a later occupation remains to be determined.

Conclusion

A major objective of the remote sensing project was to bring data together from various ground-based, aerial, and satellite testing methods in the hope of increasing the reliability and the applicability of remote sensing in the field of cultural resource management. In contrast to traditional field methods, the use of multisensor remote sensing "offers an opportunity to recover a great deal of information about archaeological site content while reducing costs associated with fieldwork and long-term curation of excavated collections" (Limp 2002).

While the overall effectiveness of remote sensing technology can be very useful in detecting subsurface archaeological features at a site, several factors may have inhibited the clear-cut results that we had hoped for at the Galphin site. One environmental factor that still looms in the minds of the archaeologists is the heavy rain that occurred at the site just prior to the execution of the geophysical surveys and what effect, if any, this may have had on the equipment readings. Researchers noted that "archaeological features were identified in many of the excavation units, but in most cases it was difficult to determine whether they were causally associated with the targeted anomalies . . . (perhaps) due to the limited amount of excavation" (Kvamme et al. 2006:316).

In a number of instances, the excavations produced no visible differences between areas of positive and negative resistance denoted as a result of the electrical resistance survey. Alternatively, the ground-penetrating radar and the magnetic field gradient surveys produced somewhat clearer results. Many of the GPR anomalies were either identified as modern cultural features, such as plowscars, or natural undulations across the landscape. Each of the 20 anomalies targeted as a result of the magnetic field gradient survey produced metal artifacts; however, only half produced historic metal artifacts consisting of colonial period nails. The other half of the collection consisted of modern tin can fragments and wire pin flag fragments. Regardless, "with *half* the samples showing historic artifacts, we believe the magnetic depiction . . . may give a reasonable portrayal of the distribution of historic ferrous iron in the site" (Kvamme et al. 2006:320).

Also, the sheer abundance of linear anomalies identified at the site makes it difficult to interpret the data. "The many subtle linear GPR anomalies could represent a low wall of brick or stone, a low berm of packed earth, a compacted trail or path, a narrow paved walkway, a line of contiguous post holes, a line of somewhat separated post holes, or a narrow slit trench or builder's trench within which wooden constructions once were placed" (Kvamme et al. 2006:315–316).

Future fieldwork will therefore rely on traditional invasive archaeological methods to interpret the maze of linear anomalies recorded during the noninvasive surveys.

Although many questions were raised, excavations conducted as a result of the remote sensing anomalies did produce some interesting results overall and a new direction for the course of study at the Galphin site. Potential evidence for the east wall of the palisade is now present in two areas of study that were not previously identified. These excavations have also resulted in the discovery of several potential structures that were previously unknown within the enclosure and a historic roadbed along the eastern edge of the site. Historical documentation and secondary sources reveal that Galphin's trading post was fortified during several important events in the early history of our country—most notably during the Cherokee War and the American Revolution (Lee 1812:89; Johnson 1822:355–356; Ivers 1971:47). Archaeologists are eager to reveal whether the palisade remained relatively unchanged through time, if changes were implemented as repairs were made, or if the compound was expanded as Galphin accrued more wealth and slaves during the third quarter of the eighteenth century.

Future research at the site will focus on delineating the exact boundaries of the palisade, as well as determining the function, size, and method of construction for the structures identified during the analysis of the artifact distributions across the site and during the remote sensing survey. We will also seek to identify activity areas located in the immediate vicinity of the palisade, such as Native American encampments, cowpens, mill sites, and other historic roads that have since been reclaimed by the forest. Archaeologists will also be analyzing artifacts from previous excavations at the site and attempting to sort through volumes of associated documents collected by a Galphin descendant. This research will culminate in a comprehensive site report of the research conducted at the George Galphin site to date.

Acknowledgments

We wish to thank the following individuals for assistance in creating and/or revising a number of the figures for this essay: Brian M. Milner, Christopher R. Moore, Christopher L. Thornock, and George L. Wingard.

References Cited

Abbeville County Office of Probate Judge

1776   Probate of the Estate of George Galphin, Box 40, Package 898. Abbeville County Courthouse, Abbeville, South Carolina.

Adair, James

1974 [1775]   *Adair's History of the American Indians.* Edited by Samuel Cole Williams, LL.D. Reprint of 1930 edition. Promontory Press, New York.

Binford, Lewis R.

1962   A New Method of Calculating Dates from Kaolin Pipe Stem Samples. *Southeastern Archaeological Conference Newsletter* 9(1):19–21.

Bleser, Carol (editor)

1981   *The Hammonds of Redcliffe.* Oxford University Press, New York.

Candler, Allen D. (editor)

1907   *The Colonial Records of the State of Georgia,* Vol. IX, *Proceedings and Minutes of the Governor and Council from January 4, 1763 to December 2, 1766.* Franklin-Turner Company, Atlanta.

Cashin, Edward J.

2000   *William Bartram and the American Revolution on the Southern Frontier.* University of South Carolina Press, Columbia.

Chapman, John A., A. M.

1988 [1897]   *History of Edgefield County from the Earliest Settlements to 1897.* The Reprint Company, Spartanburg, South Carolina.

Chesnutt, David R. (editor)

1985   *The Papers of Henry Laurens,* Vol. X, *Dec. 12, 1774–Jan. 4, 1776.* South Carolina Historical Society, University of South Carolina Press, Columbia.

Herron, Tammy Forehand, and Robert Moon

2006   *Ground Truthing of a Multi-Sensor Remote Sensing Survey at the George Galphin Site: Silver Bluff Audubon Sanctuary, Aiken County, South Carolina.* Technical Report Series 26, Savannah River Archaeological Research Program, South Carolina Institute of Archaeology and Anthropology, University of South Carolina.

Ivers, Larry E.

1971   *Colonial Forts of South Carolina 1670–1775.* Tricentennial Booklet Number 3. Reprint of 1970 edition. University of South Carolina Press, Columbia.

Johnson, Joseph, M.D.

1851   *Traditions and Reminiscences Chiefly of the American Revolution in the South.* Walker and James, Charleston, South Carolina.

Johnson, William

1822   *Sketches of the Life and Correspondence of Nathanael Greene, Major General of the Armies of the United States in the War of the Revolution.* 2 vols. A. E. Miller, Charleston, South Carolina.

Jones, Charles C., Jr., LL.D.

1883   *The History of Georgia,* Vol. II, *Revolutionary Epoch.* Houghton, Mifflin and Company, Boston.

Kvamme, Kenneth, Eileen Ernenwein, Michael Hargrave, Thomas Sever, Deborah Harmon, and Fred Limp

2006   *New Approaches to the Use and Integration of Multi-Sensor Remote Sensing for Historic Resource Identification and Evaluation.* SERDP Project SI-1263, University of Arkansas, Center for Advanced Spatial Technologies, Fayetteville.

Lee, Henry

1812   *Memoirs of the War in the Southern Department of the United States.* 2 vols. Bradford and Inskeep, Philadelphia.

Limp, Dr. Fredrick

2002   New Approaches to the Use and Integration of Multi-Sensor Remote Sensing for Historic Resources Identification and Evaluation. Strategic Environmental Research and Development Program. Electronic document, http://www.serdp.org/research/CS/CS-1263.pdf (accessed April 22, 2004).

McDowell, William L., Jr. (editor)

1992   *Journals of the Commissioners of the Indian Trade September 20, 1710 – August 29, 1718.* Reprint of 1955 edition. South Carolina Department of Archives and History, Columbia.

Maki, David

n.d.   *Ground Based Geophysical Investigations of Two Archaeological Sites: Kasita Town 9CE1 and Silver Bluff 38AK7.* Archaeo-Physics Report of Investigation Number 66, Archaeo-Physics, LLC, Minneapolis.

Moore, Sue M.

2003   Cowhands and Wenches: The Archaeology of George Galphin's Georgia. In *The Savannah River Valley to 1865: Fine Arts, Architecture, and Decorative Arts,* edited by Ashley Callahan, pp. 29–39. Georgia Museum of Art, University of Georgia, Athens.

Noël Hume, Ivor

1991   *A Guide to Artifacts of Colonial America.* Reprint of 1969 edition. Vintage Books, New York.

Rogers, Vergil A.

1985   *Soil Survey of Aiken County Area, South Carolina.* United States Department of Agriculture, Washington, D.C.

Scurry, James D., J. Walter Joseph, and Fritz Hamer

1980   Initial Archeological Investigations at Silver Bluff Plantation, Aiken County, South Carolina. *Research Manuscript Series, 168.* Institute of Archeology and Anthropology, University of South Carolina, Columbia.

Sheftall, John M.

1980   Ogeechee Old Town: The Story of a Georgia Plantation. Manuscript, Savannah River Archaeological Research Program, New Ellenton, South Carolina.

1983   George Galphin and Indian-White Relations in the Georgia Backcountry during the American Revolution. Unpublished master's thesis, Corcoran Department of History, University of Virginia, Charlottesville.

South Carolina Department of Archives and History (SCDAH)

1736–1737   *Colonial Plat Books* (copy series), 3:309, S213184, Columbia, South Carolina.

Thomas, David Hurst

1990   *Archaeology.* Reprint of 1989 edition. Holt, Rinehart and Winston, Fort Worth, Texas.

LELAND FERGUSON

Middleburg Plantation, Berkeley County, South Carolina

EXCAVATIONS AT MIDDLEBURG PLANTATION (38BK38) began as part of an archaeological survey of the East Branch of Cooper River in the South Carolina lowcountry.* The goal was to locate the settlements and work places of enslaved Africans and African Americans in anticipation of a larger study aimed at exploring the development of an African American community under the stress of slavery. Founded in the 1690s, Middleburg was one of the oldest plantations on the river, and we anticipated finding evidence of early pioneering settlements similar in layout to West and Central African villages. Instead, we found mostly late-eighteenth- and early-nineteenth-century complexes. While the abundance of locally made pottery called colonoware testified to the origins and resourcefulness of those enslaved, the village layout illustrated the wealth display of plantation owners, the rigid control placed on slaves after the American Revolution, and the fear of insurrection following the Denmark Vesey rebellion conspiracy of 1822.

African Americans planted, cultivated, and harvested rice in Middleburg's swampy fields. A short distance north and west of the South Carolina coast, the briny water of the estuaries meets the fresh flow of creeks and rivers moving toward the ocean. Lighter fresh water tends to float atop salty water, and in a narrow band a few miles from the coast, the tidal water that ebbs and flows through the swamps and across the flats is relatively free of salt and suitable for growing rice; the changing tide provides the flooding and draining necessary for successful large-scale rice agriculture (Figure 1). Taking advantage of this natural phenomenon, many of South Carolina's planters became rich growing a crop they called "Carolina Gold." They also became a minority white population, surrounded by thousands of enslaved Africans who built the earthen banks and

*This article is a revised version of the Overview and Background statement for Middleburg Plantation on the Digital Archaeological Archive of Comparative Slavery website, http://DAACS.org.

Figure 1. View of Cooper River near Middleburg Plantation. Courtesy of the Digital Archaeological Archive of Comparative Slavery (http://www.daacs.org/sites/middleburg/#images).

dikes required for this massive enterprise. Middleburg was one of the earliest of these rice plantations; it had the first steam-operated rice mill on the coast; and its nineteenth-century owners were among the richest families in the nation. Their bondsmen and -women—by nature of large population size and skill—were at various times considered a critical resource, a symbol of wealth, and a grave threat.

Archaeological exploration at Middleburg began in 1986 with test excavations that located a slave village on a ridge northeast of the plantation house. In subsequent field seasons, student excavators explored the village layout, excavated the majority of one house, and investigated outlying settlements and work sites. This work resulted in several graduate and undergraduate theses and two documentary films; the author also used data from the site in the book *Uncommon Ground: Archaeology and Early African America, 1650–1800.*

Documentary Evidence

In 1940 representatives of the Historic American Buildings Survey (HABS) recorded that "Benjamin Simons, a Huguenot immigrant, built his house, 'Middleburg,' in time for the fifth of his fourteen children to be born there in the spring of 1699. It is probably the oldest wooden house in South Carolina" (Figure 2). The HABS documentation includes drawings and photographs of the house as well as a photograph of a barn and stable northeast of the house. The caption of a small map with the drawings identifies the plantation location as the "COOPER RIVER (EAST BRANCH)."

Rising no more than thirty miles north of Charleston Bay, Cooper River is little more than an estuary, and the East Branch, which flows by Middleburg, is barely 13 miles long. Nevertheless, more than twenty plantations similar to Middleburg were seated along the East Branch and its tributaries; and, by the early nineteenth century, enslaved workers had built more than 55 miles of rice field banks along this short stretch of river. The small numbers of white people who owned and planned these plantations were a close-knit group of families. The

Figure 2. Middleburg Plantation house, 1986. Courtesy of the Digital Archaeological Archive of Comparative Slavery (http://www.daacs .org/sites/middleburg/#images).

Simons, Lucas, and Ball families owned Middleburg in the seventeenth, eighteenth, and nineteenth centuries, and the three were related by marriage. In turn, from plantation to plantation their enslaved workers were also closely related. Marriages and liaisons between plantations were common, and both white and black had kin up and down the river. Thus, the documentary evidence from one location often sheds light on the history of two, three, or more other plantations. These sources have served as the basis for several historical works, including two dissertations on demography and social history (Cody 1982; Terry 1981), as well as Edward Ball's 1998 book *Slaves in the Family*, in which Middleburg figures as one of the family seats.

In the 1951 book *Charleston Gardens*, Loutrell Briggs mentioned the Middleburg slave quarters:

> [At Middelburg] there is the avenue of gnarled old live oaks leading to an ample grass forecourt on which the house faces flanked by massive magnolias. To one side, at some distance, are farm buildings, and on the river side beyond the garden, a rectangular pond which was no doubt the "duck pond" to be seen on *a very old map of the plantation*. This drawing also shows a forecourt with a square formal garden on each side. Beyond one garden are twelve cabins for the Negroes and beyond the other, a barn and machine house with other accessory buildings. [Briggs 1951:113; emphasis added]

Brigg's description of the "very old map" matches a 1786 Middleburg map by surveyor Joseph Purcell (Figure 3). The "twelve cabins," labeled "Negro Houses" on the map, were located about 100 yards northeast of the plantation house. A

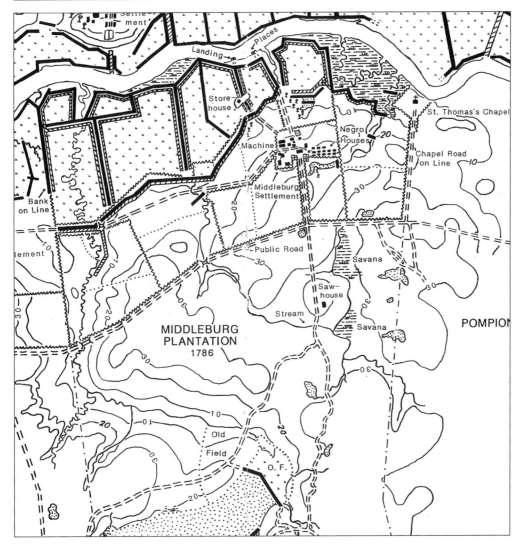

Figure 3. Middleburg Plantation based on a map by Joseph Purcell, 1786. Courtesy of the Digital Archaeological Archive of Comparative Slavery (http://www.daacs.org/sites/middleburg/#images).

1794 land-division map that appears to be based largely on Purcell's map shows only nine houses. The Purcell map shows rice banks and fields, landing places, and a storehouse on the waterfront, fences, roads, a saw house, and dependencies near the plantation house.

The first slaves came to Middleburg sometime in the late seventeenth or early eighteenth century, but the first population counts come from the last quarter of the eighteenth century. Estate inventories list 87 slaves living at Middleburg in 1772 and 89 in 1789. The activities of the Middleburg workforce, represented by tools and materials in the lists, included blacksmithing, tanning, cooperage, shoe and saddle making, spinning, lumbering, dairying, animal husbandry, and the cultivation of oats, peas, corn, and rice. Locally made folk pottery was not listed in these inventories or any other plantation documents so far discovered. However, the archaeological recovery of more than 21,000 fragments of this pottery, called colonoware, emphasizes the resourcefulness of the African American population, the narrow conception of value represented by the inventories, and the limitations of the documentary evidence as a source for accurately describing day-to-day plantation activities (Affleck 1990:20–56).

From early in the 1700s, the plantation owners had businesses and dwellings in Charleston and on the coast as well as at Middleburg, and nineteenth-century censuses show that the white presence at the plantation was often no more than a young man serving as overseer. All along the Cooper River there was an overwhelming black majority.

Middleburg and Hurricane Hugo, 1989

In 1986 when the Middleburg archaeological project began, the plantation looked much different than it does today. Then, visitors approaching the "big house" from Cain Hoy Road drove through a wide live-oak avenue that formed a sort of tunnel. Branches draped with Spanish moss arched over the road, and the white frame plantation house stood almost hidden at the end. In 1989 the plantation house and the solid oaks along the avenue withstood the devastation of Hurricane Hugo. However, the violent winds ripped away the massive oak branches,* providing a vista somewhat similar to the way it looked in the early nineteenth century soon after the owner's bondsmen transplanted the trees. Reinforcing this scene, the severely damaged pine forest on either side of the avenue was clear-cut after the storm, opening fields that slaves also cleared in the early days of the plantation. Although the hurricane opened the forest, providing a prospect similar to that of the early nineteenth century, it destroyed several architectural features from that period.

The plantation house and a handful of outbuildings had survived for more than a century and a half, and there were also impressive ruins of other structures. Behind the house, and flanking the remnants of an old formal garden, were two dependencies—a dilapidated servants' duplex on one side and on the other a kitchen/washhouse with an adjacent privy.† Before the hurricane, the owner had the servants' quarter dismantled and was rebuilding the kitchen/washhouse. The hurricane totally destroyed the latter, so the restoration became a rebuilding.

A few hundred yards southeast, and situated on the same low ridge as the house, stood the two imposing barns described in the HABS report. The barn closest to the house—a brick, two-story, European-style‡ edifice—was called a "commissary" by plantation owners and a "slave jail" by many local African-Americans. Beyond the brick barn stood a carriage house. There, raised brick piers supported a wooden superstructure, and the building included spaces for horses, carriages, or wagons. Architectural historians dated both of these buildings to the first half of the nineteenth century, and our archaeological investigations showed that near the end of the first quarter of that century, these barns had replaced the "Negro Houses" shown on the 1786 and 1794 maps. The brick building survives into the twenty-first century (Figure 4); the carriage house collapsed in the hurricane.

The plantation house sits about 300 yards north of the public road and the Cooper River is about the same distance north of the house. Near the old river landing, a brick smokestack stands high above surrounding trees, and in the

---

*According to plantation representative Max L. Hill III, National Park Service representatives selected some of the limbs for repairs to the USS *Constitution*.

†Amateurs excavated this privy in the early 1980s.

‡Barile (1994) describes this as resembling a "Czech Barn" with "unmistakable Dutch influence."

Figure 4. View of the Middleburg commissary, 2007. Courtesy of the Digital Archaeological Archive of Comparative Slavery (http://www.daacs.org/sites/middleburg/#images).

jungle-like growth below are the boiler and giant gears of Middleburg's nineteenth-century rice mill. Adjacent to the machinery, overgrown brick foundations outline the ghost of the multistory mill. In the woods not far from the giant flue is a smaller chimney and building mound, said to be the ruins of the plantation blacksmith shop. In the mid-1980s the small tollhouse for the mill was still standing. The chimneys and mill ruins survived the hurricane; the tollhouse did not.

From 1986 through 1999, graduate and undergraduate students conducted the Middleburg survey and excavation under the direction of the author. The devastating hurricane hit three years after the project began, and it changed our perception of the plantation and altered some of our plans for work. Moreover, as we focused on learning about human power relations and the creation of an African American community under extreme social duress, the hurricane reminded us that Middleburg's black villagers also faced the ever-present natural dangers of this low-lying land.

Excavation History

In the middle 1980s, Ferguson and graduate student David Babson (1986) prepared a composite map of eighteenth- and nineteenth-century plats on the East Branch of Cooper River.* This map and the accompanying report were to serve as tools for both archaeological research and cultural resource management. Although the original map included more than 20 plantations, Ferguson and Babson found no plats for several plantations, including Middleburg. Babson discovered the 1786 and 1794 maps after the archaeological project began.

In 1986 three factors combined to initiate a search for the Middleburg quarters. The Department of Anthropology of the University of South Carolina asked Ferguson to teach an archaeological field course; Middleburg was a blank

*This project was funded by the Department of Anthropology of the University of South Carolina and a Survey and Planning grant from the South Carolina Department of Archives and History.

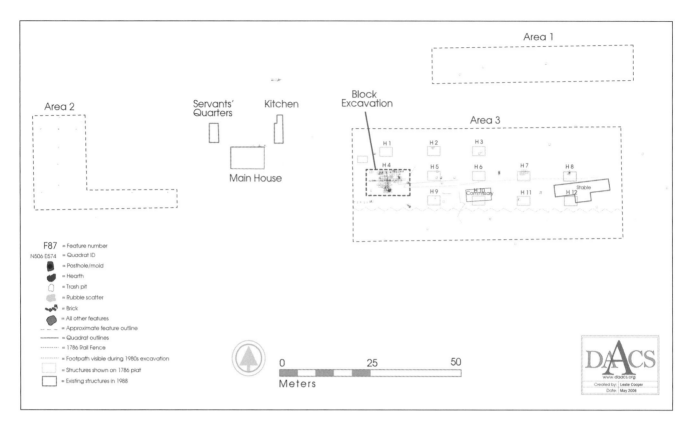

Figure 5. Middleburg Plantation map showing main house in relation to excavation areas. Created by Leslie Cooper for the Digital Archaeological Archive of Comparative Slavery. (http://www.daacs.org/sites/middleburg/#images).

place on the East Branch map; and the owners—the Max L. Hill family—had responded enthusiastically to a mailing to landowners along the river. The ensuing field research included four field schools and spanned more than a dozen years.

The search for the Middleburg slave quarters was a typical archaeological game of trial and error—that is, hypothesis testing. In the beginning, with no period maps of the plantation, we had clues to the quarter location from two sources. First, John Gibbes, a descendant of a previous plantation owner, claimed the quarters were in a low area northeast of the plantation house, a place we designated Area 1 (Figure 5). Second, Briggs's book *Charleston Gardens* referred to a "very old map" that he said showed barns on one side of the house and "Negro Houses" on the other. We associated the "commissary" and "carriage house" on the ridge east of the house with the barns described by Briggs. Thus, we suspected that if the quarters were not found in the spot specified by Gibbes, they were most likely west of the plantation house in a location designated Area 2. The ridge east of the house with the present-day barns was designated Area 3. Based on the information, we expected the quarters were most likely in Area 1 and least likely in Area 3. Archaeology and subsequent historical research demonstrated our prediction wrong. We discovered the quarters in Area 3.

In our search for the quarters, four 1 m^2 tests northeast of the house in Area 1 produced no features and only a sparse scattering of artifacts. West of the house, in Area 2, artifacts recovered from ten 50-by-50-cm tests and three post-hole tests were consistent with barns but not habitation.

As we tested Area 2, we also monitored utility workers in Area 3 using a "ditch witch" to excavate a 6-in-wide trench from the plantation house to the brick commissary building. Artifacts from this excavation included colonoware

and European ceramics, shards of glass, broken bricks, and hundreds of rusty nails—just the kinds of artifacts expected from an early slave quarter.

Monitors sifted all the dirt thrown up by the ditch digger through ¼-in screen and plotted the frequencies of various artifact types. Based on a high artifact frequency in the vicinity, we placed a series of eight 1-in cores in the hot spot, and began excavating two squares. These tests strongly implied that we were wrong in guessing that the contemporary barns were in the same location as those barns described by Briggs on the "old map."

As other students conducted these field tests, David Babson, searching the private archive of an adjacent landowner, discovered a copy of Joseph Purcell's 1786 map of Middleburg—apparently the map described in Briggs's garden book. In the vicinity of our Area 3, the map showed 12 small buildings labeled "Negro Houses." Our excavations appeared to be in the village, and the two nineteenth-century barns sat on top of the ruins of some of the houses.

Based on our findings and the map, we expanded excavations and began finding the postholes of an earthfast building—that is, a building with posts in the ground as foundation. Subsequently, we followed the paths of two linear features, possibly fence lines of the easternmost garden shown on the Purcell map. Confident we were in the vicinity of the village, we excavated a series of 17 1-m test squares aimed at locating the other houses. As a hedge against our predictions, we also selected eight test locations we believed to be just beyond the village, as well as 16 random locations within the predicted boundary. We used a stratified, unaligned, random-sampling technique.

In the vicinity of our Area 3 tests, we eventually exposed a two-room, earthfast house with ruins of a central brick chimney (Figure 6) (Adams 1990). Sometime after construction, several of the earthfast posts appeared to have been shored with brick and mortar, for fragments of those materials were found around and over most of the postholes. The mortar and brick fragments suggested that bricks had been salvaged after razing the building. With the outline exposed, the house measured approximately 14.8 by 29.5 ft (Figure 7).

The house-plan measurements together with the centrally located chimney suggested that the building was a duplex with two rooms measuring approximately 14.8 sq ft with doors on the southern elevation. The room diagonals

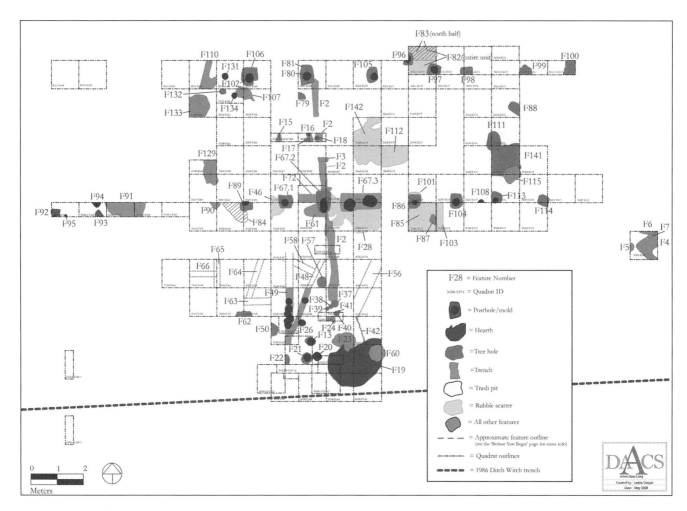

Figure 7. Composite map showing block excavation in the "Negro Village." Created by Leslie Cooper for the Digital Archaeological Archive of Comparative Slavery. (http://www .daacs.org/sites/middleburg/#images).

measured 7 yds, suggesting the Euro-American technique of laying out a square room by first striking a diagonal with a string, then using a carpenter's square to turn 90 degrees at the midpoint and measuring a second diagonal the same length. The ends of the diagonals thus form the corners of a square room with the perpendicular intersection in the center of the square (see Glassie 1975:23; Adams 1990:72–73). Adams observed that the technique "fits well with the European control displayed in the settlement layout."

The 1786 map showed three rows of houses—a northern line of three structures, a middle line of five, and a southern line of four. Those who laid out the village appear to have aligned the northern walls of the northern line of the "Negro Houses" with the northern wall of the plantation house. West of the houses at the edge of a wooded area was a rail fence, and a rail fence ran between the southern line of houses and a dammed waterway. We believed we were likely seeing the remains of the western-most house of the middle row of houses on Purcell's 1786 map. Aiming to locate the village more securely, we laid out a number of 1-m test squares. Students placed eight squares outside the presumed village to the north, east, and south. We anticipated, and discovered, negative evidence for houses in these tests. Sixteen more 1-m tests were placed within the approximately 3.2-acre rectangle of the presumed village, some within and some between predicted house locations. In addition to tests laid out in and between predicted house locations, we laid out 20 1-m squares in a stratified, unaligned random pattern within the presumed village; however, because of time limitations we excavated only two of these randomly located squares.

Digging at Middleburg

Diggers excavated units with shovels and trowels, usually in 10-cm levels or following natural stratigraphy and sifting all soil through ¼-in screen. The natural soil profile at Middleburg consists of three strata: (1) a surface level of gray/brown, sandy/loam, (2) a second zone with less organic material and a light yellow loamy sand, and (3) a sandy clay subsoil that is frequently rust colored. Deeper postholes could be easily identified by the varied colors of the mixed soils filling the holes.

When sifting, excavators collected faunal and botanical materials as well as artifacts. In addition, during a portion of the excavation, particularly the block excavations of 1988, samples from six selected units were separated and screened using water flotation and screening. Limited faunal analysis shows evidence of catfish, turtle, quail, and deer as well as domesticated chicken, swine, and beef. Similar floral studies identified a variety of nondomestic as well as domestic plant foods. These data support conclusions from historical sources that people enslaved on the South Carolina coast supplemented rations provided by plantation owners through fishing, hunting, and gathering in local waterways and woodlands.

Lesser and Greater Middleburg

The Middleburg plantation house, the slave quarter ruins, the barns, and old rice fields fit our common notion of an antebellum plantation with a stable core of plantation buildings and outlying fields. To convey such an image, however, would be a gross simplification—and distortion—of the history and cultural geography of this place. It was much more complicated.

Settlement began in the 1690s with Benjamin Simons's warrant for 100 acres of wilderness. Through the following century what started as a small pioneering farmstead grew to more than 3,000 acres that included at least three satellite settlements, often called plantations themselves, and a variety of agricultural lands. In 1785 Benjamin Simons III sold a portion of the plantation known as Campvere to a relative. Following the death of Simons III in 1789, estate executors for the decedent's daughters divided the remaining lands into three plantations: Middleburg, Horts, and Smoky Hill. In the 1840s and 1850s, John Ball, a neighboring landowner, purchased all these plantations and more. Ball owned the plantations into the early twentieth century, when the properties were again divided with the tract called Middleburg returning to boundaries somewhat similar to the middle eighteenth century.

For the African Americans who cleared and worked these lands, the various plantation boundaries may have held little significance. The owners were friends and relatives, who frequently shared resources and labor, and there is well-documented evidence of enslaved African Americans moving from village to village along the river. Lowcountry rice agriculture was concentrated, producing high yields on relatively small, intensively managed fields. At its largest, the five Middleburg settlements were within a mile and a half or less from one another. And this is only for Middleburg; on nearby plantations there were even more villages. From the middle of the eighteenth century through the Civil War, hundreds of African Americans lived within an easy walk, or short canoe paddle, from Middleburg; within a day's travel, there were thousands.

Under the direction of Rick Affleck, student archaeologists surveyed and tested four of these "greater Middleburg" sites. A database, analyses and discussion of this work is available in Affleck's thesis: "Power and Space: Settlement Pattern and Change at Middleburg Plantation" (1990).

Middleburg and the Denmark Vesey Conspiracy

Student archaeologists working at Middleburg established links between changes in the plantation landscape and the fear and anxiety inspired by the slave revolts and threats of insurrection in the late eighteenth and early nineteenth centuries. In the summer of 1822, Middleburg and the entire lowcountry barely escaped a wholesale rebellion. Together with six compatriots, Denmark Vesey, a free black man, planned a revolt that was set to erupt one quiet Sunday morning. A single informant spoiled the plan, and planters quickly arrested the conspirators.

Retribution was swift and harsh. A Charleston court sentenced Vesey, his lieutenants, and 28 others to hanging. New laws severely controlled the movement of blacks, and planters were encouraged to reorganize their plantations to protect property and assert control. Kerri Barile (1999) has demonstrated that in response, many planters, including Middleburg's owners, concentrated barns and storehouses near plantation houses and moved slave quarters to dispersed settlements away from plantation-house yards.

Correlation of Middleburg data with this reactionary period following the conspiracy developed over several years of research. First, archaeologists working in the Middleburg quarters established that slaves moved into this village during or before the third quarter of the eighteenth century and that they were likely gone by sometime in the 1820s (Affleck 1990; Adams 1990). Historical documents and the archaeology of Patti Byra (1996) indicated that the oak avenue and the formal garden north of the house were laid out and planted in the 1820s or early 1830s. Then, Barile, investigating the commissary and stable, found that these buildings were built sometime in the 1820s or early 1830s over the ruins of the village. Moreover, she showed that Jonathan Lucas Jr.—who had married Sarah Lydia Simons and thereby came to own Middleburg—was closely involved with investigating the conspiracy and the repressive reaction. With these pieces of the puzzle, Barile argued that because of the threat posed by their slaves, the Lucases razed the quarters near the plantation house (those we had excavated) and moved residents to other locations—so far unidentified. Apparently they also abandoned a vulnerable storehouse near the river, replacing it with the brick commissary built on top of a portion of the old village. Nearby the new storehouse, they built a carriage house. Thus, according to Barile, in reaction to the fear of rebellion, the plantation center became a bastion of formal gardens and secure property—a concrete illustration of the reaction to the "painful degree of anxiety" inspired by Vesey, his conspirators, and their followers.

Summary

Aimed at better understanding the growth of an African American community under the oppression of slavery, historical archaeology at Middleburg plantation has illustrated the resourcefulness and resilience of the enslaved population as well as planters' attempts to control their black workers and their response to threats of rebellion.

Combining archaeological discovery with eighteenth-century plats and documents, student archaeologists discovered the location, layout, and many particular features of a late-eighteenth- to early-nineteenth-century African American village. Discovery of early European ceramics in tests from the eastern portion of the village suggests that undiscovered features in this area may date to the early eighteenth or even late seventeenth century. The archaeological survey mapped and tested several settlements closely related to Middleburg.

Eighteenth-century planters arranged the settlement in a rigid alignment based on the orientation of the plantation house, and the excavation of one house revealed an earthfast structure laid out in European fashion. Nevertheless, the white minority could not completely control the large number of workers. The prodigious amount of folk-made pottery, together with fishhooks, gunflints, and a wide range of plant and animal remains, testifies to independent activities of Middleburg's black majority—activities that likely included active as well as passive resistance to domination.

Nineteenth-century changes to the Middleburg settlement correlate with fearful reactions to the Denmark Vesey conspiracy. Like many others, Middleburg's owners had barns and storehouses built close to the plantation house, and the slave quarters moved away. At least one quarter-house was burned prior to construction of a new brick commissary. This period saw many cruel and repressive responses from planters throughout the lowcountry. Nevertheless, their reactionary movement of slave quarters away from plantation houses to more remote locations may have reminded some black Carolinians of Br'er Rabbit being thrown in the briar patch. Through the nineteenth and twentieth centuries, the remoteness of these lowcountry communities allowed the Gullah people to flourish as one of America's most distinctive subcultures—their survival due in part to their ancestors' competent resourcefulness and threats of rebellion.

References Cited

Adams, Natalie

1990   Early African-American Domestic Architecture from Berkeley County, South Carolina. Unpublished master's thesis, Department of Anthropology, University of South Carolina, Columbia.

Affleck, Richard M.

1990   Power and Space: Settlement Pattern Change at Middleburg Plantation, Berkeley County, South Carolina. Unpublished master's thesis, Department of Anthropology, University of South Carolina, Columbia.

Babson, David

1987   Tanner Road Settlement: The Archaeology of Racism on Limerick Plantation. Unpublished master's thesis, Department of Anthropology, University of South Carolina, Columbia.

Ball, Edward

1998   *Slaves in the Family.* Farrar, Straus and Giroux, New York.

Barile, Kerri Saige

1999   Causes and Creations: Exploring the Relationship between 19th Century Slave Insurrections, Landscape and Architecture at Middleburg Plantation, Berkeley County, South Carolina. Unpublished master's thesis, Department of Anthropology, University of South Carolina, Columbia.

Briggs, Loutrell

1951   *Charleston Gardens.* University of South Carolina Press, Columbia.

Byra, Patti L.

1996   The Contextual Meaning of the 1830s Landscape at Middleburg Plantation, Berkeley County, South Carolina. Unpublished master's thesis, Department of Anthropology, University of South Carolina, Columbia.

Cody, Carol Ann

1982   *Slave Demography and Family Formation: A Community Study of the Ball Family Plantations, 1720–1896.* Ph.D. dissertation, University of Minnesota. University Microfilms, Ann Arbor, Michigan.

Ferguson, Leland, and David Babson

1986   *Survey of Plantation Sites along the East Branch of the Cooper River: A Model for Predicting Archaeological Site Location.* Report submitted to the South Carolina Department of Archives and History, Columbia.

Glassie, Henry

1975   *Folk Housing in Middle Virginia: A Structural Analysis of Historic Artifacts.* The University of Tennessee Press, Knoxville.

Terry, George

1981   "Champaign Country": A Social History of an 18th Century Lowcountry Parrish in South Carolina, St. Johns Berkeley. Unpublished Ph.D. dissertation, Department of History, University of South Carolina, Columbia.

MARTHA A. ZIERDEN

Charleston

Archaeology of South Carolina's
Colonial Capital

WHETHER THE PERSPECTIVE IS POPULAR or scholarly, the city of Charleston occupies a central place in the history of South Carolina. Site of the first permanent European settlement in Carolina, the town has been continuously occupied since 1680. Historical studies of the colonial capital began as early as the late eighteenth century, and new volumes appear every few years. The city is famous for its well-preserved architecture and for its long-standing programs in historic preservation. Recognition, study, and preservation of the city's archaeological resources are more recent developments. Controlled archaeological explorations occurred sporadically in the twentieth century, but archaeology was not recognized as an important source of information until the 1970s. In the ensuing four decades, archaeology has become a key source of data on city life, sometimes confirming trends known from documentary sources but more often providing a more complex and sometimes fundamentally different view of the way things were.

The majority of the research and excavation projects in Charleston have been conducted by the Charleston Museum; nearly 30 projects have been conducted since Elaine Herold's research in the 1970s (Figures 1 and 2). Several private archaeological firms have worked in the city, each bringing a broader perspective to interpretations of urban life. The archaeological story of the city is also selective, based on the way sites have been chosen, or avoided, for excavation and study. Some time periods and types of occupation have been studied extensively, while others not at all. But all research, regardless of the size of the project or the type of site, has been united under a guiding paradigm, devised in 1984 and revised in subsequent years (Zierden and Calhoun 1984; Rosengarten et al. 1987). As with most historical archaeology, research has focused on daily life in the city, on issues of subsistence, material culture, landscape layout and development, and social relations, and is skewed toward the wealthy and literate.

Figure 1. Map of Charleston, showing location of sites. Map by Martha Zierden, the Charleston Museum, Charleston, South Carolina.

Charleston Sites

Public Sites

1. McCrady's Tavern
2. Dock Street Theatre
3. Lodge Alley
4. Powder Magazine
5. Atlantic Wharf
6. Exchange
7. South Adgers Wharf
8. Vendue/Prioleau
9. Beef Market/City Hall
10. Chas. Co. Courthouse

Residential/Commercial

11. Chas. Judicial Center
12. First Trident
13. Visitor's Center
14. Charleston Place

Upper Status Residences

15. Aiken-Rhett
16. Joseph Manigault
17. William Gibbes
18. John Rutledge
19. Post Office/Courthouse
20. Nathaniel Russell
21. Miles Brewton
22. 14 Legare St.
23. Heyward-Washington

Modest Status

24. 66 Society St.
25. 40 Society St.
26. 70 Nassau St.
27. 72 Anson St.
28. President St.
29. 82 Pitt St.

All the materials retrieved from Charleston sites have been retrieved, organized and quantified in the same way. All materials have been screened through ¼-in mesh. The assemblages, singly and together, have been grouped into functional categories following Stanley South's Carolina Artifact Pattern (South 1977). Under this method, artifacts are quantified in relative proportions to each other within eight broad categories, based on the function, or use, of the item in household activities. South's methodology has been widely used by historical archaeologists, allowing for direct comparison among sites, and all of the Charleston data have been organized in this manner.

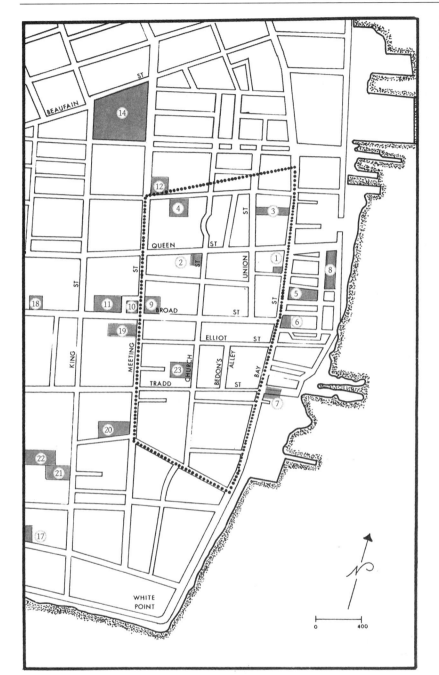

Figure 2. Detail map, sites excavated in the eighteenth-century portion of Charleston. Map by Martha Zierden, the Charleston Museum, Charleston, South Carolina.

No matter the particular history of the property, all urban sites share certain characteristics. Urban centers are defined principally by density and complexity of settlement; the amount of human energy expended per unit of land is considerably greater than the surrounding region (Staski 1982). Density and complexity are reflected in an archaeological record that is usually deep, dense, and highly stratified. Moreover, the archaeological record is often reorganized and redeposited, the result of continuous occupation and the intrusion of later deposits into earlier ones. Reorganized soils can be removed to a new place, resulting in deposits that are secondary and even tertiary. This means that on sites of continuous occupation, the earliest occupations can be compromised by disturbances of later ones. The scale and the nature of urban archaeological deposits require specific field and analysis techniques that differ somewhat from traditional archaeological methods (Staski 1982; Honerkamp and Fairbanks 1984).

The Charleston Peninsula

Though not the first site of human habitation in South Carolina, and not even the first site of European habitation in Carolina, Charleston is readily identified as central to the history of the state. Charleston occupies the peninsula formed by the Ashley and Cooper rivers flowing into the Atlantic Ocean; in its most popularized form, historical sources joke that here the Ashley and Cooper rivers "form" the Atlantic Ocean. This exaggerated comment underscores the centrality of the city to state, regional, and even national history.

Albemarle Point is the site of the first permanent European settlement in South Carolina. In April 1670 three English ships sailed into Charleston Harbor to claim by occupation lands awarded to eight British noblemen. Well aware of their tenuous hold on the new colony, "in the very chaps of the Spaniard" (Joseph Dalton to Lord Ashley, September 9, 1670, in Crane 1981:3), the settlers chose the readily defensible location on the Ashley River. Here, English and Africans built a small community lasting a decade. They settled a land occupied by small groups of native people, already in flux from two centuries of Spanish incursion. At Charles Town Landing, eminent archaeologist Stanley South found ample evidence of continuous occupation of the point by native peoples, climaxing in development of a ceremonial center in the twelfth century and continuing into the early eighteenth century (South 2002; South, this volume).

Deemed unhealthy and indefensible, the English setters soon cast their eye on the peninsula. The new site was situated on a good natural harbor, both defensible and well situated for transatlantic trade (Salley 1928:105; Mathews 1954:153). The peninsula featured a ridge of high land running along the center, while numerous creeks and marshes transected the eastern and western margins of the land.

If the peninsula was well situated in the eyes of European settlers, it did not seem to measure up to native standards. Very little evidence of native occupation has been recovered from archaeological sites in the city, even as displaced artifacts in later contexts. The southern tip of the peninsula, known as White Point because of a bank of sun-bleached oyster shell, may have been native in origin, or may have been a natural bank. As this bank was subject to filling and/or erosion throughout the subsequent centuries, the site has not been investigated. The current archaeological record would suggest that native use of the peninsula was limited.

Historian Robert Weir notes that the peninsular location was not without its shortcomings (Weir 2002:66); indeed, the town's survival was questionable through the end of the seventeenth century. The bar at the harbor entrance was shallow, making entry into the harbor difficult for larger vessels. The water table on the low-lying peninsula was high, so that underground cellars were impractical and wells were shallow, compromising the quality of drinking water. Mortality rates were high, and population growth was slow. Food was relatively plentiful, however, and by the end of the first decade of settlement, the colony was supplying food to islands in the West Indies (Weir 2002:69).

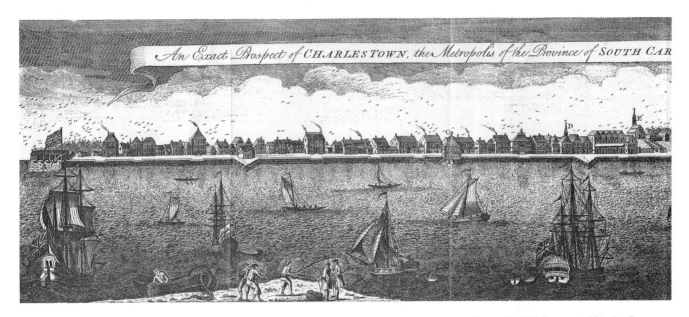

Figure 3. 1738 Prospect of Charles Town Harbor by Bishop Roberts, 2010.5.97. Charleston Museum, Charleston, South Carolina.

Foodstuffs, lumber, and deerskins from trade with native peoples were the colony's first lucrative trade items. Beginning in the 1690s, the production of rice and naval stores brought economic stability to Carolina and with it increases in the population of the city. With the development of rice as a profitable export came the increased importation of Africans as enslaved laborers, many of whom contributed knowledge and skills to growing and harvesting the grain (Weir 2002: 70; Carney 2001). By 1708 the majority of Carolinians were black (Wood 1974).

Artifacts of the earliest European settlers are common, but undisturbed contexts from the first 50 years are extremely limited. Even excavations within the limits of the city wall (built by 1704) have revealed few contexts predating the 1720s. Somewhat more common are sites with occupations dating to the 1730s. These are particularly valuable, as fire destroyed much of the city in 1740, and the rebuilt landscape was significantly different.

The early plan of Charleston, devised in 1672, was known as the "Grand Modell." This plan divided the peninsula into deep, narrow lots characteristic of seventeenth-century British colonial towns and guided development of the city until the second quarter of the eighteenth century (Poston 1997:48). Charleston's plan featured broad streets and lots reserved for a church, town house, and other "publick structures," including a public market (Thomas Ashe in Bridenbaugh 1938:10). But the plan on paper had to be adapted to the realities of the terrain of the peninsula (Saunders 2002:200). The highest land between Vanderhorst's and Daniel's creeks was chosen, as this was the section of the Cooper River where the deepest water and narrowest marsh was found.

The Colonial City

Our view of pre-1740 Charleston is based on the harbor prospect by Joseph Roberts, completed a year before the fire (Figures 3 and 4). The waterfront view emphasizes the brick seawall, conveniently removing the numerous wharves that already spilled into the harbor; a plan by the same cartographer published a year later shows eight wharves in front of the wall. The prospect shows a crowded

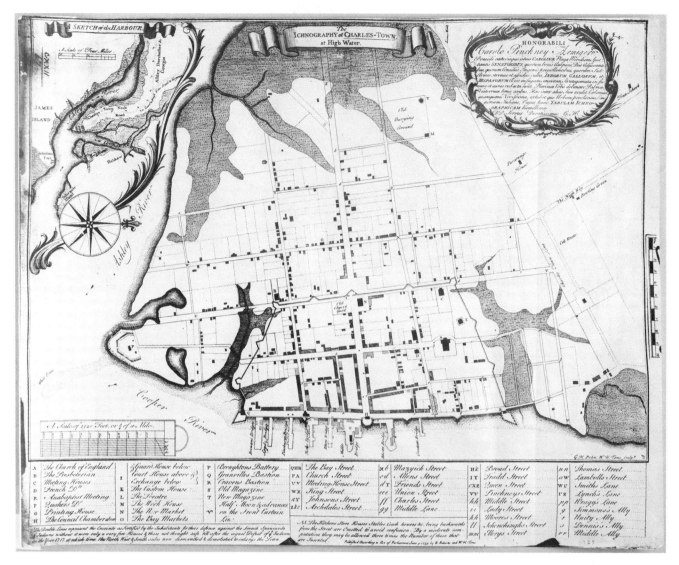

Figure 4. *Ichnography of Charles-Town at High Water,* 1739, by Bishop Roberts and W. H. Toms, MY 153. Charleston Museum, Charleston, South Carolina.

street front with a range of building styles and materials (Poston 1997). Most dwellings were two rooms to a floor or featured an asymmetrical plan. The substantial merchants' dwellings along East Bay Street and elsewhere featured stores on the first floor and dwellings above. Archaeological evidence, such as that of John Milner's house on Church Street (Herold 1978) and 96 Broad Street at the Charleston Judicial Center (Hamby and Joseph 2004), suggests that the relatively small houses of this period fronted directly on the street.

Recent archaeological work at the Charleston Judicial Center site (Figure 2, no. 11) by J. W. Joseph and New South Associates suggests that the early city featured diverse lot layouts as well as house forms (Hamby and Joseph 2004; Joseph 2002). The project explored an entire city block at Meeting and Broad streets, adjacent to the gates of the city walls and occupied from the earliest decades of the eighteenth century. The use of exploratory trenches and block stripping allowed exploration of landscape features on a scale previously unavailable in the city. This revealed an urban landscape that evolved to fit the needs of a growing population throughout the colonial period.

The earliest architecture described by Joseph featured modest houses fronting directly on the street. Most interesting was exposure of a house of earth-fast construction, consisting of clay walls set in trenches. There was evidence for a variety of building styles and materials, "ranging from African earth-walled structures to European half-timbered dwellings to lowcountry tabby structures to Caribbean buildings of Bermuda stone" (Joseph 2002:224).

More revealing was Joseph's research on land use and lot layout. Hamby and Joseph recovered a range of work-yard features in the immediate rear yards of the homes along Broad Street. These included root cellars, storage pits, structures, wells, and privies. The center of the block, in contrast, was free of features during the early period. Joseph suggests that prior to the 1740 fire more than half of the urban lots were used for agricultural purposes, for fields and livestock. Joseph attributed this layout to cultural preference, as well as the need to devote considerable space to production of food and fodder (Joseph 2007). Work-yard functions were concentrated near the house and the street frontage, in contrast to the long, narrow layout of single-house lots that typify the late eighteenth and nineteenth centuries. Only rarely is an entire city block, particularly one in the oldest section of the city, cleared for archaeological exploration. Data from the Judicial Center dig suggests that the remains of early colonial Charleston may lie beneath the foundations of later structures and not in the open rear courtyards of these properties.

Joseph's model was reflected in the earliest occupation at the Heyward-Washington house (Figure 2, no. 23) (Herold 1978; Zierden and Reitz 2007). Here, gunsmith John Milner's modest wood house fronted directly on Church Street, and his work yard and smithy were located immediately behind it (Figure 5). Elaine Herold's excavations revealed the foundations of the house and a concentration of work-yard features directly behind the dwelling. These included wells, forges, sheds, and large refuse pits. Milner's home, shop, and business were burned in the town's catastrophic fire of 1740. Herold recovered numerous metal artifacts in a matrix of ash (Herold 1978).

The concentration of features noted by Herold was supported indirectly by data retrieved by the author in 2002; excavations inside the existing stable building provided the opportunity to test areas of the site beyond the limits of Herold's work. The ash from the 1740 fire—or, more precisely, from the structures burned in the fire—was concentrated near the front of the stable and diminished markedly in the rear of the building. Only a few post features and an abandoned well pit were located here. The small sample suggests that the rear lot saw little use.

This additional sample supported Herold's interpretation of a compact settlement, with Milner's house located directly on the street front and business directly behind (Zierden and Reitz 2007). The foundations of Milner's house and other early features were well preserved beneath Thomas Heyward's 1772 three-story double house and paved work yard. Like the Judicial Center site, this suggests that evidence for the earliest city lies buried under later colonial and antebellum structures but may be undisturbed.

A Commercial Center

Perhaps the most remarkable evidence of site preservation was discovered recently in the basement of City Hall, a massive public building constructed in

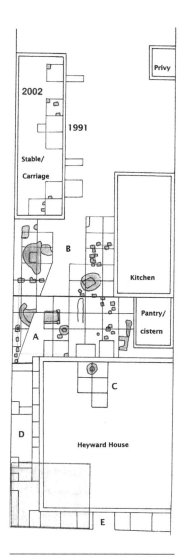

Figure 5. Map of the Heyward-Washington house showing existing late-eighteenth-century buildings and features associated with the John Milner occupation (1730–1740). Map by Martha Zierden, Charleston Museum, Charleston, South Carolina.

Figure 6. Excavations in the basement of City Hall, showing foundations for the 1760 market building. Photo by Martha Zierden, Charleston Museum, Charleston, South Carolina.

1800. City Hall was built on the site of Charleston's colonial market, set aside by the legislature in 1692 and renamed the Beef Market in 1760 (Figure 2, no. 9). According to the 1686 Boyd map (Leland and Ressinger 2006), two principal streets terminated in a square of common lands, which gradually came to be recognized as a public square. This square was later established as the public market and was nestled behind the city gates and drawbridge on the western edge of town (Bridenbaugh 1938:193; Saunders 2002). The site remained the town's principal marketplace for the next century and featured two market buildings, constructed in 1739 and 1760, respectively.

The opportunity for archaeological excavation of the market and the chance to retrieve data on provisions sold in the colonial city arose from plans for renovation of City Hall in 2004. Testing outside the building in 1984 suggested that extensive evidence of a meat market remained, but excavations were confined to the basement of the building, as that was the only part of the site to be disturbed. The extensive footprint of the building was viewed as an impediment to retrieval of intact evidence, and we expected the site beneath City Hall to be compromised by the massive foundations. Instead, the opposite was true (Figure 6). The many layers of colonial occupation, filled with artifacts and bone reflecting marketing activity, were undisturbed except for narrow construction trenches. Nearly the entire colonial site was preserved beneath the Federal structure (Calhoun et al. 1984; Zierden and Reitz 2005).

Excavation of 18 units inside City Hall revealed evidence of continuous uses from the 1690s through the 1790s in seven successive zone deposits. The site exhibited early soil layers that appear natural, and midden layers that reflect construction and refuse accumulation (Figure 7). The bone refuse was considerably denser than any other Charleston site and exhibited unique characteristics (Reitz 2007).

The foundation of the 1760 market was well preserved in the basement site. The contiguous brick foundation measured 45 ft by approximately 100 ft, and was four courses deep. The south side featured a central projection approximately 36 ft by 4 ft, while the interior was fitted with a central well and vaulted drain system. A hard-packed sand surface, surmounted by water-washed sand filled

Figure 7. Soil profile for the eighteenth-century beef market. Photo by Martha Zierden, Charleston Museum, Charleston, South Carolina.

with small fragments of hacked bone, may be an original market surface or may represent wash beneath flooring that no longer exists. Associated postholes along the center of the market and outside the south wall may have supported a series of hooks and pegs for displaying meat and other produce. The market walls were likely a series of arched openings, and the roof may have been pantile. Little architectural evidence of the 1739 building was recovered. The deepest deposits suggest that the early market did not include a formal structure (Zierden and Reitz 2005).

The market evidently sold all types of meats and foodstuffs. Evidence of a rich array of wild game and fish, as well as the range of domestic mammals, was recovered from the market proveniences. Moreover, the meats available at the market became more diverse, even as the market's designation was changed to suggest a narrower role. Smaller meats, such as fishes, were sold more frequently at the end of the eighteenth century. Data suggest that at least some of these animals, including cattle, were slaughtered on site. Hacking was the most common way to prepare and sell portions of beef. The intensely organic characteristics and very high levels of phosphorous and other chemicals in the deepest zone suggest that the animals were present at the site and that animal products were key to site-formation processes there.

Artifacts recovered from the multiple layers of refuse suggest that the market was the scene of socializing. Kitchen or cooking wares dominated the assemblage, which also featured an elevated number of tobacco pipe fragments. Clothing and other luxury items were noticeably absent. Activity items included those associated with on-site manufacture, such as scraps of brass and lead. Also notable was the recovery of quantities of English flint debitage, suggesting on-site manufacture of gunflints or other stone implements. But if the flint tools being knapped on site were used in butchering, they left little physical evidence on the animal bones, as cut marks were relatively rare.

The range of ceramics was narrower and more stylistically conservative than elsewhere in the city. An unusually large number of drinking vessels—drinking pots, tankards, canns—were present in the ceramic assemblage, while expensive tea wares were less common. Utilitarian cooking wares were common. This, plus the tobacco pipes in large numbers, suggests that the market was a vibrant public space, one used for gathering and socializing and possibly for drinking and eating. Moreover, the market assemblage remained remarkably consistent through the eighteenth century, despite architectural changes to the site and social changes throughout the city. The archaeological evidence of a vibrant city market reflects Charleston's growth as a commercial center throughout the eighteenth century.

The struggle between growth of the commercial sector after 1730 and maintenance of the city's defenses played out along the Charleston waterfront. From the time of earliest settlement, threats from Spanish and French necessitated defense of the harbor, while fear of attack by Native Americans called for defense of the landward approaches. A brick seawall was begun along the east side of the Bay Street (East Bay Street) in the 1690s and constructed gradually, as the town was beset by a series of misfortunes, including a fire in 1698, a yellow fever epidemic in 1699, and a hurricane in 1700 (Fraser 2006). The wall was complete by 1706, when a French and Spanish fleet mounted an unsuccessful invasion (Saunders 2002). The interior walls were likely earth and wood, as the legislation implies considerably less time and money invested in these features. Excavations in 1993 revealed evidence of the moat surrounding the gate at Meeting and Broad streets, beneath the historic Courthouse (Figure 2, no. 10) (Joseph and Elliott 1994). In 1999 construction revealed a line of cedar pilings, 9 in^2 and sharpened to a fine point, set on 2-ft centers. Revelation of the moat and ravelin confirmed a 1721 version of the walled city (Saunders 2002).

Charleston's Waterfront

Charleston's economic expansion in the 1730s was matched by physical expansion. The 1739 plan by Roberts and Toms indicates that the city's walls were still in place, or at least acknowledged, but that the city had spread far beyond the boundaries (see Figure 4). The inland walls, likely of earth, were demolished long before the brick seawall, which remained in place until after the Revolution. But by the mid-eighteenth century, concerns over defense were overshadowed by the issues of commerce and quality of life. The port was constantly expanding as new docks and wharves were built, resulting in a struggle between maintenance of the curtain line along the waterfront and opportunities to breach this curtain line for efficiency of transportation. A 1736 law allowed the parapet to be opened on Bay Street "for all bridges that extend twenty Feet beyond Low Water mark" (Stevens 1988 in Joseph et al. 2000:5). The 1739 map shows eight such wharves or bridges. The fire of 1740 provided an impetus for rebuilding, but the major hurricane of 1752 completely destroyed the waterfront, including buildings, stores, and their contents. The brick seawall itself was heavily damaged and required considerable rebuilding (Butler 2008; Fraser 2006; Calhoun 1983; Herold 1981). The defensive wall continued to be compromised, and numerous plats and documents show openings in the wall. By 1770 there were 17 bridges, and 22 by 1788. In 1786 East Bay Street was widened and the curtain line demolished, its foundations paved over. An imposing new Exchange and Customs House was built on filled land on top of the Half Moon Battery in 1771, providing a new landmark for ships entering the harbor (Stevens 1988:502 in Joseph et al. 2000).

The evolution from a defensive to a commercial waterfront is dramatically reflected in the stratigraphic record at South Adger's Wharf (Figure 2, no. 7). The mayor's Walled City Task Force, a consortium of specialists, took advantage of some street construction and, with the mayor's blessing, excavated this location in January 2008. The discovery was guided by a series of maps and documents. The cannon-mounted redan shown in the 1738 prospect (Figure 3) was clearly delineated on a 1785 plat. The plat suggests that the curtain line was intact but that the redan had been recently demolished to ground level. The city's Lower Market, constructed in 1750, sat on a bridge (or on filled land) in front of the wall. Market customers had to cross the wall through one of the many openings to shop at the market. After the wall was demolished, the market was expanded 29 ft to the west, covering the redan. In response to citizen complaints of a dirty, crowded market, the area was paved before all the downtown markets were closed in 1799.

The impetus for the excavation was exploration of the redan, though recovery of evidence for marketing activities was also important. But determination of the level of site disturbance—on a public thoroughfare used continually from the early eighteenth century to the present day—was the first priority. Exploratory backhoe excavation to a depth of 7 ft below surface revealed 11 undisturbed, superimposed layers that reflected use of the site from the 1740s to the 1990s. (Cultural deposits continued beneath this level, but excavation was halted at the water table.) The intact foundation of the north face of the redan, discovered 3 ft below surface, was 3.5 ft wide, with a flat surface. A superimposed parapet, 13 in wide, was indicated by a break in the brick bond, and demolished sections were found in front of the wall. White sand fill, followed by layers of brown water-washed sand, suggested an occupation surface on the interior of the redan, 3 ft below the top of the wall. Outside the wall, dark soil filled with large rubble, stone, and boulders appears to be a surrounding moat from the 1750s, this bolstered by the presence of a double line of wooden posts, likely a palisade. Demolition of the wall is suggested by rubbish-laden fill, identical on both the interior and exterior of the redan, a lens of sand fill, and a layer of crushed brick and mortar, matching the sections of parapet and the wall itself. Expansion of the market over the surface of the wall was indicated by a cap of orange clay. This continued over the wall, and expanded in thickness closer to the market footprint. This was followed by layers in 1789 (Figure 8).

The paved market street surface now sits 3 ft below the present road. In between are areas of brick and mortar rubble, reflecting demolition of the market, and then multiple layers of subsequent street paving. The earliest is a hard-packed surface of small flint cobbles, later replaced with sand and a rail line. The present surface of large flint cobbles sat in a bed of sand, and now in a bed of cement (Butler 2008).

The soil profile described above and the events reflected in this layering point to the complexity—and the clarity—of the urban archaeological record. Here, events described in documents and shown on maps can be tied to particular archaeological features, while the surrounding zone deposits can be dated from these events and from the artifacts contained in the soil. Artifacts from

Figure 8. Soil profile from South Adgers Wharf. Photo by Martha Zierden, Charleston Museum, Charleston, South Carolina.

some of the zone deposits can be associated specifically with the Lower Market, though most of the debris from the market was likely deposited in the water. The bone sample from the late-eighteenth-century deposits is particularly valuable for comparison to the Beef Market faunal assemblage. The mid-eighteenth-century soils in front of the wall contained quantities of debris, likely discarded in front of the wall from locations throughout the city. Thus, the materials inform on life in Charleston in general but cannot be used to study site-specific behavior. In the 1970s, when urban archaeology was a relatively new field of study, archaeologists were soon overwhelmed with urban fill and how to analyze it. Some argued that materials that cannot be related to specific events should be ignored. Other scholars (Honerkamp and Fairbanks 1984; Honerkamp and Council 1984) argued that discard and disorganization on a large scale reflect the realities of urban life and that scholars must adjust their scale of analysis to address the particular characteristics of such sites.

Excavations at the South Adger's site and other waterfront locations such as Atlantic Wharf (Figure 2, no. 5) and the Exchange Building (Figure 2, no. 6) have produced large artifact assemblages that portray daily life in the colonial city, even if the original source of the artifacts is unknown. They have also produced a number of unique artifacts that can occasionally be traced to the other city locations. Excavations at the Charleston Judicial Center on the northwest corner of Meeting and Broad streets revealed the remains of Philip Meyers's Sugar House, and pottery associated with refining muscovado sugar from the Caribbean (Joseph and Hamby 2007). Dozens of the distinctive red-clay cones used in the refining process were recovered from waterfront fill in front of the Exchange

Building at the foot of Broad Street (Herold 1981). The Atlantic Wharf site yielded a number of Spanish and Caribbean ceramics, as well as the remains of tropical fish (Zierden and Reitz 2002). The Exchange site, built on top of the Half Moon battery (a few blocks north of the South Adgers redan), yielded a layer of debris from the 1752 hurricane (Herold 1981). This layer was characterized by tar and pitch from barrels of naval stores, awaiting shipment when they were destroyed by the storm. The pitch created an unusual preservation environment, and the materials produced fabric, leather, and wood. Wood shavings and scrap suggest that the barrels were constructed on the wharf.

Filling of the land in front of the seawall eventually created new land, and today's waterfront continues some three blocks east of East Bay Street. The original wall lies buried beneath the street and is visible only in the basement of the Exchange Building, left exposed after archaeological excavation in the 1960s. The only other explorations of the wall—Granville's Bastion in 1925, the City Gate in 1993, and the redan at South Adger's in 2008–2009 were, by necessity, backfilled (Lapham 1925; Joseph and Elliott 1994; Agha and Poplin 2008; Butler et al. 2012). But all the projects suggest that the wall remains intact a few feet below the asphalt and that only the superstructure was removed in 1799.

Living in the City

Beyond the bustling late-colonial waterfront, Charleston's merchants and planters used their newly acquired wealth to build new townhouses, sometimes on a grand scale. The fire of 1740 cleared real estate for newer buildings at a time when the city's individual and collective wealth was expanding. New architectural styles, for both the main house and service buildings, combined with different requirements for daily life, resulted in changes to lot layout in the city. Joseph notes that by the mid-eighteenth century, at the Charleston Judicial Center, features associated with food storage and agriculture were reduced in number. Moreover, servants' quarters were removed from the immediate rear yard to mid-lot, and the work yard was reduced in size. Lots were often subdivided, further reducing the available yard space. The spaces were segregated with fences and other barriers. Joseph suggests that this reflects a decrease in the amount of agriculture in place on urban lots and the increased availability of foodstuffs at the city markets (Joseph 2002, 2007). Movement of the slave quarters and segregation of the work yard reflects changing race relations and increasing fear of the slave population following the Stono Rebellion in 1739 (Wood 1975). The development of formal gardens, accessed around—and sometimes through—the work yard, became part of the retinue of material trappings of wealthy urbanites, used to signal their social station.

Two new architectural styles emerged during the mid-eighteenth century, and these dominated the urban landscape for the next two centuries. The single house is one room wide and two deep, with central hall; the narrow, or gable, end faced the street. The double house, as its name implies, features four rooms per floor, with central hall (Poston 1997). Main houses fronted directly on the street, and a retinue of service buildings and associated work yard were aligned behind the house on one or both sides of the lot. Properties were often enclosed with walls or fences, and internal subdivision was also common. Moreover, this segmentation and enclosure (Herman 2005; Zierden and Herman 1996) increased in

Figure 9. Rear view of the Heyward-Washington house, circa 1930, showing work yard, outbuildings, and garden, MK 18768a. Charleston Museum, Charleston, South Carolina.

the early nineteenth century, as household security became a priority following the Denmark Vesey slave insurrection of 1822.

Study of townhouse lots from the mid-eighteenth century through the mid-nineteenth century was a focus of archaeological research for two decades, and the study sample includes seven upper-class residences and five middle-class residences (Figure 1). Together, the sites define the archaeological signature of daily life in the city.*

The Heyward-Washington house provides an example of these changes through the eighteenth century. After the fire of 1740 destroyed the home and shop of gunsmith John Milner, he and his son continued the business together. When John Milner Jr. inherited the Church Street property in 1749, he constructed a brick single house on the northern edge of the property and a series of brick outbuildings behind. These included a two-story kitchen and slave quarters behind the single house and a one-story stable/carriage house on the south property line. When wealthy planter Thomas Heyward acquired the property in 1772, he razed the single house and built a substantial and elaborate double house directly on Church Street, keeping the service buildings (Figure 9). He likely added the brick privy and a formal garden in the rear yard, accessed through the work yard. Large features were far less numerous in the work yard during this period; instead, refuse was recovered from the basement of the kitchen, the lower

*The upper-status residential sites studied include the following: Aiken-Rhett house at 48 Elizabeth Street (Zierden, Calhoun, and Hacker 1986; Zierden 2003), William Gibbes house at 64 South Battery (Zierden, Buckley, Calhoun, and Hacker 1987), John Rutledge house at 116 Broad Street (Zierden and Grimes 1989), Miles Brewton house at 27 King Street (Zierden 2001a), Nathaniel Russell house at 51 Meeting Street (Zierden 1996), the Simmons-Edwards house at 14 Legare Street (Zierden 2001b), the Heyward-Washington house at 87 Church Street (Herold 1978; Zierden and Reitz 2007). Modest-status residences include 66 Society Street (Zierden, Grimes, Hudgens, and Black 1988), 40 Society Street (Zierden 1989), 70 Nassau Street (Zierden 1991), 72 Anson Street (Zierden 1992), and President Street (Zierden and Raynor 1988).

Figure 10. Artifacts from Thomas Heyward's Church Street home, ca. 1790. Photo by Sean Mooney, staff, Charleston Museum, Charleston, South Carolina.

levels of the privy, and in the cellar of the main house (Herold 1978). Refuse was also recovered beneath the wood floor of the central tack room in the stable in 2002 (Zierden and Reitz 2007). The upheaval of the Revolutionary War, during which Thomas Heyward was imprisoned in St. Augustine, resulted in discard of quantities of household goods. The privy and kitchen, in particular, contained discarded remains of the finery used by the Heywards, including Chinese porcelain tea wares, creamware dining services, and elaborate glassware (Figure 10). Numerous wine bottles were affixed with the seal of G. A. Hall 1768 (George Abbot Hall was Mrs. Heyward's brother-in-law) and discarded as well (Zierden and Reitz 2007). Likewise, British occupation of the 1769 Miles Brewton house evidently resulted in cleanup (Figure 2, no. 21). Piles of Brewton's trash, including a monogrammed bottle and silver spoon, were found during excavation of an adjoining lot at 14 Legare Street (Figure 2, no. 22) (Zierden 2001b).

Townhouses constructed after the Revolution continued this trend. The Nathaniel Russell house, constructed in 1808 by the Rhode Island merchant and his lowcountry wife, was completed when the couple was older, their economic and social position established. The neoclassical single house and a retinue of service buildings were constructed along the northern side of the double lot, and the remainder used for formal garden (Figure 2, no. 20). The work yard, and the area beneath the kitchen building, was filled with Canton porcelain, imported in Russell's own ships, as well as fragments of eighteenth-century porcelain dinnerware, likely inherited by Mrs. Russell. Buckles and buttons from Mr. Russell's coats and brass hardware from upholstered and fine wooden furniture were among the material recovered on site. This relates to the possessions and landscape of the Russells documented in journals, inventories, and visitor accounts (Zierden 1999).

In addition to the bits of finery discovered on these townhouse sites, the archaeological deposits are filled with large numbers of everyday containers, less expensive glass and ceramics, tools, and food remains that are not described in documents. Refined living diminished behind the main house and garden, as the work yard was the scene of repetitious chores that held little glamour and entailed hard work. Most of these tasks, and the resulting archaeological debris, were the work of the enslaved African Americans who also lived on the urban lots. Their imprint on the city's archaeological record is extensive but nearly impossible to isolate on residential properties, as the refuse of master and slave was discarded in the same locations.

Some of the archaeological materials recovered in the city on residential properties can be ascribed to bondsmen and other anonymous urban dwellers. Inexpensive annular-ware bowls and glass beads were likely owned by African residents. The Russell house site contained artifacts that suggest cultural continuity, social cohesion, or defiance, such as Spanish coins pierced to be worn as charms, quartz crystals, and cowrie shells. Charleston sites are full of colonoware, a locally made, low-fired earthenware attributed to African and/or Native American potters. Colonoware averages 5 percent of Charleston ceramics and is recovered in larger amounts on sites from the mid-eighteenth century and earlier.

One constant facet of Charleston's archaeological past is the presence of a considerable animal population in the city. Faunal remains recovered from Charleston sites have been analyzed by Dr. Elizabeth Reitz of the University of Georgia since 1982. When individual sites are considered, the sample recovered is often too small for statistical validity. When the unit of study is the city, each of the analyzed samples becomes part of a larger research sample, subdivided by function and temporal association. Taken together, the Charleston vertebrate assemblage consists of over 129,298 vertebrate specimens, representing an estimated minimum number of 2,069 individuals.*

An often-overlooked aspect of the urban colonial landscape is the quantity and variety of domestic, commensal, and feral animals living in the city. Like the people who lived there, the activities of these animals shaped and were shaped by the urban landscape. Many aspects of the urban environment were designed to accommodate and restrict animals living in the city. Unlike other environmental components, though, the animals were active players in the affairs of daily life (Zierden and Reitz 2009).

The resident animals were part of the larger effort to provision the city. Zooarchaeological research has shown that lowcountry residents of all backgrounds took advantage of the bounty of the woods and waters of the coastal plain, and many of these animals came to live in the city. A host of wild game, fish, and shellfish formed the basis of many lowcountry dishes, and use of wild

*Reports on faunal studies are included as appendixes or chapters in the following site reports: Aiken-Rhett house at 48 Elizabeth Street (Zierden, Calhoun, and Hacker 1986; Zierden 2003), William Gibbes house at 64 South Battery (Zierden, Buckley, Calhoun, and Hacker 1987), John Rutledge house at 116 Broad Street (Zierden and Grimes 1989), Miles Brewton house at 27 King Street (Zierden 2001a), Nathaniel Russell house at 51 Meeting Street (Zierden 1996), the Simmons-Edwards house at 14 Legare Street (Zierden 2001b), the Heyward-Washington house at 87 Church Street (Zierden and Reitz 2007), and the Post Office/Courthouse annex (Bastian 1987; Trinkley 1998). Modest-status residences include 66 Society Street (Zierden, Grimes, Hudgens, and Black 1988), 40 Society Street (Reitz and Dukes 1993), 70 Nassau Street (Reitz 1990; Armitage 1990); 72 Anson Street (Zierden 1992), President Street (Zierden and Raynor 1988), and 82 Pitt Street (Poplin and Salo 2009). Faunal materials analyzed from public sites include McCrady's Tavern and Longroom (Zierden, Reitz, Trinkley, and Paysinger 1983), Lodge Alley (Zierden, Calhoun, and Paysinger 1983), Powder Magazine (Zierden 1997), Beef Market/City Hall (Calhoun, Reitz, Trinkley and Zierden 1984; Zierden and Reitz 2005), South Adger's Wharf (Butler, Pemberton, Poplin, and Zierden 2012), and Dock Street Theatre (Zierden, Agha, Colannino, Jones, Poplin, and Reitz 2009). Mixed residential-commercial sites include First Trident (Zierden, Calhoun, and Pinckney 1983), Visitor's Center (Grimes and Zierden 1988), and Charleston Place (Honerkamp, Council and Will 1982; Zierden and Hacker 1987). Synthetic studies of the zooarchaeological record in Charleston include Reitz 2007; Reitz and Ruff 1994; Zierden and Reitz 2009; and Reitz, Ruff and Zierden 2006.

game by Charleston's elite continued into the twentieth century. Archaeological evidence demonstrates that the crowded and messy conditions of the urban work yard were exacerbated by the presence of these animals and their remains. The work yard was crowded with debris, livestock, horses, and people. Archaeological analysis has clearly demonstrated that Charlestonians maintained animals on their townhouse lots and butchered these animals there despite the presence of the markets (Reitz et al. 2006; Zierden and Reitz 2009). The number of cattle in the city declined after the mid-nineteenth century, but fowl and other small animals remained on site until the twentieth century.

The Postbellum City

Charleston's archaeological record visibly diminishes after the mid-nineteenth century. As the city developed new infrastructure for transportation, drainage, sewage, and refuse disposal, the individual site activities that resulted in a robust archaeological record were abandoned. Instead of privy pits, building cellars, and yards strewn with rubbish (now considered artifacts), yards of the last century feature pipes and drains, small lost items, and pet burials (Honerkamp and Council 1984; Honerkamp and Fairbanks 1984). Structural features, such as building trenches and postholes, may contain no artifacts and therefore become difficult to date. But these archaeological features nonetheless reflect the realities of urban life in the late nineteenth century. Careful excavation, combined with analysis of the documentary record, can tease data from archaeological proveniences of this period, and provide new information. The Aiken-Rhett house was built in 1817 (Figure 1, no. 15) and was the first house on the property, located in Charleston's northern suburbs. The late date of construction and occupation, combined with owner William Aiken's progressive habits, resulted in an archaeological record that contains numerous features but very few artifacts. Still, stratigraphic sequencing and soil color suggest extensive activity at the site in the late nineteenth century, including remodeling of the house and garden (Zierden 2003). These changes are in contrast to the general history of the area, which suggests that Charleston's economy was depressed from the Civil War until World War II.

If some townhouses and townhouse owners prospered after the war, others did not. The widow of Robert F. W. Allston, owner of the Nathaniel Russell house, opened a girls' school to make ends meet. The Sisters of Charity continued the use of the property as a school until new owners in the twentieth century returned the house to its original use as a single-family dwelling. Toys and religious items were recovered from late-nineteenth-century contexts, along with refuse that was discarded near the rear walls rather than carted off-site (Zierden 1996). Descendants of Miles Brewton retained the elegant Georgian double house at 27 King Street but sold the rear half of the garden, took in boarders, and gave tours to keep the property. The number of resident servants went from 36 slaves before the war to three freed persons after the war. General maintenance was deferred, and the property fell into some disrepair. The brick-lined cellar beneath the kitchen building filled with soil and debris, this event clearly dated by recovery of an 1863 coin at the base of excavation (Zierden 2001a).

It was the neglect of historic properties occasioned by economic depression that resulted in the birth of the historic preservation movement in Charleston in the early twentieth century. The city and its key preservation organizations, the Preservation Society and Historic Charleston Foundation, remain at the forefront of the preservation movement. Preservationists did not embrace the field of archaeology until the 1980s, but in the past quarter-century efforts of the two groups have become intertwined (Fraser 1989; Weyeneth 2000; Bland 1999).

Much of the archaeological research has been mandated by these groups, and the ability to work with specialists from preservation has resulted in research projects that are truly interdisciplinary. At sites such as the Nathaniel Russell House, the Aiken-Rhett house, and 14 Legare Street, archaeologists worked under a team of architectural historians and garden historians. The South Adgers Wharf project included preservationists, historians, field archaeologists, and military specialists. Archaeological specialists, such as zooarchaeologists, palynologists, ethnobotanists, and soil chemists are regularly part of the research team. Projects in the 1980s were usually federally mandated, or funded by federal and state grants. Historic Charleston Foundation became a leading advocate for archaeological research and preservation in the 1990s, and funded dozens of projects throughout the city. Following this example, private citizens with the means to do so included archaeological research in the preservation of historic properties. The impetus for archaeological research often comes at the request of landscape architects and restoration architects. The analyzed faunal sample is the largest historic faunal sample in the country. Archaeology has become a key player in the ongoing study, restoration, and interpretation of Charleston's past.

Plate 1. Bend-break tools and blades from
the Pleistocene terrace, Topper site (38AL23).
Courtesy of the South Carolina Institute of
Archaeology and Anthropology.

Plate 2. Blades and unifaces from the Pleistocene sands, Topper site (38AL23).
Courtesy of the South Carolina Institute of Archaeology and Anthropology.

Plate 3. Clovis points from South Carolina (private collections). Courtesy of the
South Carolina Institute of Archaeology and Anthropology.

Plate 4. Red Stone points from private collections. Courtesy of the
South Carolina Institute of Archaeology and Anthropology.

Plate 5. Early Archaic points from South Carolina. Bottom row: Dalton points (private collections). Middle row: Taylor points (Charles site 38AL135, left; Big Pine Tree site 38AI143, center; Topper site 38AL23, right). Top row: Kirk corner-notched points (private collection, left; Nipper Creek 38RD18, center and right). Courtesy of the South Carolina Institute of Archaeology and Anthropology.

Plate 6. Middle Archaic points from South Carolina. Bottom Morrow Mountain points left
Clarendon County private collection, middle Calhoun County private collection, right Top Row Big
Pine Tree Site (38Al143). Middle Guilford Points left Top Big Pine Tree Site (38Al143), middle and right
Clarendon County private collection. Top Allendale Points all Big Pine Tree Site (38Al143). Courtesy
of the South Carolina Institute of Archaeology and Anthropology.

Plate 7. Late Archaic points from the Moody site. Photograph courtesy of Kenneth E. Sassaman.

Plate 8. Early Woodland Mack points from South Carolina (private collections).
Courtesy of the South Carolina Institute of Archaeology and Anthropology.

Plate 9. Woodland points from Big Pine Tree Site (38Al143). Bottom row: Yadkin points. Middle rows: Woodland notched and stemmed points. Top row: Woodland triangular points. Courtesy of the South Carolina Institute of Archaeology and Anthropology.

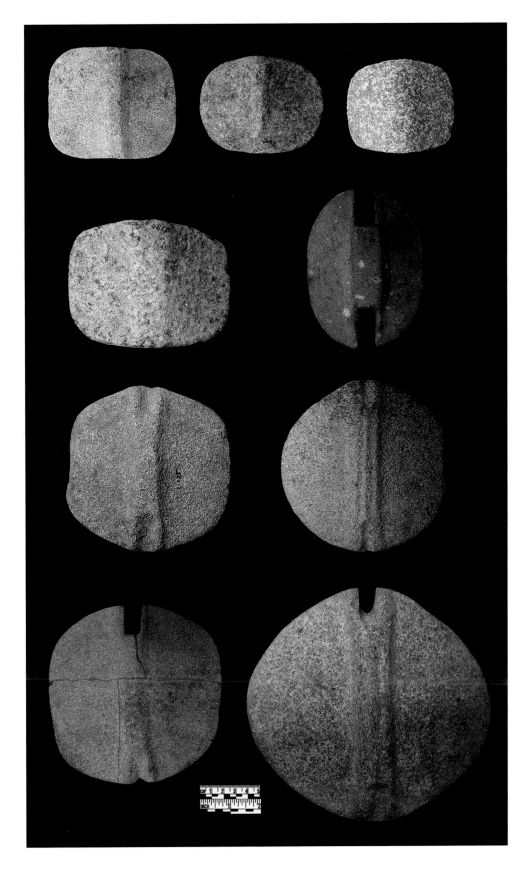

Plate 10. Southern ovate (top row and left on second row from top) and notched southern ovate bannerstones from the middle Savannah River valley, South Carolina and Georgia. The bottom two rows are unfinished bannerstones. Photograph courtesy of Kenneth E. Sassaman.

Plate 11. (right) Grooved axes. Photograph by George Wingard, courtesy of the South Carolina Institute of Archaeology and Anthropology.

Plate 12. Late Archaic soapstone cooking stones. Photograph by George Wingard, courtesy of the South Carolina Institute of Archaeology and Anthropology.

Plate 13. (left) Stone celts. Photograph by George Wingard, courtesy of the South Carolina Institute of Archaeology and Anthropology.

Plate 14. Portion of a Stallings fiber-tempered pot, excavated on Parris Island in Beaufort County. Stallings is the earliest pottery type in North America; this example dates to about 4,000 years ago. Courtesy of the South Carolina Institute of Archaeology and Anthropology.

Plate 15. Stallings fiber-tempered pottery with drag-and-jab punctuation designs. Photograph courtesy of Kenneth E. Sassaman.

Plate 16. (left) Middle Woodland herringbone-variant, linear-check-stamped jar recovered from 38AK228 by the Savannah River Archaeological Research Program. Photograph by James B. Legg, courtesy of the South Carolina Institute of Archaeology and Anthropology.

Plate 17. Mississippian-period plain bowl recovered from 38AK228. Photograph by James B. Legg, courtesy of the South Carolina Institute of Archaeology and Anthropology.

Plate 18. (right) Mississippian compli-
cated stamped jar with cob-impressed neck
recovered from 38AK390 by the Savannah
River Archaeological Research Program.
Photograph by James B. Legg, courtesy of the
South Carolina Institute of Archaeology and
Anthropology.

Plate 19. Plain Mississippian jar decorated
with cane punctations and punctated nodes,
dating to ca. A.D. 1250–1350, Richland County.
Courtesy of the South Carolina Institute of
Archaeology and Anthropology.

Plate 20. Mississippian jar decorated with a complicated stamped design, cane punctations, and punctated nodes, dating to ca. A.D. 1250–1350, Richland County. Courtesy of the South Carolina Institute of Archaeology and Anthropology.

Plate 21. (right) Sixteenth-century
Native American cooking jar recovered from a
Spanish trash pit at Santa Elena (38BU51/162).
A significant portion of the ceramics used at
Santa Elena (1566–1587) was Native Ameri-
can. Courtesy of the South Carolina Institute
of Archaeology and Anthropology.

Plate 22. Spanish redware recovered
from the site of a pottery kiln at Santa Elena,
1566–1587 (38BU51/162). Courtesy of the South
Carolina Institute of Archaeology and Anthropology.

Plate 23. (above, left) Spanish 1 *real* silver coin of Phillip II, minted in Mexico City, recovered at Santa Elena (38BU51/162). Courtesy of the South Carolina Institute of Archaeology and Anthropology.

Plate 24. (above) Spanish silver coin dated 1737, recovered during SCIAA investigations in 2012 at Fort Motte in Calhoun County. British-held Fort Motte was captured by forces led by Francis Marion and Henry Lee in May 1781. Courtesy of the South Carolina Institute of Archaeology and Anthropology.

Plate 25. Eighteenth-century colonoware bowl recovered from the Cooper River in Berkeley County. Courtesy of the South Carolina Institute of Archaeology and Anthropology.

Plate 26. (above) Eighteenth-century colonoware vessels. The bowl on the left was recovered from the Black River in Georgetown County; the other two vessels are from the Cooper River in Berkeley County. Courtesy of the South Carolina Institute of Archaeology and Anthropology.

Plate 27. Chinese-export porcelain, 1770s, from a deposit at the South Carolina Society Hall. Photo by Sean Mooney, staff, the Charleston Museum, Charleston, South Carolina.

Plate 28. Artifacts from the battlefield of Camden in Kershaw County, where the British destroyed the American southern army on August 16, 1780. SCIAA archaeologists have conducted investigations on the site since 1998. Courtesy of the South Carolina Institute of Archaeology and Anthropology.

Plate 29. A complete brass candlestick buried in a pit feature in Francis Marion's 1780–1781 camp near Dunham's Bluff in Marion County. The camp, 38MA207, was investigated by SCIAA archaeologists in 2007. Courtesy of the South Carolina Institute of Archaeology and Anthropology.

Plate 30. Eighteenth-century English slipware chamber pot (left) and cup (right) in the SCIAA collection, recovered from Coastal Plain river sites. Courtesy of the South Carolina Institute of Archaeology and Anthropology.

Plate 31. English wine bottles in the SCIAA collection, recovered by divers from Coastal Plain river sites. From left to right, the bottles date ca. 1690, 1740, 1770, and 1800. Courtesy of the South Carolina Institute of Archaeology and Anthropology.

Plate 32. Bottle seals marked G. A. Hall 1768, recovered from the Heyward-Washington House. Photo by Sean Mooney, staff, the Charleston Museum, Charleston, South Carolina.

Plate 33. (above) Charleston domestic slave tag, recovered from Dean Hall Plantation (38BK2132). Courtesy of DuPont South Carolina and Brockington and Associates.

Plate 34. Alkaline glazed stoneware vessel made by the enslaved potter Dave (1801–ca. 1880), who worked in the Edgefield District of South Carolina and was taught to read and write. Inscription reads "April 16, 1862." Recovered from 38AK953 by the Savannah River Archaeological Research Program. Courtesy of the South Carolina Institute of Archaeology and Anthropology.

Plate 35. Union soldier's shoe revealed in a Charleston Museum excavation on the north end of Folly Island, 1990 (38CH1213). Folly Island was occupied by Union troops from 1863 to 1865 during the Siege of Charleston. Photograph by Ron Anthony, courtesy of the Charleston Museum, Charleston, South Carolina.

Plate 36. English hand-painted whiteware ceramics recovered from the co-joined wrecks of the blockade runners *Georgiana* and *Mary Bowers,* sunk at the same location near the entrance to Charleston Harbor in 1863 and 1864. Courtesy of the South Carolina Institute of Archaeology and Anthropology.

Plate 37. Ceramics recovered from an early-nineteenth-century cellar in Cambridge (38GN5), a town that once existed adjacent to the site of eighteenth-century Ninety Six in Greenwood County. Courtesy of the South Carolina Institute of Archaeology and Anthropology.

Plate 38. U.S. Marine Corps brass hat insignia recovered from the site of a World War I basic training camp on Parris Island in Beaufort County. The temporary camp was located on the same site as the Spanish town of Santa Elena (38BU51/162). Courtesy of the South Carolina Institute of Archaeology and Anthropology.

References Cited

Agha, Andrew, and Eric Poplin

2008 Preliminary Report: Archaeological Investigations at South Adgers Wharf. Report on file, Historic Charleston Foundation, Charleston, South Carolina.

Armitage, Philip

1990 Remains of *Rattus norvegicus* from 70 Nassau Street, Charleston, SC. Manuscript on file, Charleston Museum, Charleston, South Carolina.

Bastian, Beverly

1987 Historical and Archeological Investigations at the United States Post Office/Courthouse Annex, Charleston, South Carolina. Report on file, General Services Administration, Atlanta.

Bland, Sidney

1999 *Preserving Charleston's Past, Shaping its Future: The Life and Times of Susan Pringle Frost.* University of South Carolina Press, Columbia.

Bridenbaugh, Carl

1938 *Cities in the Wilderness: the First Century of Urban Life in America, 1625–1742.* Ronald Press, New York.

Butler, Nicholas

2008 Rediscovering Charleston's Colonial Fortifications. Mayor's Walled City Task Force. Electronic document, http://walledcitytaskforce.org (accessed February 12, 2010).

Butler, Nicholas, Katherine Pemberton, Eric Poplin, and Martha Zierden

2012 *Archaeology at South Adger's Wharf: A Study of the Redan at Tradd Street.* Archaeological Contributions 45. Charleston Museum, Charleston, South Carolina.

Calhoun, Jeanne

1983 *The Scourging Wrath of God: Early Hurricanes in Charleston, 1700–1804.* Charleston Museum Leaflet no. 29, Charleston, South Carolina.

Calhoun, Jeanne, Elizabeth Reitz, Michael Trinkley, and Martha Zierden

1984 *Meat in Due Season: Preliminary Investigations of Marketing Practices in Colonial Charleston.* Archaeological Contributions 9. Charleston Museum, Charleston, South Carolina.

Carney, Judith

2001 *Black Rice: The African Origins of Rice Cultivation in the Americas.* Harvard University Press, Cambridge, Massachusetts.

Crane, Verner W.

1981[1956] *The Southern Frontier, 1670–1732.* W. W. Norton, New York.

Fraser, Walter J.

1989 *Charleston! Charleston! The History of a Southern City.* University of South Carolina Press, Columbia.

2006 *Lowcountry Hurricanes: Three Centuries of Storms at Sea and Ashore.* University of Georgia Press, Athens.

Grimes, Kimberly, and Martha Zierden

1988 *A Hub of Human Activity: Archaeological Investigations at the Visitor's Reception and Transportation Center Site.* Archaeological Contributions 19. Charleston Museum, Charleston, South Carolina.

Hamby, Theresa, and J. W. Joseph

2004 *A New Look at the Old City: Archaeological Excavations of the Charleston County Judicial Center Site, Charleston, SC.* New South Associates Technical Report 1192. On file, Charleston County, Department of Capital Projects, Charleston, South Carolina.

Herman, Bernard L.

2005 *Town House: Architecture and Material Life in the Early American City, 1780–1830.* University of North Carolina Press, Chapel Hill.

Herold, Elaine B.

1978 Preliminary Report: Excavations at the Heyward-Washington House. Report on file, Charleston Museum, Charleston, South Carolina.

1981 Archaeological Research at the Exchange Building, Charleston: 1979–1980. Report on file, Charleston Museum, Charleston, South Carolina.

Honerkamp, Nicholas, and R. Bruce Council

1984 Individual versus Corporate Adaptations in Urban Contexts. *Tennessee Anthropologist* 9(1):22–31.

Honerkamp, Nicholas, R. Bruce Council, and M. Elizabeth Will

1982 An Archaeological Investigation of the Charleston Convention Center Site, Charleston, South Carolina. Report on file, City of Charleston Office of Downtown Revitalization, Charleston, South Carolina.

Honerkamp, Nicholas, and Charles H. Fairbanks

1984 Definition of Site Formation Processes in Urban Contexts. *American Archaeology* 4(1):60–66.

Joseph, J. W.

2002 From Colonist to Charlestonian: The Crafting of Identity in a Colonial Southern City. In *Another's Country: Archaeological and Historical Perspectives on Cultural Interactions in the Southern Colonies,* edited by J. W. Joseph and Martha Zierden, pp. 215–234. University of Alabama Press, Tuscaloosa.

2007 Agriculture in Colonial Charleston: Landuse, Landscape, and the Lost Colonial City. *South Carolina Antiquities* 39:18–33.

Joseph, J. W., and Rita F. Elliott

1994 *Restoration Archaeology at the Charleston County Courthouse site (38Ch1498), Charleston, South Carolina.* New South Associates Technical Report 194. On file, Charleston County Capital Projects, Charleston, SC.

Joseph, J. W., and Theresa M. Hamby

2007 Sugar Production in Charleston: Archaeological Investigations of the Philip Meyers Sugar House. *South Carolina Antiquities* 39:104–115.

Joseph, J. W., Theresa Hamby, and Jennifer Langdale

2000 *The Vendue/Prioleau Project: An Archaeological Study of the Early Charleston Waterfront.* New South Associates Technical Report 772. On file, City of Charleston, Charleston, South Carolina.

Lapham, Samuel

1925 Notes on the Granville Bastion, 1704. *South Carolina Historical and Genealogical Magazine* 25:224.

Leland, Harriott Cheves, and Dianne W. Ressinger

2006 "Ce Pais Tant Desire," This Much Longed-for Country. *Transactions of the Huguenot Society of South Carolina* 110:1–41.

Mathews, Maurice

1954 A Contemporary View of Carolina in 1680. *South Carolina Historical Magazine* 5:153–159.

Poplin, Eric, and Edward Salo

2009 Archaeological Investigations at 82 Pitt Street, Charleston, South Carolina. Brockington and Associates. Report on file, Historic Charleston Foundation, Charleston, South Carolina.

Poston, Jonathan

1997 *The Buildings of Charleston: A Guide to the City's Architecture.* Historic Charleston Foundation and University of South Carolina Press, Columbia.

Reitz, Elizabeth J.

1990 Vertebrate Faunal Remains from 70 Nassau Street, Charleston, South Carolina. Manuscript on file, Charleston Museum, Charleston, South Carolina.

2007   Animal Remains from the Eighteenth-Century Charleston Beef Market. *South Carolina Antiquities* 39:87–103.

Reitz, Elizabeth, and Joel Dukes

1993   Vertebrate Fauna from 40 Society Street and 72 Anson Street, Charleston, SC. Manuscript on file, Charleston Museum, Charleston, South Carolina.

Reitz, Elizabeth, and Barbara Ruff

1994   Morphometric Data for Cattle from North America and the Caribbean Prior to the 1950s. *Journal of Archaeological Science* 21(5):699–713.

Reitz, Elizabeth J., Barbara L. Ruff, and Martha A. Zierden

2006   Pigs in Charleston, South Carolina: Using Specimen Count to Consider Status. *Historical Archaeology* 40(4):104–124.

Rosengarten, Dale, Martha Zierden, Kimberly Grimes, Ziyadah Owusu, Elizabeth Alston, and Will Williams III

1987   *Between the Tracks: Charleston's East Side during the Nineteenth Century.* Archaeological Contributions 17. Charleston Museum, Charleston, South Carolina.

Salley, Alexander (editor)

1928   *Records in the British Public Records Office Relating to South Carolina 1663–1684.* Foote and Davis, Atlanta.

Saunders, Katherine

2002   "As regular and fformidable as any such woorke in America": The Walled City of Charles Town. In *Another's Country,* edited by J. W. Joseph and Martha Zierden, pp. 198–214. University of Alabama Press, Tuscaloosa, Alabama.

South, Stanley

1977   *Method and Theory in Historical Archaeology.* Academic Press, New York.

2002   *Archaeological Pathways to Historic Site Development.* Kluwer Academic/Plenum Publishers, New York.

Staski, Edward

1982   Advances in Urban Archaeology. In *Advances in Archaeological Method and Theory,* Vol. 5, edited by Michael Schiffer, pp. 97–150. Academic Press, New York.

Trinkley, Michael

1998   *Management Summary of Archaeological Data Recovery at 38Ch1644, 85–93 Broad Street, Charleston, SC.* Chicora Research Contribution 250. Chicora Foundation, Columbia, South Carolina.

Weir, Robert

2002   Charles Town Circa 1702: On the Cusp; In Firestorm and Ashes, the Siege of 1702. *El Escribano* 39:65–79. St. Augustine Historical Society, St. Augustine, Florida.

Weyeneth, Robert R.

2000   *Historic Preservation for a Living City: Historic Charleston Foundation 1947–1997.* University of South Carolina Press, Columbia.

Wood, Peter

1974   *Black Majority; Negroes in Colonial South Carolina from 1670 through the Stono Rebellion.* Alfred A. Knopf, New York.

Zierden, Martha

1989   Field Report: Testing at 40 Society Street. Manuscript on file, Charleston Museum, Charleston, South Carolina.

1991   Management Summary: Excavations at 70 Nassau Street. Manuscript on file, Charleston Museum, Charleston, South Carolina.

1992   Management Summary: Testing at 72 Anson Street. Manuscript on file, Charleston Museum, Charleston, South Carolina.

1996   *Big House/Back Lot: An Archaeological Study of the Nathaniel Russell House.* Archaeological Contributions 25. Charleston Museum, Charleston, South Carolina.

1997   *Archaeology at the Powder Magazine: a Charleston Site through Three Centuries.* Archaeological Contributions 26. Charleston Museum, Charleston, South Carolina.

1999   A Trans-Atlantic Merchant's House in Charleston: Archaeological Exploration of Refinement and Subsistence in an Urban Setting. *Historical Archaeology* 33(3):73–82.

2001a   *Archaeology at the Miles Brewton House, 27 King Street.* Archaeological Contributions 29. Charleston Museum, Charleston, South Carolina.

2001b   *Archaeology at 14 Legare Street.* Archaeological Contributions 28. Charleston Museum, Charleston, South Carolina.

2003   *Aiken-Rhett House: Archaeological Research.* Archaeological Contributions 31. Charleston Museum, Charleston, South Carolina.

Zierden, Martha, Andrew Agha, Carol Colannino, John Jones, Eric Poplin, and Elizabeth Reitz

2009   *The Dock Street Theatre: Archaeological Discovery and Exploration.* Archaeological Contributions 42. Charleston Museum, Charleston, South Carolina.

Zierden, Martha, Suzanne Buckley, Jeanne Calhoun, and Debi Hacker

1987   *Georgian Opulence: Archaeological Investigation of the Gibbes House.* Archaeological Contributions 12. Charleston Museum, Charleston, South Carolina.

Zierden, Martha, and Jeanne Calhoun

1984   *An Archaeological Preservation Plan for Charleston, South Carolina.* Archaeological Contributions 8. Charleston Museum, Charleston, South Carolina.

Zierden, Martha, Jeanne Calhoun, and Debi Hacker

1986   *Outside of Town: Preliminary Investigation of the AikenRhett House.* Archaeological Contributions 11. Charleston Museum, Charleston, South Carolina.

Zierden, Martha, Jeanne Calhoun, and Elizabeth Paysinger

1983   *Archaeological Investigations at Lodge Alley, Charleston, South Carolina.* Archaeological Contributions 5. Charleston Museum, Charleston, South Carolina.

Zierden, Martha, Jeanne Calhoun, and Elizabeth Pinckney

1983   *An Archaeological Study of the First Trident Site.* Archaeological Contributions 6. Charleston Museum, Charleston, South Carolina.

Zierden, Martha, and Kimberly Grimes

1989   *Investigating Elite Lifeways through Archaeology: The John Rutledge House.* Archaeological Contributions 21. Charleston Museum, Charleston, South Carolina.

Zierden, Martha, Kimberly Grimes, David Hudgens, and Cherie Black

1988   *Charleston's First Suburb: Excavations at 66 Society Street.* Archaeological Contributions 20. Charleston Museum, Charleston, South Carolina.

Zierden, Martha, and Debi Hacker

1987   *Charleston Place: Archaeological Investigations of the Commercial Landscape.* Archaeological Contributions 16. Charleston Museum, Charleston, South Carolina.

Zierden, Martha, and Bernard Herman

1996   Charleston Townhouses: Archaeology, Architecture, and the Urban Landscape, 1750–1850. In *Landscape Archaeology: Reading and Interpreting the American Historical Landscape,* edited by Rebecca Yamin and Karen Metheny, pp. 193–227. University of Tennessee Press, Knoxville.

Zierden, Martha, and Robert Raynor

   1988   *The President Street Site: An Experiment in Public Archaeology.* Archaeological Contributions 18. Charleston Museum. Charleston, South Carolina.

Zierden, Martha, and Elizabeth Reitz

   2002   *Excavations on Charleston's Waterfront: The Atlantic Wharf Garage Site.* Archaeological Contributions 30. Charleston Museum, Charleston, South Carolina.

   2005   *Archaeology at City Hall: Charleston's Colonial Beef Market.* Archaeological Contributions 35. Charleston Museum, Charleston, South Carolina.

   2007   *Archaeology at the Heyward-Washington Stable: Charleston Through the 18th Century.* Archaeological Contributions 39. Charleston Museum, Charleston, South Carolina.

   2009   Animal Use and the Urban Landscape in Colonial Charleston, South Carolina, USA. *International Journal of Historical Archaeology* 13:327–365.

Zierden, Martha, Elizabeth Reitz, Michael Trinkley, and Elizabeth Paysinger

   1983   *Archaeological Excavations at McCrady's Longroom.* Archaeological Contributions 3. Charleston Museum, Charleston, South Carolina.

STEVEN D. SMITH

The Submarine *H. L. Hunley*

Confederate Innovation
and Southern Icon

ON A CRISP, CLOUDLESS SUNDOWN in mid-February 1864, a long, thin, iron water-craft cleared Breach Inlet, South Carolina, and entered the open sea.* Less than three miles dead ahead lay its objective, the Union sloop-of-war USS *Housatonic*, at anchor, but with a full head of steam. On board, the *Housatonic*'s crew was alert, keeping an eye out for a rumored Confederate torpedo boat seeking targets among the Union fleet blockading Charleston. In fact, the iron vessel bearing down on them was the *H. L. Hunley*, a true submarine and a glimmering example of the South's innovative attempts to overcome the might of the Federal navy.

About nine that evening, months of experimentation, failure, and re-experimentation came to an end. Yankee sailors aboard the *Housatonic* spotted the approaching dark shape some yards away and, while blazing away with rifles and pistols, attempted to bring to bear their larger guns. With the *Housatonic*'s confused crew watching, the *Hunley* rammed its spar-mounted torpedo into the Union ship's side and backed away. There was a jarring explosion. The *Housatonic* quickly rolled to port and settled in 30 feet of water, its men seeking safety in the rigging. The era of submarine warfare had begun. The *Hunley* was the first submarine to sink an enemy vessel in combat (Kloeppel 1992:59–81; Ragan 1995:132–140: Schafer 1996:113–125). But for what would eventually become a weapon of shock and deadly efficiency in World Wars I and II, it was an unassuming dawn, for the *Hunley* failed to return to port (Ragan 1995:141).

The mystery of the *Hunley*'s fate has been the subject of debate by military historians, wreck salvors, and professional archaeologists practically since its

*This essay, with some slight editorial differences and without the final section that brings the *Hunley* story up to date, was originally published in *Archaeological Perspectives on the American Civil War*, edited by Clarence R. Geier and Stephen R. Potter, pp. 29–42, University Press of Florida, Gainesville, 2000. Reprinted with permission.

loss. In early May 1995 the *Hunley* controversy radically changed when the submarine was discovered (Hall and Wilbanks 1995). Overnight, dispute concerning the *Hunley*'s fate was secondary to quarrels respecting its discovery, ownership, and future. These wrangles soon broadened to higher philosophical questions of states' rights and, ultimately, the vessel's ideological meaning. Now the *Hunley* is serious business, embroiling private citizens and citizens' groups, state governments, the U.S. Congress, the U.S. Navy, the media, and the literary elite in a struggle for control over its destiny and especially its meaning. Although its archaeological significance is first on everyone's lips, it often seems from the clamor, alas, to be last in the struggle for its control. This essay examines the *Hunley*'s past as a unique example of Confederate innovation, its discovery and recent assessment by the National Park Service and the South Carolina Institute of Archaeology and Anthropology, and its future as an icon of Southern culture. The *Hunley* is no mere historic underwater artifact, and its multilayered symbolism continues to grow as government agencies attempt to raise and display it.

Confederate Innovation

In creating an entirely new navy to challenge the Union, Confederate secretary of the navy Stephen Russell Mallory faced a daunting and ultimately insurmountable task. The South was rural and agrarian, while the North had a strong industrial infrastructure. Although there was a "Southern industry," it served the agricultural community and hardly could be described as diverse. In terms of capital alone, Northern industrial investment was nearly eight times as large as the South's (Genovese 1965; Luraghi 1996:34). Among Mallory's immediate industrial needs were shipyards. At the beginning of the war, the U.S. Navy had eight shipyards, while the Confederacy had captured only a small yard in Pensacola, Florida, and the prominent yard in Norfolk, Virginia. Both sides had numerous small private yards, but, overall, the South was decidedly at a disadvantage. Indeed, the South had no navy to begin with, while the U.S. fleet was 90 strong; and if most Federal vessels were old and aging, a few were among the most modern steamers in the world. The rest could be repaired or at least used as floating batteries (Luraghi 1996:32). In his classic study of the Confederate navy, French admiral Lepotier summed up the situation by noting that the Civil War was probably the only occasion in history when, as two ocean-facing nations prepared for conflict, one had total dominion of the seas (Luraghi 1996:61).

Essentially, Mallory had to build a navy from the keel up, while the North only had to rig for war. The Confederacy faced numerous challenges, but four stand out as decisive. The first was a decided lack of raw materials. Specifically, the South lacked pig iron. William Still has stated that it "is nearly impossible to exaggerate the effect of iron production on the entire Confederate war effort" (Still 1987:47). Lacking both iron reserves and iron ore at the beginning of the war, the Confederacy could not even get started building an iron fleet. Second, while the South had abundant timber for wooden ship construction, there was no way to get the timber to its naval yards. Its transportation infrastructure was wholly inadequate—there were only a few railroads and dirt roads—and there was no means for rapid improvement of the situation. The critical demand for iron actually worked against the need to build up the transportation system as operational railroads were raided for their iron rails to construct armored vessels (Still 1987:50–510). The third critical need was skilled labor. The South had genius at the level of invention, but invention has to be engineered and such skills were scarce south of the Mason-Dixon Line. As Confederate naval historian Raimondo Luraghi noted, the South's lack of mechanics, technicians, and engineers—or the existence of a true industrial machine—was the basic reason for the South's defeat (Luraghi 1996:346). Finally, the Confederacy lacked time. The time to build a transportation system, cut timber, forge iron, and construct a Confederate navy was simply not available (Still 1987:80–81).

Mallory did his best to meet these challenges. As he worked desperately to build a navy, he looked for any advantage. There were a few. First, there was hope that the Confederacy could purchase part of its navy from European powers. Second, there were its timber resources, both wood and resin products such as tar and pitch. If it could get these resources to its naval yards, wooden ship production could be sustained. Third was private investment. Southern patriotic fervor and the possibility of profit motivated Southern venture capitalists to invest in privateering and blockade running. The former was largely ineffective, the latter quite successful (Wise 1988). The Confederacy primed this investment fever with loans, giving the government some control over the required new industries and what they would produce (Luraghi 1996:39). Most critically, private investment provided the Confederacy with the fuel to sail its one ship of hope—the hope of technical innovation. Free from bureaucratic restraints faced by the Federal navy (Wills 1998:23) and spurred by men of genius, Mallory looked to novel technological inventions to float the Confederate navy.

Mallory's initial vision was "based on a four-fold technical surprise: armored ships, rifled naval guns, commerce destroying, and submarine weapons" (Luraghi 1996:69). It is important to understand that reliance on technical innovation was not simply a side issue in Mallory's overall strategy; rather, it was at its core. Mallory was well versed in the recent progress in maritime technology and, according to one contemporary, was responsible for the initiation of Confederate submarine warfare (Luraghi 1996:236). "To hold that this evolution influenced his strategy understates the case. In reality, technology affected Confederate naval strategy in its very bases and ground rules, in the cardinal point upon which the talented secretary built it: technology would be the tool that appeared to offer a breath of hope in facing a war that otherwise would be hopeless or lost before it began" (Luraghi 1996:61).

Although submarine weapons were one of Mallory's fourfold elements in his hope of technical surprise, his intentions lay with the development of torpedoes (or mines, as we call them today) rather than with submersible boats. Clearly, Southern innovation is no better illustrated than in its development of torpedo warfare, through which these examples of "Rebel barbarity" were forged into a "formidable strategy" (Schafer 1996:3,180). Even when they didn't cause havoc with vessel destruction, they caused the Union fleets to proceed with caution. In the end, torpedoes were remarkably successful, causing more destruction to Union vessels than did Confederate warships (Schafer 1996:12). But mines are largely passive instruments, drifting ambuscades. To wrest control of the seas, the Confederacy had to take the offensive, and this meant either self-propelled torpedoes in the modern sense or the delivery of the torpedo by a submersible vessel. The Confederacy worked to develop both.

The Union made the first attempt at a submarine, and although it developed the famed submersible the Intelligent Whale, Northern submarine development was thwarted by an indifference to underwater warfare induced by its domination of the surface (Luraghi 1996:251). Submarines were left to the South, and the South went at it at the Tredegar Iron Works in Richmond, Virginia, the Leed's Foundry in New Orleans, Louisiana, the Park and Lyon's Machine Shops in Mobile, Alabama, and the Confederate naval facilities at Selma, Alabama (Wills 1998:24).

The *Hunley* was the product of two earlier prototypes, the *Pioneer* and the *American Diver,* built by a team of machinists and businessmen who began their efforts at Leed's Yard in New Orleans, perhaps as early as August 1861. The machinists were Baxter Watson and James McClintock. These practical men were joined by entrepreneurs Horace L. Hunley, John K. Scott, Robert Ruffin Barrow, and Henry J. Leovy. The core of this group was McClintock and Hunley. They kept the dream of a fully submersible submarine alive after numerous failures. Their first attempt, the *Pioneer,* was made of quarter-inch iron plate, about 34 ft long, 4 ft at the beam, and 4 ft in depth. Shaped somewhat like a cigar, the main body, where four men propelled the vessel with a hand crank, was about 10 ft in length. From this 10-ft central section the vessel tapered to a conical bow and stern (Ragan 1995:20). The *Pioneer* gained notoriety and a Letter of Marque by successfully sinking a schooner and two target barges using a towed torpedo in Lake Pontchartrain in February 1862 (Wills 1998:24). Its potentially deadly future was cut short when New Orleans fell to the North and the vessel had to be abandoned. McClintock, Watson, and Hunley made their way to Mobile, Alabama. At Thomas Park and Thomas Lyons's machine shop, they met Lieutenant William Alexander, who was instructed by the Confederate army to assist them in their next venture.

The second effort at a submersible was funded entirely by Horace Hunley. Using the success of the *Pioneer* as a starting point, the machinist innovators experimented with the propulsion system in the form of, amazingly, an electromagnetic engine. Though this engine did not work, it gives us a measure of their advanced thinking (Ragan 1995:22). Next they tried steam. Historian Mark Ragan points out that although many others criticized their attempts at steam propulsion in a submersible craft, these machinists were steam-gauge manufactures by civilian trade and must have known something about their chances of success. Though their steam-propulsion effort failed, they were eventually vindicated by the French, who successfully operated a steam submarine after the Civil War (Ragan 1995:24). Finally, the team settled on a hand-cranked propeller turned by four men. The vessel, known as either *Pioneer II* or the *American Diver,* was about 36–40 ft in length, 3.5 ft in the beam and 4 ft in depth (Wills 1998:25). This vessel had two major problems. First, four men could not crank hard enough to gain sufficient speed to maneuver against an enemy vessel. Second, its armament consisted of a towed torpedo similar to that of the *Pioneer.* The sub had to dive under an enemy vessel, its crew hoping that the towed torpedo would hit its victim. Before the inventors could find solutions to these problems, the *Pioneer* sunk in Mobile Bay and could not be recovered.

Undaunted (or at least only slightly daunted), the team looked for more funds for another attempt. At this time, Mobile, Alabama, saw the formation of a group of entrepreneurs seeking to take advantage of the Confederate government's offer of 50 percent of the value of all Federal vessels destroyed to the privateers who sank the vessels. The leader of this group was E. C. Singer, whose uncle was the inventor of the Singer sewing machine and who himself was the innovator of the Singer underwater contact mine (Ragan 1995:26). The Singer Submarine Corps invested in the McClintock team's next adventure, with Hunley once again adding funds. The new vessel would eventually be named after its financier and champion, Horace Hunley.

Historical sources regarding the *Hunley*'s design are vague, but from what is known, it was the next logical step in the designs used previously but incorporated new innovations based on experiences with the two prototypes. Memories of the *Hunley* indicate that it was from 30 to 40 ft in length, between 4 and 3.5 ft at the beam, and between 4 and 5 ft in depth (Wills 1998:29). The 1996 assessment expedition found that it is 39 ft, 5 in, in length; 3 ft, 10 in, at the beam; and 4 ft, 3 in, in depth. Unlike the previous two subs, the *Hunley* was built from a cylindrical steam boiler rather than plate metal. The inventors cut the boiler longitudinally, inserting two 12-in boiler-iron strips in her sides. Both bow and stern tapered smoothly to wedge-shaped ends. Near each end, a bulkhead formed water-ballast tanks to raise and sink the vessel. The tanks operated by opening seacocks that flooded them for diving. A force pump ejected the water for surfacing. Movement up and down was performed by lateral diving planes, which pivoted like airplane flaps to direct the submerged vessel.

Propulsion, still a problem, was partially solved by a larger crew of eight, who still hand-cranked an ordinary propeller. Men sat on the port side and cranked the shaft bracketed to the opposite wall. There was so little room inside that it was impossible to pass from fore to aft, so half the crew entered from a forward hatch and the other half from the rear. Outside, the propeller connection to the shaft was guarded by a wrought-iron ring. The commander sat in the forward hatch, navigated using a compass, controlled the diving planes and rudder, and watched a mercury gauge that gave some general indication of depth below the surface. Just behind the fore hatch was a snorkel box, to allow some air from the surface while running submerged (Ragan 1995:26).

The team initially experimented with a towed torpedo, as this system had been somewhat successful in Mobile Bay. But in rough waters the torpedo became as dangerous to the *Hunley* as it was to its prey, so a new system was devised. Exactly how the new system worked is not known. A boom with a socket torpedo was used, however, and attached somewhere on the bow (Wills 1998:30). With this configuration, the *Hunley* would ram, securing the torpedo in its victim, and then back away. The attached torpedo was detonated by a lanyard.

The shallow waters of Mobile Bay were less than ideal hunting grounds for the *Hunley* and permission was secured to move the vessel to Charleston, where Confederate general Pierre Gustave Toutant Beauregard welcomed its arrival on August 12, 1863 (Ragan 1995:35). At Charleston it underwent further testing. The history of the *Hunley* in Charleston is as fascinating and incredible as any human adventure. Twice during trials the vessel sunk. In the first instance, five crew members were lost, and the second claimed the life of Horace Hunley and many of the experienced mechanics who had been with the team in Mobile (Wills 1998:32). Since by this time the Confederate army had full control of the *Hunley*, the new team was led by Lieutenant George Dixon, who would command the *Hunley* on its historic mission. Under Dixon's command, a new crew began a rigorous training program on Sullivan's Island, South Carolina, which was in fact the first submariner's school in the world (Luraghi 1996:256). The crew endured a physical training regime and long hours in the sub. Once, the crew survived a 2-hour-and-25-minute submersion at the bottom of Back Bay, South Carolina (Ragan 1995:120–122). By December 1863 they were ready, and General Beauregard issued orders for them to begin operations against the Federal fleet.

Discovery

Exactly what happened that night of February 17, 1864, is clouded in speculation as documentary sources are contradictory, most being later reminiscences rather than contemporary records. The sheer genius of this vessel continues to be better appreciated as historians and archaeologists search tenaciously for new documents. The murky interpretations resulting from these documents could be clarified by the incontrovertible facts of archaeological excavation, as the *Hunley* has been found.

In May 1995 the *Hunley* was discovered, but controversy will probably continue as long as it exists. Several groups and individuals searched for the *Hunley* after its loss. The Union fleet dragged for it during the war while assessing the damage to the *Housatonic* (Ragan 1995:156). Again in 1872 and 1873, the U.S. government searched the area. Exactly who was the first in modern times to search for and discover the *Hunley* is one of many controversial issues that continue to be debated. One individual claims to have found it and/or the *Housatonic* in 1970 and filed for their discovery in Federal court (Ragan 1995:204–203). Another claims to have started his search in 1974 (*Hunley* Project web page 1997). Fiction author Clive Cussler and the South Carolina Institute of Archaeology and Anthropology (SCIAA) jointly and unsuccessfully searched for it in 1980–1981 and again in 1994. This set the stage for its confirmed discovery in 1995 by the National Underwater and Marine Agency (NUMA), Cussler's nonprofit foundation, which searches for shipwrecks (Hall and Wilbanks 1996). Inevitably, with such intense interest by salvors, archaeologists, and adventurers, the sensational underwater discovery soon created a storm of charges and countercharges, which the media happily devoured.

During these exchanges, the SCIAA, the state agency responsible for South Carolina's underwater antiquities, was a highly visible target of much of the acrimony. Although often frustrating and sometimes amusing for its staff, the professional and legal responsibilities that kept the institute from entering the fray were played out in the press, on the Internet, and in various popular publications. The archaeological community was not always unaffected by this rancor either. In the confusing days immediately after the discovery, the institute attempted to organize a committee of experts into a "*Hunley* Project Working Group," its duties being to advise the institute regarding the vessel's protection and preservation. While some colleagues were genuinely concerned with the *Hunley* and were enthusiastic and helpful, others were hesitant and dissembling when asked to join the group. It was obvious that they did not wish to commit themselves until it was clear where the institute would emerge in the perceived political power struggle among various public and private factions.

Frankly, the SCIAA was momentarily caught flatfooted by the worldwide attention resulting from the announcement and the deep rancor developing among the various parties competing for discovery credit. The initial and immediate problem was determining legal responsibility, and that depended on the vessel's location, which was not known because Cussler refused to turn over coordinates to the institute. If the vessel was located in state waters as suspected, the underfunded institute was now the manager of what the media were calling the nation's most important underwater find of the decade, a find demanding the utmost in continual protection from rediscovery by looters.

To the institute at least, their responsibilities were clear, if widely misunderstood. Under national antiquity law, the vessel belonged to the U.S. government, specifically the General Services Administration. The Abandoned Shipwreck Act and the National Historic Preservation Act placed local responsibility with the State Historic Preservation Office (SHPO). In South Carolina, active management of underwater resources rested at that time with the institute, with SHPO oversight and cooperation as defined by the state's underwater act and a memorandum of agreement between the SHPO and the institute. Immediately after the announced discovery, the institute contacted the Naval Historical Center and began a collegial dialogue, including development of a draft memorandum for the vessel's security and possible recovery. Informed of the pending agreement, South Carolina's attorney general ordered the institute to cease negotiations with the navy and also cease any further discussions with Cussler. Only 10 days after the discovery, state representatives introduced a concurrent resolution in the state legislature to create the South Carolina *Hunley* Commission, which would seek state ownership from the federal government and—critically for the institute—the commission was to become the ultimate state authority over the *Hunley*. When the bill passed later that month, it left both the institute and the State Historic Preservation Office in a perplexing situation. Did a state resolution legally absolve state agencies with federal oversight of their federal preservation responsibilities? Amid this great excitement and rapidly changing events, the subtle changes in authority were not clear to the stimulated public and concerned professional colleagues, who demanded action from the institute. Despite demands, all through the following year the commission's authority solidified, and the institute's duties became clearly defined when the state attorney general issued an informal opinion that the institute's role was *only* that which it was assigned by the commission (Cook 1996).

Throughout 1995 and into 1996, interest in the future of the *Hunley* continued to intensify. The state commission, with the assistance of South Carolina's national congressional representatives, vigorously sought ownership, and bills were introduced in the U.S. House and Senate to convey title to the state. Representatives from Alabama also sought to have the vessel displayed, when eventually raised, in Mobile (Neyland and Amer 1998:8). As federal interests were arranged, the Naval Historical Center became the lead organization acting on behalf of the General Services Administration. Naturally, they sought advice from an oversight committee consisting of the Advisory Council for Historic Preservation, the National Park Service, the National Oceanic and Atmospheric Administration, and the Smithsonian. Although the summer of 1995 saw negotiations breaking down between South Carolina and the federal government, the fall brought increased cooperation. In October, Cussler released the coordinates of his find to the Naval Historical Center.

With the location now known, in November 1995 the Commission and the Naval Historical Center decided to jointly oversee an expedition to verify the discovery and assess the vessel's condition. This project was jointly led by the institute on behalf of the state commission and the Submerged Cultural Resources Unit of the National Park Service on behalf of the federal government. One year after its discovery, the institute and the Park Service made the first scientific assessment of it (Murphy et al. 1998). The expedition partially uncovered the *Hunley*, providing an initial look at this long-sought artifact. One important finding was recognition of its advanced hydrodynamic design. Drawings of the *Hunley* indicated a rather blocky, blunt, crude design, but the expedition revealed a sleek, thin, tubular vessel designed for submerged running. Hatch portholes were found only on the port side and deadlights ran along the top between the hatches. The only damage seen was to the forward hatch; a hole was found where there should have been a forward-facing viewport. The ragged hole adds fuel to the continuing debate about the *Hunley*'s demise.

Cooperation between the National Park Service and the institute in the field, with joint oversight by the state commission and the U.S. Navy, resulted in a successful expedition in spite of intense media scrutiny and vocal naysayers. This effort went a long way toward ironing out misunderstandings between federal and state interests. Eventually, in August 1996 the commission and the navy signed a Programmatic Memorandum of Agreement (PMOA), giving title to the federal government, while the state had control over the *Hunley*'s fate, including its future interpretation (Memorandum 1996). The final PMOA was remarkably similar in overall content to that initially drafted by the institute and the navy.

Confederate Icon

Control of the *Hunley*'s future now rests in the hands of South Carolina's *Hunley* Commission and the federal government's Naval Historical Center. These two agencies, but especially the commission, exert a powerful control over the vessel's recovery, conservation, and display. The navy's mission is clear—to make sure that recovery and conservation are done correctly. The commission shares that responsibility and desire, but it has another concern that goes far beyond the *Hunley* as an archaeological artifact. Indeed, the controversy surrounding the *Hunley*'s discovery and the commission's actions must be understood in a much broader sense. The *Hunley* is no mere sensational archaeological find. Yes, it is a unique example of military engineering and an invaluable artifact of naval history and military technology. It is apparently in excellent condition—literally a time capsule encased in shell and sand—and our knowledge of submarine history will be greatly enhanced by its conservation and display. These facts alone make it a national treasure. But while significant, these facts may be secondary to its meaning to the modern South and the struggle for the *Hunley*'s interpretation. This struggle will bring to practical application all realms of political and philosophical discourse concerning who owns and who controls the past, since the *Hunley* may become the new icon of southern heritage.

The historiography of Southern history is as fascinating as the history of the South. Through each generation, historians of the South have sought to define and explain southern history and, by extension, its ultimate expression in the Confederacy. The question of how we interpret the South and the interrelated question of how we interpret the Civil War have been at the core of historical scholarship since 1865. The changing responses to these questions go far in defining each succeeding generation (Pressly 1965). Even the appellations used for the war of 1861–1865 are demonstrative of these changing meanings. The war of the rebellion, the War between the States, the needless war, the irrepressible war, and now, most often, the Civil War—all these epithets offer sometimes subtle but more often distinctly different interpretations of the "late unpleasantness." Today it is safe to say that the dominant paradigm, in academia at least, emphasizes the issues of slavery and race. Today the Civil War is interpreted as the war to end slavery, a perspective supported by noted historians such as James McPherson, Richard H. Sewell, David M. Potter, and William J. Copper (Toplin 1996:29). Indeed, regardless of initial causes, it cannot be debated that from the moment of Lincoln's Emancipation Proclamation, the war became the war to end slavery in America (Smith 1994:5). This perspective was not always dominant but gained strength as the civil rights movement informed political and social change beginning in the 1950s. Today in academia, the slavery issue and the African American experience are manifest in almost all aspects of historical and social study disciplines. In archaeology this focus is expressed in studies of slave life, plantations, and the whole issue now being labeled as the African Diaspora (see McDavid and Babson 1997). Based on paper and symposium titles from the 1998 Society for Historical Archaeology annual meeting, for instance, 85 of the 396 papers presented, or 21 percent, dealt with African Americans, Diaspora, race, or slavery. The effect of this focus is, naturally, a decided avoidance of any aspects defined as traditional Southern culture, and of things Confederate. Back in 1969, Frank E. Vandiver wrote, "Currently the tide of historical interpretation is running against the Confederacy," pointing to scholars' avoidance of defending the Confederacy and especially its position on the institution of slavery. Vandiver added that "even Southern historians have shied away from a positive approach" (Vandiver 1969:148). Certainly this is even more apropos today.

Today academe seeks to project its paradigms into the public arena. Regarding the current paradigm, it does so by revising educational materials, by controlling government-sponsored research through revision of the requirements of grants-in-aid, by revising national historical contexts, and by revising the focus of federal and state park battlefield interpretation. Curiously, while there are numerous examples of academe's success, there is also a public countermovement diverging from academe's interpretations of the past. The war, as Shelby Foote has so well stated, is for Americans at "the crossroads of our being" (Cullen 1995:2), and with its multilayered complexity, it is difficult for the public's interest to be completely channeled. Spurred by Ken Burns's monumental film, public interest in the Civil War is at a peak not seen since the centennial. This interest seems—at least in South Carolina and, I would venture, throughout the South—focused on the war itself rather than on its ideological causes and effects. Contrary to academe, this perspective largely avoids divisive racial issues. Public interest is focused on the fate of the common man, both black and white, during the Civil War. The most visible manifestation of this interest is the rapid growth of black and white reenactor organizations. It is heartening to see black and white men and women work side by side to preserve a "memory" of the war that acknowledges but does not exploit or focus on the race issue. This public does not deny slavery or the horrors of racism but rather appears to want to focus on understanding what happened to *people*, not their underlying hatreds. The result is a healing and an interaction worthy of encouragement. There are other manifestations of this movement that can be easily gleaned on the Internet from an increasing number of institutions focusing on the Civil War, such as the United States Civil War center at Louisiana State University, which proclaims a "pro-truth, anti-agenda" philosophy (http://www.cwc.lsu.edu). Further, Civil War magazines, roundtables, and discussion groups are stronger than ever. This renewed interest has also strengthened an undercurrent of renewed defense of southern cultural traditions, again both black and white, and within the latter, strongly figures the Confederate traditions of honor and chivalry. Evidence of this is seen in the sustaining of Southern fraternal organizations such as the Sons and Daughters of Confederate Veterans.

Public interest in the war and its military aspects also runs counter to academe's growing bias against military history. The study of military history has "always been something of a pariah in U.S. Universities," and it faces an increasingly "hostile environment" (Lynn 1997:777–778). From a peak around 1970, interest in academic military history continues to drop, and "two major universities—Michigan and Wisconsin—have recently virtually abandoned the field" (Coffman 1997:775). This attitude "ignore[s] a literate lay audience that consistently has manifested an interest in the Civil War" (Gallagher 1996:42). Yet military aspects of the war (especially in the experiences of the common soldier) continue to attract the public, and again the interest extends into studies of the Confederate army. It would be wrong to state that this interest is totally ignored by universities. University presses today actively compete for and publish new works on the Civil War, especially diaries and war reminiscences. But when the Confederacy is discussed, it is usually about its military aspects. Also, as often as not, the authors of these works are outside academe. Regardless of source, these books are rapidly and avidly purchased by the public. It is virtually impossible to keep up with the literature as one pursues specialty book catalogs. Recent works on the *Hunley* or works including chapters on the *Hunley* are perfect examples of this trend (Campbell 1996; Kloeppel 1992; Ragan 1995; Schafer 1996).

It is within this context of divergent interests that the *Hunley*'s interpretation will be debated and its iconography will be established in the future, for the *Hunley* has been found at a unique period in South Carolina's history. It is widely known that South Carolina has the distinction of flying the Confederate battle flag over its statehouse. The public—stirred by media, politicians, and academics—is increasingly divided about its symbolism and meaning, some seeing it as a symbol of racism, others seeing it as a symbol honoring Confederate dead. The pro-flag forces, many of whom are active in Civil War reenactments, are decidedly in the minority and at a disadvantage on this ideological battlefield. Tagged with a flag whose former noble symbolism has been superseded by a history of Jim Crow and KKK hatred, the flag came down in July 2000. In war, the battleground must be chosen to one's advantage, and this battleground is an indefensible position.

Upon this scene of tension and ideological conflict comes the *Hunley*. The *Hunley* represents some of the few positive aspects of the Confederacy that can be proudly touted in a world dominated by a growing dogmatic, decidedly anti-Confederate, intelligentsia. The *Hunley* represents the underdog against a formidable foe. It represents Confederate innovation and invention. It represents youthful independent American ingenuity against the old-established order of Northeastern industrialism. Indeed, it *is* a shining example of human bravery in the face of overwhelming odds. No matter what one's ideological stripe, one has to stand in awe of the courage it took to enter a tiny 3-ft-10-in-by-4-ft iron tube—a tube that had already cost the lives of at least 13 people—and sail out on an open sea with little hope of return. The *Hunley* is an icon of the Confederacy that the battle flag can no longer be. Those defending the flag, the South, and the Confederacy need the *Hunley*. The *Hunley* Commission, made up mostly of Sons of Confederate Veterans, understands its importance. For this reason, they have repeatedly made it clear that they want total control over the interpretive displays for the *Hunley*. What they fear most is a Smithsonian revision of the Confederacy reminiscent of recent controversies surrounding the *Enola Gay* display (Harwit 1996; Minutes, October 11, South Carolina *Hunley* Commission).

The *Hunley*'s iconography is much broader than Confederate innovation and bravery, and includes just about all aspects of Confederate dialectic. Foremost is the issue of states' rights. During the yearlong negotiations with the federal government, this issue was at the heart of negotiations over the question of *Hunley* ownership. At one point, a commission member stated in a semiserious tone that South Carolina had once before gone to war over the issue, and would do so again. Although the senator's statement was taken as the humorous *bon mot* that was intended, the senator was wrong. South Carolina twice has gone to "war" over the issue. The second time was in April 1961 during the commemoration of the Civil War centennial at Fort Sumter in Charleston, South Carolina. The U.S. Civil War Centennial Commission, established by Congress, arranged a ceremony at Fort Sumter. Among the "national assembly" was an African American representative from New Jersey, who reported that she was denied a room at a Charleston hotel. State commissions from several Northern states said they would not take part in the ceremonies in protest of this treatment, and the president of the United States announced that the ceremonies would take place at the nonsegregated U.S. Naval Yard. On cue, the South Carolina Centennial Commission seceded from the national commission, and Charleston became the host of two centennial meetings (Pressly 1964:8). With regard to the *Hunley*, it is extremely doubtful that South Carolina would actually secede. It was clear from the negotiations, however, that the situation was serious, and both U.S. senators and at least one U.S. representative worked behind the scenes to ensure that the state and the commission became a full partner with the Naval Historical Center in shaping the *Hunley*'s future.

Beyond states' rights and Confederate symbols, the *Hunley* will continue to swirl in controversial waters. As this is being written, archaeologists working for the commission and the navy are diving on the 6.67-ton *Hunley* in preparation for its raising. By the time this essay is read, the *Hunley* may be in its conservation tank, awash in a mixture of chemicals designed to preserve it forever. If so, the commission and the navy are to be congratulated. They would be the first to raise a whole Civil War vessel successfully, and their efforts would go a long way toward erasing the memory of the broken *Cairo,* a gunboat that collapsed during its raising from the Mississippi River (Bearss 1980). Another issue is the *Hunley*'s contents. It is possible that it contains not only valuable archaeological information but also human remains. The *Hunley* is a war grave. Reburial and repatriation concerns have not been at the forefront of the debate, but they are an undercurrent that could add to the tension surrounding the vessel's future.

Still another problem will be keeping public interest in the project while conservation drags on. The conservation process is estimated to take up to ten years. This brings us back to the control of the *Hunley*'s meaning. Can the commission keep the *Hunley*'s iconography alive long enough for its second raising—the one that will take it out of the conservation tank and to the display room? Will they be able to control its interpretation in a world increasingly hostile to all things Confederate? What is the future of Confederate history? Luraghi, in his exhaustive study of the Confederate navy, concluded that "the Confederates showed an outstanding sagacity not only in creating new war tools but in using them in exceptional and creative ways so as to transform them from technical curiosities into tested elements that would change radically and forever the conduct of war at sea" (Luraghi 1996:346). This much can be said of the commission: it too has the sagacity displayed by the Confederate naval program and the tools to succeed in raising and conserving the vessel. But the ultimate question is how will their *Hunley* be remembered? Can a submarine become what a battle flag cannot—the icon of southern heritage?

15 Years Later

The essay above was written a little over 15 years ago amid swirling controversy and uncertainty as to the *Hunley*'s fate as a Civil War artifact. Much of the fiery rhetoric expressed by *Hunley* champions and naysayers at the time of the vessel's discovery has thankfully abated, but currents still run under a calm surface. If I may be permitted to continue the sea metaphor: like a surfer staring at a shark fin I find it reasonable to anticipate that the *Hunley* will continue to incite controversy amid the present five-year run of sesquicentennial events commemorating (or revising and refighting) the Civil War (2011–2015). As I seek here to update the past 10 years of *Hunley* research and its continuing iconography, it remains clear that the *Hunley* is still a vessel at war.

First, the *Hunley* Commission's amazing success must be acknowledged. Against high political odds and incredible logistical challenges, the *Hunley* came home in August 2000. The commission created a 501(c)(3), the Friends of the *Hunley,* Inc. (http://www.hunley.org/), to assist in fundraising for the recovery, conservation, and ultimate exhibition of this historic vessel. With a host of collaborators, divers, and engineers, the commission turned to Oceaneering International, Inc., to raise the *Hunley.* Oceaneering constructed a cradle, raised the *Hunley,* and brought it to shore amid the cheers of thousands of enthusiastic boaters and sightseers lined along Charleston Harbor (Chaffin 2008:221–222) (Figure 1). Today the *Hunley* resides safely at the Warren Lasch Conservation Center in North Charleston (Figure 2). The *Hunley*'s interior was found to be filled with sediment, which has been painstakingly excavated through the last twelve years (Figure 3). The remains of its eight crew members, found in an excellent state of

Figure 1. (top) The *Hunley* breaks the surface again after 136 years. Courtesy of the South Carolina Institute of Archaeology and Anthropology.

Figure 2. A computer-generated illustration of the inside of the Hunley after excavation. Courtesy of Friends of the *Hunley*.

Figure 3. The *Hunley* in its cradle and being sprayed during transport to land. Courtesy of the South Carolina Institute of Archaeology and Anthropology.

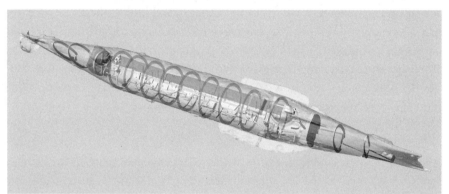

preservation, were reburied in 2004 with full military honors, next to previous *Hunley* crews. Some 30,000–40,000 people attended various memorial events during the week in which the remains were laid to rest (Jacobsen et al. 2005:14). Meanwhile, conservation of the vessel continues. Archaeologists and conservators have learned as much about conservation techniques as they have about the *Hunley*. Indeed, the conservation technology used has been cutting edge, thanks to a combination of private donations and federal and state support.

It was the latter source of funding that saw another *Hunley* battle. In 2006 the *State* newspaper in Columbia ran a series of articles questioning the cost of the *Hunley*'s recovery and conservation to South Carolina taxpayers. State Senator Glenn McConnell, chair of the *Hunley* Commission, defended the expenses in the *State,* and the story soon lost traction. At least part of the reason was the support McConnell has provided the state senate's black caucus and a promise to secure state lottery funds for South Carolina's historically black colleges (Chaffin 2008:252–253; *Journal of Blacks in Higher Education* 2006:35). In any case, state support is only a small part of the overall effort contributing to the *Hunley*'s successful recovery and conservation. A large part is the result of a wise effort by *Hunley* organizers to draw together a diverse coalition of contributors, including the Department of Defense, the Legacy Resource Management Program, the National Park Service, the National Geographic Society, the Naval Historical Center, the Smithsonian Institution, the South Carolina Department of Archives and History, the South Carolina Institute of Archaeology and Anthropology, Clemson University, the College of Charleston, Coastal Carolina University, Texas A&M University, the University of Tennessee, and the Charleston Museum, to name just a few (*Blue Light* 2011a:8). Some institutions are providing funds, but many are providing matching services in the form of expertise and equipment use, such as the MRI- and CT-scanning services provided by the Medical University of South Carolina. Less recognized but no less critical are the multiple private and corporate donations that fund the daily expenses of conserving the *Hunley* at the Lasch center. The *Hunley* conservation work is an example of a successful public-private cooperative effort.

In my 2000 essay I expressed doubt about keeping the public's interest during the long process of excavation and conservation. I was wrong; that has not been as serious problem. At this point there seems to be exactly the right amount of public interest. Public tours of the conservation facility to see the conservation in progress continue to be popular with the public and are part of Charleston's tourism attractions. Some 500,000 visitors have visited the Warren Lasch Conservation Center to view the *Hunley*. This visitation rivals many well-known museums in the United States and is testimony to the public's support (*Blue Light* 2010a:7). School groups regularly tour the *Hunley,* and study units about the *Hunley* are available on the web for teachers. South Carolinians who are seriously interested in the *Hunley* can purchase state license plates to show their support. They can join the Friends of the *Hunley* and receive newsletters and updates (*Blue Light*). At the same time, the *Hunley* is no longer the focus of constant media attention. The news, when the *Hunley* is news, is generally positive.

Keeping the public's attention alive has been enhanced by the slow excavation of the vessel's interior, and with each spoonful of sediment, new discoveries have added to our knowledge of its innovative character. The submarine is 40 ft long, with tapered ends and two cylindrical conning towers fore and aft, 16 ft, 3 in apart. The towers are equipped with glass viewing ports and hatch covers sealed with rubber gaskets. The submarine's navigation system consists of a long rod running from fore to aft to the rudder, connected to a vertical rod like a joystick. This turned the vessel port and starboard. Another lever operated two dive planes to raise and lower the vessel in the water.

As noted in the original essay, the vessel was armed with a single torpedo (bomb) mounted at the end of a 17-ft spar. Recovery of the vessel has revealed that the spar is made of iron, rather than wood, and connected to the submarine at the bottom of the bow. The idea was to ram the torpedo into an enemy vessel and then back off, leaving the torpedo attached to its target by a barbed tip. Once the *Hunley* was a safe distance away from the enemy ship, a line linking the torpedo to the submarine was pulled to detonate the torpedo.

The interior consists of three compartments, separated by iron bulkheads and consisting of a forward ballast tank, crew compartment, and aft ballast tank (*Blue Light* 2003:3). The ballast tanks have separate pumps, but they are also connected by a pipe allowing them to be filled simultaneously. Each tank has a seacock open to the sea and the vessel was submerged by filling the ballast tanks. To rise to the surface, the crew used hand pumps to empty the water in the tanks.

A bellows system, mounted on the hull, replenished the air in the vessel. It consisted of wood, leather, and rubber components, which have made conservation a challenge (Jacobsen et al. 2005:16). Along the bottom of the vessel's crew compartment, from the forward to the aft ballast tanks, were strewn some 100 loose pig-iron ballast blocks weighing 4,453 lbs (*Blue Light* 2010b:5; Jacobsen et al. 2005:15). These were probably placed as needed to trim the vessel. In the forward section where Lieutenant Dixon sat, archaeologists found a metal tube containing mercury, indicating its function as a depth gauge. The crew sat on one side of the vessel on a pine plank and cranked a shaft that ran the length of the crew compartment to propel the vessel forward.

There has been strong interest in the *Hunley*'s crew. Seven of the crew members' remains were found on the floor of the submarine, indicating that they died at their stations. Lieutenant Dixon's remains were found in the forward section below the forward hatch at his station; however, his remains were found trapped by mud and sitting slightly upright. Stable isotope analyses indicate that half the crew were born in the United States, but the other half were foreign born and probably from northern Europe (Jacobsen et al. 2005:9). Through a combination of historic and archaeological research, the remains of seven crew members have been matched to known individuals. The eighth crew member's name has not been confirmed. Facial reconstructions have been completed and are on display at the Warren Lasch Conservation Center. Personal artifacts found in the submarine include pocket knives, clothing remnants and buttons, eight canteens, shoes, and leather belts. Also found was the ID tag of Ezra Chamberlain, a private in the Seventh Connecticut. Research revealed that Chamberlain was killed in action on Morris Island, and the tag must have been a battlefield souvenir (http://hunley.org/main_index.asp?CONTENT=IDTAG).

One of the most exciting finds from the public's perspective was a $20 gold coin engraved with the words "Shiloh, April 6th, 1862, My life Preserver, G.E.D." in four lines. The coin had been warped by a blunt impact and confirms the story that Dixon's life was saved when a bullet hit the coin in his pocket at the Battle of Shiloh. Indeed, forensic evidence of the bullet wound was found on Dixon's upper left femur (Jacobsen et al. 2005:9). Besides the coin, a compass, the depth gauge, wrenches, nuts and bolts, a whip staff, and tiller were found with Dixon (*Blue Light* 2011b:5).

Researchers still do not know what sank the *Hunley*. It is expected that more clues will be revealed as the exterior of the submarine is better exposed and conserved. Upon recovery, a large hole on the port side of the forward conning tower led to speculation that the *Hunley* had been hit by fire from the *Housatonic* or was damaged when the torpedo exploded. However, in 2003 divers found a nineteenth-century grappling hook that may have been used after the war in an attempt to find the *Hunley* (*Blue Light* 2009:8). The hook could have caused the hole in the tower. There are two more holes in the *Hunley*, one on the starboard side at the aft ballast tank and the other at the forward ballast tank on the same side (Jacobsen et al. 2012:3). Careful analyses, combining a geological study of the sediments inside the hull, the location of the holes, and experimental archaeology, indicate that the holes are actually the result of a combination of corrosion and the scouring of sand against the hull as a result of tidal currents. In other words, the holes were not the result of any battle-related damages (Jacobsen et al. 2012:9). Twelve years later, so much more is known about the *Hunley*, but there is still much to learn.

In 2000 I ended my *Hunley* essay with the question, "Can a submarine become what a battle flag cannot—the icon of southern heritage?" Within South Carolina, and especially around Charleston, I think the answer is: yes, it has already. Many South Carolinians are proud of the *Hunley* and the efforts of the commission. Those who still dissent on the basis of its recovery costs or its increasingly problematic Southern heritage should at least by now see it as an archaeological treasure in its own right.

Of course, the *Hunley* will never heal the deep wounds of the Civil War or mitigate the state's continuing flag controversy. At this moment, the divisions seem even deeper, and thus the *Hunley* remains a flash point. I have met few people since 2000 who are indifferent about the *Hunley*. This has been demonstratively brought home to me from the reactions to my original essay. It has been popularly received and lauded. But it has also evoked strong negative reactions from some in academe. This is understandable, given that one point of the essay was to illustrate modern trends in the teaching of the Civil War, how these trends continue to diverge from the public's interests in the war, and how this divergence is reflected in reactions to the *Hunley* then, now, and in the future. The *Hunley* will continue to play an important iconographic role, both positive and negative, in the ongoing reshaping of South Carolina history, just as the "late unpleasantness" continues to haunt us.

References Cited

Bearss, Edwin C.

 1980 *Hardluck Ironclad: The Sinking and Salvaging of the Cairo.* Louisiana State University Press, Baton Rouge.

The Blue Light: The Official Newsletter of the Friends of the Hunley

 2003 Excavation Update. Vol. 10 (November):3.

 2009 Grappling Hook. Vol. 33/34 (Fall/Winter):8.

 2010a Historical Awareness. Vol. 36 (Fall):7.

 2010b The Hunley's Ballast Block System. Vol. 35 (Summer):5.

 2011a Institutional Fellows. Vol. 37 (Winter):8.

 2011b Why Is Dixon's Station Suspicious? Vol. 40 (Winter):5.

Campbell, R. Thomas

 1996 *Gray Thunder: Exploits of the Confederate Navy.* Burd Street Press, Shippensburg, Pennsylvania.

Chaffin, Tom

 2008 *The H. L. Hunley: The Secret Hope of the Confederacy.* Hill and Wang, New York.

Coffman, Edward M.

 1997 The Course of Military History in the United States since World War II. *Journal of Military History* 61:761–775.

Cook, Robert F., assistant deputy attorney general of South Carolina

 1996 Informal opinion to Glenn F. McConnell, state senator, April 16.

Cullen, Jim

 1995 *The Civil War in Popular Culture: A Reusable Past.* Smithsonian Institution Press, Washington, D.C.

Friends of the *Hunley*

 2012 Website. http://www.hunley.org. Accessed June 20.

Gallagher, Gary W.

 1996 How Familiarity Bred Success: Military Campaigns and Leaders in Ken Burns' "The Civil War." In *Ken Burns' "The Civil War": Historians Respond,* edited by Robert Brent Toplin, 37–59. Oxford University Press.

Genovese, Eugene D.

 1965 *The Political Economy of Slavery: Studies in the Economy and Society of the Slave South.* Pantheon Books, New York.

Hall, West, and Ralph Wilbanks

 1995 Search for the Confederate Submarine H. L. Hunley off Charleston Harbor, South Carolina. National Underwater Marine Agency. Submitted to the Naval Historical Center, Washington Naval Yard, Washington, D.C.

Harwit, Martin

 1996 *An Exhibit Denied: Lobbying the History of the Enola Gay.* Copernicus Books, New York.

Hunley Project Web Page

 1997 http://members.aol.com/litespdcom/index.html

Jacobsen, Maria, V. Y. Blouin, and W. Shirley

 2005 *H. L. Hunley Project: 2004 Archaeological Findings and Progress Report.* Legacy Resource Management Program, Department of Defense, Washington, D.C.

 2012 Does Erosion Corrosion Account for Intriguing Damage to the Hull of the Civil War Submarine H. L. Hunley? *Proceedings of the 2012 International Marine Forensics Symposium.* American Society of Naval Engineers, Marine Technology Society, and Society of Naval Architects and Marine Engineers, National Harbor, Maryland, April 3–5.

Journal of Blacks in Higher Education

 2006 How a Confederate Navy Submarine Restoration Project Helped Support Black Colleges and Universities. Summer, no. 52:35.

Kloeppel, James E.

 1992 *Danger Beneath the Waves: A History of the Confederate Submarine H. L. Hunley.* Sandlapper Publishing, Orangeburg, South Carolina.

Luraghi, Raimondo

 1996 *A History of the Confederate Navy.* Translated by Paolo E. Coletta. Naval Institute Press, Annapolis, Maryland.

Lynn, John A.

 1997 The Embattled Future of Academic Military History. *Journal of Military History* 61:777–789.

McDavid, Carol, and David W. Babson (editors)

 1997 In the Realm of Politics: Prospects for Public Participation in African-American and Plantation Archaeology. *Historical Archaeology* 31(3): 1–152.

Murphy, Larry E., Daniel J. Lenihan, Christopher F. Amer, Matthew A. Russell, Robert S. Neyland, Richard Wills, Scott Harris, Adriane Askins, Timothy G. Smith, and Steven M. Shope

 1998 *H. L. Hunley Site Assessment.* A cooperative project of the National Park Service, the Naval Historical Center, and the South Carolina Institute of Archaeology and Anthropology, funded by the South Carolina Hunley Commission and the Department of Defense. Legacy Resources Program, Santa Fe, New Mexico.

Neyland, Robert S., and Christopher F. Amer

 1998 Administrative History. In *H. L. Hunley Site Assessment,* edited by Larry E. Murphy, 5–13. National Park Service, the Naval Historical Center, and the South Carolina Institute of Archaeology and Anthropology, funded by the South Carolina Hunley Commission and the Department of Defense. Legacy Resources Program, Santa Fe, New Mexico.

Pressly, Thomas J.

 1965 *Americans Interpret Their Civil War.* Free Press, New York.

Ragan, Mark K.

 1995 *The Hunley: Submarines, Sacrifice, and Success in the Civil War.* Narwhal Press, Miami.

Schafer, Louis S.

 1996 *Confederate Underwater Warfare: An Illustrated History.* McFarland, Jefferson, North Carolina.

Smith, Steven D.

 1994 Archaeological Perspectives on the Civil War: The Challenge to Achieve Relevance. In *Look to the Earth: Historical Archaeology and the American Civil War,* edited by Clarence R. Geier and Susan E. Winter, 3–20. University of Tennessee Press, Knoxville.

South Carolina *Hunley* Commission

 1996 Minutes, October 11. Copies on file, South Carolina Institute of Archaeology and Anthropology.

Still, William N., Jr.

 1985 *Iron Afloat: The Story of the Confederate Armorclads.* University of South Carolina Press, Columbia.

Toplin, Robert Brent

 1996 Ken Burns' "The Civil War" as an Interpretation of History. In *Ken Burns' "The Civil War": Historians Respond,* edited by Robert Brent Toplin, pp. 17–36. Oxford University Press, New York.

U.S. Civil War Center, Louisiana State University

 Website: http://www.cwc.lsu.edu. November 10, 1997.

Vandiver, Frank E.

    1969   The Confederacy and the American Tradition. In *The Civil War,* edited by William R. Brock, pp. 148–56. Harper and Row, New York.

Wills, Richard

    1998   Historical Context. In *H. L. Hunley Site Assessment,* edited by Larry E. Murphy, 21–36. National Park Service, the Naval Historical Center, and the South Carolina Institute of Archaeology and Anthropology, funded by the South Carolina Hunley Commission and the Department of Defense, Legacy Resources Program, Santa Fe, New Mexico.

Wise, Stephen R.

    1988   *Lifeline of the Confederacy: Blockade Running during the Civil War.* University of South Carolina Press.

CHRISTOPHER F. AMER
AND JAMES D. SPIREK

Exploring the United States Naval Legacy in South Carolina

SOUTH CAROLINA'S COASTLINE EXTENDS some 200 miles from North Carolina to Georgia. Inlets, bays, and estuaries add approximately another third to that distance, making approximately 270 miles of actual shoreline. The sandy, shifting seabed remains shallow, less than 30 ft, out from 3 to 5 miles from the shore and only deepens to twice that depth from 12 to 25 miles offshore. From the sixteenth century on, the inlets and bays of South Carolina's coast were visited by vessels of exploration, colonization, war, and commerce. Many of these early ships failed to negotiate successfully the constantly shifting, often treacherous shallows and became permanent reminders of the dangers of the coastal waters. Some stricken craft were carried ashore in storms, and some were abandoned, while others sank because of the guns of war. Of the hundreds of vessels that sank or were otherwise wrecked on South Carolina's coast, only a few score have been located and investigated by archaeologists. Many of the submerged archaeological sites in the state are not located on the coast but within the 11,000 linear miles of rivers, streams, and navigable waterways that flow through the state.

South Carolina claims title to all constantly inundated land beneath these watercourses and to the ocean bottom of the state's territorial sea (out to the 3-mile limit) pursuant to the Submerged Lands Act of 1953. All told, the area of submerged lands in the state constitutes some 2,873 square miles or 1,838,720 acres. The state also claims title to, and therefore responsibility for, the submerged cultural resources that lie on, or are embedded in, that land. The demands and pressures made on those finite resources, notably historic shipwrecks, are increasing with every passing year. The demands come from several special interest groups, including sport divers, archaeologists, and the historical preservation community, developers, and professional treasure hunters.

The monumental task of managing and protecting these vestiges of our state's maritime past falls to the staff of SCIAA's Maritime Research Division (MRD). With three full-time maritime archaeologists and two archaeological technicians, just locating and inventorying the shipwrecks and other submerged cultural sites is challenging and involves the use of diverse methods and techniques. One of our primary methods of learning about previously undiscovered shipwrecks and other submerged cultural resources is by the sport-diving community. South Carolina is one of the few coastal states that have an active program for managing sport divers and the data they collect. Through SCIAA's Sport Diver Archaeology Management Program (SDAMP), a sport diver may apply for a hobby license, which entitles the diver to collect artifacts and fossils that lie on the surface of the river beds and seafloor. In return for this privilege, each hobby diver is obliged to report his/her findings to the program's manager on a quarterly basis. In the 32 years the program has been in existence, numerous shipwrecks, historic and prehistoric canoes, rice flats and ferries, and colonial dock structures and ship-yards have come to the program's attention through hobby-diver reports. Hobby divers have participated in site-specific investigations such as historic barges in the Waccamaw River (Harris 1992) and themselves conducted regional surveys (Harris et. al. 1993).

Likewise, underwater contractors, working on harbor and channel deep-ening and improvement projects, bridge realignment undertakings, and beach renourishment activities frequently encounter submerged cultural resources in the course of completing their work. Commercial fishermen and shrimpers fre-quently come across ballast piles that are often the only overt manifestations of buried wrecks. Reports of shipwrecks and other submerged or semi-submerged archaeological sites have led MRD researchers to investigations of specific sites—for example, the Malcolm Boat on the Ashley River (Amer et. al. 1997), the In-gram Vessel near Cheraw (Amer et. al. 1995), the Browns Ferry Vessel raised from the Black River in 1976 (Albright and Steffy 1979; Amer 1997b), and a canoe recovered from the Chattooga River in 2004, to name a few.

By far the most costly but most reliable method of locating shipwrecks and other cultural constructs is through archaeological projects and regional surveys. While the ideal situation would be to survey every square mile of submerged lands in the state to locate and record the state's submerged legacy, comprehen-sive funding for such an undertaking is unlikely to be forthcoming. Instead, SCIAA's MRD staff has identified select areas that have a high likelihood of con-taining historic shipwrecks and other vestiges of the state's past to investigate. These relatively small, regional surveys are funded through a variety of sources, including government grants, foundations and other not-for-profit entities, and private donations. During the last 10 years, staff of the MRD have conducted a number of these surveys, which includes surveys of Port Royal Sound and environs (Spirek et. al. 1999), Winyah Bay (Amer 2006), a 43-km (26.7-mile) stretch of the Pee Dee River from the site of the Confederate Mars Bluff Navy Yard to the head of navigation at Cheraw, and several regions containing U.S. Naval shipwrecks, notably Charleston Harbor (Spirek and Amer 2004; Spirek 2012).

The latter survey (Spirek and Amer 2004), which exemplifies both the division's survey strategy and site-specific-investigation techniques in managing the state's submerged cultural heritage, is the concern here.

Navy Wreck Survey

Among the countless wrecked watercraft in state waters lies a body of naval vessels spanning the years from the American Revolution to modern times. From the time when the first keel was laid for a U.S. warship or when the first private vessel was co-opted and converted for naval purposes, the U.S. Navy has had a presence in South Carolina. U.S. warships patrolled the Palmetto State's coastline during the Jeffersonian era and blockaded the ports of Charleston and Georgetown during the Civil War. Aging New England whaling ships and merchant vessels were commissioned into the U.S. Navy during that war and deliberately sunk across Charleston's harbor entrance to enhance the blockade and used as the floating foundation of a warship-repair factory for the South Atlantic Blockading Squadron stationed at Port Royal Sound. During the twentieth century, the U.S. Navy formalized its presence by establishing a navy base, first on Parris Island and then in Charleston, the latter enduring for 95 years until its closing in 1996.

It is hardly surprising that, over the 200-plus years of the navy's presence in the state, that it suffered some losses of their fleet in state waters. The first U.S. Navy ship that met its end in South Carolina was a French-built vessel named *Queen of France,* which was scuttled in 1779 to block the approach to Charleston. The last U.S. Navy ship to be lost was USS *Hector,* a collier that foundered off Cape Romain in 1916. Between these two losses, 46 vessels commissioned by the U.S. Navy made South Carolina their permanent home.

Between 2000 and 2004, working from a grant provided by the Department of Defense Legacy Resource Management Program, the MRD undertook to explore the history and cultural context of each of the 46 naval craft. The first phase of this two-phase project called for compiling historical and cultural data to document United States Navy vessels lost in South Carolina waters. The resultant information included the number of vessels, vessel types, and known shipwreck locations, along with previous salvage or archaeological investigations, natural and cultural threats, and management recommendations for the sites. The Naval Historical Center (now the Naval History and Heritage Command) provided SCIAA with a database of shipwrecks in or near state waters to which the navy laid claim. Using the information amassed during the first phase of the project, MRD staff updated that database to reflect more accurately the status of the naval shipwrecks in state waters.

The second phase of the project included conducting remote sensing operations on a limited number of known or suspected U.S. Navy shipwrecks and naval usage sites. Additionally, the division conducted some prospecting surveys in areas where naval vessels are thought to have been lost. Prior to this project, SCIAA, along with other federal and state agencies, had archaeologically investigated only one U.S. Naval shipwreck in South Carolina, USS *Housatonic* in 1999 (Conlin et al. 2005). Two research areas of the project, one at the site of USS *Harvest Moon,* sunk by a torpedo in Winyah Bay, and the second, a survey of Station Creek, site of the South Atlantic Blockading Squadron's repair facility, both related to the Civil War, illustrate the MRD's diverse role in managing the state's submerged cultural resources, from gathering baseline cultural and environmental data on known sites to prospecting for previously unknown ones.

USS *Harvest Moon* (38GE440)

USS *Harvest Moon* was a 193-foot long, 546-ton, side-wheel steamer built in Portland, Maine, in 1863 (Figure 1). Purchased at Boston on November 16, 1863, by Commodore John B. Montgomery from Charles Spear for $99,300, *Harvest Moon* was soon fitted out for blockade duty at the Boston Navy Yard and commissioned on February 12, 1864. Under the command of Acting Lieutenant J. D. Warren, the vessel was dispatched to duty with the South Atlantic Blockading Squadron on February 18, 1864, and arrived at its base of operations off Charleston Harbor on February 25 (U.S. Dept. of Navy, *ORN*, ser. 1, vol. 2:99; Mooney 1991:266).

Within 24 hours after its arrival off the South Carolina coast, Rear Admiral John A. Dahlgren, commander of the squadron, made the large side-wheel steamer his flagship. After several months of blockading duty, the *Harvest Moon* reported to the Washington Navy Yard for additional modifications and repairs. The vessel was reported to have carried four 24-pounder howitzers, one 20-pound Parrott rifle and one 12-pounder rifle. Following the repairs, the *Harvest Moon* returned to its regular blockading duties on June 7, 1864, off the South Carolina and Georgia coast. For the next nine months the steamer served off Tybee Island, on the North Edisto River, and off Charleston Harbor. Its duties during the closing months of the war included both acting as a picket steamer and dispatch vessel, as well as Dahlgren's flagship (Mooney 1991:266).

While proceeding in company with the tug *Clover* on the morning of February 29, 1865, the *Harvest Moon* accidentally struck a submerged Confederate torpedo, or mine, in Winyah Bay. From the log book of the *Harvest Moon* comes the following lines describing the loss of the vessel:

> At 7:45 A.M., when about 3 miles from Battery White, we ran on a torpedo. It blew a hole through the starboard quarter, tearing away the main deck over it, which caused this ship to sink in five minutes in 2½ fathoms of water. Tug <u>Clover</u> immediately came to our assistance. The admiral and staff went on board <u>Clover</u>, the ship's officers remaining on board to save everything possible. Sent gig in charge of Acting Ensign D. B. Arey to the Pawnee for assistance. Sent three boats up the river to drag for torpedoes. John Hazard, wardroom steward,

Figure 1. Contemporary drawing of USS *Harvest Moon*. U.S. Dept. of the Navy, *ORN*, ser. 1, vol. 16:282-283.

missing, supposed drowned, he being in the hold at the time of the explosion. From 8 A.M. to midnight: Ship sank in Swash Channel, Winyah Bay, 3 miles S. E. by E. from Battery White, in 2½ fathoms water (U.S. Dept. of Navy, *ORN*, ser. 1, vol. 16:285).

From Rear Admiral Dahlgren's official report, the exact location of the vessel is revealed:

Flag-steamer <u>Nipsic</u>, Georgetown Roads, March 1, 1865. Sir: My latest dispatches Nos. 82 and 83 had been closed, and not hearing anything of General Sherman at this place, I was on my way to Charleston, but was interrupted for the time by the loss of my flagship, which was sunk by the explosion of a torpedo. This took place at 7:45 A.M. to-day, and the best information I now have is from my own personal observation. What orders may have been noticed will be elicited by the court of enquiry which I shall order.

<u>Harvest Moon</u> had been lying near Georgetown until yesterday afternoon, when I dropped down to Battery White, 2 or 3 miles below, intending to look at the work and leave by the next day. Accordingly, this morning early <u>Harvest Moon</u> weighed anchor and steamed down the bay. She had not proceeded far when the explosion took place. It was nearly 8 o'clock, and I was waiting breakfast in the cabin, when instantly a loud noise and shock occurred, and the bulkhead separating the cabin from the wardroom was shattered and driven in toward me. A variety of articles lying about me were dispersed in different directions.

My first impression was that the boiler had burst, as a report had been made by my engineer the evening before that it needed repair badly. The smell of gun powder quickly followed and gave the idea that the magazine had exploded. There was naturally some little confusion, for it was evident that the vessel was sinking, and she was not long in reaching the bottom. As the whole incident was the work of a moment, very little more can be said than just related. But one life was lost, owing to the singular fortunate fact that the action of the torpedo occurred in the open space between the gangways and between the ladder to the upper deck and the wardroom, which is an open passageway, occupied by no one, and where few linger safe for a moment.

Had it occurred farther aft or forward the consequences would have been fatal to many. A large breach is said to have been made in the deck just between the main hatch and the wardroom bulkhead. It had been reported to me that the channel had been swept, but so much has been said in ridicule of torpedoes that very little precautions are deemed necessary, and if resorted to are probably taken with less care than if due weight was attached to the existence of these mischievous things. As I close this communication Colonel Brown has arrived here with a portion of the New York One hundred and fifty-seventh, and I have directed all the posts ashore at Georgetown held by the Navy to be turned over to the Army. I have the honor to be, very respectfully, your obedient servant, J. A. Dahlgren, Commanding South Atlantic Blockading Squadron (Record Group 45, M89, no. 152, National Archives).

Extensive salvaging took place after the sinking by the Union navy. After removing the machinery, supplies, and other materials, *Harvest Moon* was abandoned on April 21, 1865.

Over the years, *Harvest Moon* has been the subject of several private surveys and projects intended to raise and recover the vessel for display. In the late 1950s or beginning of the 1960s, a survey of the wreck was undertaken by the New England Maritime Museum, which claimed the vessel was in a remarkable state of preservation. In 1963 Southern Explorations Association, Inc., announced its intention to raise and to restore the ship. The group found 20–30 ft of mud covering the vessel, consequently making little headway in their endeavor (Mooney 1991).

A decade later, SCIAA issued salvage license no. 20 to the Confederate States Historical Foundation, Inc., to investigate the remains of the *Harvest Moon*. The group conducted an initial survey of the site on April 21, 1974. They located five feet of the smokestack, with the deck cowl around the tube, protruding above the surface at low tide. Investigators probed along a 30-ft centerline with 5-ft rods but did not touch down onto the cabins. They surmised that the upper cabins were missing because of previous federal salvage work. Mud overburden covering the hull was approximately 4–5 ft thick. The smokestack listed 15 degrees, which, they opined, may also correspond to the list of the ship. Probing also revealed a large cylindrical object due south of the stack. The group proposed a two-stage excavation strategy. The first phase would include dredging down to remnants of the superstructure and establishing hull characteristics. Work during the second phase would include dredging a channel to the wreck in order to clear a section of the hull from the extant top to the bottom of the keel. According to an undated and unnamed newspaper article, the group began excavations over a weekend to remove mud from the hull to uncover wood and iron objects on the deck. The artifacts were reportedly in good condition. Up to 15 divers and 30 technicians and engineers were noted as participating in the project. The group planned to raise the vessel and house it in Georgetown as a museum. These plans to raise the shipwreck were never realized. No documents or the disposition of any recovered artifacts concerning this weekend project are on file at SCIAA. To this day, the wreck of the *Harvest Moon* remains firmly embedded in the sediments of Winyah Bay.

SURVEY

Staff from the MRD conducted work on the *Harvest Moon* site during the weeks of March 17 and April 1, 2003. The first week was spent conducting remote sensing and performing water probing. The bulk of the second week was reserved for the probing operation. Identification of the site was fairly straightforward. Not only was the location of the wreck marked on the nautical charts and in the state site files, but also the smokestack protruded above the water at all but the highest tides.

A concern about conducting work at the site was the depth of water. The *Harvest Moon* lies deeply buried beneath the sediments of a wide, flat area some 500 m from the navigation channel through Winyah Bay. At the highest tides, the mud bottom lies only 1.5 m (5 ft) below the water's surface, while, at low water, there is often less than 15 cm (6 in) of water over the site. Because the division's survey-and-work boat draws a little over half a meter (2 ft) of water at the motors, effective work time each day was restricted to approximately six-hour windows of opportunity in calm conditions. If a southeastern wind got up, waves began building along the 3-km (1.86-mile) reach of the bay, effectively diminishing the work time available to us.

The magnetometer and side-scan sonar survey was completed concurrently on March 17 and 18. During those days, MRD staff ran more than 57 lanes, covering an area of 58,820 m^2, centered on the smokestack. The division ran 37 lanes in a NNW-SSE direction, estimating this to be the orientation of the long axis of the ship. Nineteen cross lanes were then run in a NE-SW orientation, as well as several nonaligned passes to further delineate magnetic anomalies and to produce clearer sonar images. Boat speed was kept to 4 knots to accommodate optimal operational constraints of the side-scan sonar, which was deployed in conjunction with the magnetometer. The length of each lane was constrained by a shoaling bottom to the N and E and by an island near the S ends of the NNE-SSE lanes.

MAGNETOMETER

Figure 2 depicts the magnetics of the site using a 200-gamma contour along with the results of hydro-probing. The field of the irregularly shaped concentration of anomalies is approximately 81 m NNW-SSE and 67 m NE-SW, encompassing an area roughly 5,427 m^2, centered on the smokestack. Viewing the site using a 1-gamma contour doubles the area of magnetic influence but is less useful for interpretation. Additionally, there are numerous outlying anomalies scattered around but close to the main concentration, as well as several anomalies located 100–160 m to the NW and N of the smokestack. The site is composed of a series of dipolar and multicomponent magnetic anomalies. The majority of centralized anomalies have gamma readings in the 500–1600 range. However, readings of a far greater magnitude are found between 18 and 26 m SW of the smokestack, where the contours reach 6,688.80 gammas, and 18 m NNE of the stack, where an 11,063.8-gamma reading is found. Ironically, the magnetic readings nearest to the smokestack are relatively low, reaching only 284.30 gammas approximately 3 m from the vertical iron tube. This may be due to the vertical orientation of the tube, which would show lower magnetic readings than if the smokestack were lying in a horizontal orientation. The smaller anomalies, located 50–160 m from the main group are in the range of 10–43 gammas and tend to be located NNE, NW, and S of the smokestack.

With the sensor moving at 4 knots, and using the 10-gamma contour, the maximum duration along the NNW-SSE axis is 29 seconds, representing a distance of approximately 59 m (195 ft), or 2 ft longer than the as-built length of the vessel. Along the NE-SW axis, the duration is approximately 22 seconds, representing approximately 45 m (150 ft), significantly greater than the historically documented 29-ft (8.8-m) beam of the vessel.

SIDE-SCAN SONAR

Little physical evidence of the remains of the *Harvest Moon* appears on the 270 sonar records that cover the entire survey area. The majority of the sonar records depict a uniformly flat mud bottom, devoid of relief. In places, the surface of the mud is scarred by trails cut into its otherwise featureless surface by the skegs of motorboats. The most prominent feature is, of course, the smokestack, which protrudes above the surface of the water. A horizontally oriented cylindrical

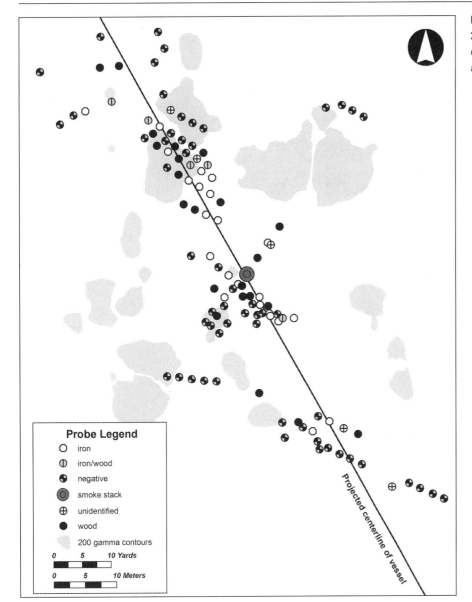

Figure 2. Results of hydro-probing with 200-gamma contoured magnetics. Courtesy of the South Carolina Institute of Archaeology and Anthropology.

Probe Legend

○	iron
⦶	iron/wood
⊕	negative
◉	smoke stack
⊕	unidentified
●	wood
	200 gamma contours

0   5   10 Yards

0   5   10 Meters

Projected centerline of vessel

object, apparently attached to the smokestack, protrudes slightly above the mud line to the SSE.

SMOKESTACK RECORDING

The smokestack is the only visible sign of wreck (Figure 3). The eroded top of the stack is visible at all but the highest tides, while at low water it protrudes more than a meter above the water of the bay. The double iron tube leans toward the SE at an angle of approximately 10 degrees from vertical. A layer of oysters covers the interior and exterior surfaces of the lower half of both tubes, with numerous loose oyster shells littering the bottom within the stack.

The 146-cm (57¾-in)-diameter smokestack is made up of two iron tubes of different diameters, one placed within the other. The inner tube is 111.76 cm (44 in) in diameter and is made up of several tube sections riveted atop one another. Each section is composed of two curved 1.27-cm (½-in)-thick wrought iron plates riveted together to form the tube section. The vertical seams of each

Figure 3. Smokestack of USS *Harvest Moon*. Courtesy of the South Carolina Institute of Archaeology and Anthropology.

section are placed at 90 degrees to the one below it. The inner tube is centered within the outer tube and held in place by courses of iron bolts spaced 38.1 cm (15 in) apart. Each course contains 16 bolts 41.5 cm (16¼ in) in length, which are fastened through both tubes with 3.8-cm (1½-in) square nuts. At low water two courses of these bolts are visible. However, above these courses there is evidence for two additional courses, although the bolts that were once present have long since succumbed to the deleterious effects of drying/inundation of the tidally influenced saltwater environment.

The outer tube appears to have been constructed in the same manner as the inner tube, with the vertical seams placed opposite those of the inner tube. One hundred seventy centimeters (67 in) below the top of the smokestack, there is an iron cylinder, lying in a horizontal orientation, protruding to the SSE. The cylinder appears to be attached to the smokestack at its NNW end. This is the same object shown in the sonar records. Probing the curved iron suggests dimensions approximating those indicated in the sonar records. Above the cylinder, a collar-like cowling angles up to meet the smokestack.

PROBING

After recording the smokestack, the crew proceeded to probe locations in the vicinity of the smokestack for evidence of ship's structure (Figure 4). However, because of high winds and building seas, this operation was terminated on March 19 after successfully probing 11 locations. A return to the site in April provided three and one half days of good conditions, during which time division staff probed an additional 101 locations. To use the 6-m-long water probe effectively in the shallow water over the site, it was necessary to work from both the 18-ft johnboat and the 25-ft C-Hawk. The johnboat provided a platform for the pumps, hoses, and accoutrements, while the C-Hawk's higher freeboard and cabin roof provided the probe operator a platform high enough to maneuver the unwieldy probe.

Hydro-probing consisted of utilizing two 10-ft lengths of ¾-in (galvanized) pipe coupled together and attached by hose to a water pump. Water under pressure was introduced through the pipe, which was inserted vertically into the mud covering the wreck site. The stream of water liquefied the subsurface sediment, allowing the pipe to descend through the sand/mud matrix until it encountered a solid object such as wood, metal, or marl.

Of the 111 locations probed in March and April, 24 produced wood contacts, 24 indicated the presence of iron, and 7 produced hard contacts that could have been either wood or iron. The remaining 56 locations produced either negative contacts (51), or the probe encountered hard-packed sand (5) (see Figure 2). All wood and iron contacts were made between .3 m (1 ft) and 4.10 m (13.5 ft) below the flat muddy bottom. However, the majority of the encounters occurred between 1.6 m (5.2 ft) and 2.6 m (8.5 ft) below the sediment. The probe encountered 3 wood contacts at greater depth between 3 and 9 m NW, and 25 m S of the smokestack.

Initial probe results suggested that the vessel lay in an orientation approximating NNW-SSE, an alignment that was later indicated when the balance of the probes was completed. Probing along that axis, and out to several meters to each side, resulted in fairly consistent wood and iron contacts for approximately 28 m (93 ft) NNW of the smokestack. To the SSE of the smokestack, positive probe results were less consistent but occurred out to 31 m (102 ft). The total length of subsurface wood and iron contacts closely approximates the 193-ft (59 m) as-built length of the *Harvest Moon*, although some wood contacts were encountered farther to the NNW. Probing NE and SW of the projected centerline of the wreck provided wood and iron contacts out to approximately 9 m (29.5 ft) to either side of the line.

DISCUSSION

The *Harvest Moon* sank in five minutes after hitting a floating mine that holed it in the starboard quarter. The ship was headed downstream when it struck the mine and sank in 2.5 fathoms (4.6 m; 15 ft.) of water approximately .5 km (.31 miles) from the main channel. Over the years, prodigious silting has taken place, covering all but the remaining vestiges of the smokestack in a thick mantle of heavy sediments. Interpretation of the wreck site follows multiple lines of evidence that include contemporary accounts of the sinking and subsequent salvage of the contents of the wreck as well as magnetometer and side-scan sonar data, data from the probing operation, and visual observations of the one remaining piece of ship's structure that is visible—the smokestack.

The smokestack provides a static point from which to anchor the survey. At first, the presence of the smokestack presented a puzzle. From the log of the *Harvest Moon* there is the following entry, "Wednesday March 22st. Steamer Sweet Brier came alongside. Delivered to her water casks, rope, rigging and smokestack for tug Catalpa." However, 170.18 cm (67 in) of the smokestack remains above the upper deck of the wreck. Undoubtedly, the original height of the smokestack exceeded that length by a considerable amount. Therefore, it can be concluded that the salvage operation removed a significant length of the iron smokestack but left the lower portion still attached to the firebox below. The entries in the ship's log for the salvage operation, which began the day after the sinking, March 2, 1865, and ended with abandonment of the vessel on April 21, 1865, were fairly specific in the objects removed from the vessel. No mention was made of the boiler or firebox, leading one to speculate that those objects remain beneath the smokestack. Furthermore, if those objects had been removed, there would have been little reason to leave the smokestack, not to mention very little structure to which the smokestack could remain attached. The document is quite clear that the salvage was comprehensive in its implementation and exerted extensive damage to the ship's hull. The 10-degree tilt of the smokestack, apparently along the length of the hull, may indicate a disarticulation of the smokestack or firebox/ boiler from the hull or suggest a corresponding slope to hull along its length.

The probing operation provides the best evidence for a NNW-SSE alignment of the hull, also providing a rough correlation between consistent wood and iron contacts and the as-built length of the vessel. Probing also delineated the horizontal cylindrical iron object projecting from the smokestack below the cowling. Both the probe data and sonar records place this object to the SSE of the smokestack, ostensibly in line with the centerline of the hull.

Depths of wood and iron encountered by the water probe tend to confirm Dahlgren's account that the ship sank in 2.5 fathoms (4.6 m; 15 ft) of water. The most consistent depth at which wood was encountered is 4.1 m (13.5 ft) below grade. *Harvest Moon* was a wooden-hulled side-wheeler with a 10-ft (3-m) depth of hold. Two accommodation decks could have added another 14 ft (4.3 m) to the height of the upper deck of the vessel. It is at the upper deck level that the cowling, located during the probing operation, would have been situated. Using the above projected heights, the keel of the vessel could be as much as 24 ft. (7.3 m) below the cowling, which currently sits at the mud line. However, the main deck, constructed of wood, would be located approximately 4.3 m (14 ft.) below the cowling, and very close to the 4.1-m (13.5-ft) depth of wood contacts encountered during the probing operation.

There is a large magnetic field around the wreck, with numerous significant anomalies, covering several thousand square meters. Given that the active salvage of the ship continued for more than a month, resulting in extensive damage to the hull, it would not be surprising to find an extensive debris field associated with the wreck. This field would contain numerous objects removed from the hull and scattered while the recovery vessels, which were anchored along either side of the stricken vessel, loaded the salvaged items. The results of the magnetometer survey tend to support this idea as most of the anomalies having the greatest readings occur NE and SW of the projected longitudinal axis of the wreck, and very few anomalies located NNW and SSE of the projected ends of the hull. The debris field should also contain many wood and other structural pieces from the wrecked hull that were dispersed during the wrecking and salvage operation and through the action of river currents and storms.

The survey confirms that much of USS *Harvest Moon* remains buried beneath the sediments of Winyah Bay, which are protecting the site from natural degradation and all but the most persistent looters. During the 1960s and 1970s, projects were initiated to conduct work on the wreck, in 1963 to raise and restore the vessel (Mooney 1991:266), and in 1974 to dredge a channel from the river to the site and salvage artifacts. It is a credit to nature's protection of the site that neither project was successful.

Station Creek Survey

After the fall of Port Royal, South Carolina, in November of 1861 to Union naval forces, Rear Admiral Samuel F. Du Pont, wanting to establish a floating repair facility for the South Atlantic Blockading Squadron in Station Creek, a tributary emptying into Port Royal Sound, wrote to Assistant Secretary of the Navy Gustavus Vasa Fox, saying, "I have just remembered that during the Crimean and China wars by England and France vessels fitted up as machine shops were used with remarkable advantage, and gunboats and large steamers were always undergoing repairs. The French floating machine shop I was on board of in Hong Kong, and she was fitted precisely as a shop on shore would have been, with shafting and gearing, etc." (U.S. Dept. of Navy, *ORN*, ser. 1, vol. 12:341).

Secretary of the Navy Gideon Welles, apparently sensing the utility of the proposal, responded to Du Pont: "Two houses, similar to the shops at Fortress Monroe, are building, and when ready will go with the machinists for the purpose of affording minor repairs to the engines at two points on the coast under your command. . . . Attempts were made to tow them from Hampton Roads, but they were driven back by gale. The Department feels confident of getting them to Port Royal by towing them empty" (U.S. Dept. of Navy, *ORN*, ser. 1, vol. 12:348).

After the second Stone Fleet arrived in 1862, Rear Admiral Du Pont kept two of the ex-whalers for use as the repair facility in Station Creek (Canney 1998:53). These were the 340-ton bark *Edward* and the 366-ton ship *India*. When the buildings arrived, Du Pont had them assembled on top of the two whalers, which had been attached broadsides, using the *India* as the blacksmith's shop and the *Edward* as a machine shop, with brass, iron, and copper foundries (Figure 5). These vessels also contained carpenter shops, barracks, mess rooms, and storerooms.

Figure 5. Contemporary drawing of the *Edward* and *India* in Station Creek. Frank Leslie, *Famous Leaders and Battle Scenes of the Civil War* (New York: Mrs. Frank Leslie, 1896), 463.

William B. Cogswell, a master mechanic, supervised the work and master mechanic W. S. Kimball supervised the entire operation (Browning 2002:78). Station Creek, an estuary opening into Port Royal Sound, was not broad enough to allow a ship at anchor to swing with the tide. However, when anchored by bow and stern, the width of the creek allowed lighters from the machine shop and coal schooners to come alongside. At high tide ships could pass by to anchor upstream or pass out to the sound. It was also used as a careenage, where vessels could be beached for bottom and rudder repairs (Hayes 1969:39; Browning 2002:297).

Within the first few months, Du Pont had the capability of undertaking minor repairs to woodwork and engines at Port Royal, but major repairs still had to be undertaken at Northern shipyards. In mid-January of 1863, the ironclads started to arrive at Port Royal. These vessels had special repair needs. In response to these needs, Welles sent General Inspector Alban C. Stimers and seven machinists to Port Royal to oversee the repairs. In April 1863 Stimers asked Secretary Welles to appoint Patrick Hughes assistant inspector of ironclads and have him put in charge of their repairs. Hughes and 40 men arrived in Port Royal on June 25, 1863, and immediately started to work on repairing three monitors (Roberts 2002:103).

The *Edward* and the *India* were used for almost two years until the size of the squadron grew too large for them to handle the scope of work needed. In the fall of 1863, W. B. Cogswell started to move the foundry ashore near the hulks, which were about to be abandoned. A small shell midden, just off the creek, was used to set up the foundry, with a wharf jutting out into the creek. The spring tides of August 1864 almost stopped repairs altogether. The *India* was lifted off the piles that were holding it in place. The current floated the vessel down the creek and beached it on the opposite side. When it was towed back, they discovered that it could not be put back in place inside the pilings and was taking on water at an alarming rate. The *India* was stranded and eventually broken up after all usable machinery had been salvaged. The *Edward* also had to be beached near the wharf, where it was also stripped of its machinery and left to the elements (Browning 2002:297).

ARCHAEOLOGICAL INVESTIGATIONS

In an effort to document the Union naval activities at Station Creek during the Civil War, the MRD launched a search in the creek to locate the two abandoned shipwrecks and any other underwater or terrestrial features related to the naval repair facility. Besides obtaining additional information about the floating and land repair facilities, historical research uncovered two nautical charts revealing the infrastructure along the creek waterfront. An 1862 nautical chart shows a dock on the north side of the creek on the hummock closest to the water, and an 1873 nautical chart illustrates two docks at the location, reflecting a build-up of the facilities as the war dragged on to 1865. Georectification of the 1873 nautical chart helped position the two docks on the modern charts. On modern charts the docks overlay into the marsh, perhaps a result of accretion in this area of the creek or as a result of positional error from georectifying the 1873 nautical chart. A pedestrian survey of the islet revealed a large mound of foundry slag, as well as a number of ceramic shards dating to the Civil War era. Additionally, a line of pilings between the islet and Station Creek clearly indicated the location of one of the docks.

Three remote sensing survey blocks were located at the mouth of Station Creek, adjacent to the island and farther upstream. Intended results included detecting the whaling vessels, incidental discards in the water, and abandoned materials associated with the repair facility. The three survey blocks extended up Station Creek from its mouth some 6 km (3.8 miles) and covered an area of over 333,000 m². A total of 147 anomalies were detected using the magnetometer and side-scan sonar. While the vast majority of these anomalies, upon inspection, were found to be modern debris, a few targets turned out to represent targets with culturally significant components, especially the survey block adjacent to the island.

STATION CREEK 2 SURVEY BLOCK

MRD staff surveyed this block on March 29, 2001, using both the magnetometer and the side-scan sonar (Figure 6). Lane spacing was set at 15 m (ca. 50 ft), and the boat operated at approximately 4 knots. The block covered a 90,785-m² area and measured 1,199 m (ca. 3,934 ft) by 147 m (ca. 484 ft). Water depth in the block ranged from 1.5 m (4.9 ft) to 9.6 m (31.5 ft). There were 38 anomalies detected: 35 magnetic anomalies and 3 sonar anomalies. Of the 35 magnetic anomalies, 21 were between 1 and 10 gammas (SC2–1, 5–12, 14–16, 19, 20, 23, 26, 30–34), and the remaining 14 ranged from 15 to 410 gammas. The sonar anomalies indicated three apparently interconnected rock mounds along the interface of the creek and marsh, which had corresponding magnetic anomalies. The rock mounds were in such close proximity to each other that they were given a single designation, *SC2-s1*. There were many medium- to large-sized magnetic anomalies in the creek, which most likely reflect the Civil War use of the creek as a workstation. The largest magnetic anomalies were detected along the marshland where the docks were located on the north shore of Station Creek.

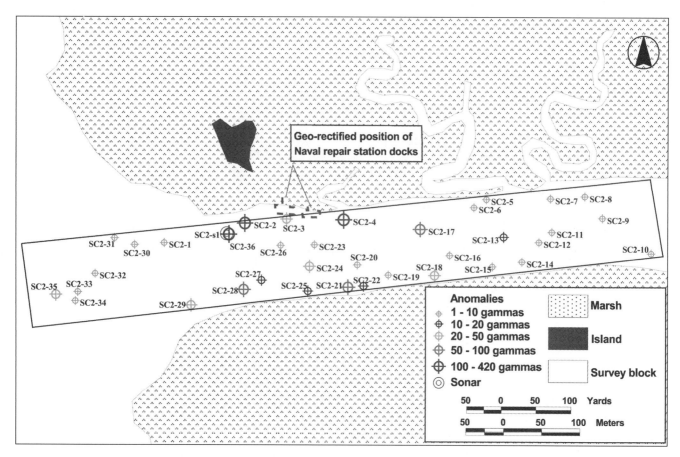

Figure 6. GIS map of Station Creek showing survey areas, including the small shell-midden hummock or islet used as a foundry during the Civil War. Courtesy of the South Carolina Institute of Archaeology and Anthropology.

MAGNETIC AND ACOUSTIC ANOMALIES

SC2-s1 was an acoustic anomaly that initially appeared to be a series of three rock mounds. The mounds cover an approximate length of 35 m (114.8 ft). Their widths varied from between 2 and 4 m (6.6–13.2 ft). The rock mounds suggest ballast piles, possibly associated with the whaling hulks, which were most likely stripped of anything of value or use and then scuttled; or alternately, the rocks were used in the construction of the inter-island causeway.

SC2–2 was a 410.7-gamma multicomponent magnetic anomaly that lasted for 35 seconds. The anomaly disturbed two lanes and an area of 4,827 m². Water depth at the anomaly was 4.8 m (15.7 ft.). The magnetics suggested the presence of several medium- to large-sized, ferro-magnetic cultural objects. This anomaly was the largest of the cluster of anomalies along the marsh, which included the rock mounds. There were no acoustic targets associated with this anomaly.

SC2–4 was a 358.1-gamma multicomponent magnetic anomaly that lasted for 31 seconds. The anomaly disturbed two lanes and a 4,805-square-meter area. Water depth at the anomaly was 7.1 m (23.3 ft). The magnetics suggested that the presence of several medium- to large-sized, ferro-magnetic cultural objects were the cause of the anomaly. This anomaly was the largest magnetic node in a cluster of other lesser anomalies.

SC2–36 was a 121.9-gamma multicomponent magnetic anomaly that lasted for 10 seconds and was also associated with the rock mounds. Water depth at the magnetic and sonar anomalies was 4.7 m (15.4 ft). The magnetic anomaly disturbed two lanes and covered an area of 811 m². The magnetics suggested the presence of several medium- to large-sized, ferro-magnetic cultural objects that were associated with the rock mounds. The rock mounds and the magnetic anomaly were also part of the cluster of magnetic anomalies connected to *SC2-2*.

SC2-2 was ground-truthed on May 29, 2003, and found to consist of two large metal rectangular objects, heavily concreted, perhaps iron stock for foundry work (Figure 7). A pine piling was also located during the circle search of the area and perhaps is related to the navy docks, or alternatively, pilings used to secure the position of the floating machine shops. Numerous other smaller metallic targets were detected by the metal detector. Hand fanning revealed the two large iron objects lying in a cruciform shape. The larger of the two weighed approximately 45 kg (ca. 100 lbs) and measured approximately 1.5 m (4.9 ft) in length, with a maximum width of .2 m (.66 ft), and tapered to a slightly lesser width at the other end. The other, smaller piece weighed approximately 34 kg (ca. 75 lbs) and was approximately .6 m (2 ft.) in length and .15 m (.49 ft) wide. The objects were resting in a muddy and sandy matrix in about 2 m (6.6 ft) of water at low tide.

SC2-4 was ground-truthed on May 26, 2003, and found to consist of a deposit of modern ferro-magnetic debris. Objects included remnants of a boat trailer, steel wire, and other indeterminate metal constructs, both exposed on the bottom and buried in the sediment. The scatter site was approximately 15 m (49.2 ft) in length and 5–7 (16.4–23 ft) in width. Water depth ranged from less than 1–2 m (less than 3.3–6.6 ft) and rested on a sand/mud matrix with oyster shells.

SC2-36 and *SC2-s1* were initially ground-truthed on May 26, 2003. Division staff deployed buoys at the magnetic anomaly *SC2-36* and at the upstream and downstream termini of the rock mound *SC2-s1*. One dive was made for the purpose of measuring and sampling the rock pile, as well as searching for evidence of a ship. Originally thought to represent three distinct mounds, visual inspection determined that there was only one contiguous mound of rocks at the site. During that dive, staff measured the rock mound at 28.3 m (92.8 ft) in length,

Figure 7. Joe Beatty and Jim Spirek holding iron bar stock. Courtesy of the South Carolina Institute of Archaeology and Anthropology.

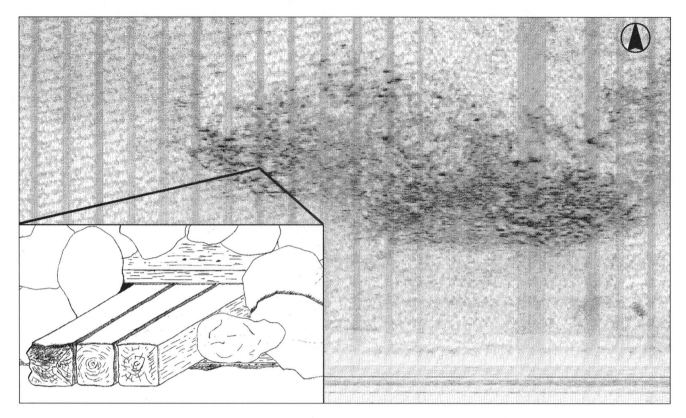

Figure 8. Side-scan sonar image of Station Creek Wreck with frame and plank drawing. Courtesy of the South Carolina Institute of Archaeology and Anthropology.

which conformed quite well to the 28-m (91.9 ft) scaled length taken from the sonar records. Scaled widths for the mound indicated that the rocks extended from 9 to 12 m (29.5 to 39.4 ft) across the site. Division staff also retrieved some flint cobbles from the mound, an iron ship nail with a fragment of wood attached, and a piece of iron stock with a brick and a bottle concreted to either end of it. Both the brick and bottle date to the Civil War era. Staff also reported large quantities of iron strewn around the site.

A return visit to the site on May 29 provided the evidence necessary to pronounce *SC2-s1* a shipwreck. The site was designated 38BU2080 in the South Carolina State Site Files, and named the Station Creek Wreck. Staff encountered and recovered a copper drift pin, wooden pulley sheave, and a fragment of a stoneware vessel, as well as locating an exposed 75-cm (2.5-ft) -long section of hull made up of the eroded ends of frames, hull planking and ceiling. The exposed timbers were recorded during that dive, and samples were taken of the wood, the copper sheathing covering the exterior surface of the hull planks, and a wooden treenail (Figure 8).

The exposed timbers are located on the south side of the ballast mound, approximately 5 m (16.4 ft) from the downstream end of the rocks. The structure lies approximately 1 m (3.3 ft) above the creek bed with rocks both below and above it. The rocks are angular, with many of them having diameters of 75 cm (2.5 ft) or less. However, several rocks near the structure exceeded 100 cm (3.3 ft) in diameter. Three frames were accessed after moving several large ballast rocks. The pine frames protrude horizontally from the ballast and perpendicular to the mound's longitudinal axis for a distance of approximately 75 cm (2.5 ft) and terminate in heavily eroded ends. Each frame has molded and sided dimensions of

23 cm (.75 ft), with a space between each timber of 1 cm, providing a room-and-space measurement of 24 cm (.78 ft).

Hull planks are attached to the outboard surface of the frames. Only one plank could be accessed because of the surrounding ballast rocks. The pine plank is 1.6 cm (.052 ft.) thick and at least 16 cm (.52 ft.) in width. The plank is attached to each frame with a wooden treenail measuring 3.4-cm (.11-ft) in diameter. Copper sheathing covers its outboard surface, fastened to the wood with .29-to-.35-cm- (.1-to-.12-ft-) square copper nails. Much of the visible plank exhibits severe shipworm (*Teredo navalis*) damage. Atop the frames, the ceiling was visible beneath the ballast. The pine ceiling is 7.5 cm (.25 ft) thick and, like the hull planks, is riddled with shipworm tubes.

DISCUSSION

The timbers recorded are located near the downstream end of the ballast mound, suggesting that they are near one end of the vessel. As the hull narrows at its extremes, one would expect to see an upward sweep to the frames, even close in to the centerline of the vessel. The recorded frames are horizontal, suggesting that the hull is heeled towards the creek channel, or that the weight of the ballast has distorted the stout timbers. Circumstantial evidence from a drift pin may point to a clue as to which end the timbers are located. The 136.4-cm-(4.5-ft-)long copper fastener was found on the creek bed approximately 2 m (6.6 ft) from the articulated timbers. It is possible that a fastener of that length would have been used in the deadwood construction of the stern.

The presence of a shipwreck at that specific location in Station Creek tends to confirm historical accounts of a vessel being abandoned there and suggests that 38BU2080 is the 340-ton bark *Edward*. The scantling and timber dimensions would not be inconsistent with a nineteenth-century sailing vessel of that tonnage. Furthermore, the large quantity of ballast associated with the wreck, perhaps as much as 560 m³, would not be surprising. The *Edward* was bought for the Second Stone Fleet with the intent of sinking it in the approach to Charleston Harbor. Additionally, the bark was no longer expected to sail but rather, along with the *India,* to provide a stable, stationary platform for the naval repair facility.

Further work is planned at the 38BU2080 once another source of funding has been identified and secured. Such work will include selectively test-excavating the wreck to map its structure, and characterizing the site to its immediate environmental and cultural setting. This will also include mapping the site into the overall complex of the once extensive naval repair facility on land. Additionally, we intend to record precise timber measurements and scantlings at selected hull locations and compare those figures to those of construction and insurance records of the *Edward,* if those records can be located through additional research. Finally, it should be noted that 38BU2080 is the first shipwreck site in South Carolina to be located solely through the efforts of the Maritime Research Division's remote-sensing operations.

Conclusion

The historical and archaeological research for this project produced a broad historical perspective of the navy in South Carolina and more focused inquiry into each individual ship and post-depositional history as a shipwreck. Additionally, remote sensing operations occurred at several selected shipwrecks and naval activity sites in Charleston, Port Royal, ACE Basin, and Winyah Bay that provided baseline environmental and archaeological data. The project allowed us to develop a Geographical Information System (GIS), which is providing us with the tools to analyze the state's submerged cultural resources and develop management policies and research strategies regarding the sites containing South Carolina's maritime legacy.

Shipwrecks in South Carolina have been the focus of attention of would-be salvagers and state cultural resource managers since the 1950s. Civil War–era wrecks, notably blockade runners, have featured in the sights of treasure hunters due in no small part to the diverse military and civilian items they carried as cargo. With the advent of state law in 1968 to address salvaging of shipwrecks, groups expressed renewed interests in recovering materials from shipwreck sites, obtaining salvage licenses from the state to salvage Union steamers such as the USS *Boston* and USS *Harvest Moon,* as well as the Confederate blockade runners *Minho, Stono* (formerly the USS *Isaac Smith*), *Georgiana,* and *Mary Bowers.* This trend continued sporadically until 1991, when the first law protecting the state's submerged archaeological sites was enacted (South Carolina Underwater Antiquities Act of 1991 [Amended 2001], SCCL 54–7–610 *et seq.*), effectively curtailing salvage of the state's maritime heritage. This has allowed MRD staff to focus on expanding our knowledge of South Carolina's maritime past through regional surveys and hobby diver reports, as well as dealing with management issues related to cultural factors such as dredging and construction and environmental factors such as submerged sites being exposed as lakes and rivers recede during drought conditions.

References Cited

Albright, Alan B., and J. Richard Steffy

1979   The Brown's Ferry Vessel, South Carolina: Preliminary Report. In *The International Journal of Nautical Archaeology and Underwater Exploration.* 8(2):121–142.

Amer, Christopher F.

2006   A Survey for Lucas Vazquez de Ayllon's Lost Capitana. *Legacy* 10 (3): 10–15. South Carolina Institute of Archaeology and Anthropology, University of South Carolina, Columbia.

Amer, Christopher F., William B. Barr, David V. Beard, Elizabeth L. Collins, Lynn B. Harris, William R. Judd, Carleton A. Naylor, and Mark M. Newell.

1993   The Malcolm Boat (38CH803): Discovery, Stabilization, Excavation, and Preservation of an Historic Sea Going Small Craft in the Ashley River, Charleston County, South Carolina. Research Manuscript Series No. 217. South Carolina Institute of Archaeology and Anthropology, University of South Carolina, Columbia, SC.

Amer, Christopher F., Jonathan M. Leader, and Frederick M. Hocker

1997   "Browns Ferry Vessel." *Underwater and Maritime Archaeology, an Encyclopedia.* James P. Delgado, ed., pp. 77–78. British Museum Press. London.

Amer, Christopher F., Suzanne Linder, William Barr, and Mark Newell

1995   The Ingram Vessel, 38CT204: Intensive Survey &and Excavation of an Upland

Rivercraft at Cheraw, South Carolina. Research Manuscript Series No. 220,. South Carolina Institute of Archaeology and Anthropology, Columbia, SC.

1995   *The Ingram Vessel, 38CT204: Intensive Survey and Excavation of an Upland Rivercraft at Cheraw, South Carolina.* Research

Manuscript Series No. 220. South Carolina Institute of Archaeology and Anthropology, University of South Carolina, Columbia.

Browning, Robert, Jr.

2002   *Success Is All That Was Expected: The South Atlantic Blockading Squadron during the Civil War.* Brassey's, Dulles, Virginia.

Canney, Donald

1998   *Lincoln's Navy: The Ships, Men, and Organization, 1861–65.* Naval Institute Press, Annapolis, Maryland.

Conlin, David, (editor)

2005   USS Housatonic Site Assessment. Submerged Resources Center Professional Report No. 19. National Park Service, Santa Fe, New Mexico.

Dahlgren, John

1865   To Gideon Welles, 1 March 1865, Area File of Naval Records Collection, Record Group 45, Entry M89, no. 152 Area 8. National Archives and Records Administration, Washington DC.

Harris, Lynn

1992   *The Waccamaw-Richmond Hill Waterfront Project 1991: Laurel Hill Barge No. 2.* Research Manuscript Series No. 214. South Carolina Institute of Archaeology and Anthropology, University of South Carolina, Columbia.

Harris, Lynn, Jimmy Moss, and Carl Naylor

1993   *The Cooper River Survey: An Underwater Reconnaissance of the West Branch.* Research Manuscript Series No. 218. South Carolina Institute of Archaeology and Anthropology, University of South Carolina, Columbia.

Hayes, John D. (editor)

1969   *Samuel Francis Dupont: A Selection from His Civil War Letters.* Cornell University Press. Ithaca, NY.

Mooney, James (editor)

1991   *Dictionary of American Naval Fighting Ships.* Naval Historical Center, Washington, D.C.

National Archives and Records Administration, Washington D.C. Area File of Naval Records Collection, Record Group 45, Entry M625, Area 8.

Roberts, William H.

2002   *Civil War Ironclads: The US Navy and Industrial Mobilization.* Johns Hopkins Studies in the History of Technology. Johns Hopkins University Press, Baltimore.

Spirek, James D.

2012   *The Archeology of Civil War Naval Operations at Charleston Harbor, South Carolina, 1861–1865.* Report prepared for the American Battlefield Protection Program, National Park Service. South Carolina Institute of Archaeology and Anthropology, University of South Carolina, Columbia.

Spirek, James D., Christopher F. Amer, Joseph Beatty, Lynn Harris, Carleton Naylor, and Laura Von Harten

1999   *The Port Royal Sound Survey, Phase One: Preliminary Investigations of Intertidal and Submerged Cultural Resources in Port Royal Sound, Beaufort County, South Carolina.* South Carolina Institute of Archaeology and Anthropology, University of South Carolina, Columbia.

Spirek, James D., and Christopher F. Amer (editors)

2004   *A Management Plan for Known and Potential United States Navy Shipwrecks in South Carolina.* South Carolina Institute of Archaeology and Anthropology, University of South Carolina, Columbia.

U.S. Department of the Navy

1894–1922   *Official Records of the Union and Confederate Navies in the War of the Rebellion (ORN).* 30 vols. Government Printing Office, Washington, D.C.

**Carl Steen, Christopher Judge,
and Sean Taylor**

Archaeology and Public Education on the Great Pee Dee River

The Johannes Kolb Site

ARCHAEOLOGISTS HAVE BEEN AT WORK at the Johannes Kolb site since 1997 (Steen and Judge 1997). The work there is done in the spirit of public education, teaching, and research. As we have worked, we have come to realize that what we are doing there is not much different from what went on in the past. The older members of the group share their knowledge of the resources available at this special place with the young and with interested neighbors. We work hard, socialize, and form bonds of friendship. Some have even found their mates and formed families, and moved on to lead projects of their own, reflecting the way groups expanded and society developed in the past. As William Faulkner (1951 act 1, scene 3) wrote, "The past is never dead. It's not even past." When people look back at our occupation of the site at the turn of the twenty-first century, they will see us as yet another group that came to the site, dug some holes, ate some local food, left a few distinctive artifacts, and went on about our ways. Here we introduce the work at the Kolb site, the geology and history of the landform, the field and lab work, and our public education efforts. This information is used to add substance to our discussion of the culture history of the Great Pee Dee.

Site Setting and Discovery

The Johannes Kolb site (38DA75) is located in Darlington County on an ancient sandbar in the middle of a vast river swamp over seven miles wide (Figure 1). It is bordered by a relic channel of the Great Pee Dee River that was cut off in the 1880s. This location has been an attractive locale for as long as people have been in the area, as artifacts from as old as about 12,000 years are found in excavation units that produce modern material. Even its discovery reflects this: the site was recorded by a local high school student, Ernest "Chip" Helms III, whose family was part of a hunt club that had its headquarters there.

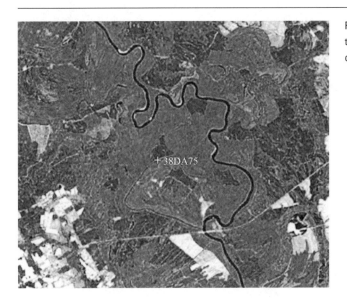

Figure 1. Location of
the Kolb Site. Courtesy
of Christopher Judge.

The Kolb site project began when Chip Helms came to visit the South Carolina Department of Natural Resources Heritage Trust Program staff in 1997. Chip detailed his early adventures on the preserve when it was a hunt club leased by his father and uncles from the Edwards Paper Company in the early 1970s. Often Chip followed behind the logging crews to look for artifacts in the places they disturbed and left bare. Historian Eugene Waddell, then at the Florence County Museum, helped Chip identify his finds and encouraged him to correspond with the Institute of Archaeology and Anthropology at the University of South Carolina in Columbia. Chip wrote articulate letters, accompanied by artifact photos and detailed and accurate sketch maps to the state archaeologist, Dr. Robert L. Stephenson. These letters ended with a request to send a team of archaeologists to investigate his sites. Dr. Stephenson wrote back to Chip with assigned site numbers and a lament that he simply did not have the staff or funds to investigate every site in the state. Years passed, and after the land was dedicated as a heritage preserve, Chip contacted Christopher Judge of the Heritage Trust Program about the possibility of some archaeological research on the sites.

Because of the presence of an eighteenth-century component, Heritage Trust Program archaeologist Chris Judge asked his colleague and friend Carl Steen to join the project as codirector. He had just wrapped up his research at the eighteenth-century backcountry site of John de la Howe's Lethe Farm in McCormick County (Steen et al 1996). Soon Judge and Steen put together a team of volunteers to spend a week in the Great Pee Dee swamp in August 1997. This crew included USC undergraduate Sean Taylor, who now holds Chris Judge's old job at the Heritage Trust Program. Because of the heat, bugs, and intense vegetation, the crew soon realized that summer was not the time to come to the Kolb site. But the project was underway, and it quickly became apparent that this was not a run-of-the-mill Coastal Plain site.

Excavation Approach: Balancing Exploration and Preservation

Excavating the site raises an ethical question. So many sites have been destroyed by development, agriculture, logging, and silviculture that the state began to buy endangered sites to protect them. The Kolb site is on a state heritage preserve, and it is protected in perpetuity, so why not let it be? As a state-owned preserve, the site offers several unique opportunities. It belongs to the citizens of the state of South Carolina, current and future, and public monies were (and are) used to acquire and manage the preserve; therefore, it is only fitting that the citizens realize a return for their investment. The return we archaeologists envisioned would be in the form of knowledge about the area's human past derived from the excavation, analysis, and interpretation of the artifacts the site's inhabitants left behind. Also, there was a gap in our knowledge of the archaeology of this region that the site was uniquely positioned to fill. Many sites have been excavated in the Coastal Zone but few in the state's interior. While excavation of the site would fill many voids in our knowledge, it also offered an opportunity for unique research and public education. Further, the project could be conducted in a publicly owned place that would be forever free from opposing land-use possibilities. Therefore, to address the question of preservation we have taken pains to address all occupations, not just the ones we as researchers are interested in, as well as to approach the excavations with a long-term sampling plan that will leave over 80 percent of the site untouched.

Geology of the Great Pee Dee River

The Great Pee Dee river system is one of the largest in the Southeast (Linder and Johnson 2000). Its headwaters nearly reach the Virginia border. It starts as the Yadkin in North Carolina and becomes the Great Pee Dee at the confluence of the Yadkin and Uwharrie Rivers. It flows about 250 miles (as the crow flies) or 430 river miles to the coast at Georgetown. It is only navigable by large vessels in the Coastal Plain (U.S. Army Corps of Engineers 1977).

The Pee Dee passes through three physiographic regions: the Mountains, the Piedmont, and the Coastal Plain (Kovacik and Winberry 1987). The first two were formed through ancient volcanic activity and long-term weathering and metamorphic processes. The Coastal Plain is relatively young, forming over the past 65 million years through sedimentary processes.

The Coastal Plain of the Southeast is traversed by large rivers with flood plains that are often wide but relatively shallow. In these flood plains, distinctive environments summarized as river swamps have developed over the past 20,000 or so years. During the last Ice Age the river was more of a braided stream than the wide flowing river seen today (Leigh et al 2004).

University of Georgia geomorphologist Dr. David Leigh took core samples at the site and at other landforms in the surrounding swamp (Leigh et al 2004). Though radiometric dating has not been completed, he feels that our sand ridge came into being during the late Pleistocene epoch, after about 25,000 years ago, when global warming was beginning to free moisture from the glacial ice after a long dry period. This moisture came to earth as rain. The Pee Dee was a braided stream in a relatively shallow valley that was periodically scoured out as water flow increased, eventually forming the broad floodplain and river swamp we see today. Sandbars like the one at the Kolb site, and larger dune formations like the one across the river on Byrd's Island formed in the distant past as a result of this periodic flooding. Artifacts from 11,000 to 12,000 years ago have been found at the site. A substantial sample of excavation units has been tested with soil

Figure 2. Sean Taylor, with large rhyolite cobbles found in the riverbed near the site. Courtesy of Christopher Judge.

augers to determine whether deeply buried deposits are present, but no artifacts have been found below about 1.3 m. Thus, occupations from more than about 25,000 years ago are not expected, but there is no reason not to expect 12,000- to 25,000-year-old deposits.

Lithic Resources

Many visitors to the site ask: "Where did they find the rocks they used for stone tools?" After all, the central Pee Dee is not noted for its large rock outcrops, and the native stone is of relatively poor quality. Many flakes and cobbles excavated at the site exhibit a rounded exterior cortex formed through eons of tumbling down the Great Pee Dee River. So, in attempting to answer the question, we began to search the local area for sources. In recent investigations of the Great Pee Dee River's main channel between Society Hill and Johnsonville, gravel bars (Figure 2) have produced large cobbles of quartz, flow-banded rhyolite, porphyritic rhyolite, argillite, and other igneous and metamorphic materials identical to the lithic artifacts being excavated from the Kolb site. This shows definitively that an abundant array of rocks can be found within the region. Lithic debitage exhibiting river-cobble cortex has been recovered from numerous archaeological sites along the river, which indicates that people were quarrying these materials locally.

This is an important discovery, since interpretations of early human behavior —especially lithic provisioning—often focus on important raw material sources such as the Uwharrie rhyolite/metavolcanic quarries and the Allendale chert quarries (Steponaitis et al 2006; Goodyear et al 1989). Early research suggested that groups were tethered to these resources and that they were central to group identity (Daniel 1998; Sassaman 1993). Our research shows that the people of the Pee Dee would have no need to visit either source unless they simply wanted to. Humans often display hard-to-explain behavior as a result of environmental and cultural pressures or simple agency, so a humanistic explanation can always be made. But from a scientific perspective there is no evidence that the people living at the Kolb site absolutely had to visit those sources. All the rocks they needed for stone tools could be gathered from the river.

While studying this we also began to understand that the site has been a place of education for at least 12,000 years. Because of the abundant lithic materials readily available from the river, it is believed that aboriginal people took advantage of this abundance to teach younger generations to make stone tools. Often excavation units produce flakes that are, in the eyes of our flintknapper, Sean Taylor, the product of a master knapper. These are often found in close association with debitage that reflects the work of an individual who possessed a lesser amount of skill. Through the observation of the unambiguous characteristics of the artifacts and the lessons learned from Experimental Archaeology (Mathieu 2002), this information has been interpreted to represent the teaching of the craft to a younger generation. It is reasonable to infer that a group of people would take the opportunity to educate others when raw materials are in abundance and easily accessible. Learning to break rocks in a predictable manner to create a useful edged tool is time consuming and can be wasteful of raw material. It has taken Sean Taylor more than 10 years to begin to become moderately proficient with certain aspects of the craft, and he has literally broken up several tons of rock in the process. A group of people who relied on the natural world for provisions and whose safety net consisted of the skills they had been taught by elders would probably not waste valuable lithic materials on education in places where these raw materials were in short supply. Realizing that we are continuing a long tradition of education through our work at Kolb is a deeply profound and unexpected lesson to learn from the archaeological record.

Chris Young (2010), one of our student volunteers at the Kolb site, has been conducting petrographic, neodymium isotope geochemistry and XRF analyses on Kolb rhyolite similar to work published for North Carolina (Steponaitis et al. 2006). Young worked under Dr. Joanna Casey in the Department of Anthropology at USC on a Magellan undergraduate research grant to commence his study. Sean Taylor provided rhyolite samples that he had collected from Mechanicsville to Johnsonville on the Great Pee Dee River, and we allowed Chris to thin-section some Early Archaic points. The project also included working with Dr. Gene Yogodzinski in the Department of Geological Sciences at USC, who not only guided in geological matters but allowed Young access to his lab for processing samples of both rhyolite raw material, rhyolite tools, and debitage.

The outcome of the studies has proven empirically that Kolb toolmakers were able to obtain rhyolite locally in cobble form from Pee Dee River shoals and need not have relied on well-known metavolcanic quarries located 160 km upstream of the site. This opens new avenues for understanding the behavior and social order of ancient Native Americans, as previous models had social groups tied to specific lithic sources (Anderson and Hanson 1988; Sassaman 1993; Daniel 1998). We understand now that this was not the case.

Clay Resources

Another important raw material for prehistoric and historic people was malleable and plastic clay that could be used to make ceramics. Clay is formed through the in-situ weathering of certain rocks and minerals. These are known as primary clays. When these erode away and are redeposited, they are known as secondary clays. More details can be found in Cardew (1969) and Rhodes (1957), but for the present purposes it is only important to understand that the clays found here are sedimentary in nature—that is, secondary clays.

When the oceans receded in the distant past, lakes, ponds, sounds, and even inland seas were formed in different places. This is seen clearly in the landscape of North Carolina's Albemarle Peninsula and Sound. There a thin line of sandbars holds a large, shallow body of fresh water. Several huge, shallow lakes are found on the peninsula. If these were to dry out, the sediment beneath them would be clearly different from the surrounding soils.

When water from the Piedmont flowed into these depressions and came to a halt, the sediment fell out, with the heaviest settling first and the lightest last. Clay molecules are actually flat and tend to float longer. When they settle or "deflocculate," lenses of pure clay can be formed. These are usually in relatively isolated deposits, though they may be intermixed with broader areas of less pure clay, sand, and rocks. Experimentation with the local clays has met with mixed success, but it is believed that local sources could have easily supplied the site occupants. Recent research on clay sourcing by archaeologists working in North Carolina used local clay as a control sample (Herbert and McReynold 2004).

EXCAVATIONS

Between 1997 and 2011 we excavated 108 2-by-2-m excavation units (EUs) and 243 test units (TUs) measuring 50 cm² each. These are shown in Figure 3. This is

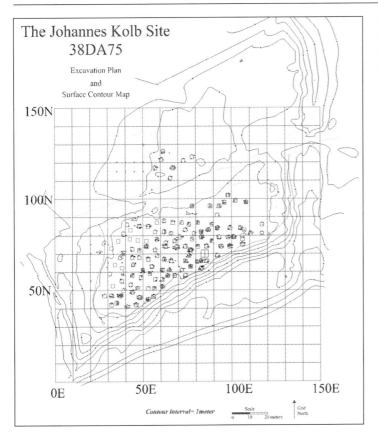

Figure 3. Kolb site plan. Courtesy of Christopher Judge.

a total of 454.25 m² of surface area. These units nearly all went to a meter below surface, if not deeper, so it is fair to say that roughly 492.75 m³ (645 cu yds) of soil have been excavated. This is the equivalent of about 98.5 single-axle dump truck loads (http://www.earthhaulers.com/faqs.html), or 1,612,500 lbs of sand, to put the level of effort in perspective. Since the soil went back into the units as backfill we can say that about 3,225,000 lbs of soil have been moved.

SAMPLING

We have taken a sampling approach to our excavations. This weighs the value of learning about the site using destructive means against the value of preserving as much of the site as possible. A two-pronged approach has been taken. First, we established a grid and set about excavating a 50-cm test unit every 5 m. This will allow us to look at a broad area at a fairly reliable level of intensity, producing a 1 percent sample. Next, we have further sampled these 5-m boxes with a randomly placed 2-m square in each one, which will yield an additional 16 percent sample. Neither sampling program has been completed at this point, but when all is said and done, we will have obtained a 17 percent sample, and left 83 percent of the site intact for future research.

BASIC PROCEDURES

At a minimum, all soils are screened through ¼-in mesh, but finer mesh has been used when appropriate, and flotation samples have been taken. The 50-cm TUs have been excavated using arbitrary 20-cm levels. In the early years we excavated the 2-m EUs in 10-cm levels. Later we broke the units into quads, and began using 5-cm levels. In both, when features or soil changes were encountered, the soils were excavated separately, while we still observed the level depths.

The EUs are dug from ground surface using a fixed datum. This has evolved from line levels to laser levels over the years. All unit corners have been recorded with a transit or total station and added to an ever-growing site map. The site as a whole has been mapped with a total station, and the data has been processed using Autocad, Surveypro, and Surfer software.

The Kolb site is dense with features. These take the form of soil anomalies and artifact deposits. We emphasize data recording as a result. This is a very important component of our teaching mission. Students and volunteers take the notes for their units, draw the floors, and clean up for photos. At some sites excavators are simply brute labor. Here we take a different approach and try to teach students to read the soil, interpret it, and record that knowledge. One way we do this that differs from other sites is that we hire professional field technicians whenever possible (though many professional colleagues also volunteer their services) so that there is a professional close enough to every crew to coach the less knowledgeable. Using volunteers, the results can be as variable as the individuals involved, so for the sake of consistency the project principals also take overview notes and unit photographs.

50-CM TU RESULTS (DISTRIBUTION STUDIES)

We concentrated on excavating the 1 percent sample in the first three field seasons. Preliminary artifact density mapping was generated when a reasonable number were completed. Using this information we can see, for instance, that

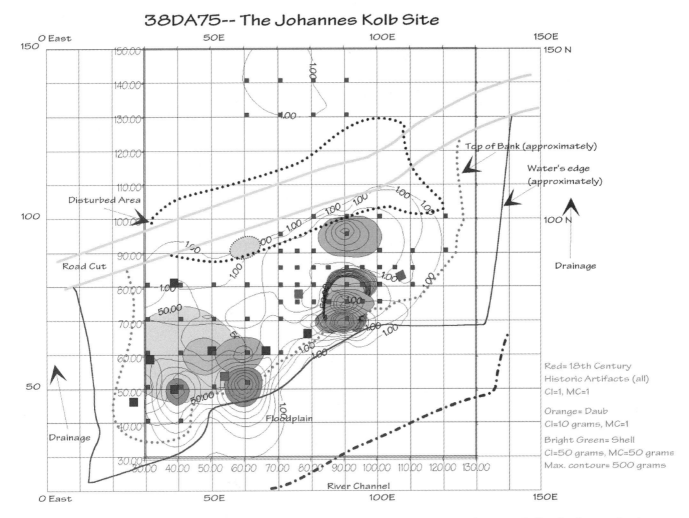

38DA75-- The Johannes Kolb Site

Figure 4. Artifact density map, showing
eighteenth-century artifacts, daub, and shell.
Courtesy of Christopher Judge.

artifacts associated with Johannes Kolb are more common in the eastern part
of the site, so when we wish to study Kolb we can concentrate there (Figure 4).
Further, this approach can be taken with any number of artifact types to see
whether relationships can be discerned that mark activity areas from the various
occupants of the site. The 50-cm TUs sample features and their distribution also.
In our first year alone, we excavated 25 TUs, which encountered eight features,
including historic posts and prehistoric pits and shell lenses.

2-by-2-m EUs

A typical EU will have a disturbed, dark gray, upper topsoil layer that is usually
about 25–30 cm thick. This disturbance dates to the 1970s. Below that another 10
cm of more compact topsoil is seen. This will contain historic artifacts. In many
of the EUs closer to the riverbank, a buried midden layer can be seen. This is
usually about 10 cm thick. The upper soils are dense with roots, but by about 40
cm below surface, the number decreases and the soil begins to change to a lighter
gray-brown. Both historic and prehistoric artifacts are found in the top 30–35 cm,
but below that the artifacts are prehistoric, except in features.

Our excavations have been aimed at understanding site-formational processes (Schiffer 1987). Artifacts are found from the ground surface to as much as
1.3 m below surface. So our basic questions are these: How did a particular artifact

end up where we found it? Was the ground surface 1.3 m lower 12,000 years ago than it is today? Did flooding cause the soil to build up, burying successive occupations? Or, was something else involved? The project principals were familiar with Jim Michie's (1990) bioturbation concept and felt that this would be an ideal site to test the idea. Including the possibility of natural factors contributing to artifact movement broadens the concept to "pedoturbation."

In the 108 EUs that have been excavated, over 500 cultural features (Figure 5) have been recorded. That is an average of about 6 per unit. This is an exceptional number that does not include the numerous vague "potential features" we have been forced to dismiss. Because the midden and topsoil are up to 50 cm thick in places and discerning edges is complicated by pedoturbation-leaching, root action, animal burrowing, and human impacts (Buol et al. 1973:89, 94; Wood and Johnson 1978:317), many features have no doubt been missed. However, our sampling approach ensures that future researchers can apply advanced techniques to control for our present-day deficiencies. For example, geoarchaeological investigations are ongoing, which should help delineate the natural and anthropogenic site-formation processes as well as the effects of environmental changes on the site and the adaptations of the site inhabitants. Dr. Mark Brooks and Dr. Christopher Moore are working on soil and sediment analyses and thermoluminescence dating. Dr. Terry Ferguson is evaluating the applicability of techniques in environmental magnetism. Preliminary results of these geoarchaeological investigations are promising (Ferguson, personal communication 2011).

Both historic and prehistoric features have been identified. The most common type of feature is a historic post. These range from small fence posts to structural posts over a meter deep. The Johannes Kolb house was built on posts, as were the slave houses from the later occupations. In fact, the last known structure on the preserve, which was moved to the entrance gate in the 1970s, was built on 10-in posts. At least three of the slave houses had subterranean storage pits or "root cellars" dating to the 1830s–1850s period. These are common on sites

Figure 5. Two-meter-by-two-meter excavation unit with features pedestaled. Courtesy of Christopher Judge.

in Virginia and the Chesapeake region, but they are not widespread on South Carolina slave sites (Gage 2009).

Prehistoric features are more difficult to read. It appears that few, if any, long-term structures were built here. Certainly no elaborate high-status structures such as council houses (Schroedel 1986) were built. This may also be a result of our inability to identify them as a result of historic disturbance. Prehistoric posts tend to be small and not very deep. However, it is also likely that temporary shelters would be erected during fishing and hunting seasons that would leave little discernible evidence in terms of soil features, at least. Artifact features, such as dense knapping floors, localized midden deposits, and other activity areas are also evident.

One type of feature we find very often is what is thought of as a storage pit (DeBoer 1988). These are large, deep pits dug to the subsoil and even a little beyond. These begin in the lower topsoil and appear to be associated with the people who used grog-tempered Hanover-type pottery primarily. We call them storage pits, but they tend not to produce many artifacts and even those seem to come from the soils removed from the pit to begin with, which ended up in the backfill. There are exceptions, however, that lend credence to the storage interpretation. For instance, Feature 02–22 contained a number of ceramic sherds, along with fish, turtle, mammal bone, and river mussels (Figure 6). This produced a carbon date of about A.D. 877 (UGA sample 13305, corrected). Ethnographic evidence and common sense tell us that protected food storage is necessary while camping, however, to protect the resources from marauding wildlife.

The dark soils and shallower features give way to a brown sand around 50 cm below surface usually, and often Stallings and Thoms Creek pottery are found at this level. From 50 to 60 cm, some soil staining from leaching and root activity is still present, but the soil becomes lighter with depth. In several cases dense beds of flakes associated with variants of the Savannah River–type point (Coe 1964) were seen at this level. The artifacts drop off in number in the levels between 60

Figure 6. Feature 02-22, a storage pit. Courtesy of Christopher Judge.

and about 80 cm below surface. The Middle Archaic is not well represented here, but it appears that the site was heavily used in the Late Archaic. Between 80 cm and about 105 cm, the Early Archaic and Late Paleoindian occupations are very well represented. Occasionally artifacts are found to as much as 1.3 m, but usually nothing is present below about 1.1 m. At about 1.1 m below surface, the sand becomes lighter and has a finer grain.

Pedoturbation has resulted in a great deal of mixing. Early tools are seen in the topsoil, and later ones at unexpected depths. Tool specimen no. 389, for instance, is a well-made rhyolite triangular point found at 75 cm below surface. Triangular points are most common in the top 30 cm, with an overall average depth of 26.1 cm below surface. The numbers decline with depth as Table 1 shows, but nearly a third of the total (as of 2005) are below 30 cm. The same pattern is seen with other broad types as well, but stepping back and applying group averages to the types we see triangular points at 26 cm, Savannah River types at 51 cm, early notched points at about 80cm and Paleo types at 107cm below surface. A rough stratification is evident, but the idea of stable occupation floors is not supported.

TABLE 1. Points by Depth

DEPTH	TRIANGULAR	STEMMED WOODLAND	SAVANNAH RIVER	MORROW MOUNTAIN	GUILFORD	EARLY NOTCHED	PALEO TYPES
0–30	93	4	3	2	4	1	
31–40	22	5	7	2		3	
41–50	10	9	5	4	4	2	
51–60	10	10	8	3	1	3	
61–70	3		4		2	6	
71–80	1		2	1	1	11	
81–90	1	1	1		2	17	
91–100			1		1	19	1
101–110					1	3	2
110–120						2	1
AVERAGE DEPTH	26 cm	47 cm	51 cm	46 cm	56 cm	80 cm	107 cm

So, was the ground surface 12,000 years ago 1.3 m lower than it is today? David Leigh's analysis of the soil-grain size did not identify any major flood deposits, and nothing to suggest a major buildup—or erosion—of soil is visible in the profiles. No doubt the site has been flooded at different times but not on a regular basis. Silica freed from decomposed leaves and tree parts and windblown sand appear to have been the primary sources of new soil. Human activity such as game and rock processing, house daubing, and pottery making have also contributed. Soil buildup may therefore have been slight and gradual, resulting in the stacking of active zones of pedoturbation. Otherwise it appears that the oldest artifacts are where they are because they have had the longest time and most opportunities to be impacted by pedoturbation, especially bioturbation.

ARTIFACTS

The number of artifacts recovered at the Kolb site has been as much of an impediment as a blessing. Since the project is privately funded, a full-time lab staff has not been available. However, basic cataloging of each year's artifacts is done on an ongoing basis. To illustrate the magnitude of the job ahead, by 2010 over 260,000 flakes alone had been cataloged, and this is simply a basic level of identification, not an intensive analysis.

For the purpose of identifying and dating artifacts, we generally refer to well-regarded references such as Coe 1964 and Daniel 1998 for stone tools; Coe 1964 and 1989, South 1976, and Cable, Styer, and Cantley 1998 for Native American ceramics; and South 1977 and Noel Hume 1970 for historic artifacts.

DEBITAGE

By far the most common artifact at the site is the simple, unmodified metavolcanic flake (231,044, preliminary count as of 2010). Many of these came from the river or from ancient gravel bars exposed in the uplands through erosion. Metavolcanic is followed by quartz (19,495), chert (7,965), and orthoquartzite (736). Most of the chert is from local sources, but material from the Allendale outcrops on the Savannah is also seen. The presence of nonlocal chert and orthoquartzite from the Santee drainage tells us that people traveled across drainages, not just up- and downstream. The debitage found here reflects all stages of lithic reduction. People were bringing cobbles here and breaking them down into usable flakes and tools, as well as maintaining existing tools.

STONE TOOLS

As of 2005, 1,166 stone tools had been analyzed. That total includes four Paleoindian point fragments; 80 Early Archaic type points-notched Hardaway, Palmer, Kirk, Taylor, and LeCroy types; about 25 Middle Archaic Morrow Mountain and Guilford types; 30 square-stemmed Late Archaic Savannah River types; and 35 stemmed Woodland-type points. Most common are triangular points, 163 of which were analyzed by 2005. Triangular points mostly replaced stemmed points after about 500 B.C. in North Carolina and South Carolina (Ward and Davis 1999; Steen and Judge 2003). The earlier examples were used as knives and spear and dart points. The bow and arrow are thought to have been introduced after about A.D. 450 and many of these are true arrowheads (DePratter 1993). As Table 1 shows, these were mostly found in the upper 30 cm of soil.

The earliest tools at the site (Figure 7, top) appear to be two crystalline quartz lanceolate-point fragments. Neither is complete enough to firmly assign a type name. One is a basal fragment that is incurvate and ground. The other is a midsection with fluting on both sides. In 2008 another early point was found (Figure 8). This is a classic example of an unbeveled Dalton-type point made of weathered basalt, dating between about 9000 and 10,500 B.P. (Morse 1997). This and the other early points all were found between about 95 and 120 cm below surface at the very base of the units.

Other stone tools include some 230 formal scrapers and 25 blade tools. These are nearly all associated with the early component. Utilized and retouched flakes were used throughout time as expedient cutting tools. Tools for other uses include bifaces made both as preforms for points and as working tools, axes, nutting stones, grinding stones, and abraders.

Figure 7. Early projectile points/knives.
Courtesy of Christopher Judge.

Figure 8. Dalton point found in 2008.
Courtesy of Christopher Judge.

38DA75 - The Kolb Site

0   1   2   3   4   5cm

38DA75 - The Johannes Kolb Site

0 10 20 30 40 50 60 70 80 90 100mm

0   1   2   3   4in

PREHISTORIC CERAMICS

All of the major South Carolina pottery groups have been recovered at the Kolb site, from fiber-tempered Stallings ware to Contact Period complicated stamped wares. Though much is shared, the overall collection does appear to differ from assemblages seen in the Cape Fear, Santee, and Savannah drainages. Intensive ceramic analysis has not been completed at this time, however, so the full range of variance cannot be quantified.

Early researchers saw the Pee Dee drainage as a borderland between the northern and southern tribes, using language groups as a defining characteristic (Coe 1964; South 1976). As long as we recognize that the border was never fixed and that it was only a border in the very broadest of terms, that is accurate.

Figure 9. Thoms Creek pottery recovered from the Kolb site. Courtesy of Christopher Judge.

People north of the Pee Dee did predominantly speak Siouan languages, while those to the south spoke Muskhogean languages; but group movement did occur, as the pottery here clearly demonstrates. Fiber-tempered Stallings and sand-tempered Thoms Creek pottery (Figure 9) are found here at depths that put them at the base of the topsoil, in context with Savannah River–type points—especially "eccentric" shaped variants—and smaller Woodland stemmed variants. This suggests that the people who appeared in the Savannah River drainage 4,000–5,000 years ago did not stop there but continued to explore, apparently by water as well as by land.

The collection here is dominated by textile-marked wares—fabric-impressed and cord-marked pottery. The idea of ceramic "types" is not emphasized at the Kolb site, because strictly considering ceramics in this way blinds us to variability that may be meaningful on the interpretive level. Our approach has been to downplay the idea of typology and use descriptive terms at the preliminary level to allow future researchers with ideas about typology to work from a relatively unbiased beginning point.

In a few cases, types defined elsewhere are clear, and examples can be identified here. Stallings, Thoms Creek, and Deptford wares are found, along with a tremendous amount of grog-tempered Hanover wares. Lithic-tempered cord- and fabric-marked wares are common as well. Inclusions range from pebbles to crushed quartz to sand tempering ranging from fine to coarse.

Complicated stamped pottery is not common at the site, though examples identified as the Pee Dee type have been found. This also reiterates the idea of a borderland, as the expansion of Mississippian culture from the Southwest essentially stopped at the Pee Dee.

HISTORIC ARTIFACTS

Historic period artifacts include early ceramics, glass, nails, and other items from the Johannes Kolb occupation as well as remains from what seem to be two

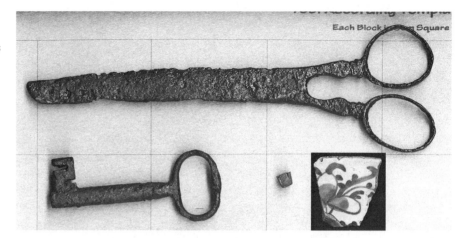

distinct slave occupations: one from the late eighteenth century and the other from the 1830s–1850s period (Figure 10). Root cellar features in particular have yielded scissors, keys, and other materials. Around the turn of the twentieth century, a sawmill was installed and the workers seem to have stayed here temporarily, as there is a burst of domestic artifacts from that period as well as a plethora of saw teeth. Shotgun shells and fishing tackle (and a beer can or two) tell us of the more recent site function. Given that we archaeologists are leaving unit nails in at least one corner of every unit we dig, and that we inevitably lose tools, keys, coins, and other things, we are making a contribution to the archaeological record, too.

Culture History

PRE-ARCHAIC TO POST-MISSISSIPPIAN

Recent research suggests a human presence in the Savannah River drainage as early as 50,000 years ago (Albert C. Goodyear, personal communication March 4, 2012). This is still strongly contested, however. Regardless, people were surely in the Eastern United States by about 18,000 years ago (Adovasio and Stukenrath 1990). Knowing the potential for deeply buried earlier components, we have tested a sample of each year's units by augering. About 3.5 m below surface all across the site, there is a layer of pea gravel that accumulated when the site was in a high-energy fluvial environment. No artifacts have been found below about 1.3 m below surface in any of our work. However, the sample size that has been taken from below that depth is much smaller in volume than the sample size taken above that mark, so the potential for new discoveries remains.

Fragments of two crystal quartz bifaces found in the deepest levels of our excavations are thought to be from lanceolate bifaces (Figure 5) that may date from 11,000 to 18,000 years B.P., but the earliest whole point we have is a Dalton type made of basalt (Figure 8). Radiocarbon dates of 10,000–12,900 B.P. have been obtained for this type of point (Morse 1997; Anderson and Sassaman 2012). When these were in use, the environment was changing from the cooler, drier Pleistocene to the warmer, moister Holocene.

The flora and fauna available changed rapidly during this period, and the number of humans exploiting the environment was growing. In order to adapt, localized foraging strategies began to evolve. The technology of bifaces changed during this time, and lanceolate forms gave way to side- and corner-notched points. Other tools, such as formal scrapers and blades continued in use until about 7,000 years ago. Evidence from this period is abundant at the Kolb site. At this time people are thought to have been organized in small groups based in the extended family. These societies are thought to have been egalitarian in nature, with no designated rulers and followers.

The population continued to grow and artifacts that have been dated to the period between about 5,000 and 7,000 years ago are found all over the state (O'Steen 1990; Sassaman 1993; Benson 2006). Points with square stems, contracting stems, and rounded bases mostly replace the more finely crafted notched points. Their wide distribution tells us that people were exploring every niche in the environment in search of food and other resources (House and Wogaman 1978). With more people on the land, more complex forms of social organization had to develop and groups are thought to have reacted by becoming more tightly knit, and placing leadership responsibilities on designated individuals.

To think that there is a smooth trajectory of change among people who were more or less based in the Pee Dee drainage throughout time is probably a mistake. Around 5,000 years ago people began making large, sometimes crude square stemmed points that are generally grouped as the Savannah River type (Coe 1964). Around 4,500 years ago people who had been making these points in the Savannah River valley also began to make clay pottery tempered with plant fibers (Waring and Williams 1968; Stoltman 1974; Sassaman 1993). Dates on this "Stallings"-type pottery range between 4500 and 3500 B.P. Sand-tempered Thoms Creek pottery with very similar decorations is found in contexts dating between about 4000 and 2500 B.P. (Trinkley 1980, Saunders 2002), so an overlap is evident. Was the difference a result of group fissioning (essentially, Sassaman's [1993] band-macro band model) or adaptation by neighboring groups—that is, diffusion?

All three phenomena are clearly manifested at the Kolb site and appear to be distinctly different from earlier deposits. Dense knapping beds are found with broken and discarded square-stemmed points in them. Thoms Creek and Stallings pottery are usually found a little closer to the ground surface, suggesting a stratigraphic succession that has been blurred by pedoturbation. This is what Sassaman (1993) refers to as the preceramic and ceramic phases of the Late Archaic. The sites of these people are found along the coast as well as up and down every drainage from the Great Pee Dee River to Florida. It has been suggested that the practice of making fiber-tempered pottery came to the Southeast from South America across the Caribbean islands (Saunders and Hays 2004). The questions again becomes these: What moved—the people or the idea? Were the "Stallings/Thoms Creek People" intrepid explorers or opportunistic early adopters?

Pottery making spread up the East Coast quickly, and by about 4000 B.P. people were making ceramic pots in North Carolina (Coe 1964), Virginia (Egloff and Potter 1982), and points north (Custer 1989). The Pee Dee drainage is seen as the core of a loose frontier (South 1977). In general, people making pottery with designs created by malleating the bodies with carved paddles tend to be found to the south and west, while people to the north and east most often decorated their ceramics with textiles—cord, net, and fabric. That said, both methods were used in both regions at different times.

The people of the Southwest were in contact with Mesoamerica and brought corn to the United States. In the Mississippi valley, maize agriculture was introduced around 2,000 years ago. It did not spread to North and South Carolina until after about 1100 B.P. Societies that rely on the weather tend to develop elaborate belief systems based on sun worship, which they hope will allow them to insure the cooperation of the weather gods. This allowed what we know as Mississippian culture to develop. It is likely that Mississippianism was as much a belief system as a set of adaptive lifeways. The Pee Dee is about the farthest north and east that the Mississippians reached. They were in the area by about 1,100 years ago, and flourished until about 650 years ago.

To the northeast, in North Carolina and Virginia, agriculture came later, and the culture that developed does not seem to have included classic Mississippian traits such as mound building. In North Carolina they did not make pottery with complicated stamped designs until about 500 years ago (Ward and Davis 1993). But their population grew so large that societies were forced to deal with issues that arise when people are forced to live together in villages. Cultural complexity increased, and some of the more objectionable aspects of complex societies arose. Warfare and feuds beginning in the prehistoric past lasted into historic times. This resulted in group conflict and mass migrations that shaped the population of the Pee Dee whom the first Europeans encountered.

HISTORIC NATIVE AMERICANS

The first known Europeans to visit the Pee Dee came through in 1521, 1526, and 1540 (Hudson 1976, 1990). For the next 200 years, the only Europeans to visit the area were travelers and traders rather than settlers. Their firsthand impact was limited, yet their indirect impact was devastating (Smith 1987). Native Americans had no resistance to the worst of the diseases brought in by the seafaring Europeans and their African slaves. Groups were cut down en masse. The fevers did not discriminate by social status, age, or social role. Chiefs, priests, and healers died alongside farmers and children, often taking the accumulated knowledge of generations with them. In 1708 a lowcountry preacher wrote that the local Native Americans still practiced a recognizable "Green Corn" ceremony but that no one could explain why or what the symbolism meant (Le Jau 1708 in Klingberg 1956). Further, the early colonists needed labor, and many southeastern Indians were enslaved to provide it. In 1730 as much as 25 percent of the slave population was Native American (Menard 1995).

Many of the remaining Coastal Plain Native Americans joined the Catawba, Cherokee, and other large groups (Merrell 1989), but a number simply stayed put and lived among the Europeans and their slaves. These so-called "settlement Indians" stopped practicing their traditional lifeways and learned to speak English and worship in Christian churches. Although they gave up their Indian identity to an extent, they still stayed together, if only on the extended-family level.

The racial dynamic of southern society of the eighteenth through the twentieth centuries placed whites, or Euro-Americans, at the top and all "people of color" below, with Africans and the enslaved at the bottom and free people of color in an uncertain position in the middle. As the three groups interbred, the lines between races were blurred, and Indians faced a new problem: often they were accused of being runaway slaves. When this happened the burden was on them to prove their heritage. In a society where permanent identification documents were nonexistent, the accused were forced to rely on the testimony of their white neighbors to prove their heritage. If this was not forthcoming, they could be enslaved. One such case from living memory was recounted by James Island author Eugene Frazier (2006).

Yet many Native Americans survived, and their families are still to be found in the Pee Dee region today. With the loosening of racial divisions in the late twentieth century, many have begun rediscovering their native roots and joined together as the Pee Dee, and Lumbee tribes. Across the state we see people with native roots organizing in groups such as the Kusso-Natchez and Waccamaw.

Johannes Kolb and Family

As Europe left the medieval period and the modern mercantile system began to evolve, both upper- and lower-status individuals were forced from their traditional lifeways. For instance, to fuel the new factories' demand for wool, sheep herds were put to pasture on what had traditionally been agricultural fields. The displaced families were forced to find new lands or move to the cities. Many chose to seek a new life in the colonies. Around the turn of the eighteenth century, a young Johannes Kolb arrived in southeastern Pennsylvania with his extended family and other members of their Mennonite Church (Cassel 1895). For over 30 years he lived and worked there, but when a group of Welsh Baptists decided to come south to take advantage of the colonial governor's offer of free land in the Welsh Neck (Figure 11), he and two of his brothers and their families joined them.

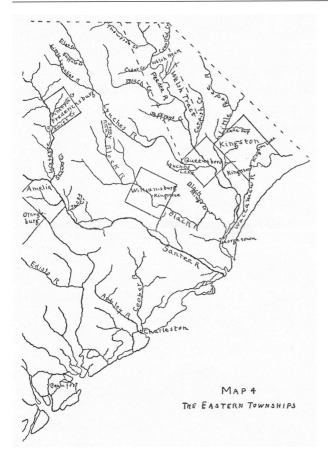

Figure 11. Map of the eastern townships (from Meriwether 1941). Courtesy of Christopher Judge.

Johannes Kolb's time in South Carolina is poorly documented. This is not unusual. Before 1768 Charleston was not just the capital but the only place in the state with courts, magistrates, a sheriff, and a land office (Wallace 1951). News from the backcountry was of little concern to the coastal rice planters, and most frontier dwellers were passed over by written history (Johnson 1997). There are a few mentions of Johannes Kolb in land records, but he is better known for being the progenitor of a lineage that touches many of Darlington County's families today. As Chapman Milling (in Ervin and Rudisill 1964:147) put it, "Most families . . . could trace their descent from James James, the Welsh leader, from Johannes Kolb, the Palatine, from Pierre Bacot, the Huguenot, or from all three."

Even the date of Kolb's death is unknown, but he appears to have died before 1762, when the Reverend Evan Pugh took the ministry at the nearby Welsh Baptist church and began keeping a record of his daily activities (Rudisill 1993). Pugh mentions a "Mr. Kulp" in 1762 and nonspecific Kolbs through the 1760s. He was minister to and friends with his sons, Martin and Peter, and his daughters, Sarah, Mary, Mehatibel, and Hannah, at the same time, however. He does not mention Johannes Kolb by name or mention the deaths of any unspecified "Mr. Kolb."

So, the archaeological record tells us much of what we know about Kolb, his family, and their lives on the Pee Dee. When Chip Helms recorded the site, he found clearly pre–Revolutionary War pottery on the surface, and with the first few test units we confirmed this in subsurface contexts. But the material record is understandably thin, reflecting the site's remote frontier setting (Lewis 1976). At sites closer to the coast and its markets, imported goods are common; but in this context people would make wooden wares for eating, buckets and gourds would be used to store and serve liquids, and wood could even serve in the place of iron nails and architectural hardware. After all, the closest major ports, Charleston and Wilmington, were over 100 miles away as the crow flies, roads were bad, and travel by water was time consuming. Artifacts we can tie to Johannes and family include sherds of English slipware and Delft, as well as bottle glass and nails. Distribution mapping shows these to be concentrated in the east end of the site. Larger excavation units there encountered historic structural posts and recovered daub, brick, mortar, and plaster. This is consistent with the expected vernacular architecture of the time (Upton 1986), so it is believed that Kolb's house was in this area.

Johannes Kolb's sons were grown when they arrived and soon purchased lands of their own across the river on Kolb's Neck—what is now called Byrd Island. After Johannes Kolb and his wife, Sarah, died, the place seems to have been abandoned. There is a hiatus in the occupation between the 1760s and 1780s, but artifacts from the 1790s to 1810s are fairly common, and another occupation from the 1830s–1850s period is also evident. Further analysis is necessary to fully evaluate this sequencing, however.

Land records for the transaction have not been found, so how or when exactly he obtained it is unknown, but when the land next changed hands in 1849, Bright Williamson transferred the land to his son, Thomas C. Williamson. It is likely that the property was passed down to one or all of Johannes and Sarah Kolb's children, who subsequently sold it to Williamson.

In 2008 we found a clue. A silver spoon was found that was marked with the initials E over LB (Figure 12). Johannes Kolb's granddaughter Elizabeth

Figure 12. Silver spoon, engraved E over LB, recovered from the Kolb site. Courtesy of Christopher Judge.

Kimbrough married Colonel Lemuel Benton around the time of the American Revolution, so it is assumed that these are their initials. The land Elizabeth inherited from her father, John Kimbrough, abuts Johannes Kolb's property. This is marked "Benton" on the 1849 plat. Colonial silver expert Grahame Long believes that this is a colonial piece, probably southern, which dates between 1720 and 1740. But, he says, it would not be unusual at all for a family to "update" an existing heirloom for a wedding gift (Grahame Long, personal communication 2008).

The Benton and Williamson Slaves

Neither the Bentons nor the Williamsons lived here. Both had homes on the high ground overlooking the river swamp, and both were slaveholders, so the people living here were African American slaves. All the documentary record tells us about these people is that there were 49 of them on all of Thomas C. Williamson's properties in 1850. He and his wife both died young, and by 1854 their children were living with their grandparents at nearby Mont Clare Plantation (Ethel Williamson, in Ervin and Rudisill 1964). The fields were probably still maintained, and slaves probably lived here until they were emancipated. This site, along with others in the river swamp, faced increasing flooding and seems to have been mostly abandoned after the war.

To date at least four slave houses have been identified at the Kolb site. These were probably post-in-ground structures, like Johannes Kolb's, as we found numerous deep structural posts. Some may have been log buildings as well, such as the standing slave cabins at Witherspoon Island, just downstream from the Kolb site. Rectangular root cellars are found beneath the floors of these buildings. They contain a variety of materials including scissors, buttons, cuff links, ceramics, and bottle glass.

Other items include an 1856 silver half-dime pierced for suspension (Figure 13). Pierced coins such as this were considered good luck charms and were often worn on an ankle bracelet (Puckett 1975). In fact it also represented a fairly valuable investment—in 1856 slave settlement dollars at least. Finally, the image on the coin is "Liberty," who holds in her hand a staff topped with a Liberty cap,

Figure 13. Pierced button and coin recovered from the Kolb site. Courtesy of Christopher Judge.

symbol of the French Revolution. The good luck the owner was hoping for may have included freedom. So this one object expresses meaning in several separate spheres at once: as a sign of a belief system, as a symbol of wealth and status, and as a sign of aspiration toward freedom and thus dissatisfaction with slave status.

Investors and Loggers

In 1874 the estate of T. C. Williamson sold the property to Darlington lawyer Berryman W. Edwards, who then passed it on to his son, George. Upstream more and more farmers were clearing fields during the nineteenth century, causing increased runoff and flooding. Planting crops in this environment became too risky a venture, and most fields in the swamps were abandoned. But the nineteenth century also brought the railroads, and with populations everywhere in the eastern United States growing, lumber and other forest products came into great demand. The steam engines that ran the trains were adapted, and narrow-gauge tram roads were run through the swamps of the Pee Dee and other rivers throughout the South to exploit a resource that had previously been too bulky to use: the giant cypresses, pines, and hardwoods of the river swamp (Southerlin 2008). The Edwardses set up a sawmill in the north part of the site and renamed the place "Riverdale." We regularly find teeth from their saws and other artifacts from this period. After the trees were cut out, the tract faced a history similar to many in this environment. It was allowed to regenerate in pines, which were cut to fuel the growing paper mills, such as the Sonoco Company's Hartsville plant, among others. It passed from lumber company to lumber company during the twentieth century before it was finally deeded to the SCDNR in 1989.

Public Education at the Kolb Site

Archaeology should serve the scientific goal of learning about past cultures, but we should always bear in mind that sharing this knowledge with the community is the ultimate goal. Archaeology that is conducted in private, which is not shared, serves no useful purpose as it destroys the resource for, essentially, the titillation of a single person.

TEACHING STUDENTS AND VOLUNTEERS

From the beginning at the Kolb site, our work has been aimed at learning about the site and the history of the Pee Dee region and at sharing our discoveries and knowledge. We do this by encouraging active participation by people who want to learn to practice archaeology. We have had everyone from crawling babies to octogenarians help us "dig in the dirt" over the years. Obviously, children cannot put in a full day's work before they are at least ten or so years old, but we still allow them to help with screening. Boy Scouts, local high school students, and other school groups come out to help as well, but we mainly concentrate on a group who are at a crossroad in their lives, college students.

From the very beginning in 1997, this project was envisioned as a public project for a number of reasons. First and foremost, our friend and benefactor, Dr. Ernest L. "Chip" Helms III, was interested in bringing our research efforts to the attention of his family, friends, and neighbors in the community of Mechanicsville, Darlington County, South Carolina. Second, the site is located within a 2,800-acre Heritage Preserve owned by the state and managed by the South Carolina Department of Natural Resources, open to the public from sunrise to sunset 365 days of the year. The Kolb site is bisected by the only vehicle-accessible road on the preserve, about three miles from the entrance, and thus it would be hard to keep this project quiet. Collectors and interested parties are invited to visit and help, and we have never had a problem with vandalism. A third reason revolves around the fact that the project principals have been committed to archaeological education throughout their careers.

The public education component of our research has been both as rewarding and important as the scientific research described throughout this essay. In our initial one-week season, the road to the site was in rather bad condition and only passable with four-wheel-drive vehicles. Undeterred by such obstacles, local game warden Sergeant Russell Galloway ferried a number of folks in and out, and Chris Judge was constantly driving back and forth to Weatherford's Country Store to pick up students, volunteers, and interested members of the public.

As noted, Native Americans in South Carolina were all but wiped out by disease and enslavement, yet some families stayed behind. In researching the history of Native Americans at the site, we have sought to include their descendants at every step to help them reclaim knowledge of their history. Among the early visitors was Chief David Locklear of the Pee Dee Indian Tribe of South Carolina. The Pee Dee have continued to be frequent visitors and supporters of our research, and many, including present-day chief James Calder, have worked side by side with us.

When our second season evolved to two weeks, we designated the middle Saturday as "Public Day" and sent press releases out to encourage visitation. Chip's sister Mary Ellen Howell and her husband, David, along with family and friends provided a BBQ lunch to all, a tradition that has continued to this day. Usually we get from 200 to 300 visitors on public day, but visitors are welcome at any time and many return year after year, often bearing food.

We were very fortunate to have a number of project members lending their unique talents to our educational program in the early years and who continue with us to the present. Sean Taylor, then an undergraduate anthropology student at Carolina, had been learning to flintknap and would leave his excavation unit to break rock for the visitors. Jason Smith, an archaeologist, was also involved in eighteenth-century and early-military reenactments and joined us in portraying Mr. Kolb in period attire, with his wife, Susan, posing as Mrs. Kolb. These efforts to breathe life into the silent and static archaeological record were extremely well received by site visitors, and that encouraged us to expend additional effort and resources in that direction.

Since those early days our educational mission has grown and evolved. Another key contributor has been Bobby Southerlin of Archaeological Consultants of the Carolinas, whose prehistoric pottery-making and -firing demonstrations combine education with research as we strive to understand the archaeology of the site. Tariq Ghaffar, an archaeologist turned high school teacher, became the main site interpreter, providing guided tours to individuals and groups who made their way out into the swamp to learn about the past. Often this is a demanding and exhausting task, but such efforts are important. We have been pleased to open the site to schoolchildren visiting as part of their classes. Having a person dedicated to the task makes their experience more rewarding.

Over the years Sean Taylor has become an expert primitive technologist. He has become involved in a regional network of such experts, so we have added a number of individuals to our public day who demonstrate everything from friction fire making, blowgun hunting, prehistoric fishing techniques, and cooking in clay pots to hide tanning and more. These interpreters include Scott Jones, Fuz Sanderson, Keith Grenoble, Tom Mancke, and Tom Ray. This has evolved into one of the best events of its kind in the Southeast. Sean has also led us in designing large posters to inform the visiting public further about our findings within the site and within a regional context. Understanding how artifacts were made and used helps us better understand the remains we find in the soil, so these demonstrations are as useful for the students and professionals as they are for the visitors.

We have provided pamphlets and posters explaining our project to the public and have lectured in schools, social clubs, and other venues in the community. Erika Shofner, as part of her M.A. studies at USC, designed an exhibit for the nearby Florence County Museum that has also been installed at the Hartsville Museum, the Native American Studies Program at USC-Lancaster, and the DNR's Florence office.

We have taken a certain amount of pride in our accomplishments at the Kolb site and we have been noticed by others as well. We were the recipients of the first-ever Archaeological Stewardship Award present in 2006 by the South Carolina Governor's Office and the first-ever Archaeological Education Award from the Archaeological Society of South Carolina. In addition, in 2007 we received the Southeastern Archaeological Conference's Public Education Grant to help fund our site interpreter, primitive technologists, and a project photographer.

Another source of pride is the fact that many who joined us as young students have become professional archaeologists and continue to be involved, even though they now have full-time jobs and families to keep them busy. We even have a number of students who have left the profession to pursue other paths, yet find their way back to the Pee Dee in the spring to assist us. Most Kolb site veterans speak of it as "our project," a visible sign that this is a project that takes diverse people from diverse walks of life to accomplish. Some 12,000 hours of volunteer service have been logged. Several friends come out for the sole purpose of cooking in the evening for 30 people, and at least one is frequently asked about when folks are planning their time with us.

As you can see, our success can be measured in terms of the people who get involved, get turned on to the mission, and then jump in and help. Of enormous help has been the loan of two hunt club houses that allow us to house our large staff. This sometimes grows around public-day weekend to 40 people. We estimate that the generosity of the C. Kirk Dunlap and Campbell Coxe families has saved us over $50,000 in motel costs. This project could not be done without their generous assistance.

The future for the Kolb site revolves around sustained funds for the research so that we can obtain the 17 percent sample, conduct the in-depth analyses needed to write reports, and find the funds and facility to curate the massive collection that has been retained by the excavations. Public and academic publications will be produced and disseminated. Many theses and dissertations could and should emanate from the Kolb site. The spirit of and for the project remains high and we ("the diggers," as we are called locally) have established a sense of place and belonging in the Great Pee Dee region. That has resulted in putting the Kolb site on the map.

Research at the Kolb site will provide a benchmark by which all future archaeological endeavors in the eastern part of South Carolina will be assessed and compared. This last fact is related to both the full set of archaeological components from the Ice Age onward, the fact that the three main ethnic groups in South Carolina are represented at the site, and the intensive level at which the site was approached and understood. There are probably other sites like this one out there waiting to be discovered and excavated. A certain magic developed around the Kolb site because of the persistence of a special person who found the site. He knew it was unusually important, and he eventually was successful in attracting the attention of archaeologists. In Chip Helms's honor, our project has been and continues to be dedicated to the memory of his parents, Mr. and Mrs. Ernest L. Helms Jr.

References Cited

Adovasio, J. M., J. Donahue, and, R. Stukenrath

1990   The Meadowcroft Rockshelter Radio-carbon Chronology 1975–1990. *American Antiquity* 55:348–360

Anderson, David, and Glen Hanson

1988   Early Archaic Settlement in the Southeastern United States. *American Antiquity* 53:262–286

Anderson, David G., and Kenneth Sassaman

2012   *Recent Developments in Southeastern Archaeology.* Society for American Archaeology Press, Washington, D.C.

Benson, Robert W.

2006   *Sumter National Forest Cultural Resources Overview.* Southeastern Archaeological Services, Athens, Georgia.

Buol, S. W., F. D. Hole., and R. J. McCracken

1973   *Soil Genesis and Classification.* Iowa State University Press, Ames.

Cable, John, Kenneth F. Styer, and Charles E. Cantley

1998   Ceramic Analysis: A Study of Taxonomy and Systematics in the North Coastal Zone. In *Data Recovery Excavations at the Big Jones (38HR809) and Maple Swamp (38HR315) Sites on the Conway Bypass, Horry County, South Carolina.* New South Associates, Stone Mountain, Georgia.

Cardew, Michael

1969   *Pioneer Pottery.* St. Martin's Press, New York.

Cassel, Daniel Kolb

1895   *Genealogical History of the Kolb, Kulp, or Culp Family and its Branches in America.* Morgan R. Wills, Norristown, Pennsylvania.

Coe, Joffrey

1964   *Formative Cultures of the Carolina Piedmont.* Transactions of the American Philosophical Society, Philadelphia, Pennsylvania.

Custer, Jay

1989   *Delaware Prehistory.* University of Delaware Press, Wilmington.

Daniel, Randy

1998   *Hardaway Revisited: Early Archaic Settlement in the Southeast.* University of Alabama Press, Tuscaloosa.

DeBoer, Warren

1988   Subterranean Storage and the Organization of Surplus: The View from Eastern North America. *Southeastern Archaeology* 7(1):1–20

DePratter, Chester

1993   The Woodland, Mississippian and Protohistoric Periods in South Carolina. *South Carolina Antiquities* 25(1 and 2):43–48

Egloff, Keith, and Stephen Potter

1982   Indian Ceramics from Coastal Plain Virginia. *Archaeology of Eastern North America* 10:95–117

Ervin, Eliza C., and Horace F. Rudisill (editors)

1964   *Darlingtoniana.* R. L. Bryan, Columbia, South Carolina.

Faulkner, William

1951   *Requiem for a Nun.* Random House, New York.

Frazier, Eugene

2006   *James Island: Stories from Slave Descendants.* History Press, Charleston, South Carolina.

Gage, James E.

2009   *Root Cellars in America: Their History, Design, and Construction 1609–1920.* Powwow River Books, Amesbury, Massachusetts.

Goodyear, Albert, Tommy Charles, and James Michie

1989   The Earliest South Carolinians. In *Studies in South Carolina Archaeology: Essays in Honor of Robert L. Stephenson,* edited by Albert Goodyear and Glen T. Hanson, pp. 19–52. South Carolina Institute of Archaeology and Anthropology, University of South Carolina, Columbia.

Herbert, Joseph, and Theresa McReynolds

2004   *Compositional Variability in Prehistoric Native American Pottery from North Carolina.* North Carolina Department of Cultural Resources, Raleigh.

House, John, and Ronald Wogaman

1978   *Windy Ridge: A Prehistoric Site in the Interriverine Piedmont.* Anthropological Studies 3 Institute of Archaeology and Anthropology, University of South Carolina, Columbia, S.C.

Hudson, Charles

1976   *The Southeastern Indians.* University of Tennessee Press, Knoxville.

1990   *The Juan Pardo Expeditions: Exploration of the Carolinas and Tennessee, 1566–1568.* Smithsonian Institution Press, Washington, D.C.

Johnson, George L.

1997   *The Frontier in the Colonial South.* Greenwood Press, Westport, Connecticut.

Klingberg, Frank J.

1956   *The Carolina Chronicle of Dr. Francis Le Jau, 1706–1717.* University of California Press, Berkeley.

Kovacik, Charles, and John Winberry

1987   *South Carolina: The Making of a Landscape.* Westview Press, Boulder, Colorado.

Leigh, David, Pradeep Srivastava, and George Brook

2004   Late Pleistocene Braided Rivers of the Atlantic Coastal Plain, USA. *Quaternary Science Reviews* 23:65- 84

Lewis, Kenneth E

1976   *The American Frontier: An Archaeological Study of Settlement Pattern and Process.* Academic Press, New York.

Linder, Suzanne C. and Emily L. Johnson

2000   *A River in Time: The Yadkin–Pee Dee River System.* Palmetto Conservation Foundation, Spartanburg, SC

Mathieu, James R.

2002   *Experimental Archaeology: Replicating Past Objects, Behaviors and Processes.* Archaeopress, Oxford, United Kingdom.

Menard, Russell

1995   Slave Demography in the Lowcountry, 1670–1740: From Frontier Society to Plantation Regime. *South Carolina Historical Magazine* 96(4):280–303

Merrell, James H.

1989   *The Indians' New World: Catawbas and Their Neighbors from European Contact through the Era of Removal.* University of North Carolina Press, Chapel Hill.

Michie, James L.

1990   Bioturbation and Gravity as a Potential Site Formational Process: The Open Area Site, 38GE261. *South Carolina Antiquities* 22:15–39

Morse, Dan F.

1997   *Sloan: A Paleoindian Dalton Cemetery in Arkansas.* Smithsonian Institution Press, Washington, D.C.

Noel Hume, Ivor

1970   *A Guide to the Artifacts of Colonial America.* Alfred A. Knopf, New York.

O'Steen, Lisa

1999   The Bear Creek Site (38FA204/205): Paleoindian and Archaic Occupation in the Lower Piedmont of South Carolina. *South Carolina Antiquities* 31:1–182.

Puckett, Newbell Niles

1975   *Folk Beliefs of the Southern Negro.* Negro Universities Press, New York.

Rhodes, Daniel

1957   *Clay and Glazes for the Potter.* Chilton Book Co., Philadelphia.

Rudisill, Horace (editor)

1993   *The Diaries of Evan Pugh (1762–1801).* St. David's Society, Florence, South Carolina.

Sassaman, Kenneth

1993   *Early Pottery in the Southeast.* University of Alabama Press, Tuscaloosa.

Saunders, Rebecca (editor)

2002   *The Fig Island Ring Complex (38CH42): Coastal Adaptation and the Question of Ring Function in the Late Archaic.* Report Prepared for South Carolina Department of Archives and History, Columbia.

Saunders, Rebecca, and Christopher T. Hays (editors)

2004   *Early Pottery: Technology, Function, Style, and Interaction in the Lower Southeast.* University of Alabama Press, Tuscaloosa.

Schiffer, Michael

1987   *Formation Processes of the Archaeological Record.* University of New Mexico Press, Albuquerque.

Schroedl, Gerald F.

1986   Toward an Explanation of Cherokee Origins in EasternTennessee. In *The Conference on Cherokee Prehistory*, edited by David G. Moore, pp. 122–38. Warren Wilson College, Swannanoa, NC.

Smith, Marvin

1987   *Archaeology of Aboriginal Culture Change in the Interior Southeast: Depopulation during the Early Historic Period.* University of Florida Press, Gainesville.

South, Stanley A.

1976   An Archaeological Survey of Southeastern North Carolina. *The Notebook* 8:1–55. South Carolina Institute of Archaeology and Anthropology, University of South Carolina, Columbia.

1977   *Method and Theory in Historical Archaeology.* Academic Press, New York.

Southerlin, Bobby and Dawn Reid, Carl Steen

2008   Toward Development of an Archaeological and Historic Context for South Carolina's Sawmill, Timber and Lumber Industries. *South Carolina Antiquities* 40: 48–88.

Steen, Carl, Daniel T. Elliott, Rita F. Elliott, and Anthony Warren

1996   *Further Excavations at John de la Howe's Lethe Farm.* Diachronic Research Foundation, Columbia, South Carolina.

Steen, Carl, and Christopher Judge

1997   *Archaeology at the Great Pee Dee Heritage Preserve.* South Carolina Department of Natural Resources, Heritage Trust Program, Columbia, S.C

2003   Excavations at Sandstone Ledge Rockshelter: 38LX283. *South Carolina Antiquities* 35:1–116.

Steponaitis, Vincas, Jeffrey Irwin, Theresa McReynolds, and Christopher Moore

2006   *Stone Quarries and Sourcing in the Carolina Slate Belt.* Research Report 25. Research Laboratories of Archaeology, University of North Carolina, Chapel Hill.

Stoltman, James

1974   *Groton Plantation: An Archaeological Study of a South Carolina Locality.* Peabody Museum of American Archeology and Ethnology, Harvard University, Cambridge, Massachusetts.

Trinkley, Michael

1980   Investigation of the Woodland Period along the South Carolina Coast. Unpublished Ph.D. dissertation, Department of Anthropology, University of North Carolina, Chapel Hill.

Upton, Dell (editor)

1986   *Common Places: Readings in American Vernacular Architecture.* University of Georgia Press, Athens.

U.S. Army Corps of Engineers

1977   *Great Pee Dee River Basin.* Navigability Study, Report 11. U.S. Army Corps of Engineers, Charleston District, Charleston, South Carolina.

Wallace, David Duncan

1951   *South Carolina: A Short History.* University of South Carolina Press, Columbia.

Ward, Trawick, and R. P. Stephen Davis

1993   *Indian Communities on the North Carolina Piedmont AD 1000 to 1700.* University of North Carolina Press, Chapel Hill.

Waring, Antonio J., and Stephen Williams (editors)

1968   *The Waring Papers: The Collected Papers of Antonio J. Waring, Jr.* Peabody Museum of American Archaeology and Ethnography, Harvard University, Cambridge, Massachusetts.

Wood, Raymond, and Donald Johnson

1978   *Advances in Archaeological Method and Theory.* Academic Press, Tucson, Arizona.

Young, Christopher

2010   A Study of the Availability and Selection of Stone Tool Raw Materials in Relation to the Johannes Kolb Archaeological Site (38DA75). *South Carolina Antiquities* 42:27–34.

JONATHAN LEADER

Archaeological Prospection

Near-Surface Geophysics

ARCHAEOLOGY'S GOAL IS TO IDENTIFY and analyze the patterns of human culture from the past. To do this, we focus on the artifacts, sites, and landscapes that our ancestors or other earlier people produced, used, and inhabited. It is a poignant contradiction that every time we dig a site we simultaneously recover and destroy the information we seek. It is in our best interest to squeeze out as much information as we can from any site or field work while simultaneously doing the least amount of harm (Joukowsky 1980; McMillon 1991). Thus, we need to figure out the best place to dig. This is probably one of the oldest questions in archaeology, as there are never sufficient funds or time available to wander aimlessly around a landscape. This is not the sort of thing that should be left to chance. So, deciding where to dig often defines the difference between a successful field season and one that is less so.

Traditionally, archaeologists rely on a fairly simple set of tools to make this determination. They engage in field walking and surface collecting, research historic documents and private papers, study old maps, and listen very carefully to local stories and legends. Landowners and amateur archaeologists often provide a great deal of meaningful information. And they frequently consult the notes and records left by the professionals who worked in the area before them. The weight or importance given to any of these data sources is tied to the specific research question they are trying to answer. All archaeology is undertaken in the effort to answer questions, never to simply acquire things (McMillon 1990; Ministry of Parks and Tourism 2008).

Still, this is pretty much a hit-or-miss affair. Archaeologists are always looking for a way to tip the scales to their benefit (Gaffney and Gater 2003). One way to do this is to incorporate any technology that may cut costs, save time, or provide data not available in other ways. This makes archaeology a major consumer of other disciplines' techniques, often in ways the original producers and inventors had neither considered nor imagined.

A good example of this was the advent of flight. When airplanes first became more or less reliable, they were almost immediately put to the task of mapping and reconnaissance. The relatively low, slow, and stable flight paths used by those early airplanes provided an ideal platform for producing remarkably detailed aerial photographs. Archaeologists quickly became aware of this use and practically overnight transformed sites that were barely lumps and bumps on the ground into stunning photographic and cartographic displays. This work was further enhanced by timing the flight and photography for the best lighting conditions and during the best seasons. The early discovery that mornings and evenings provided raking light, which produced the most contrast between the culturally modified and unaltered landscape, is still of great importance almost 100 years later (Crawford 1923).

Winter and summer became the favored seasons for opposite reasons. The lack of vegetation in winter removed foliage that could hide features, while the drying conditions of summer tended to enhance the effect that underground features had on crop growth, making the resulting "crop marks" that much more noticeable. The use of special films that focused on specific spectra of visible and invisible light wavelengths, such as infrared, were quickly seized upon as they provided even more contrast for the interpretation of the landscape and the identification and analysis of sites, regardless of time of day or season (Wilson 2000).

It is important to note that there are some serious considerations archaeologists must take into account when adopting a technology. These include the initial and maintenance costs, the need for specialized training, the construction of support facilities, and the relative difficulty or ease in putting the technology into play in the field. Again, archaeology tends to gravitate towards those technologies that are the most manageable, least costly, most easily learned, and most simple to operate.

Enter geophysics, the application of physics to the dynamics of the earth. The term was first used in Germany in the mid-nineteenth century. It was most notably attached to the earth sciences, such as geology. As a science, geophysics relies on the study of seismic waves, gravity, heat flow, magnetism, and electrical conductivity to produce its information. At first blush, it may not be very clear how this could be of any benefit to archaeology. But first impressions are often misleading. The common threads among all the groups that use geophysics is that they are trying to identify, assess, and efficiently recover hidden assets (Buntebarth1981; Clark 1996).

The adoption of geophysics by archaeology did not really take off until after World War II. The reason for this was the intervention of that other great consumer and producer of applied technology—the military. Prior to the war, geophysics was both expensive and relatively obscure. The military's need to remotely sense and assess hidden threats in a variety of environments and locations resulted in a tremendous amount of research and development. This was coupled with the equally important need to produce the various units in bulk to maximize their effect on field operations—not to mention some pretty strenuous testing far beyond the rigors likely to be encountered by most field researchers.

Once the infrastructure was in place, the advancements declassified, and the equipment commercially available, archaeologists were very quick to see their utility and reapply them to peaceful pursuits.

What Are the Most Common Forms of Archaeological Geophysics?

Geophysics encompasses a remarkably diverse set of techniques, not all of which are really applicable to archaeology (Kearey et al. 2002; Lowrie 2007). Archaeologists, as always, have cherry-picked those techniques they believe to be the most useful (Witten 2006). The resulting list that follows is not written in stone. As the techniques have evolved in the primary arenas of geophysical research, there is a constant reassessment of what may or may not be useful. And some of the largest purveyors of geophysics, such as NASA, have in recent years made common cause with archaeologists and other secondary users. This enlightened attitude has been to everyone's benefit and fueled innovation (Johnson 2006).

The near-surface geophysical techniques used in archaeology can be divided into passive and active forms. Passive techniques include such things as visible and invisible light recorders, magnetometers, gradient magnetometers, and electromagnetic detectors. Active techniques include metal detectors, seismic resonance devices, electrical resistivity, and ground-penetrating radar. In each instance, the intent is really very much the same: to identify and accurately locate differences in the surrounding soils or environment that can then be linked to either natural or cultural processes. The most common forms of archaeological geophysics can be further reduced to those most likely to be encountered in the field. These include metal detectors, electrical resistivity, gradiometers, and ground-penetrating radars.

METAL DETECTORS

Most people are familiar with metal detectors. Originally designed to detect landmines for the military, they seem to have made an effortless shift to civilian pursuits, which is to say that practitioners first relied on military-surplus detectors. The technology involved was not declassified for several decades. Modern detectors operate using a couple of different methodologies. These are very low frequency (VLF), pulse induction (PI), and beat-frequency oscillation (BFO). The best detectors tend to be the VLF format. This equipment takes a coil-within-a-coil approach. The search head has an outer coil that produces an electromagnetic field and a shielded interior coil that acts as the receiver. The polarity of the outer coil's magnetic field is shifted back and forth very rapidly. This moves the field above and below the coil and into the ground, where it interacts with natural and cultural materials. These subsurface materials form weak magnetic fields in response, which are then picked up by the receiver coil. The signal is then passed to the sensors in the control box, which interprets it. With the best devices of this type, there is some fairly sophisticated software put to use that provides not only a best guess as to the nature of the metal (such as iron and gold) but the size and depth of the artifact as well.

In the hands of a trained operator, a metal detector is a remarkably simple, inexpensive, easily transported, and highly accurate device for locating and plotting metal or mineralized artifacts (Figure 1). In the hands of an untrained operator, it is a good stick to scare away snakes from the site. Most people seem

Figure 1. University of South Carolina anthropology students using VLF metal detector at Williamston Farm Battlefield. Courtesy of the South Carolina Institute of Archaeology and Anthropology.

to fall somewhere in between the two extremes. Metal detectors have been used to very good effect in battlefield analyses and other historic contexts. The discovery of uniform items such as unit badges, buckles, hook attachments, and the plotting of spent cartridges and shot have in several instances rewritten our understanding of how battles were undertaken and fought. The National Park Service's research at the Custer Battlefield site in South Dakota and Dr. Steven D. Smith's work at the Camden Battlefield site in South Carolina are excellent examples (Scott and Connor 1986; Smith et al 2007, 2008). It has also allowed for the discovery of the graves of otherwise unidentified soldiers and civilians killed in action and buried on the field. In other settings metal detectors have been instrumental in noting the location of and plotting artifacts associated with farmsteads or seasonal habitations. This has enriched our understanding of landscape use long after the visible above-ground remains have ceased to exist. Nail patterns from wooden structures are often all that remains of outbuildings.

Unfortunately, there is a downside to metal-detector use. Their simplicity, lack of expense, transportability, and accuracy make them the tool of choice for professional looters and unethical collectors. It is important to note that the vast majority of people who use metal detectors are law abiding. Unfortunately, it only takes a few rotten apples to wreak havoc on the archaeological heritage and damage the reputation of the majority of users. This has been addressed recently here in South Carolina by the passage of a new state law (South Carolina Code of Laws 2010).

The problem is easy to see. Metal detectors only identify artifacts that interact with the magnetic field. Many, if not most, of the artifacts and features on a site do not respond to these machines. Therefore the focus on those artifacts that are locatable by this technology actually endangers the survival of those that are not. Archaeologists and reputable metal-detector users recognize this problem. The recovery of any item located by a metal detector requires that very careful mapping and excavation be done to ensure that no other potentially more valuable data is damaged or destroyed in the pursuit of the "goody." The most common response encountered when dealing with unethical individuals called to account for the damage that they have done is that they "are preserving history by saving these precious items from being lost." On the face of it, this sounds pretty good. Unfortunately, the reality is that it is tantamount to saving the staples in a library while destroying the books.

Fortunately, here in South Carolina the institute has made common cause with a number of metal-detecting clubs and practitioners to the mutual benefit of both and the preservation of the archaeological heritage. And for many people metal detectors are their first experience in geophysics. It can be a good experience and is a valuable technique.

ELECTRICAL RESISTIVITY SURVEY

Originally based on mining and soils-science applications, electrical resistivity surveys have been used in archaeology since the late 1940s. A longstanding favorite in Europe, it has been less used in the United States, although this is beginning to change as more people embrace geophysical techniques and look for inexpensive options. There were some early adopters who championed the technique here in the United States. Gary Shapiro and Mark Williams stand out for their pioneering work in Michigan, Georgia, and Florida and their subsequent influence on South Carolina research (Shapiro1983; Williams and Shapiro 1982; Williams and Shapiro, eds. 1990).

The equipment is deceptively simple (Figure 2). In its most common current configuration, it is made up of two pairs of stout metal probes, a battery, a voltmeter, a considerable length of two-strand wire for the connections, and a digital data logger. One set of probes is kept stationary and placed off-site when possible. The other set is attached to a mobile frame that supports the battery and electronics and is linked by electrical cable to the stationary set. The mobile frame is moved from location to location for the testing. The natural salts dissolved in the moisture naturally found in the earth provide the pathway for the current to run between the mobile probes and against the constant reading of the stationary probes. This difference is then logged and can be downloaded

Figure 2. University of South Carolina anthropology students using a simple resistivity set at Williamston Farm Battlefield. Courtesy of the South Carolina Institute of Archaeology and Anthropology.

later via any one several sets of commercially available software (including Geoplot, Archaeosurveyor, and Snuffler) for analysis. The result is a two- or three-dimensional horizontal plot of the data.

Electrical resistivity surveys require very careful mapping of the test lanes if one wishes to produce an accurate horizontal plot. The lanes are most often in the form of a grid nominally of 10 by 10, 20 by 20, or 30 by 30 m in size. This translates to 32.5 by 32.5, 65 by 65, or 97.5 by 97.5 ft. Most archaeology, as well as most scientific research, relies on the metric system. Since the earth, and most sites, do not come neatly packaged this way, modern equipment has the ability to enter "dummy" data in areas that are not tested.

How deep the equipment tests is a function of the distance between the probes and the soils in which it is operating. As a rule of thumb, the expectation is that the depth sampled is equal to 1.5 times the space between the mobile probes. A very common configuration used by archaeologists is either .5- or 1-m spacing. A quick bit of math then reveals that, all things being equal, the depth reached is .75 or 1.5 m respectively. In the English system this equates to 2.4 and 4.8 ft. Greater depth is possible by using greater spacing, but there is a problem. If one makes the spacing greater to reach a greater depth, the outcome is a less clear delineation of the data. In other words, the deeper one goes, the more "blurred" the results. And in archaeology, a "fuzzy" picture is not a good picture, which tends to keep this technique operating very near to the surface.

One way to get around this issue and increase the depth is the use of multiplexers. A multiplexer is a hardware and software interface that allows the equipment to have multiple probes mounted on the mobile frame at different widths. The probes are activated in pairs at each test location, effectively multiplying the total number of tests and providing "stacked" data that provides a much better plot of the area.

But what exactly is being plotted? The equipment is testing and recording the resistance of the soil to the passage of the current. This means that in those areas where there is a lot of moisture, there will be less resistance recorded. And in those areas with less moisture, the resistance will be higher. Compacted areas such as roads, living floors, foundations, and building rubble all tend to limit the amount of moisture available to pass the current. Ditches, canals, trenches, burials, and storage pits tend to collect moisture and therefore potentially have a lower resistance to the surrounding areas. Using this equipment requires that the operator pay very careful attention to both ends of the spectrum and, for that matter, even the smaller nuances in between. Archaeologists often spend a lot of time post-processing the data to get the best or clearest picture they can.

An additional consideration is that soil moisture can change drastically over time. There is no guarantee that the same results will be had if an area is retested at a later date. This is especially true in regions that suffer broad climate swings. Here in the Southeast we have been afflicted with episodes of severe drought. Experience has shown that a site tested during the rainy months and revisited during the height of the summer drought can provide drastically different data. A great deal of care needs to go into the planning and scheduling of field work to take this into account. Best practice calls for the work to be done in a single season under very similar conditions.

One of the dividends of the popularity of this technique in Europe is that a plan to build a quite serviceable resistivity unit is available online through a popular electronics magazine (Becker 2003a, 2003b). Any competent do-it-your-selfer with electronics experience (such as with circuit boards and soldering) can produce a professional-grade product at a greatly reduced cost. In fact, the popularity of this kit in England resulted in the production of freeware to interpret the results (for example, Snuffler). Though not as glitzy as the commercial offerings and lacking in some of the bells and whistles, it will do the trick with a minimum amount of fuss and at very little cost.

GRADIOMETER

Magnetic gradiometers are rapidly becoming the geophysical tool of choice in the United States. There are several good reasons for this preference. The first is that they are eminently suited to work on prehistoric sites. The second is that they are quick (Aspinall et al. 2008).

Originally designed for mining surveys, gradiometers are a special form of magnetometer. Most people are familiar with compasses and the magnetic field that surrounds the earth. In practical terms, this means that we are surrounded by magnetic fields that are shifted and distorted in our immediate locations by both natural and introduced elements in the environment. Additionally, soils contain varying amounts of minerals that are magnetic. Cycles of wetting and drying of soils can enhance their magnetic signature through what is known as the fermentation effect. As the name implies, there are bacteria that act on the soils and increase the magnetic effect. Ore deposits and other magnetic geologic formations, such as bedrocks, also contribute to an area's signature.

Human activities can disturb the natural magnetic levels. Trenching or digging pits reorders the magnetic particles in the soil, making them contrast with the undisturbed soils around them. Lighting fires or using hearths also changes the local magnetic field in marked contrast to the "background." And the introduction and discard of fire-altered materials such as pottery, brick, and stone are particularly noticeable to the equipment. It goes without saying that any metal artifact produced or discarded at a site is also very noticeable. On the other hand, what may not be apparent is that as the organic materials (such as trash or wooden structures) left on site decay, these may be identifiable as well.

In other words, gradiometers are remarkably sensitive. Things we would not normally consider to be magnetic actually *are* at a minute degree and can, in some circumstances, be picked up by the equipment. This is why gradiometers have made such an impact on archaeological research in South Carolina and the United States. So much of our archaeological past is precontact and lacking in the grandiose architectural features so common to the Old World that distinguishing sites from the background using other geophysical techniques can be very difficult. Gradiometers bridge this gap very nicely.

Another point in their favor is that gradiometers are designed to work at a steady walking pace, which makes them considerably faster than resistance surveys (Figure 3). They also operate without touching the ground, which means that one does not have to worry as much about vegetation or obstacles. If you can walk through it, chances are very good that you can test through or over it as well. Water has little or no effect on them unless they are immersed, which should be

Figure 3. University of South Carolina anthropology students using a dual gradiometer rig at a historic farm site in Lower Richland. Courtesy of the South Carolina Institute of Archaeology and Anthropology.

avoided. As with electrical resistivity surveys, close control over the areas being tested is very important. The grids, and indeed the software, are the same for both. Gradiometers also have the ability to enter "dummy" data for areas that are either inaccessible or excluded for other reasons, such as property or site boundaries.

There are some drawbacks to using gradiometers. The very sensitivity of the equipment means that the operator and anyone else nearby must be acutely aware of their surroundings, clothing, and equipment. Anything with a battery, such as a watch or cell phone, or made from metal, such as pins, snaps, zippers, and eyeglasses, may be picked up by the device and produce false readings. Mechanical pencils used to record data in field books are often overlooked and need to be carefully considered. Steel-toed shoes or support shanks cannot be used, nor can most cameras in the immediate vicinity. Nor can most snake leggings, as they often rely on wire mesh as the snake-proof barrier. Metal fences, overhead power lines, or localized heavy telecommunications chatter can adversely affect the sensitivity of the equipment.

Fortunately, most modern equipment comes with filters or other means to remove or limit the effects of most obstacles. And one rapidly comes to appreciate not carrying a cell phone everywhere. Hiking and outdoor supply stores are unaware of it, but they often carry field clothing and shoes that contain no metal or other items that react with the gradiometer. When in doubt, the researcher must test personal items or clothing with the equipment prior to going into the field to ensure that it is acceptable for use. And a word to the wise: it is always a good idea to invest in a good pair of nonreactive snake proofs. It is hard to walk through snaky areas at a constant speed and keep an eye on both the equipment and the critters.

Gradiometers come in single, double, or multiple configurations. The choice of which to use depends on several factors such as funding, staffing, and time constraints. The most cost-effective is the dual gradiometer. It costs slightly more but covers twice as much ground. The cheapest and easiest to maneuver in the field is the single gradiometer, although it will take twice as long to gather the same information as the double gradiometer. Any configuration beyond this is a specialized case with limited applications and usually a premium price.

There is one aspect in the operation of any gradiometer that takes some getting used to. Rather than pressing a button to log a reading, modern gradiometers take readings at set time intervals. To ensure that the same amount of ground is being covered during each testing period, the manufacturers have adopted a metronome-like beep. The time between beeps can be modified somewhat, but once it is set, the operator must walk to the steady tempo. This takes some practice to do well.

Again, the popularity of this device in Europe has led to the online publication of plans to build a quite serviceable gradiometer unit (Becker 2004a, 2004b). Any competent do-it-yourselfer with electronics experience (in circuit boards and soldering) can produce a professional-grade product at a greatly reduced cost. However, great care must be taken in the orientation of the upper and lower magnetometer arrays during building. Any error will significantly impact the equipment's abilities and accuracy. And while it is possible to produce dual gradiometer setups from these plans, it is not suggested. Aligning two magnetometers correctly to make a single functioning unit is exciting enough. Aligning four magnetometers to make the dual unit can be very frustrating. If you have decided to make your own, then it is much better to produce the single version and get on with it. Properly done, it will do the trick at a much lessened cost.

GROUND-PENETRATING RADAR

Remarkably, the first ground-penetrating radar (GPR) survey was done in 1929 to sound the depth of a glacier in Austria (Buntebarth 1981). This was five years before the term "radar" (radio detection and ranging) was actually coined. It then lay pretty much forgotten until the 1950s when a series of mishaps with U.S. Air Force planes attempting to land in Greenland brought it back into the light. As it turned out, the plane's onboard radar systems could not distinguish the ice landing surfaces very well, instead penetrating below it and providing faulty distance data that led to several crashes. The military from several countries pumped research and development funds into the technology. The culmination was that ground-penetrating radar was developed and eventually evolved into the forms we have today.

Archaeology came to GPR fairly late after the equipment was declassified in the 1970s. Modifying the technique to make it useful for archaeology has not been particularly easy and has taken the better part of two decades. It is probably one of the most expensive of the commonly used geophysical techniques employed by archaeologists. Potentially it is the most valuable.

Radar operates by sending out radio waves that impact an object and reflect back to a receiver. This sounds pretty simple but actually is not. The radio wave has to reach the object, which means that it has to pass through whatever is between it and the target, and then return through the same medium. And the target does not only reflect the radio wave, but it also partially absorbs it and sends it back as a series of radio waves. For that matter, every inclusion or density shift in the medium through which the radio wave passes also partially absorbs and reflects back at different rates. Complicating the situation further is the speed at which the survey is being done. In other words, the equipment is moving in relation to the target, which means the reflectance is coming back at a variety of angles to the machine.

The computations and adjustments to the early equipment both in terms of hardware and software to make this work was an engineer's dream but most other people's nightmare. It is common knowledge that the math competency in the United States is not all that high. We rank 27 out of 40 worldwide at the high school level, according to the 2006 PISA survey (Programme for Independent Student Assessment 2006). Archaeologists reflect the national norms. A rather unkind engineering colleague once quipped that archaeological GPR surveys should be done with one shoe off to keep up with the computations.

Fortunately, the rapidly advancing software packages commercially produced specifically targeted this issue. They also targeted the problem of interpreting the reflected radio-wave data. Modern GPR units available to archaeologists can produce results in 2-D or 3-D on the fly and are capable, under the very best of conditions, of resolving targets to centimeters (for example, 2–4 in or less). Until recently the best software was very expensive, licensed on a yearly basis, and required either a hardware key or a "dongle" to provide access. Failure to keep up your license could in some instances deprive you of access to your previously gathered data. Fortunately, this is no longer the case.

GPR units come with a wide choice of antennas to produce the radio waves (such as 40MHz, 100MHz, 120MHz, 200MHz, 300MHz, 400MHz, 500MHz, 900MHz, and 1.5GHz). The rule of thumb is that, under most circumstances, the lower the frequency, the deeper the penetration and the lower the resolution. In terms of depth this means that antennas can cover from less than a meter (0–39 in) down to 5,400 m (17,550 feet). Clearly, most of these antennas are not applicable to archaeology. Archaeologists tend to stay pretty much between the 200–900MHz ranges. In South Carolina the most commonly used antennas are the 400 or 500MHz models. Most serious practitioners will have access to or outright ownership of multiple antennas. Antennas with frequencies ranging above or below may be used if special conditions warrant. Some of the newer and much pricier units come with a variable antenna array capable of acquiring data from all the antennas at the same time and stacking the data (for example, Mala Mira, or 3d RADAR VX-Series).

The radio wave that goes into the ground most closely resembles a cone with the narrow end at the surface. Just as with the gradiometer and electrical resistivity surveys, control over the test lanes and grids is crucial. Painting an object by overlapping the cones at depth is a very useful technique. But the lanes must be very carefully laid out. The best 3-D results tend to occur with lanes that are .25 m (9.75 in) apart.

The earliest GPR units resembled vacuum cleaners or some futuristic pull toy (Figure 4). The current models more closely resemble supermarket trolleys or lawn mowers (Figure 5). The early versions were very maneuverable but unstable and difficult to keep on line or to measure distance covered. The current models stay on track very well and do a bang-up job of measuring distance. They are less maneuverable and can be useless in earthwork or trench situations, as the wheel base tends to hang up. For this reason, it is common for archaeologists to retain the earlier, somewhat obsolete versions to use in tight quarters, while

Figure 4. Older sled-style ground-penetrating radar in use at Campfield Plantation. Courtesy of the South Carolina Institute of Archaeology and Anthropology.

Figure 5. (below) Current trolley-style ground-penetrating radar in use at Clemson University's Calhoun Cemetery. Courtesy of the South Carolina Institute of Archaeology and Anthropology.

relying on the more advanced software to post-process the data and make it fully useful.

Unfortunately, no one has developed software at this writing that can handle all three instruments' data at the same time. Thus, at least two separate sets of software are routinely used by archaeologists, who then have to fold the results into a single coherent picture when possible. This situation will undoubtedly change in the near future.

So, What Does It All Mean?

Near-surface geophysics is nondestructive and can produce remarkable information that can dramatically influence the plans for field research. In some instances, it can answer the primary research question outright. It is unlikely that it will ever replace excavation; there will always be the need to "truth" the majority of anomalies identified. But it is very clear from the numerous projects, studies, reports, and books written by or available to archaeologists that geophysics is now an expected technique and practice. Best practice calls for the explicit inclusion of geophysical techniques at the earliest stages of field work. This has been recognized by internationally acclaimed stewardship and research organizations, such as English Heritage. South Carolina is fortunate in that we independently came to this conclusion very early on.

The use of near-surface geophysics in South Carolina has helped cut field costs and has been a major contributing factor to the success of several nationally and internationally recognized projects. It has also been a low-cost and effective support to local and agency projects. It is not an overstatement to say that the way archaeology is conceptualized and accomplished has changed for the better through the incorporation of these techniques.

We are very fortunate that in this state the public has an abiding and often very direct connection to our shared history. Unlike populations of some of the other states in our region, South Carolinians tend to be multigenerational and stable in their locales. This provides a wealth of information and insight into the historical patterns that archaeologists are interested in studying. It also tends to provide a depth of volunteer and collegial participation that is not common elsewhere in the United States. It is rare that a field project looking for volunteers is not blessed by an abundance of public interest.

All the near-surface geophysical techniques discussed here are suitable for trained volunteers to operate. The opportunity this provides for public outreach and education cannot be stressed enough. We live in a rapidly changing world with competing agendas and perspectives. The more people we involve in archaeology, the better. Medicine and archaeology should share the same motto, *Primum non nocere*, "First, do no harm." Preservation and protection of the archaeological record is a paramount concern. Near-surface geophysics is one of the best methodologies whereby volunteers can make a substantive and important contribution to field research without fear of doing any harm.

References Cited

Aspinall, Arnold, Chris Gaffney, and Armin Schmidt

2008 *Magnetometry for Archaeologists.* AltaMira Press, Lanham, Maryland.

Becker, John

2003a Earth Resistivity Logger, Part 1. *Everyday Practical Electronics* 32(4):288–295.

2003b Earth Resistivity Logger, Part 2. *Everyday Practical Electronics* 32(5): 360–368.

2004a Magnetometry Logger, Part 1. *Everyday Practical Electronics* 33(7):469–476.

2004b Magnetometry Logger, Part 2. *Everyday Practical Electronics* 33(8):543–547.

Buntebarth, Gunter

1981 Zur Entwicklung des Begriffes Geophysik. *Abhandlungen der*

Braunschwiegischen Wissenschaftlichen Gesellschaft 32: 95–109.

Clark, Anthony J.

1996 *Seeing Beneath the Soil. Prospecting Methods in Archaeology.* B. T. Batsford, London.

Crawford, Osbert Guy Stanhope.

1923 Air survey and archaeology. *Geographical Journal,* May, 324–366.

Gaffney, Chris, and John Gater

2003 *Revealing the Buried Past: Geophysics for Archaeologists.* Tempus Publishing, Stroud, Gloucestershire, United Kingdom.

Johnson, Jay K.

2006 *Remote Sensing in Archaeology. An Explicitly North American Perspective.* The University of Alabama Press, Tuscaloosa.

Joukowsky, Martha

1980 *A Complete Manual of Field Archaeology: Tools and Techniques of Field Work for Archaeologists.* Prentice-Hall, Englewood Cliffs, New Jersey.

Lowrie, William

2007 *Fundamentals of Geophysics.* 2nd ed. Cambridge University Press, New York.

McMillon, Bill

1991 *The Archaeology Handbook: A Field Manual and Resource Guide.* John Wiley and Sons, New York.

Ministry of Parks and Tourism

2008 *Avocational Archaeology Field Manual.* Archaeological Resource Management Section (ARMS) of the Heritage Resources Branch, Regina, Saskatchewan, Canada. Electronic document, http://www.tpcs.gov .sk.ca/FieldManual (accessed November 11, 2009).

Programme for International Student Assessment (PISA)

2006 Science Competencies for Tomorrow's World, Volume 1, Analysis. Organisation for Economic Co-operation and Development, Paris.

Scott, Douglas D., and Melissa A. Conner

1986 Post-Mortem at the Little Bighorn. *Natural History* 95:46–55.

Scott, Douglas D. and Richard A. Fox Jr.

1987 *Archaeological Insights into the Custer Battle.* University of Oklahoma Press, Norman

Shapiro, Gary

1983 A soil resistivity survey at 16th century Puerto Real, Haiti. *Journal of Field Archeology* 11:101–110

Smith, Steven D., James B. Legg, Tamara S. Wilson, and Jonathan Leader

2007 *"Obstinate and Strong": The History and Archaeology of the Siege of Fort Motte.* South Carolina Institute of Archaeology and Anthropology, University of South Carolina, Columbia.

Smith, Steven D., James B. Legg, and Tamara S. Wilson

2008 *The Archaeology of the Camden Battlefield: History, Private Collections, and Field Investigations.* South Carolina Institute of Archaeology and Anthropology, University of South Carolina, Columbia.

South Carolina Code of Laws

2010 Archaeological Resources Act.

Williams, J. Mark, and Gary Shapiro

1982 *A Search for the Eighteenth Century Village at Michilimackinac: A Soil Resistivity Survey.* Archaeological Completion Reports No. 4. Mackinac Island State Park Commission, Mackinac Island, Michigan.

Williams, J. Mark, and Gary Shapiro (editors)

1990 *Lamar Archaeology: Mississippian Chiefdoms in the Deep South.* Tuscaloosa, University of Alabama Press.

Wilson, David R.

2000 *Air Photo Interpretation for Archaeologists.* 2nd ed. Tempus Publishing, Stroud, Gloucestershire, United Kingdom.

Witten, Alan J.

2006 *Handbook of Geophysics and Archaeology.* Equinox Publishing, London.

Forty Years of Historical Archaeology in South Carolina at SCIAA

A Personal
Perspective

HERE I SUMMARIZE my personal perspective on historical archaeology in South Carolina as I experienced it from 1968 to the present. The events involving historical archaeology are told as grants were received and projects launched by my colleagues and me through the years. They are listed in chronological order, from my employment at SCIAA to various sites I explored; I touch base as well on some of the projects carried out by colleagues as funding became available.

I do not attempt to go into detail regarding the culture process represented by what we found, nor do I attempt a broad perspective on the known history of the sites we examined and the lives of the people who occupied them. That broad theoretical goal, shared by historian, anthropologist, and archaeologist, is presented in my reports on the projects and the studies listed in the References Cited. The illustrations are selected from some of the sites I have excavated.

South Moves South to South Carolina

I first thought of leaving my North Carolina position as archaeologist at Brunswick Town State Historic Site as I was having a beer at the Southeast Archaeological Conference with John Combes. He had been excavating at the mid-eighteenth-century historic site of Fort Prince George, South Carolina (see Williams 1998; South 2005:204). John had recently been hired by Dr. Robert L. Stephenson, director at the University of South Carolina's Institute of Archaeology and Anthropology (SCIAA). Bob had only recently come to the institute after previous director William Edwards resigned to take a position in Colorado.

John told me that SCIAA would soon be letting a contract for a historical archaeologist to excavate at the site of Charles Towne Landing, where the South Carolina Tricentennial Commission was preparing a park to commemorate the 1670 settlement on Albemarle Point, across the Ashley River from where the city of Charleston was later established (South 2005:204). I told him I would be interested in applying. He was surprised because he knew I was well entrenched in historical archaeology in North Carolina, and he had no idea I would be willing to leave that position.

I told him that they were trying to make an administrator out of me and had taken me out of historical archaeology research at Brunswick Town to an office in Raleigh. Incidentally, my book on historical archaeology at Brunswick Town has been published by the North Carolina Department of Archives and History (South 2009a). Also, for my work in historical archaeology in North Carolina, Governor Mike Easley presented me with that state's highest civilian honor, "The Old North State Award," in 2006.

Excavating the Original Charles Towne Landing Site

But, back to the past: John Combes recommended to Bob Stephenson that I be hired on a contract basis in 1968 to undertake the Charles Towne challenge. I completed my report on that exploratory project as the first in SCIAA's Research Manuscript Series (South 1969; South 2005:205, 209). Riley Macon, the University of South Carolina Provost for Research at the time, saw the need for an unclassified faculty position at SCIAA with the anticipation that more such positions would be established in the future with the goal of anchoring SCIAA's archaeological research mission within the academic framework provided by the university.

John Combes and I lived in a trailer on the Charles Towne site, and it was there that Bill Kelso (see Tolson 2007:64–67), now archaeologist at Jamestown, Virginia, volunteered to dig with us for a week, which proved to be a rewarding experience for the three of us. Having recently worked with Ivor Noël Hume in Williamsburg, and having learned the detailed methodological approach used there, he was surprised to see my method using machinery. He told me he had never seen so much data recovered in so short a time.

I told him that it was time that archaeologists stop "peeping through keyholes" using 5-ft squares and shovel tests and move on to opening "football field"–size units that would open broad windows to the past, allowing us to view that vast landscape of our cultural heritage. Later in Virginia, using my model, he introduced there the use of machinery as an archaeological tool to open those archaeological windows to the past. More recently, I published a paper entitled "Using the Telescopic Boom Hydraulic Excavator: The Ultimate Archaeological Shovel" (South 2002a [1998]: 30(1):37–42).

Following the Trail of an Avocational Archaeologist and the Original Palisade Ditch

I published my book on my work at Charles Towne Landing in a volume entitled *Archaeological Pathways to Historic Site Development* (2002b), which tells not only of the 1670 settlement but also of a Native American moundless ceremonial center I also excavated there. I have reviewed those fluorescent years in historical archaeology in South Carolina in my autobiography, including a chapter on tales from the Charles Towne Landing adventure (South 2005:211–226).

At that site I followed an avocational archaeologist, Johnny Miller, who had exposed a number of features, including a section of the original 1670 fortification ditch along the north side of the original settlement site. I followed that ditch, excavating and stabilizing it by rebuilding the parapet and placing a

Figure 1. Parapet reconstruction from the archaeologically revealed fortification ditch protecting the original Charles Towne site (South 1969). Courtesy of the South Carolina Institute of Archaeology and Anthropology.

Figure 2. Excavation underway at the corner of the Native American ceremonial compound found at Charles Towne State Historic Site (South 1969). Courtesy of the South Carolina Institute of Archaeology and Anthropology.

treated-post palisade beside the original posthole pattern found during excavation (South 1969, 1971a, 2005:218) (Figures 1 and 2).

Method and Theory in Historical Archaeology

I drew on my experience at Brunswick Town and Charles Towne Landing to write *Method and Theory in Historical Archaeology,* which is still in paperback in a fifth printing 30 years after it was first published (South 1977a; South 2002c). My vision was that historical archaeology should not only focus on the specific details of the archaeological record, which we archaeologists so enjoy doing, but to concentrate on the cultural, historical, and social processes responsible for creating that record. For too long, I felt, archaeology had looked not far beyond describing the grains of sand being removed by its brushes. It was time to sit up straight and stare at the big processes that created those bits and pieces being revealed by trowels. That was the message I tried to get across in that book, in which I explored theoretical and analytical techniques and revealed culture process through the formula concept using ceramics to demonstrate the Brunswick Pattern of Refuse Disposal (South 1977, 2002c).

I felt that archaeologists should stop simply describing what they found and instead link those objects and features to the past processes responsible for putting them there. That linkage, described by Raab and Goodyear (1973) in their seminal paper on middle-range theory, is the connection between the archaeological record and the past I was trying to get across to my colleagues in 1975 when I wrote the method and theory book (South 1977a, 2002c; see also Goodyear, Raab, and Klinger 1978).

Another discovery at Charles Towne was a fan-shaped redoubt that had been placed by Hessian soldiers under British command during the Revolutionary War in the siege of Charleston. This feature was also stabilized as an interpretive exhibit for the public visiting that historic South Carolina site which was so important in the founding of the British presence in the state (South 2005:215–217). That public is vastly interested in what archaeologists do, and archaeologists have a responsibility to respond by showing them results of the archaeological process through interpretive reconstructions based on research and archaeology and thus keeping their strong interest in archaeology alive.

Charles Towne Landing Revisited

After a few decades away from Charles Towne, I received a grant from the South Carolina Department of Parks, Recreation, and Tourism to search for archaeological evidence of the first structures inside the fortified area of Charles Towne. Michael J. Stoner managed a crew under my direction and found a small structure inside the fortified area of the site, in which we placed posts to show visitors where the building once stood. We published our report on this project, which provides the details of our discovery at that time, as do those simple interpretive posts marking the location of the original holes dug by the colonists (Stoner and South 2001; see also South 2005:355–356).

I was able to show South Carolina governor Jim Hodges the results of Stoner's archaeology, which revealed the evidence for the original English settlement in the state. For my overall contribution to historical archaeology in South Carolina, historian Walter Edgar nominated me to receive "The Order of the Palmetto," South Carolina's highest civilian award. Mike and I have recently published a second edition of our volume on our dig at Charles Towne Landing—*1670 Charles Towne: The Barbadian Connection* (Stoner and South 2007). Mike also published his report on "The Brunswick Pattern and the Interpretation of a 1670 Charles Towne Structure" (Stoner 2005:73–80).

Saving South Carolina's Underwater Heritage for Taxpayers

Shortly after my arrival in South Carolina, Bob Stephenson asked that I be the SCIAA representative to divide the artifacts being recovered through the underwater salvage law of 1969. The concept was that the taxpayers could then have a representative collection of each diving license issued by SCIAA. Our dream was that this collection would insure that a sample of South Carolina's historical and archaeological underwater heritage would be preserved in perpetuity for research and interpretive museum displays at SCIAA. Under the authority provided by this law, I undertook the first division of underwater artifacts recovered from the wreck of the Civil War vessel thought to be the *Mary Bowers* or the *Georgiana* (South 1971b; see also South 2005:227–228). The division we decided on was 75 percent to the divers for their discovery, expense, and effort in recovering the cultural resources from wrecks, with 25 percent going to the state of South Carolina through SCIAA.

Political Intervention

Before underwater archaeology was introduced, however, in order to establish an underwater division within SCIAA, I offered to approach Rembert C. Dennis, chairman of the Senate Finance Committee, to request a position for a state underwater archaeologist, a budget, and a station wagon. This was done and the Underwater Division was established (South 1971b).

This move on my part resulted in Bob's receiving some flak from university officials, who threatened to acquire a new director if such intervention in their process occurred again within SCIAA. As a result, I had to back off on further dealings with Senator Dennis. I have told the details of this story elsewhere (South 2005:228–231). My view is that Bob had great courage and hope for the future of underwater archaeology in South Carolina by authorizing me to bypass that process and to take that leadership responsibility to move ahead where his superiors in the administration had failed to do so. I told him I would take the flack because I had done the deed, but he pointed to the quote displayed on his desk: "The Buck Stops Here." Our opportunity for further funding for underwater research through Senator Dennis also stopped.

Unfortunately, as the underwater program at SCIAA developed, the managers at SCIAA found that making such a division and conserving the resulting artifacts was a daunting task, so they had the law changed. Since that time, no such division is required by law on behalf of the taxpayers except in the rare case when a salvage license is granted. The focus changed from acquiring and curating past underwater resources to helping hobby divers in their search for collecting relics to sell at flea markets. I still believe SCIAA's mission is to conduct research, acquire cultural resources, conserve those resources, and curate those symbols of past cultural, social, and historical processes for the future (South 2005:227–231).

A New Era

SCIAA is presently on the threshold of a new horizon with strong support from the university's Dean Mary Fitzpatrick at the College of Arts and Sciences and SCIAA's director, Charles Cobb. They are moving forward from simply maintaining the status quo to creating new archaeological research positions within the Research Division. This is a long-needed step to insure that SCIAA archaeologists not only comply with current contractual requirements for fulfilling the minimum state and federal salvage responsibilities to cultural resource management but also to initiate through grant procurement the funding necessary to pursue long-range, university-driven research goals through the Research Division and to curate the resulting cultural resources within SCIAA.

Edgefield Alkaline Glazed Stoneware

In the summer of 1970, a pediatrician, Dr. Georgeanna Greer, visited SCIAA and introduced me to her research on alkaline glazed stoneware and Edgefield pottery history. Her work was so impressive that I urged her to publish the results of her efforts, which she did (Greer 1971; South 1971f, 1971g). Later she was to become the leading authority on that ceramic type with the publication of her fine book (Greer 1993). She is an excellent example of someone in a nonarchaeological position becoming fired up and challenged by a strong desire to learn something about the past—a passion that well serves anyone who is inspired by intellect and interest to "plow new ground" in the reach to discover what lies ahead and to take part in that adventure.

Bob Strickland's Historical Archaeology at the Cornwallis House

In 1970, shortly after my arrival in South Carolina, Bob Stephenson and I visited the dig conducted for Historic Camden by Bob Strickland at the Cornwallis House in conjunction with SCIAA. On this visit I became aware that local groups interested in preserving their history were searching out old log cabins, barns, and other buildings and moving them to historic sites to aid in interpreting their past. I later ran into this phenomenon at Ninety Six, and I became concerned that this trend was leading to pseudo–log cabin towns "springing up like mushrooms to attract tourists." As a result, I published a paper, "The Log Cabin Syndrome," which later became "The Role of the Archaeologist in the Conservation-Preservation Process" (South 1970d, 1971d, 1971e, 1972c, 1972d, 1973f; see also South 2005:232–233). My view is that archaeologists must at times stand up from troweling on their knees to address larger issues demanding attention.

Tom Hemmings's Archaeological Exploration of Land's Ford Canal

In December 1969, as I was working on my report on Charles Towne Landing, Tom Hemmings was using a backhoe to explore the profiles of Land's Ford Canal, built between 1820 and 1823, on the west bank of the Catawba River in Chester District, South Carolina (Hemmings 1970). Helping local historical groups to accomplish their goals is part of SCIAA's mission.

Exploratory Excavations at the Price House

In June 1970 I conducted a project at the Price House in Spartanburg County, with one of the crew being my son, David. The large brick dwelling house was still standing, with an attached servant's quarters whose cellar was full of scorpions when we began excavation. We were looking for the flanking buildings on each side of the house. On the east side we found the foundation for a structure we interpreted as a possible kitchen. Near that we found a cellar we interpreted as a cold cellar dating from around 1794.

On the west side of the house we located the foundation wall of bricks for a 14-by-27-ft structure. The scarcity of ceramics and other refuse from the early nineteenth century found there revealed that this was not a kitchen but may have served another function, perhaps as an office (South 1970a, South 2005:267).

This house represents the movement of pioneers (such as the Moravians) from Virginia, Pennsylvania, and other northern states to the southern Carolina frontier in the eighteenth century and during the early years of the nineteenth century. This broad process was largely responsible for the development of the Piedmont region of the Carolinas.

This process of assisting local groups to better understand their history through their resources and collections has been a major function of Tommy Charles for many years. Tommy has helped many people better understand the information their collections contain, and in the process he has provided valuable information to SCIAA.

Exploratory Historical Archaeology at Ninety Six

In 1970 and 1971 I conducted three projects at the site of Ninety Six, South Carolina, where I dug at the 1751 Goudy's Trading Post, Fort Ninety Six of 1759 and 1761, Moultrie's New Stockade of 1761, the town of Ninety Six, the fortified jail in Ninety Six, Williamson's Fort of 1775, the anti-Cherokee fort of 1776, Colonel Cruger's "square palisade" fort of October 1780, Lieutenant Haldane's Star Fort of December 1780, Lieutenant Haldane's *caponier* of December 1780, Holmes' Fort of 1780, "Light Horse Harry" Lee's approach trenches of 1781, General Nathanael Greene's parallels of 1781, Kosciusko's mine of 1781, and British major Green's traverse of 1781 (South 1970b, 1971a–1971e, 1971h:35–50, 1972c–1972e; see also South 2005:239–265). The reports on those projects have been published and illustrated extensively. I was assisted there by Richard Polhemus (1971a–1971d), Steve Baker (1972), and John Jameson (ed. 1997), who made their own contributions to historical archaeology in the decades to follow.

Excavation at Revolutionary War Williamson's and Holmes' Forts

On the hill above the eighteenth-century town of Ninety Six, at the British Holmes' Fort site of 1780, I excavated the hornwork fortification ditch built on the site of the earlier Williamson's Fort and left it open. I then reconstructed the parapet beside the ditch as an interpretive exhibit revealing the results of the archaeological process (South 1971c, 1972a) (Figure 3).

In 1775 a stockade had been built connecting some of John Savage's barns, and these were used as bastions from which the Whigs inside the fort defended against a Tory attack. During that attack, a Whig, James Birmingham, and a Tory, Captain Luper, were killed (South 1972a; see also South 2005:244–245). I recovered the remains of one burial and another empty grave inside the area of Williamson's and Holmes' forts. Who the individual may have been is still something of a mystery that only DNA analysis may someday address.

When the National Park Service took over the site, it placed palisade posts to help with the interpretation of this Revolutionary War feature and built log barns to indicate where Savage's barns had once stood, as reveled by our archaeological

Figure 3. Using machines and a "schnitting" crew to reveal what Holmes Fort of 1780 had to say in 1971. Courtesy of the South Carolina Institute of Archaeology and Anthropology.

evidence. A marker in memory of James Birmingham has been erected on the site by the Daughters of the American Revolution to commemorate this first American casualty of the revolution in the South (South 1971c, 1971h, 1972a).

Sadly, there is no marker for the Tory, Captain Luper. What group, interested in "the rest of the story," will research his heritage, discover why his loyalty to the British had cost him his life, and place a marker on his grave? Failure to represent both sides is an instance of honoring only one side of the story and thus rewriting history.

Count Kosciusko's Tunnel at the Star Fort

I also found an entranceway into the mined tunnel dug by Count Kosciusko at the Star Fort in an attempt to blow it up (South 1972f). My son David, my crew chief, Randy Luther, and I crawled inside and mapped its extent. A photograph of Randy and me taken by David inside the tunnel in 1970 is on the cover of my autobiography, wherein the story of our tunnel adventure is retold (South 2005:249–250).

The National Park Service cleared all the trees from over the tunnel located at the Star Fort at Ninety Six (which had been protected for 200 years by the forest soaking up the rain water). As a result of this landscaping, the tunnel has since been collapsing and is probably no longer safe to enter.

When we were sitting inside the tunnel, we were fascinated by the original pick marks made by Kosciusko's sappers as they excavated the tunnel while awaiting the 600 pounds of black powder they had ordered to blow a hole in the parapet wall of the fort. It arrived too late, and Nathaniel Greene lifted the siege and moved on to fight another day (Figure 4).

SCIAA Research at Fort Motte and the Camden Battlefield Site

Recently, as part of SCIAA's continued outreach mission, Steve Smith, Jim Legg, Tamara Wilson, and Jonathan Leader (2006) reported on Fort Motte in Calhoun

Figure 4. Randy Luther and Stan South in Kosciusko's tunnel 1970. It was dug to blow up the Star Fort at Ninety Six, but that never happened. Courtesy of the South Carolina Institute of Archaeology and Anthropology.

County, South Carolina, a 1781 fortified house that served as a British supply depot for convoys to Ninety Six from Charleston.

Legg and Smith (2007) have also conducted a metal-detector survey of the Camden battlefield site and have recovered remains of that important Revolutionary War engagement between British and Continental forces. Steve Smith's Applied Research Division continues to serve a major function for SCIAA in mitigating adverse impacts to cultural resources.

Historical Archaeology at Fort Watson

When I was digging away at Ninety Six in 1971 and 1972, Leland Ferguson, who at that time was at SCIAA, began excavation on what was known as the Santee Indian Mound on the bank of Scott's Lake (38CR1) (Ferguson 1973, 1975a, 1975b, 1977). As it turned out, he found the remains of Revolutionary War–period Fort Watson and was not able to dig deeper into the Mississippian Period mound before funding ran out. Ferguson left SCIAA to pass his knowledge on to students for many years.

Lewis's Archaeological Frontier Model

An example of SCIAA's research loss and academia's gain is Kenneth E. Lewis. Ken was with SCIAA for a decade on a soft-money contract basis. He was hired away from SCIAA to teach at Michigan State University. His interest in archaeological model building led him to develop his model for frontier settlements based on his research at the town of Camden (Lewis, 1976, 1977a:151–201, 1977b).

In recent years Ken has periodically returned from his teaching to conduct archaeological research in Camden.

SCIAA's Role in Research-Driven Archaeology

In the early 1970s some of us at SCIAA had a dream that as more staff archaeologists were hired to conduct research in their chosen fields of specialization to fulfill the university-oriented research mission, we would become a major national leader in drawing grants, colleagues, and students to South Carolina to fulfill that mission. But with the advent of national and state mandates for cultural resource management, the emphasis turned to contractual assistance to help manage national CRM contractual requirements.

There have been other cases where the dream of fulfilling the university research-driven goals of long-range archaeological research has not come about. Consequently, researchers once affiliated with SCIAA went on to make their mark elsewhere. Among those are Natalie Adams, David Anderson, Paul Brockington, Linda Carnes-McNaughton, Joe Joseph, Chris Judge, and Carl Steen.

Finally, in 2007, with the hiring of Adam King, a new researcher was added to the Research Division. Highly qualified archaeologists Steve Smith, Chris Clement, Chris Gillam, James Legg, Michael Stoner, Keith Stephenson, Adam King, Mark Brooks, and Richard Brooks have made their contributions to SCIAA in goals outside the Research Division, primarily depending on their support from beyond SCIAA and the university.

As I have periodically brought this point up to university provosts, deans, and presidents through the decades, I have been told that the university was backing away from funding research positions unless those hired could generate their own salaries through grants and contractual arrangements from other agencies. Chester DePratter and I were told by one dean that our positions as university-paid researchers were "as dead as a dodo" when the time came for us to vacate those positions.

However, the good news is that the present dean, Mary Anne Fitzpatrick of the School of Arts and Sciences, and the director, Charles Cobb, have a more optimistic vision for the future of SCIAA. Research Division archaeologists Tommy Charles, Chester DePratter, Al Goodyear, and I have made our contributions, and now the future is looking much brighter with the new leadership in place.

Survey Archaeology in South Carolina in the 1970s

Interspersed with major research projects such as that at Ninety Six were survey projects I undertook to mitigate adverse impact to cultural resources before they were destroyed through development. That was before the Applied Research Division was created, so I conducted various projects throughout the state (South 2005:267–274).

Susan Jackson and I conducted a survey around the future site of the interchange of U.S. I-20 and I-95 on Byrd Trust land near Florence (South 1973b). Also, I did a survey of Jenkins Island in Beaufort County (South 1973c) and another on the north end of the Isle of Palms north of Charleston (South 1973d). All this occurred in those days soon after the passage of the National Historic Preservation Act, which resulted in the explosion within archaeology of an emphasis on salvaging cultural resources before they are destroyed through the cultural process of land development. As a result, the Applied Research Division under Steve Smith's direction was created to mitigate adverse damage to cultural resources.

SCIAA's 1971 March into Georgia

As the need for historical archaeology investigations increased, I was asked to examine the site of Fort Hawkins in Macon, Georgia, and assess the potential for historical archaeology there (South 1970c). As a result of that study, SCIAA hired Richard Carrillo to conduct exploratory excavations there. Richard and I went to the site of the rebuilt blockhouse, and after he opened archaeological trenches revealing the location of the ditches where palisades once stood in the area, I transit-mapped the data and Richard wrote his report (Carrillo 1971). Richard worked for SCIAA as a historical archaeologist for a number of years in the mid-1970s and dug at the eighteenth-century tabby fort ruin at Fort Dorchester (Carrillo 1976). He went on to form his own company in Colorado.

SCIAA and South March into an Attic in Georgia

Later on, I marched into Roswell, Georgia, where I studied the artifacts accumulated for 100 years in the attic of the Archibald Smith House, in an ATTIC (Archaeological Techniques to Inventory Collections) project. There, Sharon Pekrul (of the SCIAA Curation Division), Tommy Charles, Joe Beatty, Ruth Trocolli, and I spent several weeks photographing artifacts and recording 15 volumes of data (South 1990a). Later, I abstracted from that study a paper on the toys stored there, dating from before and during the Civil War (South 2004a). Such interactive projects with agencies in other states have long been a mission of SCIAA in its goal of discovering, recording, and conserving past knowledge for future generations.

Polhemus's Pipeline Investigations and the Fox House Project

In October and December 1971, Richard Polhemus conducted pipeline surveys necessary to mitigate possible damage to cultural resources during the development of the Charles Towne Landing site for interpretation to the public (Polhemus 1971a and 1971b). In the same year Richard published his report on the exploratory historical archaeology excavation he carried out in the yard of the John Fox House (38LX31) in West Columbia (Polhemus 1971c) and at the Brown House at Charles Towne Landing (38CH1) (Polhemus 1971d). Such projects, carried out through local sponsors, were typical of SCIAA's activities in the early days of its growth—a mission continued through the Applied Research Division.

The Pawley House Project

At the request of the owner of the Pawley House on Pawley's Island, South Carolina, I agreed to study the house to determine its age of construction. The rumor was that it was the original Pawley House from which the island got its name. It was hard to imagine that a beach house could have stood 200 years, given the frequency of hurricanes that sometimes wiped the beaches clean of structures. But in September 1971, my daughter Lara, my son Robert, Richard Carrillo, and I visited the house. There I took photographs and measurements and later wrote a report recording the details of what is a rare, surviving eighteenth-century beach house (South 1971i; South 1973a; see also South 2005:268–270) (Figure 5).

Figure 5. Robert and Lara South in 1971, on the steps of the Pawley House, a rare eighteenth-century beach house on Pawley's Island, South Carolina. Courtesy of the South Carolina Institute of Archaeology and Anthropology.

Most of SCIAA's projects are carried out at the request of (with funding often provided by) contractors or local historical or archaeological societies. This one, however, was sponsored by an individual property owner where no threat to the property was present. Most cultural resource management projects are motivated by legal requirements designed to mitigate cultural resources before a development is undertaken, and the research potential and interpretive value are destroyed forever.

A Native American Site on Hilton Head Island

In 1973 a mitigation of damage to cultural resources on a future condominium site on Hilton Head was called for, and I was sent to carry out the project. The owner furnished food and lodging, so the crew and I, along with my daughter Lara, son Robert, and wife, Jewell, enjoyed eating "high on the hog" there for a week (South 1973g). We "crucified" the site with two trenches at right angles, which revealed the edges of a Native American shell deposit dating from around 700 years ago. We also found evidence indicating that the site had been occupied around 4,000 years earlier.

Archaeology on the Horseshoe at USC

In the spring of 1973, at the urging of Vice Provost George Terry, I conducted a project on the University of South Carolina's horseshoe-shaped plaza and located the original driveway to the president's house, along with several wells once used by the students and others during the early years of the nineteenth century. In that project I also found the foundation ditch for the originally planned location of DeSaussure College (South 1973e; South and Steen 1992; see also South 2005:271–272; Bryan 1976). This project involved many university students, who volunteered to assist with the excavation.

One skeptical colleague, upon hearing my interpretation of the ditch I had found, said that the change, had it occurred as I surmised, would have been written about somewhere for historians to find. I reminded him that the whole purpose of archaeology was to explore the archaeological record to discover information *not* recorded only by the fickle finger of history. Months later the doubting colleague reported that while he was researching the early financial records of the university, he had found the misfiled minutes of the Board of Trustees meeting in which the vote had been taken to move the planned location of that building 100 feet to the north (Figure 6).

Excavation in front of the Elliott/Harper College revealed a domed well shaft built over the original well. This well contained discarded medicine bottles, microscope slides, test tubes, and other school-related artifacts. Other wells also revealed the activities of students through lost coins, marbles, poker chips, an earring pendant, pencil ferrules, a thimble, and a Union army button, probably lost there during the fire that burned Columbia on February 17, 1865. Lamp

Figure 6. Students revealing the top of the Elliott/Harper College well in 1973. Courtesy of the South Carolina Institute of Archaeology and Anthropology.

lighting of the Horseshoe common in the nineteenth century was revealed by carbon electrodes for arc lights. In 2008 I wrote a essay for an edited book by Russ Skowronek and Kenneth Lewis on archaeology on college campuses.

Exploratory Archaeology at Fort Johnson

In May 1973 I conducted a two-week project at the site of Fort Johnson on the south side of Charleston Harbor (South 1974f, 1975a, 1975b). We found a long barracks building, where our excavation cut a telephone cable—not once, but twice on consecutive days! I also discovered a part of a totally buried fortification wall.

Later on, Randolph Widmer and I conducted an archaeological sampling strategy on another site near Fort Johnson and a subsurface sampling strategy for archaeological reconnaissance (South and Widmer 1976 and 1977:119–150), resulting in the discovery of a posthole pattern for a Woodland Period house.

Palmetto Parapets at Fort Moultrie National Monument

Another major 10-week project was undertaken through the National Park Service at Fort Moultrie in the fall and winter of 1973 (South 1974a:viii). The size of the "Palmetto Parapets" report on this exploration of the original 1775 moat of Fort Moultrie prompted the creation at SCIAA of the Anthropological Studies Series of monographs, becoming the first in that series.

We found British regimental buttons thrown from the parapet onto the berm beside the moat, and buttons from William Moultrie's Second South Carolina Regiment in the moat itself, along with black powder, palmetto logs, and other refuse discarded there during the use of the fort by American forces during the American Revolution (South 2005:274–278). An impressive amount of colonoware pottery was also recovered. In the report on that project (South 1974a:242–247), I included a chart on the evolutionary development of buttons. Some colleagues began using the Fort Moultrie report as a text in their courses on historical archaeology (Figure 7).

Figure 7. Stan South and his archaeological crew during excavation at Revolutionary War–era Fort Moultrie in 1973. Courtesy of the South Carolina Institute of Archaeology and Anthropology.

Examining Human Burial Remains

At the request of David Hurst Thomas at the American Museum of Natural History, I examined the hardware and other artifacts associated with three antebellum burials from the Georgia Coast (South 1976; Thomas et al. 1977).

Later on, with Susan Jackson, I excavated the graves of William Moultrie and his family (South 1977d, 1979d), at Windsor Hill, where relic collectors had been carrying off tombstones with the names of famous men to be sold as paving stones on patios. We salvaged a group of these, placed beside an access road to be loaded and hauled off, and relocated them at Goose Creek Cemetery in the hope that they would be safer there.

Exploring Method and Theory in Historical Archaeology

In the 1970s I began writing my book *Method and Theory in Historical Archaeology* 1977a), which grew out of a number of papers I published in the early 1970s on various aspects of method and theory (South 1974b–1974e).

In 1975 I took my book manuscript to New Mexico to visit Lew Binford, a classmate from my Chapel Hill days, to seek his opinion. Liking what he read, he agreed to write the foreword. It was published in 1977 (South 1977a, 2002c). The message I delivered there, often with the zeal and passion of a religious zealot, was quickly adopted as a text for the field at many universities and remains in print 30 years later (South 2002c) for use in training students.

A Summer with Schiffer and Colleagues at SCIAA

Shortly after I finished my method and theory book, Michael Schiffer of Arizona State University visited SCIAA to spend the summer interacting with his colleague Al Goodyear. Al, Mike, and I had a few beers together during our frequent discussions. While he was here, I invited him to contribute an essay to the edited book I was putting together at that time on archaeological research strategies. He agreed, and his contribution, "Toward a Unified Science of the Cultural Past," became the second essay in that book (Schiffer 1977:13–40).

Pattern Recognition in Historical Archaeology

During the years following the publication of my method and theory book, I continued to compile *Research Strategies in Historical Archaeology* (South, ed. 1977) and explore archaeological pattern recognition (1977b), guidelines for the preparation and evaluation of archaeological reports (1977c), contemporary patterns of material culture-a pull-tab study (South 1978a–1978c, 15 1980b), exploring analytical techniques (1978d), pattern recognition in historical archaeology 16 (1978e), historic site content, structure, and function (1979a), and deep water and high ground 17 (South and Hartley 1980).

I was touched by the kiss of death when my wife, Jewell, learned of her lung cancer while Hartley and I were in the field. When she died, my world as I had known it collapsed, but I was saved by my passion for archaeological research. After my recovery, I was ready for a change—and a new direction—which soon came.

Figure 8. Marking features revealed through excavation at sixteenth-century Spanish Santa Elena near the golf course on Parris Island (South 1983). Courtesy of the South Carolina Institute of Archaeology and Anthropology.

The Spanish Santa Elena Long-Range Research Program

By 1979 I was an eager listener when the editor of the *National Geographic* magazine, Joe Joseph, met with me and SCIAA director Bob Stephenson to urge us to submit proposals to the magazine for excavation at the sixteenth-century site of Spanish Santa Elena (38Bu51 and 38Bu162), on Parris Island, South Carolina. This launched a new direction for future adventures in the field of historical archaeology through Spanish colonial research (Figure 8).

I received grants for three years from the National Geographic Society, which were followed by a series of grants from the National Science Foundation, the National Endowment for the Humanities, the Explorers Club of New York, and others.

After a decade, I was joined in that challenge by my colleague Chester De-Pratter and many other volunteers and colleagues, including Bill Hunt, Gary Shapiro, John Goldsborough, Susan Jackson, Mike Harmon, Ken Sassaman, Richard Polhemus, Kathy Deagan (South and Deagan 2002), Jim Legg, Mike Stoner, and many others, who through the years have helped and inspired me to continue my passion to record, conserve, preserve, restore, and interpret the past (South 2005:317, 354)..

My report on my search for Spanish Santa Elena was published (South 1979b), and that search for understanding of the Spanish presence in the New World has continued to the present. The first sampling of the site revealed the moat of Fort San Felipe (South 1980a, 1980c, 1980d). Those early reports on Santa Elena were followed by others (South 1982b), including a search for French Charlesfort of 1562 (South 1982a). Not having found French Charlesfort, I continued my research and publication at Santa Elena (South 1983, 1984, 1985a, 1985b, 1988a–1988e, 1989; South and Hunt 1986; South et al. 1988; see also South 2005:293–334). Since 1989 the research has continued with my colleagues Chester DePratter and Jim Legg, assisted by others (DePratter and South 1990, 1995; South and DePratter 1996).

Michie Explores Native American and Historical Archaeology

Before SCIAA was created, Jim Michie was excavating Native American archaeological sites in South Carolina. By the 1980s he began examining historic sites (Michie 1982, 1984, 1987, 1989; Michie and Mills 1988). His work at Wachesaw/Richmond Hill and at Fort Congaree clearly demonstrated his ability to examine historic sites as well as Native American ones such as the Taylor site.

Legg and Smith Explore Historical Archaeology of the Civil War Period

Military historical archaeology of the Civil War period has been conducted by Jim Legg, Steve Smith, and their colleagues at Folly Island, South Carolina, where they investigated an African American graveyard (Smith 1993 and 1994; Legg and Smith 1989; Zierden et al. 1995). This area of history has long been a popular one for South Carolina historians, and their work at Folly Beach and elsewhere has brought new data to light on this important period in South Carolina's history.

Historical Archaeology in SCIAA's Applied Research Division

Steven D. Smith (1993, 1994) in association with colleagues, has led the Applied Research Division on many historic site research projects through his career at SCIAA in past decades. That division conducts research projects obtained through competitive bidding. In this process Steve has become recognized as a highly qualified researcher in the field of applied research archaeology. His publication record (too numerous to list here) includes his authoring 2 books, 6 booklets, 10 chapters, and 14 technical reports.

Legg Explores Historical Archaeology of World War I

Archaeologist Jim Legg has provided research expertise on many archaeological projects at SCIAA for decades. One of the areas of most interest to him is the period of the First World War (Legg 2005). In his excavation with me and Chester DePratter on the Spanish site of Santa Elena, Jim became familiar with evidence we uncovered reflecting the Marine Corps Training Depot on Parris Island during that war. His study reveals the material remains of the architecture, arms and equipment, uniforms, personal possessions, subsistence, indulgence, and hygiene of that era on the site. This study helps fill lacunae into that period of historic site investigation in South Carolina.

Scientific Methodology, Evolution, and Explanation through Energy Theory

In 1989 I was invited to Canada to the Chacmool conference as the keynote speaker to present my archaeological views on the theme "Households and Communities." I saw this as a way to urge archaeologists to recognize the broad energy processes that drive cultures and social systems to do what they do. I presented there a specific example from Santa Elena of the arguments of relevance (middle range theory) necessary to connect the archaeological record to the processes needed to explain the broad cultural and social movements driving cultural activity of the past (South 1989).

The response encouraged me to present a book chapter, "From Thermodynamics to a Status Artifact Model," to emphasize the role played by the second law of thermodynamics in the processes of culture (1990b).

By 1993 I had become more aware of the strange fruit of the alien, humanistic, anti-science plant I had seen blooming at the 1975 Society for Historical Archaeology meeting in Charleston. Concerned at that time about this perspective, I hoped that interest in the application of science to archaeological method and theory was so strong that only naïve students would fall for that anti-science noise (South 1993a). I was wrong, however.

By 1996 I had begun to express my concern to Halcott Green, who has had a longtime interest in energy theory and shared my concern about the direction historical archaeology had taken away from scientific method and theory. As a result, we wrote papers in 1996 and 1997 on evolution in historical archaeology and energy theory in relation to material culture studies. After having been turned down by historical journals as not in keeping with current thinking in the field, the papers were finally published (South and Green 2005a, 2005b), in a festschrift my colleagues presented in my honor, entitled *In Praise of the Poet Archaeologist: Papers in Honor of Stanley South and His Five Decades of Historical Archaeology* and edited by Linda Carnes-McNaughton and Carl Steen (2005; see also South 2005:349–352).

These papers reflect our concern that the field of historical archaeology was moving away from the scientific pursuit of data collecting and quantitative analysis toward subjective storytelling, which is the mainstay of the novelist, who imagines stories to elaborate and "improve" on the facts with the goal of entertaining readers. This is a different goal from educating the reader to the realities revealed by the archaeological record and using that information to help explain past culture process.

It has become popular to fire shots at processualists and their scientific efforts—terming their efforts old fashioned, "myopic," and out of date in the post-processual, postmodern world; thus, subjectivity rather than objectivity has become the mantra. However, as Lew Binford said in 1975 at the SHA meeting in Charleston, "No one ever said science was easy!" So many jumped on that bandwagon.

DePratter and Legg at French Charlesfort of 1562

In the 1980s I made unsuccessful efforts to locate French Charlesfort (South 1982a; DePratter and South 1990). In the 1990s, while still railing at the anti-scientific trend in historical archaeology, I continued excavating and publishing with my colleagues (DePratter et al. 1996a, 1996b). Through Chester DePratter's initiative, this cooperative venture continued to pursue the elusive French Charlesfort of 1562.

We finally found it beneath the Spanish Fort San Felipe I had dug in 1984 but failed to recognize the French sherds (South 1985a). Jim Legg was able to identify the Charlesfort pottery from his familiarity with French stoneware, which he had gained while visiting French museums and the French countryside. His dad had crash-landed his glider in France during the D-Day invasion of World War II, which later inspired Jim to conduct research in that country.

I sometimes say that my search for the 1562 French Charlesfort site was finally resolved as a result of that invasion. Resolving that question was important, so University of South Carolina President John Palms was present on the site in 1990 to make the announcement to the world of the discovery of that famous French attempt to settle and lay claim to the New World.

The Search for John Bartlam's Staffordshire Pottery

One of the most exciting recent projects undertaken was the search for the kiln and pottery remains of the Staffordshire potter John Bartlam at Cain Hoy [Cain-hoy], South Carolina (South 1993b:1–66, 1999a, 1999b, 2004b, 2005:344–345). I was assisted on those Cain Hoy projects by Carl Steen, James Legg, and Brad Rauschenberg (1999), who were as passionately driven by the search as I was. Bartlam was making his creamware and tortoiseshell earthenwares at his manufactory on the north bank of the Wando River north of Charleston in the late 1760s.

Figure 9. John Bartlam's attempt to make America's first porcelain at Cain Hoy. Courtesy of the South Carolina Institute of Archaeology and Anthropology.

Later in Charleston in 1771, he advertised for young African American apprentices to assist with his manufacture of the earthenware and "china" (his effort to make porcelain) (South 2004b:169). He was familiar with pottery manufacture from his work in Staffordshire (Figure 9).

This ware has come to be known to archaeologists as "Carolina Creamware" (South 1993b:14). The manufacture of this ware by Bartlam and later by William Ellis, who taught the Moravian potter Rudolph Christ how to make the Staffordshire earthenware, is told in my book *Historical Archaeology in Wachovia*, stimulated by my historical archaeology done at the Moravian settlements at Bethabara and Old Salem, North Carolina, but that is a story that unfolded before I came to SCIAA (South 1999a, 2004b).

The Long-Range Research Division Program at Santa Elena Continues

Upon occasion, short excursions away from historical archaeology at SCIAA sometimes intervene in my schedule, such as invitations to speak in Uruguay, Argentina, Canada, Mexico, France (at the Sorbonne), and Spain. Meanwhile, Chester DePratter, Jim Legg, and I continue our research, analysis, interpretation, writing, and publication of results of our Spanish Santa Elena/French Charlesfort saga (South 1996a, 1996b; South and DePratter 1996; DePratter and South 1998a–1998c; DePratter, South, and Legg 1996a, 1997, 2001).

South and Stoner

My most recent project was a return to Ninety Six with Michael Stoner and Jim Legg to find further evidence of the fortifications built around the town. We were searching for a fortification ditch located in the woods east of the town, but our search was not successful (unpublished ms. on file at SCIAA).

A recent project of the Research Division was sponsored by the William Sullivan family on Callawassie Island, South Carolina (South and Stoner 2007). Michael Stoner and I photographed, measured, and excavated test units and shovel tests in and around an early nineteenth-century tabby ruin in Bill and Shanna Sullivan's backyard, where Jim Michie and Tommy Charles had conducted a survey (Michie 1982). It was thought by historians and architects that the 40-ft-sq structure represented the home of James Hamilton Jr., but our research there failed to reveal any architectural or archaeological evidence of the Brunswick pattern of refuse disposal usually associated with domestic household ruins of that period. We suspect it may have served as a storage area for shipment of cotton and sugar mill products (see also South 2007, 2008) (Figure 10).

Future Historical Archaeology at SCIAA

In this personal perspective on historical archaeology from my 50 years in the field, almost 40 of which have been experienced at SCIAA, I have summarized my views on the developmental changes I have seen take place there during the growing-up period for the field. That was an era when the field was represented in America by only a handful of archaeologists, while multitudes represent that profession today. During that time the field has evolved from an endeavor focused on artifacts plucked from the body of the earth to be placed in private collections with little concern for understanding the cultural body from which they originated.

Figure 10. The northeast corner of the Sullivan Tabby Point Ruin on Callawassie Island. Courtesy of the South Carolina Institute of Archaeology and Anthropology.

Through the insistence of Lewis Binford and others, archaeologists were admonished to use the methods of science to derive a larger meaning behind the objects—the processes that caused them to be found in their archaeological context by archaeologists. This idea of explaining the archaeological record in terms of the cultural, historical, and social processes that formed it transformed historical archaeology from the level of glorified relic collecting into an interdisciplinary field of science combining archaeology with history, oral history, ethnography, and the stuff of folklore—storytelling. The latter aspect has become a focus in the field in recent years, and I will attempt to explain the relationship, as I see it, between the use of the scientific perspective in historical archaeology and storytelling.

Artifact Form, Use, Function, Context, Explanation, and Storytelling in Archaeology

Historical archaeology is a field requiring methodological rigor and hard work, dealing on the one hand with a focused concern on detail, while on the other with the translation of those data-picked details from excavations to the larger cultural processes represented. Archaeologists have long used ethnography, history, and oral history as an explanatory bridge between the form of the artifact held in their hands and its past role in the cultural process of which it was once a part.

Entering this interpretive process in recent years in historical archaeology is an emphasis on storytelling as a tool. A stone projectile point, a knife, and a gun, though different in form, can be described from the visual appearance through observation of the material of which they are made and their shape or form. This is a relatively simple first-step descriptive process that can be done in the absence of knowledge of the function they were designed to perform or the use to which they were put. The cutting edge of a spear point or an arrowhead and the shape of the stem can be described as facts. With sharply defined edges, their function was to cut. There seems to be little room here to open the door to storytelling.

Artifact use, however, opens that door. It is at this level in the artifact-interpretive process that storytelling begins to catch on when some practitioners are faced with the many uses to which artifacts can be put.

A projectile point was used attached to a shaft: to send a message, to kill food, to refine a skill, to stop an enemy, to pick the teeth, and so on. A knife was used as a subsistence tool, a protection tool, a construction tool, a clothing tool, a personal-grooming tool, a back scratcher, or a means to remove a scab or cut an umbilical cord.

A gun was used as a weapon, an indication of status, a subsistence-procurement tool, a deterrent to enemies, or as an instrument to kill enemies, to drive nails, to make threats, to display in an exhibit case to impress others; the list goes on. It is this many-optioned range of possibilities for artifact use that opens the door for some to tell a story about the artifacts they have found. But those stories chosen to tell must be underwritten by more than creative imagination.

For those concerned with scientific explanations, it is here where the importance of archaeological context comes into play. For instance, finding a thimble in an archaeological level with no other artifacts limits severely the range of possible scientific or storytelling options. The explanation for the thimble cannot move beyond the simple function that the form implies by its currently known use and raises the possibility of loss behavior as a possible explanation based on the archaeological record. To tell a story about the person who lost the thimble and the circumstances involved in the loss may be good entertainment, but without that anchor to the archaeological record, it is fiction.

However, finding a thimble in contextual association with a number of others, with pins, needles, and scissors in quantity, within a series of rooms in a structural ruin, allows for the introduction of an explanation for sewing activity beyond that of a thimble found alone—raising the possibility of a tailor shop. In this case, contextual association has allowed this interpretive, explanatory "story" to be told, anchored in archaeological fact. That is the reason why quantitative sampling of artifact distributions vertically (to elicit temporal changing-form relationships), and horizontally (to elicit spatial cultural relationships) is so important in explaining the archaeological record beyond simply the artifacts themselves. Context enriches and expands the interpretive possibilities.

Carrying this example one step forward, when the thimbles, pins, needles, and scissors are demonstrated through historical research to have come to an American site from another part of the world, the cultural processes of colonization within a world economic trade network are introduced into the interpretive explanation—based on the archaeological record and not simply by imaginatively selecting one of the many uses to which an artifact may have been put in the past in order to make the story more "interesting."

It is my hope that future historical archaeology research will build on the scientific foundation already laid by those few who still believe in that method as a necessary tool in our efforts to decipher and interpret the past behavior and cultural processes represented in the archaeological record.

Historical archaeologists must begin to *demonstrate* their arguments of relevance between those details we pick from the earth and their *explanation* of what the processes were that caused them to be there. Only then will historical archaeology be living up to its potential as a scientific endeavor, fully contributing to our understanding of a past culture as well as our own—not simply telling stories because they are more fun to read.

I have written a book, *Talking Artifacts: The Twentieth Century Legacy* (2009b), using artifacts covering 100 years in time. It is a photographic and descriptive record, similar to a probate inventory, accompanied by stories the artifacts have to tell through my personal association with them. Some talk louder than others, and I am selecting those stories to form the primary text for the reader more interested in stories than in researching illustrations of twentieth-century artifacts. So, I too see a place for storytelling in archaeology.

However, the stories those artifacts tell through me are not from my imagination. They are true stories, told for entertainment and for sharing knowledge about artifact form, function, and use with which many readers may not be familiar. In this context it is my expectation that the book will be a learning experience for material culture researchers, archaeologists, and historians interested in the century just past, as well as for those who enjoy reading stories that have emerged from a personal association with artifacts.

These stories are not archaeology, but they speak the truth through artifacts nonetheless, as archaeologists do in their attempts to elicit truth from the archaeological record. This inventory of mundane things and the associated stories speaks of a southern middle-class family in the twentieth century—of a child bride, of multiple murders, of suicide, of love, childhood joys, dreams, learning from artifacts, ambition, and death. It represents a pattern to be seen in attics and basements of homes occupied by extended families throughout the South and elsewhere in America. This personal account is the appropriate oral-history venue, I believe, for storytelling. While it may cast some insight on historical archaeology, that discipline still requires the rigor of science to elevate its position within the humanities.

Acknowledgments

I want to thank Chester DePratter, James Legg, and Michael Stoner for the discussions we have had over the points I have raised in this essay and their suggestions for improving it. Also, I would like to thank other colleagues at SCIAA for reading parts of it and offering their comments.

References Cited

Baker, Steven G.

1972 *A House on Cambridge Hill (38GN2): An Excavation Report*. Research Manuscript Series 27. South Carolina Institute of Archaeology and Anthropology, University of South Carolina, Columbia.

Bryan, John Morrill

1976 *An Architectural History of South Carolina College 1801–1855*. University of South Carolina Press, Columbia.

Carnes-McNaughton, Linda, and Carl Steen

2005 *In Praise of the Poet Archaeologist: Papers in Honor of Stanley South and His Five Decades of Historical Archaeology*. Publications in South Carolina Archaeology 1. Council of South Carolina Professional Archaeologists, Columbia.

Carrillo, Richard F.

1971 *Exploratory Excavations at Fort Hawkins, Macon, Georgia: An Early Nineteenth Century Military Outpost*. Research Manuscript Series 14. South Carolina Institute of Archaeology and Anthropology, University of South Carolina, Columbia.

1976 *Archaeological Investigations at Fort Dorchester (38DR4): An Archaeological Assessment*. Research Manuscript Series 86. South Carolina Institute of Archaeology and Anthropology, University of South Carolina, Columbia.

DePratter, Chester B., and Stanley South

1990 *Charlesfort: The 1989 Search Project*. Research Manuscript Series 210. South Carolina Institute of Archaeology and Anthropology, University of South Carolina, Columbia.

1995 *Discovery at Santa Elena: Boundary Survey*. Research Manuscript Series 221. South Carolina Institute of Archaeology and Anthropology, University of South Carolina, Columbia.

1998a Return to the Kiln: Excavations at Santa Elena in the Fall of 1997. *Legacy* 3(1): 6–7. South Carolina Institute of Archaeology and Anthropology, University of South Carolina, Columbia.

1998b *Santa Elena/Forts San Marcos, Felipe, Charlesfort, Excavation and Analysis*. Report to the Department of the Navy. South Carolina Institute of Archaeology and Anthropology, University of South Carolina, Columbia.

1998c Search for Santa Elena Forts. *Legacy* 3(2): 4–5. South Carolina Institute of Archaeology and Anthropology, University of South Carolina, Columbia.

DePratter, Chester B, Stanley South, and James Legg

1996a The Discovery of Charlesfort. *Transactions of the Huguenot Society of South Carolina* 101:39–48.

1996b Charlesfort Discovered! *Legacy* 1(1)–1(5):8–9. South Carolina Institute of Archaeology and Anthropology, University of South Carolina, Columbia.

1997 Santa Elena Excavations, Fall 1996. *Legacy* 2(1):4–5. South Carolina Institute of Archaeology and Anthropology, University of South Carolina, Columbia.

2001 *38BU162U: Excavations for an Irrigation Pipeline on the Santa Elena Site, Parris Island, Beaufort County, South Carolina*. Research Manuscript Series 229. South Carolina Institute of Archaeology and Anthropology, University of South Carolina, Columbia.

Ferguson, Leland G.

1973 *Exploratory Archaeology at the Scott's Lake site (38CR1) Santee Indian Mound Fort Watson Summer 1972*. Research Manuscript Series 36. South Carolina Institute of Archaeology and Anthropology, University of South Carolina, Columbia.

1975a Analysis of Ceramic Materials from Fort Watson, December 1780–April 1781. *Conference on Historic Site Archaeology* 8(1):2–28. South Carolina Institute of Archaeology and Anthropology, University of South Carolina, Columbia.

1975b *Archaeology at Scott's Lake, Exploratory Research 1972, 1973*. Research Manuscript Series 68. South Carolina Institute of Archaeology and Anthropology, University of South Carolina, Columbia.

1977 An Archaeological-Historical Analysis of Fort Watson: December 1780–April 1781. In *Research Strategies in Historical Archaeology*, edited by Stanley South, pp. 41–71. Academic Press, New York.

Goodyear, Albert C., L. Mark Raab, and Timothy C. Klinger

1978 The Status of Archaeological Research Design in Cultural Resource Management. *American Antiquity* 43(2):159–172).

Greer, Georgeanna

1971 Preliminary Information on the Use of the Alkaline Glaze for Stoneware in the South. *Conference on Historic Site Archaeology* 5:155–170. South Carolina Institute of Archaeology and Anthropology, University of South Carolina, Columbia.

1993 *Great and Noble Jar: Traditional Stonewares of South Carolina*. University of Georgia Press, Athens.

Hemmings, E. Thomas

1979 *Archaeological Exploration of Land's Ford Canal, Chester County, South Carolina*. Research Manuscript Series 2. South Carolina Institute of Archaeology and Anthropology, University of South Carolina, Columbia.

Jameson, John H., Jr. (editor)

1997 *Presenting Archaeology to the Public: Digging for Truths*. Alta Mira Press. Walnut Creek, California.

Legg, James

2005 The Great War at Santa Elena: The Incidental Archaeology of World War One Marine Corps Training on Parris Island, South Carolina. In *In Praise of the Poet Archaeologist: Papers in Honor of Stanley South and His Five Decades of Historical Archaeology*, edited by Linda Carnes-McNaughton and Carl Steen, pp. 120–140. Publications in South Carolina Archaeology 1. Council of South Carolina Professional Archaeologists, Columbia.

Legg, James, and Steven D. Smith

1989 "The Best Ever Occupied...": Archaeological Investigations of a Civil War Encampment on Folly Island, South Carolina. Research Manuscript Series 209. South Carolina Institute of Archaeology and Anthropology, University of South Carolina, Columbia.

2007 Camden: Salvaging Data from A Heavily Collected Battlefield. In *Fields of Conflict: Battlefield Archaeology from the Roman Empire to the Korean War*, edited by Douglas Scott, Lawrence Babits, and Charles Haecker, pp. 208–33. Praeger Security International, Westport, Connecticut.

Lewis, Kenneth L.

1976 *Camden: A Frontier Town in Eighteenth Century South Carolina*. Anthropological Studies 2. South Carolina Institute of Archaeology and Anthropology, University of South Carolina, Columbia.

1977a Sampling the Archaeological Frontier: Regional models and Component Analysis. In *Research Strategies in Historical Archaeology*, edited by Stanley South, pp. Academic Press, New York.

1977b *A Functional Study of the Kershaw House Site in Camden, South Carolina*. Research Manuscript Series 110. South Carolina Institute of Archaeology and Anthropology, University of South Carolina, Columbia.

Michie, James L.

1982 *An Archaeological Investigation of the Cultural Resources of Callawassie Island, Beaufort County, South Carolina.* Research Manuscript Series 176. South Carolina Institute of Archaeology and Anthropology, University of South Carolina, Columbia.

1984 *An Initial Archaeological Survey of the Wachesaw/Richmond Plantation Property, Georgetown County, South Carolina.* Research Manuscript Series 191. South Carolina Institute of Archaeology and Anthropology, University of South Carolina, Columbia.

1987 *Richmond Hill and Wachesaw: An Archaeological Study of Two Rice Plantations on the Waccamaw River, Georgetown County, South Carolina.* Research Manuscript Series 203. South Carolina Institute of Archaeology and Anthropology, University of South Carolina, Columbia.

1989 *The Discovery of Old Fort Congaree.* Research Manuscript Series 208. South Carolina Institute of Archaeology and Anthropology, University of South Carolina, Columbia. Originally published 1976.

Michie, James L. and Jay Mills

1988 *The Search for Architectural Remains at the Planter's House and the Slave Settlement, Richmond Hill Plantation, Georgetown County, South Carolina.* Research Manuscript Series 205. South Carolina Institute of Archaeology and Anthropology, University of South Carolina, Columbia.

Polhemus, Richard

1971a *Exploratory Excavation in the Yard of the John Fox House (38LX31).* Research Manuscript Series 13. South Carolina Institute of Archaeology and Anthropology, University of South Carolina, Columbia.

1971b *Archaeological Investigations of a Proposed Pipeline Ditch at Charles Towne Site (38CH1).* Research Manuscript Series 15 (August–September). South Carolina Institute of Archaeology and Anthropology, University of South Carolina, Columbia.

1971c *Archaeological Investigations of a Proposed Pipeline Ditch at Charles Towne Site (38CH1).* Research Manuscript Series 17 (December). South Carolina Institute of Archaeology and Anthropology, University of South Carolina, Columbia.

1971d *Archaeological Investigations in the Vicinity of the Brown House, Charles Towne Site (38CH1).* Research Manuscript Series 22. South Carolina Institute of Archaeology and Anthropology, University of South Carolina, Columbia.

Raab, L. Mark, and Albert C. Goodyear

1973 On the Value of Middle Range Theory in Archaeological Research Strategies. Ms. on file at the South Carolina Institute of Archaeology and Anthropology.

Rauschenberg, Bradford

1999 John Bartlam, Who Established "New Pottworks in South Carolina" and Became the First Successful Creamware Potter in America. *Journal of Early Southern Decorative Arts* 17(2):1–66.

Schiffer, Michael B.

1977 Toward a Unified Science of the Cultural Past. In *Research Strategies in Historical Archaeology,* edited by Stanley South, pp. 13–40. Academic Press, New York.

Skowronek, Russell, and Kenneth Lewis

2010 *Beneath the Ivory Tower.* University of Florida Press, Gainesville.

Smith, Steven D.

1993 *Whom We Would Never More See: History and Archaeology Recover the Lives and Deaths of African American Civil War Soldiers on Folly Island, South Carolina.* South Carolina Department of Archives and History, Columbia.

1994 Archaeological Perspectives on the Civil War: The Challenge to Achieve Relevance. In *Look To The Earth: Historical Archaeology and the American Civil War,* edited by Clarence R. Geier Jr. and Susan E. Winter, pp. 20. University of Tennessee Press. Knoxville.

Smith, Steven D., James B Legg, Tamara S. Wilson, and Jonathan Leader

2006 *"Obstinate and Strong": The History and Archaeology of the Siege of Fort Motte.* South Carolina Institute of Archaeology and Anthropology, University of South Carolina, Columbia.

South, Stanley

1969 *Exploratory Archaeology at the Site of 1670–1680 Charles Towne on Albemarle Point in South Carolina.* Research Manuscript Series 1. South Carolina Institute of Archaeology and Anthropology, University of South Carolina, Columbia.

1970a *Exploratory Excavation at the Price House (38SP1).* Research Manuscript Series 5. South Carolina Institute of Archaeology and Anthropology, University of South Carolina, Columbia.

1970b *Exploratory Archaeology at Ninety Six (38GN1–38GN5).* Research Manuscript Series 6. South Carolina Institute of Archaeology and Anthropology, University of South Carolina, Columbia.

1970c *An Examination of the Site of Fort Hawkins in Macon, Bibb County, Georgia, with an Evaluation of the Potential for Historical Archaeology, with a View Toward Historic Site Development.* Research Manuscript Series 21. South Carolina Institute of Archaeology and Anthropology, University of South Carolina, Columbia.

1970d The Historical Archaeologist and Historic Site Development. *The Notebook.* 2(9–12):16–21; 8:1–55. South Carolina Institute of Archaeology and Anthropology, University of South Carolina, Columbia.

1971a Excavating the Fortified Area of the 1670 Site of Charles Towne, South Carolina. *Conference on Historic Site Archaeology Papers* 4, pt. 1:37–60. South Carolina Institute of Archaeology and Anthropology, University of South Carolina, Columbia.

1971b A Comment on the Relationship Between the State and Salvage Diving Operations. Historical Archaeology Forum, *Conference on Historic Site Archaeology Papers* 4, pt. 2:107–13. South Carolina Institute of Archaeology and Anthropology, University of South Carolina, Columbia.

1971c Exploratory Archaeology at Holmes' Fort, the Blockhouse, and Jail Redoubt at Ninety Six, South Carolina. *Conference on Historic Site Archaeology Papers* 5, pt. 1:35–50. South Carolina Institute of Archaeology and Anthropology, University of South Carolina, Columbia.

1971d The Historic Site Archaeologist and Historic Site Development. *Conference on Historic Site Archaeology Papers* 5, pt. 1:90–103. South Carolina Institute of Archaeology and Anthropology, University of South Carolina, Columbia.

1971e The Log Cabin Syndrome. *Conference on Historic Site Archaeology Papers* 5, pt. 1:103–14. South Carolina Institute of Archaeology and Anthropology, University of South Carolina, Columbia.

1971f A Comment on Alkaline Glazed Stoneware. *Conference on Historic Site Archaeology Papers* 5, pt. 2:171–88. South Carolina Institute of Archaeology and Anthropology, University of South Carolina, Columbia.

1971g Comment on Alkaline Glazed Stoneware from Various States. *Conference on Historic Site Archaeology Papers* 5, pt. 2:188–92. South Carolina Institute of Archaeology and Anthropology, University of South Carolina, Columbia.

1971h   *Historical Perspective at Ninety Six, with a Summary of Exploratory Excavation at Holmes' Fort and the Town Blockhouse.* Research Manuscript Series 9. South Carolina Institute of Archaeology and Anthropology, University of South Carolina, Columbia.

1971i   *The Pawley House (38GE15).* Research Manuscript Series 16. South Carolina Institute of Archaeology and Anthropology, University of South Carolina, Columbia.

1972a   *Archaeological Excavation at the Site of Williamson's Fort of 1775, Holmes' Fort of 1780, and the Town of Cambridge of 1783–1850s.* Research Manuscript Series 18. South Carolina Institute of Archaeology and Anthropology, University of South Carolina, Columbia.

1972b   Evolution and Horizon as Revealed in Ceramic Analysis in Historical Archaeology. *Conference on Historic Site Archaeology Papers* 6, pt. 2:71–117. South Carolina Institute of Archaeology and Anthropology, University of South Carolina, Columbia.

1972c   The Role of the Archaeologist in the Conservation-Preservation Process. Paper presented at North American International Regional Conference, Williamsburg, Virginia, and Philadelphia (conducted under the auspices of the International Centre for Conservation, Rome, Italy).

1972d   *The Role of the Archaeologist in the Conservation-Preservation Process.* Research Manuscript Series 26. South Carolina Institute of Archaeology and Anthropology, University of South Carolina, Columbia.

1972e   Historical Archaeology Reports: A Plea for a New Direction. Conference on Historic Site Archaeology Papers 7, pt. 3, sec. 1:151–57.

1972f   The Archaeological and Interpretive Proposal for the Kosciusko Tunnel at the Star Fort at Ninety Six, in South 1972a:103–110.

1973a   The Pawley House (38GE15). *The Notebook* 5(1):13. South Carolina Institute of Archaeology and Anthropology, University of South Carolina, Columbia.

1973b   *An Archaeological Survey of the Area of a Proposed Industrial Park Located on the Byrd Trust Lands in Florence County, South Carolina.* Research Manuscript Series 41. South Carolina Institute of Archaeology and Anthropology, University of South Carolina, Columbia.

1973c   *An Archaeological Survey of Jenkins Island Beaufort County, South Carolina.* Research Manuscript Series 42. South Carolina Institute of Archaeology and Anthropology, University of South Carolina, Columbia.

1973d   *Archaeological Survey of the North End of the Isle of Palms, Charleston County, South Carolina* (with Robert L. Stephenson). Research Manuscript Series 53. South Carolina Institute of Archaeology and Anthropology, University of South Carolina, Columbia.

1973e   Exploratory Archaeology Project on the Campus of the University of South Carolina. Manuscript on file, South Carolina Institute of Archaeology and Anthropology, University of South Carolina, Columbia.

1973f   A Statement on the Master Plan for the Development of Ninety Six. Memo: South to Stephenson, June 28, 1973. Manuscript on file, South Carolina Institute of Archaeology and Anthropology, University of South Carolina, Columbia.

1973g   Research Design, Progress Report, and Daily Report for the Indian Spring Site (38BU24) on Hilton Head Island, South Carolina. South Carolina Institute of Archaeology and Anthropology, University of South Carolina, Columbia.

1974a   *Palmetto Parapets.* Anthropological Studies 1. South Carolina Institute of Archaeology and Anthropology, University of South Carolina, Columbia.

1974b   The Horizon Concept Revealed in the Application of the Mean Ceramic Date Formula to Spanish Majolica in the New World. *Conference on Historic Site Archaeology Papers* 7, pt. 3, sec. 1:96–23. South Carolina Institute of Archaeology and Anthropology, University of South Carolina, Columbia.

1974c   The Function of Observation in the Archaeological Process. *Conference on Historic Site Archaeology Papers* 7, pt. 3, sec. 1:123–37. South Carolina Institute of Archaeology and Anthropology, University of South Carolina, Columbia.

1974d   Methodological Phases in the Archaeological Process. *Conference on Historic Site Archaeology Papers* 7, pt. 3, sec. 1:138–45. South Carolina Institute of Archaeology and Anthropology, University of South Carolina, Columbia.

1974e   Evaluation of Analysis Situations Relative to the Archeological Data Bank. *Conference on Historic Site Archaeology Papers* 7, pt. 3, sec. 1:146–51. South Carolina Institute of Archaeology and Anthropology, University of South Carolina, Columbia.

1974f   *An Archaeological Survey of an Area of Fort Johnson.* Research Manuscript Series 62. South Carolina Institute of Archaeology and Anthropology, University of South Carolina, Columbia.

1975a   *Fickle Forts on Windmill Point: Exploratory Archaeology at Fort Johnson.* Research Manuscript Series 81. South Carolina Institute of Archaeology and Anthropology, University of South Carolina, Columbia.

1975b   *Preliminary Assessment of the Site of the Southeastern Utilization Research Center and the Waste Treatment Plant at Fort Johnson, Charleston County, South Carolina.* Research Manuscript Series 79. South Carolina Institute of Archaeology and Anthropology, University of South Carolina, Columbia.

1976   *Comment on Ceramics and Buttons from a Burial in the Cunningham Field Mount D on St. Catherine's Island, Georgia.* Research Manuscript Series 98. South Carolina Institute of Archaeology and Anthropology, University of South Carolina, Columbia.

1977a   *Method and Theory in Historical Archaeology.* Academic Press, New York.

1977b   Archaeological Pattern Recognition: An Example from the British Colonial System. In *Conservation Archaeology: Models for Cultural Resource Management Studies,* edited by Michael B. Schiffer and George J. Gummerman, pp. 427–33. Academic Press, New York.

1977c   Guidelines for the Preparation and Evaluation of Archaeological Reports. The Management of Archaeological Resources (with Keith Anderson, Hester Davis, Rob Edwards, Michael B. Schiffer, and Gwinn Vivian), in *The Airlie House Report,* edited by Charles R. McGimsey III and Hester A. Davis, pp. 64–77. Special Publication of the Society for American Archaeology, Washington, D.C.

1977d   The General, the Major, and the Angel. *Transactions of the Huguenot Society of South Carolina* 82:31–49.

1978a   Contemporary Patterns of Material Culture or Hansel and Gretel in the Modern World: Following the Trail of Pull Tabs to "The Pause That Refreshes." *Conference on Historical Site Archaeology Papers* 12:57–106. South Carolina Institute of Archaeology and Anthropology, University of South Carolina, Columbia. Reprinted in *South Carolina Antiquities: The First Ten Years,* edited by Wayne Neighbors, pp. 400–412. Archaeological Society of South Carolina, Columbia, 1980.

1978b   Research Strategies for Archaeological Pattern Recognition on Historical Sites. *World Archaeology* 10(1):36–50.

1978c   Evolution and Horizon as Revealed in Ceramic Analysis in Historical Archaeology. In *Historical Archaeology: A Guide to Substantive and Theoretical Contributions,* edited by R. L. Schuyler, pp. 68–82. Baywood Publishing, New York.

1978d   Exploring Analytical Techniques. In *Historical Archaeology: A Guide to Substantive and Theoretical Contributions,* edited by Robert L. Schuyler pp. 253–266. Baywood Publishing Co., New York.

1978e   Pattern Recognition in Historical Archaeology. *American Antiquity* 43(2): 223–230.

1979a   Historic Site Content, Structure and Function. *American Antiquity* 44(2): 213–237.

1979b   *The Search for Santa Elena.* Research Manuscript Series 150. South Carolina Institute of Archaeology and Anthropology, University of South Carolina, Columbia.

1979c   *An Archaeological Survey of an Area of Fort Johnson.* Research Manuscript Series 62. South Carolina Institute of Archaeology and Anthropology, University of South Carolina, Columbia.

1979d   *The General, the Major, and the Angel: The Discovery of General William Moultrie's Grave.* Research Manuscript Series 146. South Carolina Institute of Archaeology and Anthropology, University of South Carolina, Columbia.

1980a   The Search for Sixteenth Century Santa Elena. *Conference on Historic Site Archaeology Papers* 13:25–37. South Carolina Institute of Archaeology and Anthropology, University of South Carolina, Columbia.

1980b   Contemporary Patterns of Material Culture or Hansel and Gretel in the Modern World: Following the Trail of Pull Tabs to 'The Pause That Refreshes." *Conference on Historic Site Archaeology Papers* 12:87–106. South Carolina Institute of Archaeology and Anthropology, University of South Carolina, Columbia.

1980c   *The Discovery of Santa Elena.* Research Manuscript Series 165. South Carolina Institute of Archaeology and Anthropology, University of South Carolina, Columbia.

1980d   Santa Elena, A Spanish Foothold in the New World. In *Excursions in Southeastern Geology: The Archaeology-Geology of the Georgia Coast,* edited by James D. Howard, Chester B. DePratter, and Robert W. Frey, pp. 206–224. Geological Society of America, Georgia Geologic Survey, Atlanta.

1982a   *A Search for the French Charlesfort of 1562.* Research Manuscript Series 177. South Carolina Institute of Archaeology and Anthropology, University of South Carolina, Columbia.

1982b   *Exploring Santa Elena 1981.* Research Manuscript Series 184. South Carolina Institute of Archaeology and Anthropology, University of South Carolina, Columbia.

1983   *Revealing Santa Elena 1982.* Research Manuscript Series 188. South Carolina Institute of Archaeology and Anthropology, University of South Carolina, Columbia.

1984   *Testing Archaeological Sampling Methods at Fort San Felipe 1983.* Research Manuscript Series 190. South Carolina Institute of Archaeology and Anthropology, University of South Carolina, Columbia.

1985a   *Excavation of the Casa Fuerte and Wells at Fort San Felipe 1984.* Research Manuscript Series 196. South Carolina Institute of Archaeology and Anthropology, University of South Carolina, Columbia.

1985b [1979]   Exploring Santa Elena. *National Geographic Society Research Reports* 20:703–715. National Geographic Society, Washington, D.C.

1988a   Santa Elena: Threshold of Conquest. In *The Recovery of Meaning,* edited by Mark Leone, and Parker B. Potter, Jr., pp. 27–72. Anthropological Society of Washington, Smithsonian Institution Press, Washington, D.C.

1988b   Project Description and Goals in Proposals and Research Design: The Santa Elena Example. *American Archaeology* 7(2).

1988c   South's work at Santa Elena featured in Joseph Judge article, "Exploring America's Forgotten Century," *National Geographic* 173(3):330–363.

1988d   Scoperto a Santa Elena. *Columbus 92* 4(6): P. 28, pp, 1-16. Genoa, Italy. Rich Man, Poor Men: Observations on Three Antebellum Burials from the Georgia Coast. *Anthropological Papers of the American Museum of Natural History* 54(3)

1988e   Articles on Santa Elena artifacts in *Features and Profiles,* January–June. Archaeological Society of South Carolina.

1989   Using Scientific Methodology and Energy Theory to Address Artifacts from British and Spanish Colonial Communities. *Proceedings of the 21st Annual Chacmool Conference,* edited by Scott MacEachern, David J. W. Archer, and Richard D. Garvin, pp. 3–12. Archaeological Association of the University of Calgary, Canada.

1990a   The ATTIC Project (Archaeological Techniques to Inventory Collections): A Smith Family Legacy. J. Lister Skinner Jr. Project. The South Carolina Research and Development and South Carolina Institute of Archaeology and Anthropology, University of South Carolina, Columbia.

1990b   From Thermodynamics to a Status Artifact Model: Spanish Santa Elena. *Columbian Consequences: Archaeology and History of the Spanish Borderlands East,* edited by David Hurst Thomas, pp. 329-41. Society for American Archaeology, Washington, D.C.

1993a   Strange Fruit: Historical Archaeology 1972–1977. *Historical Archaeology* 27(1):15–18.

1993b   *The Search for John Bartlam at Cain Hoy: America's First Creamware Potter.* Research Manuscript Series 219. South Carolina Institute of Archaeology and Anthropology, University of South Carolina, Columbia.

1996a   *Archaeology at Santa Elena: Doorway to the Past.* Popular Series 2. South Carolina Institute of Archaeology and Anthropology, University of South Carolina, Columbia.

1996b   Arqueología en Santa Elena Entrada al pasado. *Osmus* 4(18):44–45 (pt. 1); 4(19):40–41, (pt. 2). Miami Beach.

1999a   *Historical Archaeology in Wachovia: Excavating Eighteenth Century Bethabara and Moravian Pottery.* Kluwer Academic/Plenum Publishers, New York.

1999b   Excavating the Pottery of John Bartlam: America's First Creamware Potter. In *Old and New Worlds,* edited by Geoff Eagan for SPMA and R. L. Michael, pp. 289-99. Oxbow Books, Oxford, United Kingdom.

2002a [1998]   Using the Telescopic Boom Hydraulic Excavator: The Ultimate Archaeological Shovel. *South Carolina Antiquities* 30(1):37–42.

2002b   *Archaeological Pathways to Historic Site Development.* Kluwer Academic/Plenum Publishers, New York.

2002c   *Method and Theory in Historical Archaeology.* With a new introduction by the author. Percheron Press, Clifton Corners, New York.

2004a [1990]   Toys in the Attic: The ATTIC Project. *South Carolina Antiquities* 34(1–2): 1–6.

2004b   *John Bartlam: Staffordshire in Carolina.* Research Manuscript Series 231. South Carolina Institute of Archaeology and Anthropology, University of South Carolina, Columbia.

2005 *An Archaeological Evolution.* Springer, New York.

2006 Ninety Six Fortification Search. Manuscript on file at the South Carolina Institute of Archaeology and Anthropology.

2008 Archaeologically Testing the Tabby Point Ruin: Callawassie Island, South Carolina. *South Carolina Antiquities* 40:42–47.

2009a *Colonial Brunswick: Archaeology of a British Colonial Town.* North Carolina Department of Archives and History, Raleigh.

2009b *Talking Artifacts: The Twentieth Century Legacy.* South Carolina Institute of Archaeology and Anthropology, University of South Carolina, Columbia.

South, Stanley (editor)

1977 *Research Strategies in Historical Archaeology.* Academic Press, New York.

South, Stanley, and Randolph Widmer

1976 *Archaeological Sampling at Fort Johnson, South Carolina (38CH275 and 38CH16).* Research Manuscript Series 93. South Carolina Institute of Archaeology and Anthropology, University of South Carolina, Columbia.

1977 A Subsurface Sampling Strategy for Archaeological Reconnaissance. In *Research Strategies in Historical Archaeology,* edited by Stanley South, pp. 119-50. Academic Press, New York.

South, Stanley, and Michael O. Hartley

1980 *Deep Water and High Ground: Seventeenth Century Low Country Settlement.* Research Manuscript Series 166. South Carolina Institute of Archaeology and Anthropology, University of South Carolina, Columbia.

South, Stanley, and William Hunt

1986 *Discovering Santa Elena West of Fort San Felipe.* Research Manuscript Series 200. South Carolina Institute of Archaeology and Anthropology, University of South Carolina, Columbia.

South, Stanley, Russell Skowronek, and Richard Johnson

1988 Spanish Artifacts from Santa Elena. Anthropological Studies 7. South Carolina

Institute of Archaeology and Anthropology, University of South Carolina, Columbia.

South, Stanley, and Carl Steen

1992 *Archaeology on the Horseshoe at the University of South Carolina.* Research Manuscript Series 215. South Carolina Institute of Archaeology and Anthropology, University of South Carolina, Columbia.

South, Stanley A., and Chester DePratter

1996 *Discovery at Santa Elena 1993: Block Excavation.* Research Manuscript Series 222. South Carolina Institute of Archaeology and Anthropology, University of South Carolina, Columbia.

South, Stanley, and Kathleen Deagan

2002 Historical Archaeology in the Southeast 1930–2000. In *Histories of Southeastern Archaeology,* edited by Shannon Tushingham, Jane Hill, and Charles H. McNutt, pp. 35–50. The University of Alabama Press, Tuscaloosa.

South, Stanley, and Halcott P. Green

2005a Evolutionary Theory in Archaeology at Mid-Century and at the Millennium. In *In Praise of the Poet Archaeologist: Papers in Honor of Stanley South and His Five Decades of Historical Archaeology,* edited by Linda Carnes-McNaughton and Carl Steen, pp. 154–189. Publications in South Carolina Archaeology No. 1. Council of South Carolina Professional Archaeologists, Columbia.

2005b Energy Theory and Historical Archaeology. In *In Praise of the Poet Archaeologist: Papers in Honor of Stanley South and His Five Decades of Historical Archaeology,* edited by Linda Carnes-McNaughton and Carl Steen, pp. 37–63. Publications in South Carolina Archaeology No. 1. Council of South Carolina Professional Archaeologists, Columbia.

South, Stanley, and Michael J. Stoner

2007 *The Sullivan Tabby Point Ruin: Callawassie Island, South Carolina.* Research Manuscript Series 233. South Carolina Institute of Archaeology and Anthropology, University of South Carolina, Columbia.

Thomas, David Hurst, Stanley South, and Clark Spencer Larson

1977 Rich Man, Poor Men: Observations on Three Antebellum Burials from the Georgia Coast. *Anthropological Papers of the American Museum of Natural History* 54(3): 393–420.

Stoner, Michael J.

2005 The Brunswick Pattern and the Interpretation of a 1670 Charles Towne Structure. In *In Praise of the Poet Archaeologist: Papers in Honor of Stanley South and His Five Decades of Historical Archaeology,* edited by Linda Carnes-McNaughton and Carl Steen, pp. 73–80. Publications in South Carolina Archaeology No. 1. Council of South Carolina Professional Archaeologists, Columbia.

Stoner, Michael J., and Stanley South

2001 *Exploring 1670 Charles Towne: (38CH1A/B).* Research Manuscript Series 230. South Carolina Institute of Archaeology and Anthropology, University of South Carolina, Columbia.

2007 *Exploring 1670 Charles Towne: The Barbadian Connection.* 2nd ed. Research Manuscript Series 230. South Carolina Institute of Archaeology and Anthropology, University of South Carolina, Columbia.

Tolson, Jay

2007 As the Ground Shares Its Secrets: A Determined Archaeologist Challenges Old Beliefs. *U.S. News and World Report.* January–February: 64–67.

Williams, Marshall W.

1998 *A Memoir of the Archaeological Excavation of Fort Prince George, Pickens County, South Carolina,* edited by Lisa Hudgins. Research Manuscript Series 226. South Carolina Institute of Archaeology and Anthropology, University of South Carolina, Columbia.

Zierden, Martha A., Steven D. Smith, and Ronald W. Anthony

1995 *"Our Duty Was Quite Arduous": History and Archaeology of the Civil War on Little Folly Island, South Carolina.* Charleston Museum Leaflet 32.

CHRISTOPHER F. AMER is recently retired from the University of South Carolina's South Carolina Institute of Archaeology and Anthropology, where he was state underwater archaeologist. He received his master's degree in anthropology through the Nautical Archaeology Program at Texas A&M University. Amer has written and cowritten numerous essays in archaeological publications including *Coffins of the Brave, That from These Honored Dead,* and the British Museum's *Encyclopaedia of Underwater and Maritime Archaeology.* For 26 years he cochaired the Government Maritime Managers meetings at the Society for Historical Archaeology's annual Conference on Historical and Underwater Archaeology. Amer is currently an archaeological consultant based in Vancouver, Canada.

CHARLES COBB is James E. Lockwood, Jr. Professor and Curator of Historical Archaeology at the Florida Museum of Natural History. He received his doctorate from Southern Illinois University in 1988, and his research focuses on Native Americans of the southeastern United States. Cobb, along with Chester DePratter, is currently pursuing research related to Native American and European interactions along the Carolina frontier.

CHESTER B. DEPRATTER is head of the Research Division at the South Carolina Institute of Archaeology and Anthropology, University of South Carolina. He received his doctorate in anthropology from the University of Georgia. DePratter's broad research interests include sixteenth-century Spanish explorations and settlement in the southeastern United States, coastal shell middens, and Civil War prisons.

ALBERT C. GOODYEAR is a research associate professor with the South Carolina Institute of Archaeology and Anthropology at the University of South Carolina. He received his doctorate from Arizona State University. He is the founder of the Southeastern Paleoamerican Survey, a program that searches for the earliest people in the Southeast. He is the director of excavations at the Topper site and other early sites in Allendale County, South Carolina.

LELAND FERGUSON is Distinguished Professor Emeritus of Anthropology at the University of South Carolina, where he teaches in the South Carolina Honors College. He is the author of *Uncommon Ground: Archaeology and Early African America, 1650–1800* and *God's Fields: Landscape, Religion, and Race in Moravian Wachovia.*

TAMMY F. HERRON is the curator of Artifact Collections for the Savannah River Archaeological Research Program of the University of South Carolina's South Carolina Institute of Archaeology and Anthropology. She received her bachelor's degree in psychology with a minor in anthropology from Georgia Southern University. Herron serves as the president of the Society for Georgia Archaeology.

CHRISTOPHER JUDGE is assistant director of Native American studies at the University of South Carolina Lancaster. He holds bachelor's and master's degrees in anthropology from the University of South Carolina.

ADAM KING is a research associate professor in the University of South Carolina's South Carolina Institute of Archaeology and Anthropology and special projects archaeologist for the Savannah River Archaeological Research Program. He holds a doctorate in anthropology from Pennsylvania State University and is interested in the early history of Native Americans, particularly during the Mississippian Period (A.D. 1000–1600). He is author of *Etowah: A Political History* and editor of *Southeastern Ceremonial Complex: Chronology, Content, Context.*

JONATHAN LEADER heads South Carolina's Office of the State Archaeologist. His research interests and background include the ancient Near East, Micronesia, eastern United States pre- and proto-history, submerged resources, cultural resource management, remote sensing and GIS, archaeometry, archaeometallurgy, and object conservation. He teaches and lectures on a regular basis in four departments at the University of South Carolina.

ROBERT MOON is a former staff archaeologist with the South Carolina Institute of Archaeology and Anthropology's Savannah River Archaeological Research Program at the University of South Carolina. He received a master's degree in historic archaeology from the University of West Florida in 2001. Currently he serves as a supervisor with the Florida Department of Law Enforcement.

ERIC C. POPLIN is laboratory director and senior archaeologist for Brockington and Associates, Inc. He received his doctorate in archaeology from the University of Calgary. He continues research of the prehistoric and historic peoples of the South Carolina coast through multiple cultural resource management projects.

KENNETH E. SASSAMAN is Hyatt and Cici Brown Professor of Florida Archaeology at the University of Florida. He received his doctorate in anthropology from the University of Massachusetts–Amherst in 1991. He is the author of *The Eastern Archaic, Historicized* and editor of the journal *American Antiquity.*

STEVEN D. SMITH is a research associate professor and director at the South Carolina Institute of Archaeology and Anthropology, University of South Carolina. He received his doctorate from the University of South Carolina in 2010. He has 38 years of experience in historical archaeology, most of that focused on military sites of the American Revolution and Civil War.

STANLEY A. SOUTH retired from his research position at the South Carolina Institute of Archaeology and Anthropology, University of South Carolina in 2011. He is an internationally recognized archaeologist based on his decades of research in historical archaeology. South's long research career focused on English and Spanish colonial towns and forts in North Carolina and South Carolina.

JAMES D. SPIREK is the state underwater archaeologist of South Carolina. He is in charge of review and compliance for the Maritime Research Division of the South Carolina Institute of Archaeology and Anthropology and conducts archaeological research in the state's waterways. His research interests lie in Civil War naval operations, shipbuilding and seafaring of the sixteenth century, ship architecture, and marine remote-sensing operations.

CARL STEEN is a native of the South Carolina lowcountry. He attended the College of Charleston and the University of South Carolina and received a master's degree in anthropology at the College of William and Mary. He is president of the Diachronic Research Foundation in Columbia.

KEITH STEPHENSON is an archaeologist with the South Carolina Institute of Archaeology and Anthropology and director of the Savannah River Archaeological Research Program at the University of South Carolina. He received his doctorate in anthropology from the University of Kentucky. His research interest focuses on the political economy of Woodland and Mississippian societies.

ALEX Y. SWEENEY is a senior archaeologist for Brockington and Associates, Inc., and serves as branch chief for the Savannah office. He received his master's degree in anthropology from the University of South Carolina. Sweeney continues research of the Yamasee Indian occupations of coastal South Carolina while managing cultural resource management projects in coastal Georgia.

SEAN G. TAYLOR, chief archaeologist for the South Carolina Department of Natural Resources, grew up in rural Lexington County, where his fascination with the prehistoric past began at a young age. His interest in archaeology further developed while attending the University of South Carolina, where he earned bachelor's and master's degrees in anthropology. He has spent over a decade in the field of cultural resource management, locating, excavating, and learning about various aspects of South Carolina's rich cultural heritage. At SCDNR he works with the department's staff to protect South Carolina heritage on all of the agency's lands.

MARTHA A. ZIERDEN is curator of historical archaeology at the Charleston Museum. She graduated from Florida State University with a master's degree in anthropology. She is coeditor of *Another's Country: Archaeological and Historical Perspectives on Cultural Interactions in the Southern Colonies* and a contributor to *Unlocking the Past: Celebrating Historical Archaeology in North America*.

All color illustrations can be found following page 132.

remains on, 147, 149, 150; importance of, 143–45; measurements of, 140; ownership of, 141–43; propulsion of, 140; prototypes of, 138–39; public interest in, 149; raising of, 147; recovery of, 136–37; search for, 141–42; sinking of the *Housatonic* by, 137; as a symbol, 143–46, 151; trials of, 140–41
Hollow Creek, 84
Hollywood, 38, 41
Holmes' Fort, 219–20
Horts, 111
Housatonic, 136
housing, 53, 55
human interments, 21–22, 27, 31, 57, 76–77
Hume, Ivor Noël, 214
Hunley, Horace L., 139
"*Hunley* Project Working Group," 141, 143
Hunt, Bill, 229
hunter-gatherer model, 16–18
hunter-gatherers, 36, 37
Hurricane Hugo, 106
hurricanes, 106, 124
Huspah, 63

Ichisi, 63
identity, 31
India, 165–67, 171
indigo, 85
indirect cooking, 20, 26
Ingram Vessel, 155
Initial Archaeological Investigations at Silver Bluff Plantation, 83
In Praise of the Poet Archaeologist: Papers in Honor of Stanley South and His Five Decades of Historical Archaeology, 230
Intelligent Whale, 139
interconnections, 17, 30, 39
Irene phase, 71–72
irrigation, 47
Isle of Palms, 222

Jackson, Susan, 222, 227, 229
Jameson, John, 219
Jenkins Island, 222
Jesuit rings, 73, 75
jewelry, 73
Jim Crow, 145
Johannes Kolb site (38DA75): architecture of, 192; artifact assemblage of, 183–88, 192–93; ceramics of, 183, 186–90, 196; clay resources of, 178–79; dating of, 182, 184, 188–89; description of area, 174–76; documentary evidence about, 192; enslaved populations of, 187–88, 193–94; excavation methodology of, 179–81; experimental archaeology at, 196; faunal assemblage of, 183; features of, 182–83; flintknapping and, 178, 189, 196; historic artifacts of, 187–88; historic period of, 191–94; importance of, 175, 178, 195, 197; imported good and, 192; lithic resouces

of, 177–78; lithics of, 184–86, 186, 188–89; Native Americans and, 188–91, 195; pottery of, 183, 186–90, 196; pre-Clovis and, 188–89; public archaeology and, 194–97; root cellar of, 187–88; sawmill of, 194; slave quarters of, 193–94; soils of, 182; storage pits of, 183
John Fox House (38LX31), 223
John Milner's house, 121
John Rutledge house, 128
Jones, Scott, 196
Joseph, J.W., 121, 222
Journals of the Commissioners of the Indian Trade, 62, 89
Judge, Chris, 222

kaolin pipes, 52, 57, 76, 89, 123
Kelso, Bill, 214
Kidder, T.R., 30
King, Adam, 222
King Lewis, 67, 70
kin groups, 41
Kirk points, 185
Knight, V. James, Jr., 39
Knoblock, Byron, 29
Ku Klux Klan, 145
Kusso-Natchez, 191

labor mobilization, 38–40, 41
lanceolate points, 2, 3, 185, 188
landscape, 37
Land's Ford Canal, 218
Last Glacial Maximum (LGM), 1
Late Archaic, 21, 35, 189
Late Paleoindian, 184
Late Woodland, 37
Late Woodland Savannah I phase, 36
Lawton phase, 37, 38, 40
Leader, Jonathan, 220–21
LeCroy points, 185
Leed's Foundry, 139
Legg, Jim, 220–22, 229–30, 231–32
Leigh, David, 176, 184
Leovy, Henry J., 139
Lewis, Kenneth E., 221–22
Locke, John, 47
Locklear, David (Chief), 195
looting, 40, 203
Lords Proprietor, 68
Lower Market, 125

Macon Plateau, 39
macro band model, 188
macroblades, 9
magnetometers, 160, 167–69, 202
maize, 48, 53
Mallory, Stephen Russell, 137–38
mammoths, 2
Mancke, Tom, 196
manifest destiny, 45
Mary Bowers, 172, 217

Mason's Plantation, 38
McClintock, James, 139
McCrady's Tavern, 130
McGillvery, Lachlan, 87
McKivergan, David A., Jr., 78–79
McPherson, James, 144
Meadowcraft Rockshelter, 1
Mennonites, 191
metal detectors, 202–4
Method and Theory in Historical Archaeology, 215–16, 227
Michie, Jim, 3–4, *3*, 24, 182, 229, 232
middens, 23, 39, 182
Middle Archaic, 184
Middleburg Plantation (38BK38): activities on, 105; archaeological methodology of, 109–10; architecture of, 106; artifact assemblage of, 105, 108–9, 113; dating of, 106, 113; description of, 102, 104–5, 106, 116; documentary evidence about, 103–5, 112; earthfast house of, 109; enslaved population of, 105–6, 111–13; faunal analysis of, 111; Historic American Buildings Survey (HABS) and, 103–4; Hurricane Hugo and, 106; maps of, 104–5, *105*, 106–7, 109, 110; owners of, 103–4, 106; postholes of, 109; rice agriculture of, 111–12; settlement pattern of, 113; slave quarters of, 104, 107–8, 112
middle-range theory, 216
Middle Woodland, 36
Miles Brewton house, 128–29, 130
military history, 145
Mill Branch, 27, 29
Miller, Johnny, 214
Milling, Chapman, 192
Mims Point, 21
Minho, 172
Mississippian, *xv*, 19, 34, 36
Mocama, 65
Mont Clare Plantation, 193
Monte Verde, 1
Moore, Christopher, 182
Moore, James, 68–69
Moore, Sue M., 86
Morrow Mountain points, 185
mortuary ceremonialism, 36, 40
mounds, 38, 39, 48
Mountain Shoshone, 17
Mount Pleasant, 52, 54–55
muskets, 49, 59, 74
Muskhogean languages, 187

Nathaniel Russell house, 128–32
National Endowment for the Humanities, 228
National Geographic Society, 228
National Historic Preservation Act, x–si, 34, 142, 222
National Oceanic and Atmospheric Administration, 142
National Park Service, 142, 143, 203, 219–20, 226